Born in Canberra in 1961, Merridy Eastman spent ten years in Melbourne and now lives in Sydney. Since graduating from NIDA in 1983, Eastman has performed in a swag of productions for the Melbourne Theatre Company, and recently for the Sydney Theatre Company. She also spent several summers leaping about botanical gardens across Australia, playing Helena in *A Midsummer Night's Dream* under the stars. In the late eighties she became a *Play School* presenter, and made papier-mâché octopi and pipe-cleaner spiders for three years until they realised how bad her singing was and replaced her. Since then she has had major roles in many sitcoms and all the commercial soap operas, playing everything from a cradle-snatching golf fanatic on *Neighbours* to an unstable funeral director on *Blue Heelers* who was so unhappy with a bad haircut, she stabbed the hairdresser with his scissors. She currently plays Eileen Unn in Channel Seven's *Always Greener*.

THERE'S
A BEAR
IN THERE
(and he wants swedish)

Merridy Eastman

A Sue Hines Book
ALLEN & UNWIN

First published in 2002

Copyright © Merridy Eastman 2002

A Sue Hines Book
Allen & Unwin
83 Alexander Street
Crows Nest NSW 2065
Australia
Phone: (61 2) 8425 0100
Fax: (61 2) 9906 2218
Email: info@allenandunwin.com
Web: www.allenandunwin.com

Extracts from the *Play School Theme* are reproduced with
permission from Mushroom Music.

National Library of Australia
Cataloguing-in-Publication entry:

Eastman, Merridy, 1961–.
  There's a bear in there (and he wants Swedish).
  ISBN 1 86508 601 0.
  1. Eastman, Merridy, 1961–. 2. Actresses – Australia –
Biography. 3. Receptionists – Australia – Biography. 4. Sex
oriented businesses – Australia. I. Title.
  331.7613067

Typeset by Pauline Haas
Printed in Australia by McPhersons Printing Group

10 9 8 7 6 5 4 3 2

To Rox and Da, living proof that life actually begins
at seventy, and whose company I love so much that
if they weren't my parents I'd have to adopt them.

If there's one thing they hate at Centrelink, it's an actor

'What else can you do?' Colin asked, without taking his eyes off his screen. 'I mean, you can't just put down "acting".'

'Well,' I began my descent, 'I've never done anything else.'

'Not even waitressing?'

I shook my head.

Colin peered at me over his glasses. 'I thought all waitresses were out of work actors.'

I laughed.

'Have you brought your CV in?' Colin asked.

'Yes,' I said, desperately searching through my black hole of a bag, 'but I don't think it's going to ... er ...'

Colin looked on with disdain as I smoothed out my crumpled three-page CV on his desk. 'Robyn Gardiner Management,' he read out loud. 'Is that an employment agency?'

'God no!' I nearly choked. 'That's my agent!'

It was an actor's joke. But Colin eyed me with as much contempt as if I'd come in wearing a doublet and hose. I considered telling him she was Cate Blanchett's agent as well, but suddenly the comparison filled me with utter, utter despair.

'You were a nurse?' Colin asked.

'Wha—?'

'Says here, "Sister Mary".'

'No! No, that's a nun.'

'A nun?'

'*Five Mile Creek*. Television show.'

Colin scanned my career. It seemed to upset him more than me. 'Are all these television shows?'

'No, most of it's theatre.'

Colin spared me his response.

'Sister Josephine?' he enquired tonelessly.

'Another nun.'

'Get a lot of nuns, do you?'

'Yes I do, actually!' I laughed. 'Must have a good face.'

Colin looked at my face.

'I mean a *good* face.'

Colin looked tired. 'Well, you can't expect to find work with this,' he announced, changing gears and leaning back in his chair.

'Oh dear,' I sighed.

'I mean, according to this,' and he gave my CV a dismissive flick, 'you have no skills whatsoever.'

'Ah ...'

'No skills whatsoever!' he repeated.

'Did you see the two Greenroom Awar—?'

'None,' concluded Colin, tossing his pen down on my papers.

I never realised fifteen years of playing character roles in largely British comedies could so offend a person. It reminded me of the time I worked for a community theatre company in Marrickville. They too found my classical theatre background offensive, and 'middle class'. I left when Alfonso, a shirtless brute who called everyone comrade, ran over my foot with the van.

Roy, at Jobfinder, was much more pleasant, and more than a little excited that I'd been on *Play School*.

'I love Noni!' He beamed.

I smiled as I searched Roy's desk for photos of his children.

'And John,' he added quickly.

If Noni knew the number of grown men who enjoyed watching her on all fours, smiling into the camera, she'd never sing again.

'So let's have a look at nannies, shall we?' Roy sang in joyful *Play School* parody, and I laughed heartily.

As I watched Roy's fingers dance merrily on the keyboard, it occurred to me that looking after other people's babies might plunge a single girl in her late thirties into a serious depression.

'Roy, do you know what I'd really like to do?'

Roy's fingers hovered mid Rachmaninov.

'I think I'd like a job answering phones.'

Roy looked terribly disappointed. 'Telesales?' he asked incredulously. 'You mean telesales?'

'No!' Lift the roof off a telesales office, and thousands of tiny unemployed actors scurry everywhere. 'I was thinking more ... a receptionist. Answering phones. Putting people on hold ... that kind of thing.'

Roy paused, then tapped something into his computer. 'Won't be a moment.' He smiled, and we waited.

'So, do you know Noni?'

'We only worked together once.'

'Both on at the same time?' Roy asked, too eagerly.

'No. We just both recorded songs on the same album, once.'

Roy's smile became strained. The printer stirred.

'Ah! Here we go.'

My heart sank as Roy read out job descriptions for receptionists needed in suburbs I'd never even heard of, all required to do much more than just put people on hold.

'What about this one?' he enthused. 'DHL Express Couriers, Alexandria!'

I'd rather nanny on antidepressants.

'Must be able to handle Commander Phone System—'

'Oh dear,' I interrupted. 'Can't.'

Roy looked hurt. 'It's just a phone with six to twelve lines.'

I winced. Roy moved on. I was running out of *Play School* mileage.

'Here's one!' he cried. 'Pleasant phone manner. Part-time.

Nights—' Roy froze mid job description. 'No, I don't think so.'
Roy twitched, screwed up my intriguing part-time night job, and
was about to throw it in the bin.

'What's wrong with it?' I piped.

'Um …' Roy's cheeks reddened. 'Not enough information.
Sounds a bit sus.'

'Oh.'

I looked from the blushing Roy to the crinkled missive and
back to Roy. It was a brothel! My heart jumped. Roy didn't know
how to tell me it was a brothel. I didn't know how to tell Roy I'd
quite like to work in a brothel. As a receptionist.

'Actually,' I blurted, 'part-time really would quite suit me,
actually.'

'Oh!' A stiff arm shot out offering me the half-scrunched paper.
'By all means.'

Sheepishly, I took it.

*And they knew that they were naked; and they sewed fig leaves
together and made themselves aprons.*

'Right then,' I said, standing.

'Well then.' Roy stood too.

'Yes—'

'See how you—'

'Let you know.' I backed into a wall. 'Oops.'

'Excellent.'

Foolishly nodding at our feet, Roy and I parted company, we
hoped forever.

In the sweltering heat of the phone booth outside, I fanned
myself as I told the girl I was answering an ad for a receptionist and
asked to speak to a 'Didi'.

'Have you worked in this industry before, Meredith?'

I usually corrected people when they got my name wrong, but
if I was going to work in a brothel, I was quite happy to be
Meredith.

'What industry is that?' I asked casually.

Muffled voices. 'Just putting you on hold.'

Half a Chopin nocturne later the girl got my details and
promised that Didi would get back to me in a day or two.

Meeting Didi

Two weeks later, on a hot February afternoon, a woman with a Slavic accent phoned me at home. Didi asked me very sweetly if I'd like to come to her suite at North Sydney the following day for an interview at twelve o'clock. Her voice was all lipstick and fingernails, and caressed with a soothing tone. Didi lived on the fourteenth floor and was looking forward to meeting me.

I'd been to a screen test for a McDonald's ad that morning so I wasn't really dressed for the sex industry when I got off the train at North Sydney at eleven-thirty in sandals and a smock dress. I swapped the sandals for the high heels in my bag, threw a belt around my waist, and undid two buttons. Then three. Then just one. During a quick detour through one of the glam arcades, and on the pretence of 'testing' new products at every cosmetics shop, I made myself up. By the time I finished doing my nails at a Revlon counter, much to the chagrin of the Revlon girls, it was time to cross the road to meet Didi, in a cloud of Chanel, Arpège and Guerlain.

I came out of the lift on the penthouse floor to be met on the other side of an iron security door by what looked like Britt Ekland, and a small dog, the sort you'd call Fifi. Even at home this woman was better groomed than an air hostess. I sensed by her poise and polite directness that Didi was a sharp businesswoman, and possibly had never worn a tracksuit in her life. She was bleached, polished, made up and sprayed in a way that suggested she might once have been a working girl herself. And good at it.

The dog's name was Max, not Fifi, and he smelt good too.

I wondered if Didi had an interior decorator, or if she had come up with the Ivanna Trump safari theme herself. Wherever I looked were brass-based pot plants on pedestals, bonsai chandeliers, mirrors, fluffy white rugs, animal skins, dog-size statues of zebras, and a moose head that looked incongruous mounted on pink floral wallpaper. I knew that somewhere around the corner there had to be a bar, with lots of mirrors, and possibly a baby grand. Standing out among all these decorative artefacts was a framed picture of a beautiful blond-haired schoolboy, and I wondered what on earth he thought his mother did for a living.

Didi led me to an intimate alcove with facing beige leather couches. She sat and crossed her shapely legs with effortless poise, recording my answers on a clipboard resting on her lap. I liked Didi's gentle manner and its mix of professional etiquette and humour, although I kept expecting her to indicate the nearest exits at any given moment. And I think Didi appreciated my cheerful disposition.

'You've got a nice face,' she said.

Before I could stop myself, I laughed and pulled such an idiotic face, I'm sure Didi regretted the compliment immediately.

'And you're tall,' she continued, with a flirtatious smile. 'Men like that.'

'Oh,' I nodded graciously, suddenly worried that Didi had confused her twelve o'clock with her twelve-thirty.

Didi was looking at me strangely, and then, with one eyebrow raised, asked if I had ever considered working on 'the other side' myself. I laughed and said no, and she laughed too. Then I said no again without laughing, and we both nodded sagely, and looked at Max. But to assure Didi I did not judge those who did work on 'the other side', I told Didi my cousin had worked as an 'escort' in London, that she'd made a pot of money, and that she and her girlfriends were handsomely ferried from Belgravia to Knights-bridge, from Isam's to Ahmed's. Once, I told Didi, I waited for her while I watched satellite television at the Lebanese Consul's. I couldn't believe the things coming out of my mouth. My cousin is an alto chorister at Westminster Abbey. Although back in the eighties, when she was a 'waitress', Briony took a lot of holidays in the Middle East, often stayed with an assistant to the Crown Prince of Abu Dhabi, and once rang me from Sam Spiegel's yacht. Anyway, Didi said softly, one of the other receptionists had recently crossed to the other side, so it was not an impossibility if I felt so inclined.

'All righty!' I said cheerfully, and changed the subject.

Didi's escort agency, which comprised sixty working girls altogether, used to be based in offices on the floor below Didi's suite in North Sydney, until two months ago. Without ever using the word *brothel*, Didi explained to me that since expanding to 'in-house' in January she had relocated the business to a house in

Darlinghurst with more room. Or rooms, to be precise. As a receptionist, therefore, I would not only be required to take phone bookings from men in hotels, I would have to 'meet and greet' clients downstairs, introduce them to the girls on roster, and take their money.

'So the girls will be . . . downstairs?' I asked gingerly.

'If they are not out on a booking, yes.' Didi smiled.

I could only think of one thing. I was going to work with prostitutes!

Didi told me to turn up for work the following afternoon at three-thirty and a receptionist called Pip would show me the ropes, metaphorically speaking. If the job appealed, I could start working three night shifts a week immediately, with two other receptionists.

'Some girls decide it is not the job for them,' Didi said with a considerate smile at the door.

Well, some girls could keep their stationery request forms, staplers and office picnics. I was going to take money from men who wanted sex! I was going to wash towels! And I was going to meet women who had sexual intercourse with complete strangers and got paid for it!

I left Didi's floating on cloud nine. I hadn't told her I was an actor. And despite having a child, she didn't recognise me from *Play School*. But what if a client recognised me from *Play School*? My agent was none too happy about this when I rang her on my mobile. I was not famous but, as she pointed out, it made a good headline. PLAY SCHOOL PRESENTER FOUND WORKING IN BROTHEL!

'And what if you open the door to some producer from Channel Nine?' she cried.

I wasn't sure, but couldn't it actually work in my favour? Anyway, I decided to go straight home and ring Mum and Dad with my news. My funny news, that we could all have a good laugh over, couldn't we? Oh God, please laugh.

Ever since they discovered the speakerphone button on their new telephone/fax machine, my parents like to stoop over this magical box, head to head, and shout. Tasmanians often think no one can hear them. But I knew by the stony silence that followed my announcement that neither parent had had any trouble hearing me at all. Finally one of them laughed, but I couldn't tell which as it was an octave higher than usual. My father, who was once an actor himself, followed my agent's lead and immediately expressed grave concern that such a job might pose a serious threat to my career.

'And do what exactly, Dad?' I asked him accusingly. 'Stop me from playing more nervous housewives in British farces?'

My parents both knew that this was the very reason I had moved from Melbourne to Sydney: to save the world, and myself, from any more repeat stage performances of the same neurotic woman, disguised in a different wig and apron, hailing from various Celtic provinces.

It was my mother, who works in children's books, who voiced the more sinister concern. In my mother's doting eyes, I have not aged since I was twelve, and she still insists on describing me, even in public, as 'shiny', 'fluffy', 'phosphorous' and, occasionally, 'velvety'. What if my new employers got it into their woolly heads, she began tremulously, that their new receptionist might make more money as a working girl? Of course, I was deemed too fluffy to be allowed any say in the matter myself.

'Don't be silly,' I laughed, deciding not to divulge that Madam Didi had already invited me to do just that. 'I'm thirty-eight, remember? As if she's going to ask an old boiler like me!'

Disappointingly, my father snorted with relief, until my mother's angry protest quickly prompted him to assure me that I was still a 'good sort', and could easily get work in a brothel, if I chose. It was the strangest compliment my father ever gave me. Judging by the silence that followed, he felt so too.

Through the arched window

Arlington House was a beautiful three-storey terrace house with two large palm trees out the front and an upstairs verandah. It looked strange in the daylight from outside. Like a set on stage between shows. I rang the door bell and a female voice on the intercom asked, 'Who is it?'

Noticing the camera above the door, I smiled and waved at it, mouthing 'Mer-e-dith!'

'*Who?*' the voice demanded through the intercom.

I dropped the charades, embarrassed. 'Meredith!'

The door finally opened slightly, revealing the top half of a blonde girl in a smart black suit, with cleavage.

'Yes?' she demanded, looking about nervously.

Her hair was pulled sharply back into a tight bun, where clearly she kept any joy.

'I'm Meredith. Here to see Pip.'

A taut little smile flashed across her face as she let me in.

I followed Victoria into the cool darkness. When my eyes adjusted I saw lots of wood panelling. We were in a beautifully renovated house, with burgundy carpets, dimmed chandeliers, and the smell of jasmine oil everywhere. On the right was a sort of waiting room, with big leather couches, lamps, a bar, and imitation antiques, including another moose. Didi obviously collected moose.

'This is where the clients wait to be introduced to the girls,' Victoria mumbled.

Everything was upstaged by a pornographic video in progress on a large television positioned in one corner. My impulse was to laugh, but something in Victoria's stony expression changed my mind. We passed a beautiful old staircase to the left, and went straight on into a large, bright and cheery kitchen.

Sitting at the kitchen table in front of me was a dishevelled young Renoir beauty. Next to her sat a harder but pretty blonde creature, who looked a lot like the American actress Heather Locklear, until she spoke.

'G'day, matey'

Despite Victoria's hasty, almost inaudible introduction, Odette and Heather looked up from their magazines and gave me a dreamy but friendly welcome. Even though it was late in the afternoon, Odette looked like she'd just got out of bed and Heather looked like she was about to go dancing. Perhaps Odette was 'in-house', and Heather was 'escort-only'.

Behind them stood a tall bench that almost divided the kitchen in half, and a large window on the right which overlooked an empty red-brick courtyard. At the far end of the kitchen was another room through which could be heard the monotonous revolutions of an industrial dryer. Inside the laundry, my guide informed me plainly, was the girls' toilet and shower. Victoria stepped into a small alcove on our right, and waited for me in front of several tall lockers.

'Coming?' she snapped.

In front of the small alcove's wall of lockers, two chairs sat at a back door, held open by an enormous terracotta ashtray that was almost full of lipstick-stained cigarette butts. Opposite this was the kitchen entrance to the girls' lounge, where I gathered they could not smoke. For the second time, I was plunged from warm sunshine into cool darkness as I followed Victoria into the airless, windowless room. It had wall to wall leather couches, rugs, a central coffee table and a television in one corner.

'Look,' said Victoria flatly as she clicked the remote control, and the television screen abruptly came to life with John and Noni singing.

If you're happy and you know it clap your hands!

Was this a joke? I looked at Victoria, but the expression on her face told me she didn't joke much. She clicked it again and in complete contrast we were now looking at a black-and-white video of an empty lounge room, with a familiar-looking moose on the wall. Had we not just been in that room?

'Yeah,' Victoria said, 'while the client sits in there watching the porn, the girls sit in here, watching *him*. Hidden camera in the telly. Good, isn't it?'

Ah. Now she smiled. Victoria was pretty. As I followed her upstairs I noticed her legs were bare and she wore black high heels. This and the cleavage made me wonder, which side did Victoria work?

On the first landing, Victoria led me into a large plush bedroom with dusty pink walls, shagpile pink carpet, and a large leopard-skin covered bed on which were placed two rich burgundy towels that matched the two rich burgundy velvet curtains. On the other side of the door hung two rich burgundy towelling dressing gowns. A tall plant in a brass pot stood in the far corner, and against the wall stood a pine tallboy, over which was hung a large framed picture of a naked lady with lots of lip gloss and lots of fluffy hair, touching her breasts as if they hurt. On one side of the bed was a chair and on the other was a bedside table with a lamp, a box of tissues, and a pump bottle discreetly encased in tortoiseshell.

'Lube.' Victoria pointed to it, rudely blowing its cover.

Next to that were various vibrators. One was so large it was positively scary.

'Crikey!' I laughed, glancing from it to Victoria, whose dead eyes snuffed my mirth in an instant.

Victoria yanked open the drawers of the tallboy. 'Towels are kept in here, along with condoms and dams.'

'Dams?'

Victoria looked at me like I was an idiot. 'All the girls use dams!'

Well, now we could all get some sleep.

'Dental dams!' she said, appalled at my ignorance.

I knew we weren't talking about saving the Franklin, but now she was suggesting girls put these 'dams' in their mouths. To cover their teeth?

'Ah.' I nodded, trying to steal a look at a 'dam'.

'For the girl's protection,' Victoria snapped, shutting the drawer.

To protect the girl's teeth from the man's penis? I no longer cared. I'd find out later from someone who didn't take the whole *dam* thing so seriously.

'This is the clients' bathroom,' she said, showing me the room next door. It was a beautiful dark green, marble-tiled bathroom with mirrored walls, and a completely mirrored ceiling. I was everywhere I looked! The fittings were fake antique brass, and big burgundy towels hung on the rails. Next to the sink was a large bottle of Listerine with a stack of plastic cups.

'You have to make sure the toilet's always flushed, there are clean towels, and the soap's refilled.'

A few stairs led up to another bedroom. This one had a fake zebra-skin cover on the bed and above the tallboy was another fluffy-haired woman wearing too much lip gloss kneeling on a fluffy rug and holding her crotch as if it hurt. Like all the rooms, the air was filled with the scent of jasmine oil, and its light was dimmed to low.

'And there's an alarm button under all the bedside tables if a girl's in trouble,' Victoria said at the door. 'And no,' she said, before I could ask, 'not while I've been here.'

Next door to that was a closed door marked *Reception*. But first we had to continue to the top of another flight of stairs to see 'the party room'. Victoria removed a gold-tasselled rope barring our way and we ascended the beautifully polished dark wooden staircase to the top. There was no door to the party room and no carpet, just polished floorboards, giving it a rather exposed disposition, but otherwise its opulence was overwhelming. One half of the room was full of huge pot plants, statues, a chaise longue and a television/video/stereo unit weighing heavily on a delicate imitation antique table. The other half housed two king-sized crimson velvet covered beds, which were separated by the usual table, lamp, dildos, vibrators, lube, tissues etc.

'It couldn't be very soundproof,' I whispered.

'It isn't,' said Victoria. 'You can hear absolutely everything underneath in reception.'

I concealed my glee and nodded disapprovingly. How awful.

'Come on,' Victoria snapped, already halfway down the stairs.

At last we were in reception and Victoria introduced me to a slim, sprightly, young woman dressed in tight black pants and top, sitting at a desk just inside the door. I was relieved to see Pip had extremely short hair like mine, wore no make-up and had no cleavage whatsoever. Pip was friendly, the room was large, and the sun shone through two sets of French windows that opened onto a balcony overlooking the palm trees. Not that Pip could see them. The two rows of solid, wooden desks, cluttered with phones, pens and other office paraphernalia, obstinately turned their backs on this airy vista, and faced the south wall instead. There were five desks in all, if you didn't count the one in the very corner that had been taken over by a large computer and a television monitor that hung from a bracket above it. A somewhat superior-looking desk sat apart from all the others, and faced the east wall nearest the windows. And I was relieved to see Victoria flop into its large, black leather chair, and swivel like a restless teenager.

'I hate going out there!' She laughed, and instantly became human.

It was only Victoria's second week but Pip had been working as a receptionist for Boris and Didi for several years. This was the first time anyone had mentioned Boris, Didi's husband, and when Pip nodded towards the spotless mahogany desk, Victoria leapt to her feet, returned Boris's leather chair to its rightful position, and skulked back to her desk behind Pip's. Would I ever get to meet Boris?

'Oh yes,' Pip assured me, 'when you do your first night shift. Boris comes in at midnight.'

The way both girls smiled, I guessed that meeting this man was going to be memorable. So who was the boss, I asked, Didi or Boris?

The girls burst into gales of laughter, and I had to wait some time for them to recover. 'Sorry.' Pip kept repeating, which was thoughtful. Finally, with one hand on her heaving chest, she gave me a pitiful look. 'Didi,' she uttered, with restrained altitude.

'Ding dong' went the front door, making Victoria involuntarily snort as she sat bolt upright and glared at the monitor in the corner.

'My God,' said Pip, looking at the young girl on the doorstep, 'it's Lola.' And through the intercom she hollered, 'Come on up, stranger.'

So that I would look like a receptionist too, I swiftly settled into the desk next to Victoria's against the wall.

'Who's Lola?' Victoria whispered.

'Doesn't work for us any more,' Pip shot back. 'Drugs. We had to ask her to leave. She used to be – Hello, princess!'

A slim girl, with lots of wavy hair, wearing tight jeans and a cut-off T-shirt, smiled anxiously in the doorway. Pip introduced the twitching Lola, whose dark eyes darted about the room in search of something.

'Hi.' Her voice broke like an adolescent boy's, and as she stepped into the light I noticed the ravaged state of Lola's young skin. 'I've come for me stuff. I left some stuff in me locker, but Sofia said it got cleaned out or somethin'.'

'Sure, sweetie,' cooed Pip, 'all the stuff from the lockers was put up there.'

Pip was pointing to something above my head. I looked up to see some plastic bags on top of a cupboard behind me, and turned back just in time to move very swiftly out of Lola's way. Whatever it was, she would be very upset if it wasn't there.

As Lola stood on my chair and noisily began hunting through various plastic bags, the other girls pretended to be busy. I stood by watching helplessly as it rained corsets and lace teddies on my desk.

'Fuck!' Lola cried as a red shoe sent my pens flying. 'It's not here!' She looked around the room desperately.

'What was it, darling?' Pip asked, as if she was a toddler.

'My fucking black leather jacket, that's what! Real fucking leather! And all me make-up!'

Lola clumsily stepped down, suspiciously eyeing the large canvas bag hanging on the back of my chair.

'So, how have you been, gorgeous?' Pip asked brightly.

Lola looked suddenly selfconscious and stepped back towards the door. 'Y'know,' she mumbled, looking from one receptionist to the next, and folded her arms protectively. 'I'm goin' up north. Just get out the city an' clean up a bit.'

We all nodded encouragingly, until a car horn beeped angrily outside.

'See yas.'

And Lola was gone.

We waited for the front door to slam.

'Leather jacket ...' scoffed Pip. '*Sure* she had a leather jacket.'

While I sat at my desk reading a frightening tome entitled *Receptionists Rules*, I listened to both girls taking incoming calls and confirming bookings. Pip and Victoria had such a practised intimate phone technique happening I could barely hear what they were saying. But I noticed they stuck religiously to the script Pip had placed in front of me.

Hello. Can I help you? ... Yes, sir, we have beautiful Asian, Australian and European ladies available. They provide the full service, *including a sensual body massage. The first hour is $200, and any extending hour is $150. What sort of lady were you looking for this afternoon/evening? . . . Would you like me to see who's available and call you straight back? . . . And are you calling from a hotel or a private home? . . .*

I watched closely as Pip surveyed the day's roster, stuck up on the wall in front of her, to find only two girls available who vaguely resembled her client's request. A few minutes later she called Derek back in Room 255 at the Airport Hilton.

'I have several young busty blondes, Derek,' Pip sang like a weather girl. 'One is a very sexy Danish girl, just back from a skiing trip, five foot five, long wavy blonde hair, blue eyes, twenty-five years old, a fantastic figure, Derek, 36–25–35. Or I have a more demure, very pretty, young strawberry blonde Australian, Derek, she's nineteen . . .'

And give or take an inch or two, Pip described the same girl four different ways. They made it sound like we had a veritable smorgasbord.

The price varied, I gathered, depending on which phone number the man used to call us. Each phone had a panel large enough to accommodate sixteen red lights that flashed madly with each incoming call, so I was somewhat relieved to see a hold button in the bottom corner. I couldn't wait to play with that. I had about twenty years of revenge to wreak with that little device.

'Why are there so many lines?' I asked my young tutor.

Pip gave a weary smile. 'Half the ads in the yellow pages are us,' she sighed with her eyes closed and then, with one finger skipping across the little buttons, she sang, 'Aussie Girls, International, Asian Fantasy Ladies, Sensual Companions, Seductress, Exotic Eurasian, Blissful Encounters, Caress . . .'

How on earth would I remember all these names? Squinting at the phone in front of me, I could just make out the worn, minute initials scrawled in gold under each button. AG, I, AFL, etc. Hopeless. AFL could never mean anything to me but football. Pip explained that all the buttons, whatever national sport they stood for, charged the same rate of two hundred dollars an hour, unless the man called on Exclusive or Cachet. Suddenly Pip swivelled around to face me and leant forward as if she had something of critical importance to impart.

'If the gentleman calls on either the Exclusive or Cachet line,' Pip announced, tapping one solid fingernail on my E and C buttons, 'there is a different spiel, and preferably spoken in a different voice.' Sounding like a late night ad, Pip demonstrated for me, and I tried hard not to laugh.

'We have university students, lingerie models and photographic models available, Asian, Australian and European, who provide the full service including a sensual body massage. The university students are two hundred and eighty dollars for the hour, lingerie models are three hundred and fifty, and the photographic models are five hundred.'

When Pip had finished I asked if there was a special stable of beautiful models to cater for such wealthy chaps. She closed her eyes and smiled. No, Pip said at last. The same girls were sent, whatever line the man called on.

'Except Genevieve,' Victoria timidly interrupted her colleague.

'Well of course you wouldn't send Genevieve on a standard booking,' Pip admonished her.

For a moment both girls forgot I was there and gushed about Genevieve's new haircut, her talented colourist at Pasha, and the Versace coat she brought back from New York. Victoria had heard you could get fake ones in Bali, but Pip assured her that Genevieve would never do such a thing. AFL was ringing, and with a sideways nod in my direction, Pip passed me to her colleague before answering it herself.

If the client called from a hotel, Victoria continued my lesson, we had to ring him back to verify a man of that name was indeed staying in that room at that hotel. But if he called from home, we had to use the computer. Victoria looked resentfully at the ancient computer sitting on the desk in the corner. With a heavy sigh, she launched herself from her desk and stomped past to collapse at her new post.

'Name?' Victoria said, turning to me. 'Any name.'

'Er, Smith,' I said, and Victoria's fingers quickly complied.

'Is Smith your ex-boyfriend?' she asked flatly without taking her eyes off the screen.

'No!' I cried, instantly wishing I'd said Beatty.

'It's all right,' Victoria muttered, 'plenty of time.'

With one Mr Smith's sexual history on display behind her tight blonde bun, Victoria explained to me that if a client was not on our files, the computer would verify his listing in the phone book and automatically open a file in his name. Once on file, we had to record which girls he had seen, how much he had paid, and 'comments'.

'Comments?'

'Things the girls think the other girls should know, or be warned about.'

While Victoria answered a call back at her desk, I expeditiously took her place at the computer and scoured the screen for 'comments'. More than once, Mr Smith in Botany had *tried to remove condom*. I scrolled down a line. *Prefers non-smoker*. And another. *NEVER SEND LOLA*.

Lola. I wondered if she'd ever make it up north.

'And look,' Victoria said, suddenly over my shoulder again, 'when anyone rings, his number comes up here.' She tapped at a tiny screen above all the buttons on the phone next to us. 'Comes in very handy when kids ring up on prank calls.'

I looked up at Victoria just in time to see her tight smile snap like a rubber band.

'Is that a client?' she asked, blanching at the monitor above.

Victoria only thawed when Pip assured her it was nothing but the shade of a palm frond moving in the breeze.

While my colleagues answered calls, I took a moment to read the handwritten signs stuck up on every spare bit of wall space in the office. They weren't so much reminders as warnings and down-right threats addressed to all receptionists.

RECEPTONISTS MUST NOT SOCIALIZ WITH WORKING GIRLS! IF FOUND OUT, SHE CAN PACK HER BAGS AND LEEVE IMMEDIATLY!

NO MOBIL PHONES ALOUD IN OFFICE. ANY MOBIL HEARD RINGING WILL BE CONFICSATED IMMEDIATLY!

NO WORKING GIRL ALLOWD IN RECEPTION!

All seemingly written by some fascist dictator possibly frustrated by his or her poor spelling skills.

When the front door bell rang again, Victoria stiffened as if she had to go downstairs and fellate the man herself. She left Pip and I checking out our visitor on the monitor. I was glad I didn't recognise the thin, balding man in a suit, holding a David Jones bag, and I wondered if Uncle Ralph had ever used a brothel. He certainly told enough jokes about them.

Once on our own, Pip showed me photos of her recent holiday in Phuket, but all I could think about was Victoria downstairs introducing Odette and Heather to the dark suit in a room with a moose. Then Pip said something that got my attention. Her boyfriend, Milton, worked in the wardrobe department on *Home and Away*. As it happened, the following week I was to play an unhappily married Christian social worker and help a prisoner escape on *Home and Away*. Should I tell Pip? I imagined myself half naked in a Channel Seven dressing room telling some guy called Milton, 'Actually, I work at the same brothel as your girlfriend,' and decided to remain the anonymous observer instead. Anyway, I soon discovered that going 'undercover' wasn't even a choice, as no one in this house was remotely interested in who I was, what I'd done, or where I'd been. The only question anyone ever asked me was if I had a cigarette. I wondered if I could quiz Pip about the dams, but she was on another call so I read more signs.

ALL GIRLS PEROIDS MUST BE RECORDED IN PEROID BOOK!

My God.

Victoria returned, flopped back in her chair and asked me if I had a cigarette. Pip obliged. Well? Which girl had he chosen?

'Oh, he's gone.' Victoria looked at Pip. 'Jerk-off.'

They rolled their eyes in stereo. Apparently this happened regularly. Men who possibly didn't even have the money just popped in for a perve, or they simply enjoyed rejecting women in their lunch hours. Oh yes, my fellow receptionists enthused, I was going to meet all sorts in this job. That's if I ever return, I felt like enthusing right back. It was the signs. They were beginning to depress me. I didn't want to work for or with anyone who thought they had the right to tell me who I could or could not socialise with; no one touched my mobile phone but me; I wasn't sure if I could demand information from other women about their menstrual cycles; and all this from someone who spelt money with two Ns!

'Come on,' Victoria laughed, slapping me on the knees. 'I'll show you where we keep the condom dispenser.'

Facing the enemy

I hadn't taken this long to choose something to wear since my disastrous date with a window-dresser.

'Have you got anything more . . . stylish?' Libby, my housemate, asked, looking sadly at my wraparound cotton dress and happy shoes. 'You look a bit . . . Amish.'

Didi told me a receptionist should dress up, but not too much. It could confuse the clients and displease the girls, neither of which I wanted to do. So for half an hour I had entertained Libby with a breathless fashion parade of every black item of summer clothing I possessed, including my new black jeans and Portman's top.

'Now you look like a hooker.'

Finally we settled on the good old white blouse and long black skirt. Looking like someone from the string section, I set off for my first night working in a brothel.

'It's me again,' I said, when my young teacher looked up from her paperwork. Pip smiled graciously and handed me the key to the front door. I listened carefully as she explained that no one could leave the house without being let out by the 'downstairs receptionist', an idea Boris had come up with to prevent in-house girls from letting themselves out before their roster ended at 5 am. To say the girls resented it was an understatement.

'Feels like a fucking convent,' a young girl in a strapless hot pink dress mumbled bitterly as she stubbed out her cigarette at the kitchen table.

There was something about the way Pip said 'Oh no, I don't ever work downstairs' that troubled me. I gathered there were two classes of receptionist. Those like me, who answered the front door, touched clients' money, picked up towels, handed out condoms etc. And those who didn't, and were repulsed by the very idea.

'I don't do downstairs either,' said the other receptionist, and then roared laughing. Raelene was a big, tough, friendly Maori mama and about as rotund as Pip was whippet. I liked her straightaway because she never forgot where we were, and she thought it was pretty funny. And Raelene found me positively hysterical. As a novice who spent her first month making one mistake after another, I provided Raelene with endless hours of free entertainment. When I flooded the kitchen, having overloaded the washing machine, she laughed so much I thought she'd have a stroke.

So there I sat, with Raelene at her desk surrounded by pens, confectionery, cigarettes and family photos, while she patiently tutored me in the art of greeting a client. I dreaded the door bell that would take me away from the security of Raelene's open family album showing her several hulking brothers at their various weddings, all protectively hugging their mum rather than their brides.

'He looks nice,' I said, pointing to one of them.

'That's Cammie. He's not speaking to me.'

'Why?'

''Cause I hit her,' Raelene said with a mouth full of Cherry Ripe, and pointed to his bride. 'We don't get on.'

The door bell rang and all eyes hit the stooped figure on the monitor, and then me. The moment had come. I now understood why, after only two weeks in her new job, receptionist Victoria had thrown in the towel, quite literally. Apparently, on Wednesday afternoon, she'd opened the front door to a client, walked straight past him, out through the gate, hailed a passing cab and climbed in. I knew just how she felt.

Sitting beside me, Raelene was rocking with laughter.

'Coming!' I sang down the intercom.

'Coming?' chortled Pip.

Oh bugger off, you patronising, upstairs brothel receptionist! One quick last glance at my list of instructions and I flew down the stairs muttering, 'video, door, menu, girls …' Raelene found it hilarious that I called the price list a menu, but that's what it looked like with its columns of services available and matching hardcore photos inside a large, laminated folder.

Before I could answer the door, I had to turn on the porn video – stupid rule because it kept the client waiting. I stood in front of the television frantically jabbing the remote control at it, but there was not a breast in sight.

'The door, Meredith!' a voice crackled through the telephone on top of the bar.

God! Was no room safe from telephone intercoms?

'Yes, yes!' I shouted at it, giving up on the video and going to the front door.

A tall frightened man in a beige safari suit far too small for him told my chest his name was Gilbert.

'Come in, Gilbert,' I said, feigning calm, and led him into the waiting room.

'Here before, have you?'

'No! No!' Gilbert shook. 'First time.'

If Gilbert was already nervous, I definitely made him worse.

'Right!' I said, too cheerfully.

Gilbert was a thin, tremulous man in his fifties and, something in his wild eyes told me, perhaps not the full quid.

'I'm from Tasmania,' he blurted.

Should I tell him I was too? No. My mother might have taught his niece. His cousin may have dated my sister. Tasmania was like that.

'How lovely,' I said instead, and thrust the price list in his lap. 'I like to call this our menu!'

Gilbert's eyes popped out on stalks. 'Are these girls here now?'

I looked over Gilbert's shoulder.

'Goodness no!' I said, my eyes landing on a photo of what looked like Pamela Anderson ingesting an enormous penis.

'Video!' came a strangled voice from the intercom.

Gilbert's terrified gaze landed incredulously on the moose.

'Gilbert,' I said without making any sudden movements, 'you

just sit there and relax because I've got some beautiful ladies who would love to meet you.'

Without taking my eyes off him I tried the remote control again. Success. The room came to life with moaning women whose pink reflections danced on Gilbert's lax face. He'd slipped into such a trance I could have amputated his leg without an anaesthetic, and so I left him there, and crept out like a mother leaves a nursery. Video, door, menu, girls ... Girls!

I had no idea which girls were in the house. The kitchen was empty except for a solitary blonde woman sitting by the back door, dressed in a smart black suit, with her round head of thick blonde hair bowed over a cigarette. As I approached she looked up at me, and I was immediately thrown to see the soft golden halo framed a face so fallen, not just with age, but sadness. We both smiled awkwardly, embarrassed, as if she'd read my thoughts. Her black suit seemed a size too large, but nonetheless revealed a generous, heavy cleavage, and although she wore too much red lipstick, her smile was sweet, like a child's.

'The others are in there,' she said softly, gesturing to the girls' lounge. 'I'm Antoinette.'

In the lounge room three other girls were checking out Gilbert on the monitor. A tall, slim, pretty blonde girl dressed in a smart red suit jumped to her feet as if she'd just stepped out of a multi-vitamin ad.

'I'm Shelby,' she announced with a broad Australian accent and a sunny smile, and shook my hand with her delicate manicured one. 'And this is Rita.'

I thought for a second that Rita was a man in drag. Reclining on a couch, she looked like one of Gauguin's Tahitian natives, if he'd kept on painting. Rita, at forty-plus years, had a solid, stocky frame that was too mature to be so barely compacted into such a tiny black dress, but her beautiful thick black hair fell luxuriously down to her waist.

'Hello, darling,' Rita purred in a deep sexy voice with an accent to match.

'And this is Maya.' Shelby gestured to a beautiful Thai woman sitting in the corner applying lipstick.

Maya looked up, nodded and smiled, then returned to her mirror. Maya was a picture of elegance in her long black evening dress trimmed with diamantes, and her hair in a neat chignon. At first I thought she was in her twenties, but Maya exuded an aura of quiet defeat that only comes with age and experience.

We all stood for a moment, watching Gilbert on the monitor. I wondered if he'd blinked since I'd left.

'What's he like?' came Antoinette's soft voice from behind me. I was surprised to see she just came up to my shoulders.

'Very nervous.'

It occurred to me that they would stay like this forever unless I prodded them.

'Okay, let's go.'

The women rose with dignity, straightened, flicked, brushed, and moved into the kitchen in a cloud of perfumes. They followed me to the waiting room door and stood behind me making more adjustments in the ornate, gold-framed mirror in the hall. I turned the handle, interrupting Gilbert, who leapt up from his video, fixed his gaze steadfastly on my chest and nodded.

One by one the girls came into the room, shook hands with Gilbert as I introduced them, and left. Gilbert mumbled and stuttered his way from one cleavage to the next. When they'd all gone I asked him if there was one he particularly liked. Wide-eyed and without hesitation, Gilbert told my chest, 'Antoinette.'

'All right, Gilbert. And would you like to see Antoinette for one hour?'

'All I want's a hand job, you know, and a bit of spanky-spanky!'

My body remained, but the rest of me fled from the room.

'Perhaps half an hour then, Gilbert?' I heard myself say.

While Gilbert twitched in anticipation, I ran upstairs clutching one hundred and twenty dollars and breathlessly asked Raelene if I should tell Antoinette about the spanky-spanky.

'Nah. Just give her the condom, tell her what room she's in, and for how long.'

I ran back downstairs to the girls' lounge, where they were immersed in *Better Homes and Gardens*. The girls never watched the negotiations taking place on the monitor, Pip told me. That would be indiscreet. But when I gave them the news about Gilbert, they barely concealed their relief, leaving poor Antoinette to graciously accept her condom and make a noble exit.

When I returned to the office the phones were going silly. This often happened, Pip explained. The first wave was overseas business-men lining up a girl for the night. The second came just before midnight when the pubs shut, and the third wave was the unsuccessful Romeos who'd staggered home from clubs at 2 am, very pissed. But now, even though it was only ten past nine, every man in Sydney seemed to have the same idea. I watched in dumb awe as Raelene and Pip worked the phones as if they were coordi-nating a fleet of jumbo jets from a control tower in peak-hour traffic.

'May-Ling, got a booking for you. Ring me back.'

'Hello, could I speak to Mr Dingermans in Room 702?'

'Patrick, pick up May-Ling at Millennium. Going to Airport Hilton.'

'Yes, we have beautiful ladies available, Australian, Asian and European.'

'She's Swiss, Mr Dingermans, very busty, double D.'

'Finished Pandora? Patrick's on his way.'

'Read out the numbers, Kimberley.'

'You're a lingerie model, May-Ling, nineteen, lots of fun, so cheer up.'

'One six or two, Kimberley? Expiry date?'

'Patrick, drop May-Ling then swing by Sheraton for Pandora.'

'No, sir, I'm afraid none of our girls provide that service.'

'Calm down, Mr Nakasawa—'

'Your number's on my screen, kid. Hang up or I'll ring back and tell your parents.'

'What you mean, girl no good?'

'Okay, Yousaf, Antoinette will be there in twenty-five minutes.'

What? Antoinette would be spanking Gilbert for at least another twenty! Raelene reminded me with a portentous look, between landing planes, that it was my job to get Antoinette out on time.

I was just about to knock on their door when Antoinette opened it. It must have looked like I'd been standing there listening the whole time.

'Oh, hello there! I was just about to ...'

Looking dishevelled and utterly wretched, Antoinette walked straight past me, revealing a limp and rather dazed Gilbert clutching his safari jacket in the corner. It was my duty to see the client out, and always ask at the door if he was happy with the service. I came to hate doing this, and even Gilbert looked at me as if I was a pervert.

I ran back upstairs, nearly knocking over Antoinette coming down with her arms full of towels.

'Oh, Antoinette, we've got you a booking at the Marriot straight—'

'Jesus Christ! Give me a fucking break!' she shouted, and stormed past.

What on earth made me think I could do this job? I could barely return a cold cappuccino let alone ask a prostitute to get cracking.

'Wait till you do an interview,' chuckled Raelene, back in reception.

'Or check a girl's arms for tracks.' Pip guffawed.

I didn't like this horrible dark house with its sad men and its moose. I wanted to go home, have a bath and watch *The Sound of Music*. I craved nuns, soap and fresh mountain air.

My night shift was supposed to end at 5 am, but at 5 am no one said anything. Boris hadn't materialised, but that wasn't unusual, said Pip. There were still a few girls to pay, so I dried more towels, put the rubbish out, loaded the dishwasher, then sprayed my allocated desk. At the end of her shift, a receptionist had to spray down her desk with disinfectant, probably to prevent the following receptionist from picking up on any of her mistakes. At least my desk was in the second row, and therefore nearer the windows behind me, but it was also against the wall, and therefore right under all of Hitler's signs. I sat down and dutifully flicked through the book I had been told was essential reading. In fact, if a receptionist did not read from 'The Bible' before she began her shift, she would be sacked on the spot. I knew because a sign next to my head said so.

The Bible was one of the largest office diaries I'd ever seen, and every bit of office news had to be recorded in it. Beside each entry were the scrawled initials of several receptionists, proving each one had indeed read that, despite having braces, Yvonne could still provide 'French'. And we were out of Lipton tea. While the others were deep in paperwork, I flicked back a month to late January and was shocked to read that the office no longer provided Viagra to clients, at thirty dollars a pop. I wondered if Didi and Boris had stopped distributing the blue pills when it occurred to them that a dead diabetic in bedroom three wasn't worth the bad publicity.

I was about to ask Raelene if Boris bought Viagra off the net when I looked up to see a tall, slim man wearing jeans, a T-shirt and runners leaning in our doorway, smiling. Surely this wasn't Boris. My colleagues greeted the man warmly, and introduced the driver to the new receptionist. I guessed by Patrick's windswept salt and pepper hair, and the laugh lines on his tanned, rugged face, that he was somewhere in his forties. After a jovial nod in my direction, he lit up a cigarette and almost danced over to Pip's desk.

Patrick was a laughing, gentle soul with an English accent. Dorset, I would have said. You play enough comic shepherdesses, you end up in Dorset. Everything about him, from his voice to his walk, seemed to lilt, even when he sat down with Pip to add up his drives. As far as I could tell, Patrick worked a few full night shifts like a taxi driver, taking orders from our office to pick up and deliver girls all over Sydney. I closed The Bible and looked around the room. All was silent, except for Raelene who was quietly counting the takings.

'It's past five,' I finally piped.

They all looked at me, then at each other, and laughed.

He'd rather you didn't talk about it

Peter and Libby, my housemates, were sitting on the couch downstairs when I finally surfaced at two the next afternoon, and I could tell by the look on Libby's face that she had been waiting for this moment for some time. Usually I was the one waiting for her. Libby worked as production coordinator on *Moulin Rouge*, and her mobile had a way of going off every twenty minutes with one fascinating crisis after another.

'Well?' she asked, hugging her knees with excitement. 'What's it like? What were the girls like? Did men come to the door? Did they think you were one of them? Do you want a cup of tea?'

Peter, who was 'resting' between acting jobs, sat next to his girlfriend reading the newspaper, either completely disinterested or pretending not to be curious. I would get used to this. Women sat on the edge of their chairs and couldn't ask enough questions, but I found that most of my male friends were much more hesitant, as if expressing any curiosity about the sex industry immediately implicated them as brothelmongers, or something.

Morris, my squash partner since drama school, became so uncomfortable when I told him about the fascinating women I now worked with, tea came out his nose. Giggling like a schoolboy, he finally managed a question. Did the girls wear knee pads, Morris spluttered, while 'giving French'? And then, with tears running down his face, Morris asked if they got '*overtime* when they got on top'. As I watched him and slowly stirred my coffee, I could see why vaudeville had died. I waited for Morris to finish his laboured impersonation of me doing phone sex and asked for the bill while he was still in hysterics over a banana in the fruit bowl at the counter. It crossed my mind to look Morris up on the computer the following night, but I decided to stop playing squash instead.

When Libby's mobile went off, Peter finally put his newspaper down and asked his first question. Did I feel safe at the brothel?

I reminded Peter that I was just the receptionist and was halfway through telling him about the alarms under the bedside tables when he interrupted me. If I was ever in any kind of trouble, ever, Peter repeated with great solemnity, he would come and pick me up straightaway, whatever the hour. I hadn't heard Pete sound this serious since he was the voice for Peugeot. But it was very sweet of him, and I told him so.

'What about the alarms under the beds?' Libby squawked when she got off her phone.

Now that she'd sorted out three hairstylists from Milan stuck in Customs with eighty ringletted hairpieces (not counting a small dog), Libby wanted to hear every detail, so Peter quietly went back to his newspaper.

Excuse me, I think you've forgotten my husband's orgasm

I'm not sure why I kept coming back. My future career in the sex industry felt precarious to say the least. But as my butterflies and I walked through the gate to begin my second weekend of night shifts at a brothel in Darlinghurst, I promised myself that if anything remotely bad happened I would walk out the door and catch the first 373 bus back to Coogee.

Of course it would be difficult explaining to Libby in the morning, but in time she would come to accept it, just as I would have to accept the time had come to join thousands of other resting actors, and do telesales.

I was about to greet my colleagues when I heard the familiar bell. Before anyone could say 'client', I threw my bag in the corner and myself into action. I tore downstairs into the waiting room, turned on the porn and opened the front door to find a well-dressed, good-looking, forty-something couple. Jocelyn and Graham greeted me with such genteel civility on this warm summer evening, I half expected one to hand me a good bottle of wine. I showed them into the waiting room where they immediately confessed to never having done this before. The very distinguished looking and proud, if bloated, Graham swayed with the alcohol that had no doubt nurtured this idea. The more sober Jocelyn let him do all the talking. She was tall and slim with short red hair and designer glasses, and she held on to her partner's arm, smiling like a mother reluctantly buying her son a dangerous toy. Graham said they wanted someone not too mature, but definitely experienced.

'Someone who'll take charge,' he said, and Jocelyn nodded unconvincingly.

There was only one girl in the house. Rita was sitting at the kitchen table eating takeaway when I burst in and asked her if she 'did couples'. Rita looked a little worried.

'I haven't done much couples, darling,' she purred. 'Does the lady want servicing too?'

'Um . . . I'll just find out.'

I ran back to the waiting room.

'Sorry, just wondered if you'd like the lady to service you as well, Jocelyn?'

'I'm not bisexual!' Jocelyn exclaimed in horror. 'I mean, she wouldn't have to go *down* on me, if that's what you mean. I certainly don't think I could go down on her.'

'Nonetheless,' said Graham, looking a little disappointed at Jocelyn, 'we should all get right into it!' And he clapped his hands together in a gesture of solitary enthusiasm.

I returned to the kitchen and told Rita she wouldn't have to 'service' Jocelyn. I loved this word, and all the trouble it saved me.

'It's all his idea, right?' Rita laughed knowingly.

I was about to tell her they wanted someone experienced, but when Rita stood up in her high heels and tugged at her tight-fitting miniature dress, flicked her long mane back and pouted into her compact mirror, I didn't think it was necessary.

I took Rita in to meet Graham and Jocelyn, and watched them as the three smiled warmly, shook hands and nervously eyed each other up and down, making pleasant chitchat as if they were meeting at a party. An awkward pause was broken by Graham leading all in a hearty laugh, followed by Rita's gracious exit. I told Jocelyn and Graham they should think about it for a moment and made my own gracious exit. I popped my head back in just to assure Jocelyn no one would have to go down on anything they didn't want to.

When I returned to the kitchen, I found Rita sitting nervously at the table like a schoolgirl. This was just like auditioning for a play, I thought.

After a few minutes, I returned to Graham and Jocelyn.

'Yes, okay.' Jocelyn sighed with relief.

'And you haven't got anyone else?' Graham smiled, less relieved.

'No,' I said, 'I'm terribly sorry. But Rita is one of our best girls. And experienced.' I felt like I was selling a car.

I ran into the kitchen to give Rita the good news, and was running up to reception with Graham's three hundred and twenty dollars when I heard a hissing sound.

'Darling!' Rita was at the bottom of the stairs. 'I look after her too. Better bring me some dams.'

'Dams?'

'Yes, there's none left in the party room. And some champagne.'

Any one-hour booking was accompanied by a complimentary bottle of St James. But curse these dams! What the hell were they?

My fellow receptionists were Maxine and, once again, Pip, who assured me I was not a burden at all but later enquired what other shifts I'd been given. Although she was the youngest at twenty-six, Pip was by far the most efficient receptionist. She weighed nothing, smoked long white cigarettes, spoke authoritatively to all the girls, added vast sums of money in her head and was fluent in Japanese. Pip was always very friendly and helpful to me, except when she was stressed. I later discovered that, despite her vast competence, Pip was a little highly strung and prone to dramatics. On a bad night, one of my mistakes could send Pip right to the very edge, and you'd wonder how such a slight frame could contain such turbulence.

Maxine, who loved to roll her eyes behind Pip's back, was also very qualified, having worked as a receptionist for the enemy. Blue Angels was a smaller and more elite escort agency run by an ex-policeman who employed a full-time make-up artist and hair-dresser for his girls, so Maxine informed me in her tiresome but friendly drone. But whereas Sam took fifty per cent, Boris and Didi took only forty, which was why a lot of Sam's girls came to us. Weighing even less than Pip, Maxine was a doll, a miniature, and claimed to be only thirty-one. With her Egyptian skin and long, stiff peroxide-white hair, Maxine looked like a negative. And she called everyone princess, gorgeous, sweetie and darling. In fact everyone called everyone sweetness, baby, dollface or pumpkin, but Maxine could use them all in one sentence.

I was looking in the top locker for the office supply of dams as Pip had told me to, but all I could see was an enormous box of condoms, a packet of surgical plastic gloves and a roll of small white plastic bags.

'Nope,' I said confidently, 'looks like we're out of dams.'

Pip had entered the stress zone, so Maxine got up to help me.

'Here they are, dollface,' she sighed, nonchalantly handing me the roll of small white plastic bags.

'Oh!' I cried, tearing off seven.

Whatever they were, that should do her.

'Here you are,' I said, almost bowling over a naked Rita adjusting the light dimmer in the party room doorway.

Averting my eyes, I noticed the pile of Jocelyn's and Graham's clothes already on one of the beds, and realised they must be in the shower.

'And the champagne, darling?' Rita asked.

Shit!

I leapt down the stairs to the kitchen, where I nearly collided with a beautiful black woman. I hastily introduced myself as I got a bottle of champagne from the fridge, found the good glasses and the tray, and then searched frantically for a bottle opener.

'You no need bottle openair for champagne,' she said with quiet incredulity and a very thick French accent.

'Of course not!' I laughed.

And like Basil Fawlty, I turned and ran back up the stairs three at a time. I arrived at the top, puffing and sweating, to interrupt a half-naked Graham and Jocelyn having a civilised pre-coital chat with the completely naked Rita.

'Here we are!' I sang, blushing crimson as I set the tray down on the bedside table, carefully not looking at anyone.

'And off I go!'

Once back in the sanctuary of reception, I flopped down at my desk, mopped my brow and studied one of the mysterious white plastic bags under the light. *Lickable Latex*, it said, *Made in Malaysia*. On the other side of the bag were instructions. The small 10 by 6 inch sheet of latex inside was to be moistened, then placed over the entire vulva or anus during oral sex. I took the sheet of latex out and held it up to the light. It smelt like a balloon. I wondered what would happen if I stretched it over my mouth and blew.

Maxine was looking at me.

'Oh,' I suddenly remembered, 'there's a black woman in the kitchen.'

Delilah, I was told, was from Africa, and because she was an illegal immigrant, she was to pay no tax. I gathered that some girls paid more tax than others, and prayed that I would never need to know more.

'She's got a fantastic French accent,' I said.

Maxine smiled. 'I know,' she said, twirling her hair, 'yet she's from Africa.'

Fifteen minutes later, Maxine and Pip were answering phones and pretending they weren't distracted by the increasingly enthusiastic moans and groans coming from the doorless room upstairs. I tried to catch their eyes to have a laugh, but they were both going to carry on as if it wasn't happening. So I sat there playing with my dental dams. I felt proud. Half an hour ago, I had introduced three adults to each other under the gaze of a stuffed moose, and now they were all having sex upstairs.

An hour later I was standing at the front door while Rita kissed her couple goodbye like old friends at the end of a dinner party, leaving me to ask the embarrassing questions. Did they enjoy the service? How did they hear about us? But no sooner had Rita disappeared to have a shower than Graham almost violently pulled me into the waiting room, followed by Jocelyn.

'Listen, Merrily, we want another girl.'

'Now?' I asked incredulously, looking from one to the other.

'Yes, but not here,' Graham growled. 'Can you send one round to our place?'

This was news to Jocelyn.

'Not now, Graham!' she cried, grabbing his arm.

Graham jerked his arm free and grabbed mine. 'We're just around the corner, Merrily, so can you send someone?'

'Yes, of course . . .' I promised Graham, freeing my arm.

'Not right now, sweetheart,' Jocelyn pleaded, and I took a step back so as not to get caught in the arm-grabbing. 'For goodness' sake, we've just had one. We don't need—'

'LOOK!' Graham suddenly shouted. 'I DIDN'T HAVE MY ORGASM!'

Graham glared at Jocelyn. Jocelyn looked at me. I looked at the moose.

Silence.

'Neither did I,' Jocelyn whimpered at last, 'but darling—'

'WELL I WANT ONE NOW!' Graham shouted.

I wondered if the girls upstairs could hear this.

'Darling, I can give you an orgasm,' implored Jocelyn, but Graham turned his back on her.

'And can she be younger?' he continued, handing me a card with his address, 'but not busty.'

I grabbed a pen to busy myself. 'Not . . . busty . . .' This was new. 'How young?'

'Eighteen,' Graham shot back.

'That's my daughter's age, for Christ's sake!' objected Jocelyn. 'Thirty,' she commanded my pen.

'Eighteen!' Graham dictated.

'Oh for God's sake, Graham!'

Diplomatically, I wrote down eighteen to thirty.

'How long will she be?' he asked urgently.

I suppressed an urge to say about a hundred and sixty centimetres.

'Oh, within half an hour?' I offered cheerily. 'By the way, how did you hear about us?'

'We're good friends of Darius,' Jocelyn smiled.

Darius?

'Darius Slade,' they chorused.

There were notes all over the walls upstairs about a Darius Slade. Notes like:

PANDORA WILL NOT SEE DARIUS SLADE!

NEW GIRLS MUST BE WARNED ABOT DARIUS SLADE!

WE DO NOT AXCEPT CHEQEUS! EXEPT FROM DARIUS SLADE.

Within twenty minutes, Maxine sent Jocelyn and Graham a girl called Bree. Apparently Bree was one of our most beautiful girls, thirty years old, smart and very good with couples, so I was surprised to hear from Sofia the following night that Jocelyn had rung to complain. Bree apparently arrived, got her three hundred and twenty, plus twenty-five dollars taxi money, asked for vegemite on toast and then settled down in front of Jocelyn and Graham's big screen television.

'But she can't do that!' I cried.

Sofia, our fascist supervisor who couldn't spell, just looked at me, bloated and heavy with the burden of her knowledge, and rubbed her face. I was reminded of Marlon Brando sitting in the cave in *Apocalypse Now*.

'*The horror.*'

Sofia, the bull

Sofia was a convincing argument for magazine astrologists. Nowhere in the world could there be a more accurate, living example of Taurus, the bull. She was even Spanish. With her stocky frame, large brown eyes and mane of curly black hair, Sofia commanded and bullied us all from her central desk like a corrupt Mexican general. Her desk was the office front line, a mess of paperwork, packets of Winfield Blue, overflowing ashtrays and coffee cups. Somewhere in her forties, Sofia reminded me, in her tired, worn-out Mediterranean way, of Anna Magnani. I said that to her once. She couldn't have cared less. I know because she told me. You always knew where you stood with Sofia. Before the night shifts, cigarettes, coffee, scotch and stress caught up with her, Sofia had been a great beauty. She told me that too.

The first night I met Sofia, she was sitting at her desk, talking on the phone and smoking a cigarette when I arrived. I smiled at her and she eyed me with vague exhaustion before swivelling her chair round to face the breeze coming through the French windows.

'I *know*, Didi,' Sofia protested down the phone. 'Yes, I know this, Didi! You don't have to tell me, Didi, I could have toll *you*! ... Well of course is not good enough. Listen ... listen, Didi ... No! I toll her! ... Well you know how many times I've toll her ... Yes, Didi! ... Oh, Chrise, Didi, I don't know ... Didi, hang on—'

Sofia put her hand over the phone, dragged on her cigarette and mumbled in my direction, 'Darling, can you pass me the thing.'

I looked at her, and Sofia vaguely gestured at something on my desk. I desperately searched among my things for a 'thing'.

'Yes, Didi,' she said, still gesturing wildly to me.

I started picking up things like a desperate contestant on a game show. Glue? Stapler? Fork? Minty?

'Didi, look, I said it to Boris — Chrise, darling!' Sofia shouted. 'The *thing*!'

And this was how it was working with Sofia. Bewildering, terrifying, and utterly exhausting. Her nightly interrogation from Didi about everything from ordering toilet paper to this week's takings set the tone, and I would spend the next twelve hours running all over that house, never knowing exactly what she was talking about, never able to understand precisely what she wanted, and giving her no end of grief. Months later, I would realise this controlled chaos was nothing more than camouflage covering Sofia's own inadequacies as manager, but even then it upset me.

Life for Sofia was indeed a bullfight. The world kept waving red flags in her face and she was as mad as hell. She huffed and puffed and swore like a trooper at all of us and our apparent relentless and determined efforts to kill her with our incompetence. Nothing anyone did was ever enough, and if it was, what did they want, 'a fucking medal?'

Sofia had worked for Boris and Didi for nearly ten years, and for the life of me I could not understand why. As manager and receptionist, she worked four shifts a week: Friday and Saturday night shifts, and the day shifts on Mondays and Tuesdays. She always arrived an hour early, puffing, having smoked all the way from her bus stop, and she always left — and this was why we hated working her shifts — well after finishing time. If you were doing the Friday or Saturday night shift with Sofia, you didn't get home until nine the next morning. Even after the answering machines went on, instead of finishing the bookwork and paying the driver, Sofia kept taking calls. She wouldn't hesitate to wake some poor Asian girl at seven in the morning to send her to drunk Kevin in Cronulla. Although there was a fifteen dollar bonus for any after-hour booking, the phones were always dead.

But Sofia would stay regardless, and expected us to do the same, with no paid overtime.

Not even as an actor had I come across such insane and financially unrewarding expectations. The mystery of this bizarre work ethic, instigated by our millionaire bosses and implemented by their faithful toreador, became even less clear to me once I met Boris.

Boris is in the building

It was my third weekend at the brothel, and I still hadn't met Boris. I'd like Boris, I was told.

'Everyone likes Boris', said Pip. 'He's funny.'

And just to prove it she went over to his majestic desk, opened a drawer, pressed a button, and some tinny contraption hidden within played 'Everybody Loves Somebody'.

'He's a bit of a Dean Martin fan.' Pip smiled.

I was hoping he'd be funnier than that.

'He's a very naughty boy, Meredith,' warned Maxine, wagging an artificially enhanced talon in my face.

Maxine had a way of infantilising grown men. Even QCs were berated for being silly, cheeky little boys. She spoke to them like mother and whore, a combination which apparently made men feel deliciously naughty. But I just couldn't understand how some of them could maintain an erection after being so excruciatingly minimised.

Both girls were doing very funny impersonations of our Bavarian boss, Boris, whom I gathered had a strange habit of patting his ears. I'd understand this better, they assured me through their laughter, when I met him at midnight.

'You'd better go downstairs and get him a clean ashtray, Meredith, sweetheart.' Maxine smiled like a Cheshire cat who didn't want to boast, but knew what pleased her boss.

I never minded going downstairs as I was keen to put any new face to one of the sixty names I had taped to the wall beside my desk. And I savoured the surprise of meeting yet another woman who shattered every preconceived notion I had of a sex worker. Not only had I met teenage university students and backpackers, I had also met housewives, single mothers and professional women, some over forty. But most refreshing was the presence, in an industry built on men's sexual desires and fantasies, of hefty, plump girls who confidently regarded their ample flesh as their sexiest asset. This was extremely inspiring to someone whose obsessive quest to be svelte once led to bulimia. I was used to an industry that puts pressure on its leading ladies to go on diets, supposedly to appeal to more male viewers. But Boris and Didi had a much broader perspective of men's preferences, judging by their employment of numerous buxom and voluptuous women who could eat whatever they wanted, so long as they gargled afterwards.

But tonight there were no new women with surprising backgrounds to meet in the kitchen, or in the girls' lounge room. I had noticed that, out of Didi's stable of sixty, only a dozen or so had embraced her transition to in-house. And as most of them only worked one or two nights a week, the downstairs lounge room seemed always occupied by the usual suspects, Shelby, Rita, Antoinette, Maya and the exotic black girl, Delilah.

Delilah was so beautiful it wasn't funny. But what really wasn't funny was that I couldn't understand a word she said. I have never been good with accents, and every time Delilah spoke, it just sounded like pure French to me. Yet all the other girls seemed to understand her perfectly well.

They were sitting around the kitchen table when Delilah stopped me in my tracks.

'Mairdite, cunyoplisussophiaowmshhtuxio?'

I looked at Delilah. She looked back at me. I looked around the table. They were all waiting for my answer.

Delilah had the most perfect skin, and she always wore a body-hugging long black or silver dress over her wonderfully curvaceous figure. Everything about Delilah was perfectly round, from her eyes and her mouth to her bum. And she was waiting for an answer.

'She wants you to ask Sofia how much tax she owes!' Shelby shouted at me, as if I was deaf.

'Right,' I said at last. 'She's not in, Delilah, but I'll ask Pip.'

Little creases appeared on Delilah's smooth brow. It seemed she didn't understand me either.

'She'll ask Pip!' Shelby shouted at Delilah.

And this was how it would always be with me and Delilah. Unless Shelby was there to translate, we got absolutely nowhere. I went back upstairs with Boris's clean ashtray.

Once I was back in reception, Pip informed me that girls could now be sent out on the Exclusive line for seven hundred dollars an hour.

'Who pays seven hundred dollars for a girl?' I cried.

'You haven't met Genevieve yet, Meredith, have you, darl?' Maxine quipped as though I would not have asked such a stupid question if I had.

Pip thought it was a stupid question too. 'Obviously not,' she scoffed, and took a deep breath.

We had one or two 'extraordinary girls', Pip exhaled, who could always be depended upon to ask for five hundred dollars or seven hundred dollars as soon as they walked through a hotel door. First cab off the Exclusive rank was Genevieve.

Or Pandora, Maxine interrupted, if she wasn't pinned, but that was another story.

I was assured by Pip, who was a personal friend of hers, that Genevieve was a true thoroughbred in a stable of Shetland ponies. A statuesque blonde with a cool disposition, classy wardrobe and an amazing body, Genevieve was the first girl we sent to any visiting dignitaries or celebrities. Then I was forgotten as my colleagues gushed over Genevieve's new Bulgari watch in the shape of a snake, until Pip suddenly shooshed her friend mid sentence with a rude finger in the air. There was a silence, followed by an outburst of laughter from the kitchen below.

'Boris's here,' Pip announced.

I followed her and Maxine's example, straightening up my desk and hiding my pizza box. I felt excited and nervously awaited my new boss's appearance.

'Ello,' said a short, fair man of about sixty at the door. He had sad eyes, a big smile and was dressed in a checked suit.

Pip and Maxine immediately fell about in cascades of giggles and 'Here's trouble!' and 'Watch out!', during which I caught Boris's sideways glance in my direction.

Feeling undeniably lovable, Boris chuckled all the way to his desk, put down his briefcase, turned to face us, rubbed his hands together, and then he did it. He patted his ears. I realise now that this was to flatten down his carefully blow-dried hair, once grey but now dyed a subtle shade of blond. It framed his pleasing, humorous face like snow on a Bavarian alp. Boris's powder blue suit was a symphony of checks and stripes that came together in a television test-pattern. His two-tone white and blue shoes shone to perfection, as did his teeth, which were surprisingly long. And I'm sure he'd sprayed something on his suit, because wherever Boris moved, so did a garden of roses.

'Orroight?' Boris smiled, clapping his hands together.

'Orroight!' chorused the girls, echoing his deliberately bad Australian accent, and we all fell about laughing.

'Ello, Meredit,' he finally said with a smile, hovering towards me, nervously patting his ears.

But as I stood to shake his hand, Boris reeled backwards, visibly disturbed that I had several inches on his five foot two.

'Are they telling you how we run this place?' he asked nervously, glancing from my head to the carpet, compulsively patting his ears.

'Yes,' I replied, quickly sitting back down. 'I think I'm getting the hang of it.'

'Goot . . . goot. And are you verking downstairs?'

'Yes,' I smiled, 'and I'm fine with that.'

'That's goot. Are you fine with that many girls in the kitchen? 'Cause I'm not!' And Boris laughed, looking from Maxine to Pip, who both turned to me with the same pitying smile.

'Have I done something wrong?' I asked.

Pip smiled sweetly and recited that as in-house receptionist it was my job to keep the numbers of girls in the house to a minimum. News to me. Didn't we need as many girls as possible downstairs to introduce to men when they came to the front door?

'Those girls who think they are too goot for in-house, they can fock off!' shouted Boris, obviously disturbed by my question.

Escort-only girls, continued Pip, were to drop in strictly to fix up their pay, and then leave immediately.

'I von't have them in my kitchen causing trouble,' Boris barked. 'Too many girls in that kitchen is too much gossip. I von't haff it!'

Perhaps a little embarrassed at his sudden outburst and the first impression he was making on the tall receptionist his wife had hired, Boris glanced at me sideways, nervously patted his ears, and sat down.

A profoundly suspicious man, I later discovered, Boris believed that any two girls left chatting at the kitchen table unsupervised for more than five minutes would inevitably compare his brothel to a better one down the road, and a collective uprising would be imminent. Boris turned to his computer. My colleagues smiled at me and turned around to their bookwork. All was silent.

Sadly, I knew that the lovable, funny Dean Martin impersonator my two bonsai colleagues enjoyed so much would be withheld from me. Some small men react to a tall woman as if asked to drive a car with the steering wheel on the outside. And now I had to go downstairs, introduce myself to any new girls, and ask the escort-onlys to leave. This job just got better and better. As I opened our door, a loud roar of laughter rose from the kitchen below. It sounded like a hen's night in full swing.

'And tell Urszula to focking keep it down,' ordered the Bavarian from his computer.

'Urszula?' I asked Pip and Maxine in a little voice.

'Sapphire,' Pip answered. 'Urszula's working name is Sapphire. She's been off for two weeks. Haven't you met her yet?'

'Don't take any shit from her, Meredith,' warned Maxine.

'Perhaps I should go down with you,' cautioned Pip.

'Her bark's worse than her bite, princess,' said Maxine.

'If she carries on about no bookings—' began Pip.

'Well, what does she expect at her age?' Maxine asked Pip.

'Have you seen how short her hair is?' Pip asked Maxine.

'*Just tell her to focking shut up!*' shouted Boris, and I was gone.

I prayed all the way downstairs. Please, God, don't let Sapphire be escort-only.

A precious stone from Yorkshire

As I approached the kitchen I could hear a rich, deep voice like Glenda Jackson's – if Glenda had come from the north of England and smoked a lot more cigarettes – entertaining the troops, and one man.

'Well, Patrick, my dear,' Glenda was shouting, 'that's because you're the only man left on this planet who's not a fooking wanker!'

I timidly opened the kitchen door to shrieks of laughter. Where had they all come from? There were girls everywhere, sitting on benches, on chairs, perched on the stove, all a captive audience to the diminutive figure before me, her hands on her hips. I stood very still. To my far right, half hiding in the lounge room, blushing and laughing and cowering over a cigarette, was Patrick. Next to him, hunched by the back door, sat Antoinette, in a cloud of smoke. The creature in front of me, clad in a black leather catsuit from her almost shaved, bleached white head to her high black leather boots, spun around.

'Who the fook are you?' she roared.

Sapphire was all teeth and cheekbones, like an albino Grace Jones. And to further disadvantage her prey, she wore large wraparound sunglasses.

'Meredith,' I stammered, looking down at her.

The room went quiet, except for a few giggles and the distant rumble of approaching humiliation. Sapphire stood back to study me in my violinist's uniform, and we all waited for the punch line. I could be funny too, but now was not the time.

'And I'm assuming, Mer-e-dith, you're not working *our* side?'

I didn't know which was worse, the girls' laughter or Patrick's pitying smile.

'No,' I answered, the blood rushing to my cheeks.

'No,' she echoed, nodding approvingly. 'And are you going to get me bookings, Meredith? Or are you as useless as those other fooking slags up there?'

Everyone laughed so I laughed too, until I realised Sapphire was waiting for an answer.

'I'm going to get you bookings,' I answered quickly.

Sapphire examined me for a moment, and no pins were dropped as we all waited for her verdict. Suddenly, she threw her head back and roared laughing. Everyone joined in, no one more relieved than me.

'Wait a minute!' she bellowed, silencing the room again.

Sapphire prowled around me in a menacing circle, eyeing me from head to toe.

'*I know you*,' she growled.

Even the tougher girls looked nervous.

'Where do I know you from, Meredith?'

'Well,' I stuttered, 'I feel like I know you too, actually.'

It was true. I felt like I'd seen Sapphire on a million television shows like *The Sweeney*, or *The Professionals*, playing a tough, foul-mouthed prostitute. Perhaps she'd fronted a punk band in the eighties? She had the kind of performance energy only a stage could contain. While we stood, regarding each other curiously in a kind of Mexican stand-off, Sapphire's audience quietly dispersed into other rooms or out the back door for a ciggie. It was Interval.

Two girls remained sitting on the bench. Marcelle, a honey-blonde Rubens, and Trixie, her petite friend with a short black bob, sat nodding at me in quiet agreement. Like Sapphire, they too felt they knew me from somewhere.

'Yeah, it's been bugging me,' Trixie grumbled, in possibly the deepest voice I had ever heard.

I smiled, shrugged my shoulders and, under their silent scrutiny, began slowly loading the dishwasher. By now I knew the recognition factor was not a welcome feeling for any working girl. After all, I could have been a friend of the family. And although I could have put them out of their misery by telling them they'd possibly seen me on *Neighbours*, *All Saints* or *Play School*, I wanted to remain the observer, not the observed.

I returned upstairs to find Boris had gone to the casino and wouldn't be back till four. A regular occurrence, my colleagues told me. Relieved that I wouldn't have to stoop all night, I asked Pip and Maxine a million questions about Sapphire.

Urszula, or Sapphire as she liked to be known, was forty-three (so her card said), a qualified martial artist, and had worked all over the world as a bodyguard, bouncer and security guard. It was rumoured she'd worked for the Mob in America, then the Mob here in Sydney. Whatever the truth, Sapphire knew every drug dealer, baron, pimp and inch of the Cross like the back of her neck-breaking hand.

'That's why she came to Boris and Didi,' said Pip, 'to get away from it all.'

I wasn't sure how one got away from the seedy world of underground crime by working as a prostitute in Darlinghurst. Wouldn't she be better off as a librarian somewhere?

'And her body is a listed lethal weapon,' Maxine added gravely.

'When you get to a certain level in martial arts,' Pip explained, 'you have to legally register your body as a lethal weapon. It's like carrying a licence for a gun.'

'She's got one of those too, hasn't she?' Maxine asked Pip.

Yes, Pip nodded thoughtfully, she did.

Apparently, Boris and Didi had shown great loyalty to Sapphire over the years, even letting her have a go as receptionist when she'd stopped pulling bookings. But her phone manner was so loud no other receptionist could hear herself think. Sapphire then returned to the fold downstairs, and very little income.

'We have got one blonde lady we could send you, Gary, a more mature lady with short blonde hair, very feisty, sexy … short hair, Gary, yes … about half an inch. Hello?'

Although Antoinette's card declared her one year older than Sapphire, her long blonde hair and double D-cup gave her extra advantage.

'And Antoinette's a lady, y'know?' said Maxine, nodding, so I nodded back.

It was true. In a tragic, Tennessee Williams kind of a way, Antoinette was a lady. Despite her forty-four or more years, she spoke in a tremulous, breathy voice, and still laughed like a little girl. But Antoinette's beauty was fading fast, and she sometimes looked bewildered at the host of young women sitting around the kitchen. Sensing she no longer fitted in, Antoinette sat as an independent island just off shore by the back door, and smoked. Some nights she looked calm, but on others she had the haggard and haunted look of someone profoundly unhappy, disturbed even.

'Where does Sapphire live?' I asked, returning to her more buoyant if disadvantaged C-cup colleague.

'She doesn't,' answered Pip.

'She's in hiding,' added Maxine.

'Has no address,' said Pip.

'No tax file number,' said Maxine.

'No Medicare card,' said Pip.

'So she sleeps here?' I asked, hopefully.

'NO!' they chorused, appalled at the question.

No girl ever, ever slept on the premises. This was a big rule. Even in a crisis, and homeless, no girl could stay in the house, with its three empty bedrooms and couches galore. No. Okay. So where did Sapphire sleep?

'In her car,' answered Pip.

'With Rex, her dog.' Maxine smiled sadly, enjoying the pathos.

My phone rang. A line marked *Kitchen* lit up. This was new.

'Hello?' I answered nervously.

'And there's no fooking milk!' she shouted.

'Hi, Sapphire.'

'And no fooking bread!'

'I'll send Patrick to get some right now.'

'And where are my fooking bookings, Meredith?'

'Getting you some right now, Sapphire.'

'That's my girl.'

Although she made me sweat, I liked being Sapphire's girl.

A necklace? You shouldn't have!

For the first two months, until the end of summer, my shifts were Thursday, Friday and Saturday nights from seven till five in the morning. Not an ideal situation for a single girl, but they were the busiest shifts, and I was slowly getting acquainted with some of the most interesting women in Sydney.

Shelby often wore the same thing on the nights she worked, as if it were a uniform. It was a two-piece red suit with gold buttons.

The skirt was short enough to show she had wonderful legs clad in skin-coloured pantyhose. The jacket came in at her slim waist and she wore a soft white blouse underneath. She always had a black shoulder bag, and matching black shoes, sensible shoes, not too high. Her long blonde hair was always brushed and off her face, and she wore only a bit of lipstick and mascara. She was a breezy, chatty and cheerful girl in her twenties, or so I thought, from the western suburbs. Shelby found my novitiate nerves a refreshing change, and leant back against the sink and smiled at me. Uneasy with her direct gaze, I complimented her on her beautiful nails.

'That's 'cause I really look after 'em,' she said, splaying her fingers. 'Here,' Shelby skipped over to me, 'feel 'em.'

I obediently felt Shelby's colourless, polished nails of steel.

'Manicare,' she said. 'Ya put a layer on. Leave it a day or two. Take it off. Ya put a second layer on. Same thing. Third layer, leave it on. Strong nails!'

I asked Shelby if she ever used colour.

'Nah. Looks tarty. And it's not right for what I do.'

I had to think about this for a second.

'What do you do, Shelby?'

'Financial consultant.' Shelby smiled, and gave me a second to catch it. 'Bank loans and personal. But I'm gunna give up the personal. Too much running around, ya know?'

Shelby was as light as a bird. Even when she crossed her long legs and leant back relaxed in her chair, she was ready to take off at any second. I asked her how she kept so slim.

'Just do. Don't exercise or nothin'. Just got a fast metabolism. It's certainly not me mum's cooking!' She laughed.

I had been instructed severely by my teachers upstairs never to use a girl's working name when calling her at home, especially if she lived with her parents. Up until now, I thought it was a joke.

'Yeah,' Shelby sighed, smiling at my incredulity, 'me and me brothers are all still at home. And we're all pretty thin.'

I no longer cared about her lack of obesity, I just wanted to know where her family thought Shelby went every night until the wee hours.

'I don't eat junk food,' Shelby continued. 'I don't even drink tea or coffee. Don't smoke and I don't drink alcohol either. Oh yeah, I look after myself.'

I asked how she juggled being a financial consultant every day with her escort work at night.

'Oh, it's hard. But not for much longer. I'm just gunna finish this year, and then I'll retire.'

Shelby had the fresh, confident smile of a woman whose house was in such good order, it gave her pleasure to talk about it. So, how did Shelby get into this line of work?

'Massage,' she smiled, and filled a glass of water from the tap.

When Shelby had studied accounting at business college by day, she worked at a massage clinic at night. When one of the girls introduced her to Boris, he told her she could be earning thousands of dollars a week. As Shelby really wanted a Prelude at the time, she thought she'd give it a go. Now she had her heart set on a Saab.

'Was it difficult,' I asked Shelby, 'crossing that line?'

'Oh yeah, the first coupla times I thought I was gunna be sick.' She laughed. 'But ya get used to it.' Shelby took a sip from her glass, and smiled. 'It's shallow water, Meredith,' she nodded sagaciously. 'You may not be able to see the bottom, but you can feel it, and it's not as deep as ya think.'

And did she have to toughen up? Did it make her cynical? Hard? Bitter? I had so many questions.

'Oh yeah!' Shelby cried. 'I don't care what anyone else says, it makes ya all those things. I could never look at men in the same way again. Not even my father and brothers. I could never trust a man, now. Not with what I know.'

Was that why she wasn't interested in marriage or children?

'Maybe.' She smiled and nodded. 'And they just don't come into my plan.'

The more I talked to Shelby, the more I noticed the thinness of her face, and the smallness of her eyes, and I realised she was actually well into her thirties. But as soon as she got a booking, Shelby would transform in front of me and breeze out the door like a teenager in a shampoo commercial.

'I wouldn't get on the wrong side of Shelby,' receptionist Trudy warned me back upstairs.

I loved working with Trudy. Although she was a struggling single mum in her early thirties, Trudy looked like a fairy with her large pretty eyes and pink-streaked hair. She spoke in quick little bursts, between long periods of thoughtful deliberation, and dismissed any bitchiness with a delightful childlike laugh.

'When an ex-client tried to expose Shelby at the Marble Bar once, she decked him.' Trudy smiled like an elf. 'Coral was with her. Laid him out cold.'

Trudy had an inherent respect for the girls, a rarity upstairs, and was acutely sensitive to each one's situation and problems. Unless we were talking about Genevieve. Trudy was the only receptionist who didn't go into sudden rhapsodies and speak in tongues about Genevieve's Cachet nose and cheekbones, her Pasha colourist or Bulgari watch. It was like getting blood out of a stone, but I finally extracted it. Trudy thought Genevieve was 'a bit of a cow, actually'.

Shelby had been with Boris for over ten years, Trudy explained to me, and was once his top earner. That's why she was allowed to work four nights a week from seven till two. Generally speaking, night shift girls weren't allowed to knock off until closing at five, but for Shelby Boris made an exception. He seldom had a kind word for any of his girls, but his loyalty towards Shelby was fierce. Shelby never hopped agencies like the other girls, she'd never taken a night off, and she paid Boris full tax. And like his wife, Shelby was an astute businesswoman and had built herself an empire out of the sex industry. Boris demanded Shelby get at least two bookings a night, which wasn't difficult. She was a tall, slim, leggy blonde, and a professional masseuse to boot. Not busty, however, and that sometimes got in her way. Or rather didn't.

I enjoyed my conversations with Shelby in the kitchen. She spoke with such candour about the most intimate things, and yet she gave away nothing of herself. There was something in her personality and voice as bright yet flat and artless as the plastic gold buttons on her jacket.

'I tell ya one thing,' she declared with a laugh, 'I wouldn't be in this game without having been a masseuse.'

Before I could guess why, Shelby explained with pride.

'I give him five minutes chat, five minutes in the shower, then spend the next forty-five sitting on his arse, giving him the best massage he's had in his life. And if he says he wants to get on with it, I just say, "Oh, honey, I'm just getting to the best part!" And I rub me tits on his back. Drives him wild. If I have to, I turn him round and give him Spanish.'

I knew that French meant fellatio, and Raelene had enlightened me that Greek meant anal, but what was Spanish?

'Ya put it between 'ere.' Shelby demonstrated by pushing her breasts together with her hands. 'An' if he comes, it's called a Spanish necklace, or a pearl necklace, see?'

Spanish necklace . . . French polish . . . Greek salad . . .

'Or,' Shelby continued, 'I'll turn 'im round and give him French if I have to.' Shelby mimed a hurried blow job. 'And just when he's about to explode, I jump on top and pop! Over in two seconds!' Shelby laughed as she rinsed her glass and left it on the sink. 'I'm an expert at avoiding the inevitable.'

Even though Shelby laughed and chatted with me and the other girls, there was something solitary about her leaning against the kitchen bench with her clear plans and her strong nails. She would generously drive any girl without transport home at the end of the night, but if one kept her waiting, Shelby would simply leave without her. No drama. She would offer, but Shelby waited for no one.

Sofia's morning appointment

Sofia never warmed to me because she did not trust that I wasn't going to do a runner, leaving her to train someone else all over again. I don't know why she took it so personally as it was the other receptionists who were doing all the training. But Sofia was suspicious of me for other reasons. I was too nice. I was playing too dumb. And the more popular I became with my fellow receptionists and the girls downstairs, the more Sofia smelt something rotten. She and Boris would speak in hushed voices just outside our office door, then come in all smiles. I tried to control my paranoia. After all, I had nothing to hide. Except that I was an actor and would leave the second I got a decent acting job.

Sofia, like Boris, presented me with a challenge. I wanted her to like me, even though she could be a cruel sadist of a boss. Besides, I was intrigued by her mysterious past, her devotion to our employers, and I have an innate respect for anyone who can speak more than one language. Sofia spoke four, fluently. Frequently, international businessmen would ring from the big hotels and ask for Sofia. I sat in dumb awe listening to exotic ribbons of French, Italian or Spanish unroll from her mouth as she juggled calls. I was struggling at the Alliance Française for the second year, and when I told Sofia I would always need Monday nights free to go to my French class I had hoped it would impress her. But she just nodded and, with a hint of a smirk as she drew on her cigarette, asked me if I'd emptied the rubbish like I should have.

We were all in the company Mercedes being driven home by Patrick, and as it had been a Friday night shift with Sofia, it was now past eight o'clock on Saturday morning. The chillier April weather meant we now kept the windows up, and I was suffocating. Patrick was smoking and, in the back seat, Sofia and Raelene had lit up too, as if they'd been deprived of their habit the whole night.

'Drop me off at the casino, will you, Patrick?' Sofia asked.

'You're not going to the casino at this hour, are you, Sofia?' I turned to ask, getting a face full of smoke.

'Well, looks like I am, darling!' Sofia chortled, sharing the joke with Raelene.

I turned back around. Sofia lived in Burwood, with whom I did not know. She had arrived for work at 7 pm utterly exhausted, and now, nearly fourteen hours and two packets of Winfield later, she was off to the casino.

'At the front, Sofia?' Patrick sang.

'Yes please, Patrick.'

'Shall I wait in case you don't find him this time?'

'No,' Sofia groaned, 'I'll find him.'

I was learning now. The less interest I showed, the more the information flowed.

'Lass time, I foun' him asleep in one of the big chairs,' she snorted.

Patrick laughed.

'It wasn't funny,' Sofia shouted, and Patrick stopped laughing. 'He was so angry with me. Shouted his fuckin' head off at me in the middle of the casino for being late.'

I tried to imagine someone shouting at Sofia.

'Then we loss everything at Black Jack and went home.'

I looked out the window as we passed the hotel I'd just sent Antoinette to, in her black evening dress, to meet Gunter in Room 3401. I noticed all the strange people on the street who'd got it so wrong, opening their shops for business, driving their kids to ballet classes. Or maybe we were the misfits. I was too tired to tell. All I knew was that Sofia had a husband who yelled at her when she finally met him at the casino in the morning, after she'd worked a thirteen-hour night shift in a brothel. You didn't hear that every day.

Blue Heelers

It's a strange way to get to know another woman. To read her card and know Theresa did golden showers before I'd even met her was irregular, to say the least. Yet by the nature of the job, I was privy to all kinds of personal information from everyone, including the girls themselves.

'I can't work tonight, Meredith. I've got thrush.'

'Who's this?'

'Alexandra. I don't think we've met.'

Even the clients would ring with frightening complaints, or compliments, about anything from the girl's intelligence to the size of her vagina. I was a walking bank of ridiculously intimate details on sixty women I barely knew. I didn't feel powerful. If anything, it was humbling.

I was filling in for Trudy. It was a cool, damp Tuesday night and I was nervous. Her name was Daphne, she was arriving at eight o'clock, and she would be my first interview. I had to ask Daphne many personal questions which I didn't honestly know if I could, from the same room. As well as this, the lounge downstairs was full of girls watching television. Not a daunting prospect in itself, but tonight, at eight-thirty, on Channel Seven, I would make an appearance on *Blue Heelers*.

This gave me great inner conflict. Half of me, the half that felt a little invisible in this strange house among its extraordinary inhabitants, craved recognition and respect. The other half knew this was not the way to get it. My role in this particular episode of *Blue Heelers* was that of an unhappy, abused funeral director's wife, so strung out that one bad haircut sends her plunging the scissors into the neck of the local gay hairdresser, whom homophobic Mount Thomas was struggling to accept; the powerful script thereby combined two social problems in one politically correct storyline. Three if you count bad haircuts.

From seven-thirty I kept finding excuses to leap downstairs and pop my head in the television room. The girls would all look up, desperately hoping it was a booking, and I'd smile, check they weren't watching Channel Seven, then disappear. It was insensitive, but I didn't care. So far so good. *Burke's Backyard*. Channel Nine.

I sat opposite Daphne in one of the spare bedrooms.

'Okay, Daphne.' I smiled, crossing my legs under my clipboard, just like Didi had with me. 'Have you worked in this industry before?'

Daphne was a plump, sweet girl in her thirties, wearing a conservative, homely skirt, floral blouse and sensible shoes. Her mousy brown hair was tied back and there wasn't a trace of make-up on her plain face. What on earth was she doing here?

'No,' Daphne smiled nervously. 'I have never, ever done anything like this in my life!'

'That makes two of us!' I laughed.

Daphne looked shocked for a second, then rocked with laughter.

'So, what do you do?' I asked.

'I'm a teacher,' she replied anxiously, leaning forward, clasping her hands in her lap.

'Tea-cher,' I wrote. 'And what name do you want to go by?'

'Daphne,' she said, a little alarmed at my short memory.

'No, not your real name. I mean, a name for work.'

Again she rocked with laughter. When she recovered, Daphne said she'd just like to be Daphne, if that was okay. It was like interviewing a sandwich hand for the chorus of the Royal Ballet.

'And you'd like to do both in-house and escort, Daphne?'

Daphne looked at me as if I was speaking Greek, and indeed I would be in a minute.

'You mean, like, do houses ... and hotels?'

As I explained what 'in-house' meant, Daphne's eyes opened wide like two saucers.

'Yeah?' she giggled nervously, as if it might be fun. 'I can do both then?'

I was now having doubts about Daphne really being a teacher, let alone seriously considering a career as a prostitute.

After I got Daphne's general details, I had to measure her. I hated this like I hated asking the clients what they thought of the service. Daphne giggled and we both apologised as I measured her 38–34–37 body. But worse was yet to come. I turned the card over. Oh dear. All these boxes to be ticked.

'So, Daphne, do you do couples?'

Her eyes widened, but she nodded.

'Lesbians?'

Another timid nod.

'Paraplegics?'

Nod.

'Quadriplegics?'

Nod.

It was twenty-five past eight. I clumsily excused myself from Daphne, and bounded down the stairs.

Ignoring the several pairs of expectant eyes looking up at me, I ogled the television. One of the Daddos, ironically patting a blue heeler, was introducing a funny ad from Sweden. Daddos meant Channel Seven. Not good. Not good at all. I ran back upstairs.

'Sorry, Daphne ... receive oral?'

Daphne looked at me. I was losing patience with her big eyes.

'Some girls don't,' I added quickly.

'Do I have to *give* ... oral?' she asked, screwing up her face.

'Yes. Yes, you do, Daphne. Generally speaking, I think you'll find that one's a bit popular in this line of work.'

'Well, if I'm going to give it, I think I'm entitled to *get* it, don't you?' she asserted boldly, then gave a nervous giggle.

'Well, you're not exactly *entitled* to get anything,' I almost snapped. Daphne's naivety was pissing me off. 'Except the money.'

'What girl in their right mind wouldn't want to receive oral sex?' she cried.

'What girl indeed?' I cried back, giving it a big tick. 'Golden showers?'

Little creases formed on Daphne's stupid teacher's brow.

'Is that like—' she squinted, and made vague hand movements over her crotch.

'It's when you urinate on a man, yes.'

'Oh no.' She shook her head. 'I don't think I could do that.' Then, terribly concerned, 'Is that all right?'

'Course it is!' I assured her, crossing it off. We were up to the Greek.

'Do you accept anal, Daphne?'

'Oh dear ... I just don't think I could—'

'Fine,' I interrupted.

It was eight-thirty.

I hastily scribbled down Daphne's home and mobile phone numbers, explaining that, no, we perhaps shouldn't take her work number, at the school. I thrust the 'Rule Book' into her arms, told her to read it, then go downstairs to meet some of the girls. Sapphire had just arrived by the sound of it, and although it felt like feeding a Christian to the lions, Daphne would soon realise that not receiving oral was the least of her problems.

I was about to fly downstairs myself when I heard Sapphire scream, and then cackle madly, joined by hoots of laughter from the other girls, and I felt sick as I remembered the shocking wig they had made me wear on *Blue Heelers*.

There were two entrances to the girls' lounge room. One was at the bottom of the stairs, and the other was through the kitchen. I took the first and burst into the room, half prepared for total ridicule and half, I'm ashamed to admit, for glory. I secretly yearned to shake off my klutzy, gauche shell of sweet incompetence and rise like a phoenix above everyone's total indifference.

Instead, I found myself hovering above three empty couches, more like a penguin. I stood in the empty room having an identity crisis as I watched myself on the screen in a muppet's wig, being interviewed by two very earnest Blue Heelers. It seemed there were three of me: the brothel receptionist, the quivering actress on television, and me. For a moment I gambled with being caught just so someone else could decide which one I was. Sapphire's voice rose from the kitchen next door, followed by the inevitable hooting, banging and cheering at the table. Her irresistible cackle made the decision for me, and I clicked the remote control at the television just as Lisa McCune was giving me the most pitying smile. With a sense of relief, I joined the women in the kitchen, happy to be swept up in the story of Sapphire's bull terrier Rex, who'd bitten the carpark attendant at the Hilton again.

The driver

Patrick was in his *late* forties, so Trudy thought, and had the sort of nervous energy that never puts on weight. Although a little ravaged by time and cigarettes, he still had a youthful bounce and boyish good looks which made him attractive, in a 'roadie' kind of way. Even when relaxing at the table drinking tea, Patrick would cross a room with weightless strides and be out the door at a second's notice. Every muscle was alive, alert, ready for anything, except perhaps a joke. If something tickled him, then Patrick liquefied into a helpless drunk, collapsed against the nearest wall, and shook with laughter.

Patrick and I were both born under a shy star. Getting to know one another was going to take time. All I knew about Patrick so far was that he drove prostitutes for a living, drank lots of tea, came from Portsmouth, and had a melodious, happy voice.

'Can you pick up Song-Lee at the Mercure Central, Patrick?'

'Oh-kayee!'

'And can you bring back some Winfield Blue for Sofia?'

'Wiiiill doo!'

Patrick was light, and fun, like a Happy Dad, and he laughed all the time. This constant gurgle of amusement and good will was due, I later discovered, to no small amount of marijuana. But on the nights of great madness, I found Patrick's somewhat trip-happy perspective a great relief.

Patrick driving us all home was the highlight of my night – or morning, I should say. Exhausted but happy, we'd all squint at the reflections of the bright morning sun on the tall glass buildings as we headed towards Bondi Junction, with the birds singing and the windows down, if it wasn't too cold. En route to our various homes, we chatted, smoked and laughed away all the tensions of the night. Unless we'd done a shift with Sofia. Then, rendered insensible, we all sat in paralysed silence, save for the farewell grunt when departing the vehicle.

Patrick always sang quietly to the radio. He seemed to know every word of every song. Sometimes I'd join him. Raelene was always too grumpy at this hour to sing, unless she heard the opening bars of Celine Dion's 'My Heart Will Go On'. Transported immediately to the watery decks of the *Titanic*, Raelene, completely tone deaf, would close her eyes and sing her heart out. Patrick and I would look out our respective windows, jaws tight, determined not to laugh.

Raelene lived in Clovelly, just up the road from my place, giving Patrick and me a three-minute window of opportunity to get to know each other. In the security of our threesome, I fancied myself hilarious, especially against the black mood emanating from the back. But after Raelene got out, I always felt a little less amusing, and from Clovelly to Coogee, I wilted slightly.

'So, Portsmouth, Patrick. That explains the Dorset accent.'

'Hampshire.'

'Right.' My shepherdess had a bigger herd than I thought. 'Do you still have family there?'

'Well, one brother's in Amsterdam, another's in France, but my dad's still there. Where's your lot, then?'

'Tasmania.'

'Here we are then!'

'Bye!'

I'd have to wait four days before we could continue the conversation.

In the meantime, however, we had our laughs, usually at the front door where I let the girls out, and Patrick always waited for his passengers to go before him. Although I was now qualified to call the girls 'gorgeous' and 'darling', I could still only do it in jest. Some of them laughed, others looked at me as if I was weird, but Patrick found my terms of endearment highly amusing, and chuckled quietly in anticipation of his turn.

'Come back soon, princess,' I'd mutter as he passed.

'Just drop this lot off, pumpkin,' he'd reply with a wicked smile.

All the other receptionists thought it was a complete drag, having to go downstairs to let girls out, but I often flew down those steps two and three at a time, just for these little exchanges.

As blonde as the ace of spades

'Did you see Genevieve as she was leaving?' Pip looked up at me, beaming with excitement.

I stood panting in the doorway, drenched in sweat. No, I had not seen the elusive Genevieve. I had missed my bus and had to run all the way from Oxford Street in clogs. Why I chose to wear heavy black wooden clogs when I was catching public transport with a twelve-hour shift of running up and down stairs in a brothel before me, I will never know.

While Maxine and Pip raved about Genevieve's Lacroix anklet, Trudy passed the day shift baton, reminding me to check the party room upstairs as it had seen a lot of action from Rita and Delilah that afternoon. Trudy knew how much I wished she wasn't leaving me with Maxine and Pip. She smiled sadly like a mother leaving her child at creche, and a mother who hadn't checked the party room upstairs for used condoms like she should have.

Maxine and Pip were deep in conversation about gourmet pizzas when I closed The Bible and got up to check the party room. As I was going downstairs anyway, said Maxine, who knew I wasn't, could I take a booking to Rita. It was a private home in Kensington and she was to go straightaway. I took Maxine's piece of paper.

'And, darl,' Maxine said as I reached the door, 'just tell her she's *supposed* to be blonde, but he won't care. She can just tell him she dyed her hair.'

I smelt a rat. A gutless rat sending a messenger to be shot. 'He's expecting a blonde' was a tricky message to give a big Filipina prostitute with thick black hair down to her waist.

'WHAT?' bellowed Rita, 'NO FUCKING WAY! YOU FUCKING TELL HER NO FUCKING WAY!'

I left pretty much straightaway, ran upstairs and communicated this message to Maxine, then continued, cursing my clogs, straight on up to check the party room. Clean towels on the beds, no wet spots on the sheets, no condoms on the floor, towels gone to the laundry ... oh dear. There, on the floor, was a used vibrator with a condom on it. There were strict rules about this. No receptionist ever had to clean up to this extent. I'd have to ask Rita or Delilah to handle it, literally. But as I went downstairs I could hear raised voices coming from the kitchen. I decided the vibrator could lie there a bit longer, and ditched the clogs.

On the pretence of doing laundry business, I walked barefoot straight into a glorious showdown between a Filipina Amazon and possibly the tiniest Egyptian blonde over twelve. Maxine was standing in the doorway while Rita paced the length of the kitchen, sucking the life out of a cigarette. Antoinette sat hunched over her cigarette in her usual corner, letting the cool night air in through the back door.

'Ah, don't be fucking ridiculous,' Rita almost spat at Maxine.

'Listen, Rita, darling,' whined Maxine, 'I'm *agreeing* with you, okay?'

'Well, I'm not fucking going!' I don't think Rita cared if Maxine agreed with her or not. 'Send Antoinette if he wants a blonde! He'll take one look at me and tell me to fuck off. You know he will! Don't you send *me* to be told fuck off!'

'Rita, honey,' persisted Maxine in treacle tones, 'I told you, *sweetheart*, the gentleman won't mind what colour your hair is, so long as you kiss.'

'HE WANTS A FUCKING BLONDE!' shouted Rita. 'Why don't *you* fucking go!'

'Rita, honey,' Maxine's voice rose, her vowels flattened slightly, 'do not speak to me in that tone, thank you very—'

'Ah, don't fucking *honey* me,' continued Rita in just that tone, 'I'm not your fucking honey.'

I felt so glad she picked Maxine up on that.

'Look!' threatened Maxine, now sounding a little more like the gutter. 'Don't you fucking speak to me—'

'AH, SHUDDUP!' boomed Rita, silencing her. 'I know you, remember? I remember you from where you *used* to work.'

Antoinette and I followed Rita's serve. While Maxine looked winded, like someone had thrown a brick at her stomach, Rita stood cool, unapologetic, and ready to fire another round. Antoinette and I watched Maxine slowly pull herself up and, with commendable but spurious majesty, limp towards the stairs. Not until Maxine was halfway up those stairs did she dare respond.

'I don't have to listen to this fucking bullshit!'

And only when she reached reception did she shout, 'SO YOU CAN GET FUCKED ANYWAY!' and slammed our office door.

Rita and Antoinette both sat at the table and lit up fresh cigarettes. I imagined Pip and Maxine upstairs doing the same. Now that Rita's anger had subsided, she looked close to tears.

'They don't care, darling,' she said to me, pointing upstairs. 'Last week, Sofia sent me to the same man twice, once as Filipina, a few days later as Malaysian.'

Antoinette nodded. It was true. She had been there. Antoinette was always there.

'The second time,' Rita continued, 'the man opens the door, takes one look at me and shuts the door in my face.'

Antoinette shook her head.

'They don't care if we get a cancellation,' continued Rita. 'I would like to see how *she* feels when ugly men look at *her* like she's not worth fucking.'

I felt ashamed that I'd harboured some vague notion that women in this profession had tougher skin that also protected them from the pain of rejection. How do you respond to being told you're not worth fucking? No matter who says it, in what context?

The two unlikely friends considered Rita's imminent punishment. They explained to me how she would now sit in the house until five in the morning, not getting one booking. And because Rita was on roster, if I let her go home, she'd be fined.

'Oh yes, darling,' Rita said, 'and what's worse, that was Antoinette's job. She's the only blonde who kisses. Everybody knows that.'

Antoinette, the only blonde who kissed, nodded sadly. We all nodded sadly. Until I asked why on earth they hadn't just sent Antoinette in the first place.

'Because I'm being punished for not answering my mobile,' Antoinette explained softly. 'I was across the road getting takeaway when they rang.'

I decided the towels could wait and sat down with them. I listened to stories of exhausted girls fined for falling asleep, for not answering phones, for refusing bookings when they were sore, for wearing pants instead of dresses, for being tardy, impolite, and so on. Management did all this fifty-dollar fining by withholding money from bookings made by credit card. And receptionists had great power, Rita warned me ominously, over how much money each girl made a night.

'Receptionists have their favourites,' Antoinette added gloomily as she shuffled over to the kettle.

As an endearing legacy of childhood ballet classes, Antoinette's slippered feet scuffed around the house in perfect turnout. Once in her high heels, the turnout remained, giving her an eccentric Chaplinesque quality, not really appropriate for an escort. This first impression did not inspire confidence, yet if a client didn't cancel as soon as he opened the door, Antoinette would usually ring an hour later to extend the booking.

I reluctantly dismissed myself from the two women, who smiled at me, grateful to have been heard. I had begun a thoughtful journey back upstairs, determined never to play favourites, when I remembered something, and ran back down.

'Oh, by the way, Rita,' I said, popping my head around the kitchen door, 'you didn't leave a vibrator on the floor in the party room, did you?'

'With a condom on it?' she asked casually.

I nodded.

'No, darling', she said. 'I saw that there and didn't touch it.'

That left Delilah. Bugger. Delilah, who I could never understand, was watching television. I'd pick the damn thing up myself.

I returned to reception to find Pip comforting a very upset Maxine.

'Rita's not to get one booking all night,' Pip decreed.

The unacceptable, rude way in which Rita had spoken to Maxine, and her stubborn refusal to go to a booking, would be reported to Boris the minute he arrived. And Rita would be fined. Maxine knew very well where I'd been for the last half-hour, so every time Pip left the room, she reminded me of her suffering. But it seemed no amount of nodding would shut her up.

'I just can't believe how upset she's made me, you know, Meredith?'

Nod.

'I was in such a good mood when I got here tonight, and she made me so upset. I'm just feeling so upset now!'

Nod.

'And now I've got such a headache.' Here came the headaches. 'You know?'

Nod.

'I'm usually such a happy person. Well, you know that. I'm not usually like this, Meredith, am I? I don't usually let people get to me like that. But she really did, and I'm just so disappointed in myself for letting her get to me. You know?'

Nod. Nod. Please die. Nod.

But Maxine's performance reminded me of a mystery unsolved. Where had she worked before, and why was it so terrifying that Rita remembered her? Wasn't it Blue Angels? And where on earth had I put my clogs?

Min's girls

Out of the twenty girls on roster each night, about one-third were Asian, including a few Eurasian. And with one or two exceptions, they were 'Min's Girls'. Min was an ancient-sounding Chinese woman who collected and looked after young Asian prostitutes. If we got a booking for any one of these girls, we called Min, and her husband, Lan, drove them to wherever they had to go. They were on a healthy commission, no doubt.

'Does she recruit them?' I asked Sofia.

'I don't know what the fuck you're talking about, darling,' Sofia answered, eyeing me distrustfully.

'Does Min go out and find young—'

'Look!' Sofia wasn't having a bar of my *Four Corners* exposé on the exploitation of young Asian girls. 'Would you rather they stay trapped in houses in Parramatta, fucking men for pimps who pay them nothing?'

'No, but—'

'Then shuddup. Min's a good woman, darling, and that's all you need to know.'

All Min's girls spoke English to different degrees, but some had such thick accents they may as well have been speaking pure Cantonese to me.

'Hive, whore, heaven, yellow yellow,' a breathy child's voice said over the phone.

It was Cho-cho, reading out the details of a credit card which apparently ended with the numbers five, four, seven, yellow yellow.

'Yellow, Cho-cho?' I asked, straining to understand.

'Yellow!' Cho-cho shouted back. 'Two yellow!'

I looked desperately at Pip, who interrupted her call to mouth, 'Ze-ro.'

'Oh … zero, Cho-cho.'

'Yeah.' Cho-cho laughed like a toddler. 'Two yellow!'

All Min's girls sounded like they were five years old, and just off the boat. Min herself barely spoke. She just did vowels.

'Min?'

'Eah ahi.'

Worse was her husband, Lan, who just grunted.

'Lan?'

'Ugh.'

'Is Min there?'

'Ugh.'

'Eah ahi?'

'Min? Is that you?'

'Eah!'

If I was lucky I got their teenage daughter Lisa, who was at university and spoke with a broad Australian accent. Lisa was always very helpful. Apparently she was studying anthropology.

Every Monday night at seven, Min would come to the house and sit down with Sofia to do the bookwork for the Asian girls. I was surprised to find the voice on the phone belonged to a sweet little lady in her fifties who laughed a lot and called everyone 'dali'. Not 'ahi'. In fact, in person I could understand Min very well. She had a great sense of humour, which was hilariously at odds with Sofia's life-or-death histrionics.

'Oh no, dali,' Min would say softly, sitting at Sofia's desk with a calculator, 'Ginjung not work tonight, dali.'

'She has to, Min!' Sofia would cry. 'We need her!'

'No, dali,' Min would laugh softly, 'she too sore from last night. Ginjung only little, dali.'

'Tell her to use more lube, Min!'

In the laundry with Maya

Although this maternal, protective side of Min was reassuring, her effect on Maya was not. Once one of Min's girls, Maya always ran for cover when Min came to the house.

'Don't you like Min, Maya?' I asked her one night when she burst into the laundry where I was folding towels.

'No,' she snapped. 'She and Lan horrible to me when I left. But I get job! I get married! I have to leave!'

Maya worked at the Hilton as a housemaid, and I wondered how the marriage was going.

'But did Min look after you, Maya, before you got married?'

Maya thought about this for a moment, then gave a reluctant nod.

'And did she recruit you, Maya? I mean, does she go out and—'

'Min get girls out of houses,' Maya shook her head, 'bad, bad houses ...'

I could tell by the way she hovered at the door that Maya wasn't comfortable talking about herself. Maya never encouraged any kind of attention, which meant she was often overlooked by clients who met her in our waiting room, and forgotten by the receptionists upstairs. Instead of showing off her slim figure in body-hugging skirts or tops with plunging necklines, Maya chose more conservative, flowing evening gowns, two in black, and one in red. She always looked more like she was on her way to a wedding reception than a booking. I imagined Maya serving clients almost like a geisha, with her quiet, sad, submissive beauty. Many of our Asian girls had a willing subservience that quite a few men preferred to the Australian way.

I continued folding towels in silence until Maya relaxed, walked around and leant against the dryer. Min got Maya out of a house in Parramatta, she told me, when she had just arrived in Australia. She was sixteen. On the pretence of seeing a girl, Lan visited the house and snuck out with his booking still in her dressing gown. I started refolding the towels from the top.

Min and Lan gave Maya a bed. They taught her English. She and a dozen other Asian girls were clothed, fed, and watched television together like a family. Lan drove as many as he could to bookings himself, and waited in the car outside, and they were paid good money. Most of the girls were illegal immigrants and didn't dare leave this safe cocoon. But not Maya. As soon as her English was good enough, she went out, got a job at the Hilton and packed her bags. Min and Lan were furious. How could she be so ungrateful and disloyal? But Maya had a family of her own. Back in Thailand she had a mother, who was looking after Maya's daughter. Towels folded twice, I began wiping down the top of the washing machine.

One of Maya's regular clients had offered her permanent residency by proposing marriage. As she was pregnant, Maya accepted, and they moved to Ashfield. When the child was at kindergarten, Maya walked into Boris and Didi's for an interview as an escort. As his two most beautiful girls at the time, Maya and Shelby made Boris and Didi a pot of money. This explained Boris's demand that they each get two bookings a night, for such long service and loyalty were rare and must be rewarded. I began madly polishing inside the lid of the washing machine.

Did her husband and son know where she worked every night? Maya laughed. Her son thought it was all housemaiding at the Hilton, which was half true. We occasionally did send Maya to the Hilton, but only in an emergency. The thought of running into one of her colleagues was understandably terrifying. But yes, of course her husband knew what she did. That's how they met, remember? And he didn't mind? Too bad if he did, she laughed. I went back to refolding the towels.

Did she really need to be working two jobs at once? Maya nodded fervently. Absolutely. Of course. She had a mother and a daughter to support back in Thailand, remember? And she squealed with excitement as she announced the imminent arrival of her daughter, who had now finished university. I stopped polishing. How old was Maya? It was wonderful to see her broad, cheeky smile.

'Twenty-six to forty all you need to know!'

Maya was rocking with laughter when the bathroom door behind me swung open, whacking me in the back.

'Fook off!' yelled Sapphire unapologetically, standing with her hands on her hips in the doorway. 'I want to fooking pee!'

When I returned upstairs, it had happened again. Raelene, Sofia and Pip were all beside themselves over Genevieve's Collette Dinnigan dress and honey blonde highlights. Apparently the goddess had dropped in, picked up a thousand dollars from last night's credit card booking, and departed for the Westin, all while I was in the laundry with Maya. Curse this fashion conscious goddess. Would she never materialise?

Patrick's pipes

Rosters were a nightmare for Sofia, and juggling every receptionist's request sent her reaching for the Black Douglas, which
explained why my request for Wednesdays meant I was now
working Sundays. I shared this shift with Maxine and Pip, who
both had their own cars. Big cars. Little women. But at least this
meant it was just Patrick and me in the Merc from the city all the
way to Coogee. Just the two of us, for twenty minutes. It would
have been twenty-five, but Patrick was too good a driver.

Patrick steered brilliantly and effortlessly with one hand. He'd
light cigarettes with the other. And he'd sing. Changing lanes was
like poetry in motion. We'd glide up behind a Mazda, say, and in a
heartbeat I'd find myself looking into a surprised woman's face on
my left before we'd take off again, without my stomach. I felt like
a kid on a ride at a show. Patrick wasn't showing off. He was
oblivious as he lit another Marlboro with his free hand. I could
drive a hundred years and I'd never be as good as Patrick. I told him
so. Patrick chuckled heartily.

It was our first long drive together, and as it hadn't been one of
Sofia's shifts, it was still dark. I asked Patrick how long he'd been
driving for Boris and Didi.

'I filled in for a friend one weekend over a year ago, and I've
been coming back every weekend since!'

I smiled. He could have answered in so many ordinary ways.

Before driving escorts, Patrick had done 'a bit of this' and 'a bit
of that', driving taxis, carpentry.

'And where do you live?' I asked, trying to find out if there was
a Mrs Patrick.

'Well, the missus threw me out a couple of years ago—' (oh
really!) '—so now I share with a couple of no-good scoundrels in
Matraville.'

Did he do anything else, I asked, when he wasn't working four
nights a week? The question seemed to tickle Patrick as he laughed
for some time.

'Well, yes. I *do* have something else that I'm *supposed* to be
doing, but do you think I can pull my finger out and *get on with it*?'

What was it, I asked, wondering if one of the scoundrels could possibly be a girlfriend.

'Well,' Patrick began cautiously, 'I've designed these pipes that carry, um, light!'

'Light?'

'Natural light,' replied Patrick throwing his body forward over the wheel, laughing. 'Yes,' he added, throwing himself back again.

'Sunshine pipes?' I suggested, sunnily.

'Yes!' Patrick beamed at me with gratitude. 'Sunshine pipes!'

I don't know if it was the sunshine or his shyness, the pipes or our strange and sudden delight, but neither of us could stop smiling as Patrick explained to me in his lilting way, nervously rocking backwards and forwards in his seat, about these pipes he had designed that could carry, with the help of mirrors, or water or petrol for all I cared, natural sunlight into windowless rooms.

'You mean, for basements?' I asked.

'For basements.' He looked at me again and smiled.

Patrick felt a bit vulnerable revealing his pipe dream to the new receptionist, I could tell. But I did not want to laugh at his pipes at all. I thought putting natural sunshine into dark basements was one of the noblest things I'd ever heard. As we drove to Coogee, I was almost moved to tears by Patrick's pipes full of mirrors and water and sunshine.

'Don't be silly!' I laughed, as Libby made us both a cup of tea the following afternoon. 'He drives prostitutes for a living! I can't go out with someone who drives prostitutes for a living.'

'Why not?' she asked. 'You book them.'

Don't pat the bull

Autumn suited Arlington House much more than summer, even if the palm trees outside our French windows did look a little sad. But now that daylight savings was over, I enjoyed coming to work when the stars were already out. A brothel feels a bit selfconscious in daylight, and doesn't like people looking at it. And I never enjoyed leaving the sun behind as I stepped into its artificially dark interior, maybe because it reminded me of doing matinees while my friends all went to the beach. But as I crossed our street on this damp, windy night and recognised, through the silhouette of two swaying palm trees, our soft office lamp light spilling onto the balcony above, I felt happy. Not only had our brothel taken on a cosy, inviting ambience with its drawn crimson velvet curtains, but it had reclaimed a bit of mystery, its rightful intrigue and, for me, its magic.

Sofia arrived upstairs, puffing and panting, and in a very good mood.

'Look what I got,' she announced to me.

Sofia flopped in her chair and threw four shopping bags on her desk, and smiled at me. Not at Pip or Raelene. At me! Why I was suddenly privy to Sofia's shopping, I did not know. I did not care. I just wanted badly to prove deserving of the honour. I smiled in anticipation. Oh please, be something nice.

'Look!' She beamed as she spread out on her desk a colourful two-piece outfit for a small child.

The little pants and top were black with bright, sporadic, hot pink and electric blue flowers, and hemmed everywhere with a simple frill.

'Oh, it's gorgeous,' I said, relieved, picking up a frilly leg. 'Who's it for?'

Sofia momentarily lost her smile.

'Monique!' she shouted at me. 'My little girl, for Chrissake!'

Pip sauntered over with an approving smile for the little outfit.

'Oh, that's just perfect for Monnie,' she said.

'Don't call her that, darling,' Sofia warned Pip. 'She fucking hates *Monnie.*'

'How old is she?' I asked Sofia.

'Four,' sighed Pip, gliding back to her chair.

I was hoping she'd get that wrong too.

Sofia showed me a photo of her little Spanish fairy, smiling in her tulle skirt and sparkly, crooked wings. Monique had long brown curly hair and long black eyelashes just like her mother's. I watched Sofia melt with pride and emotion at the sight of the little fairy, so much that I felt guilty at the thought: who looked after the fairy when Mummy and Daddy were at the casino all morning?

Sofia told me that although she and Arturo had been together ten years they had not planned to have children at all. Monique's arrival into this world was a welcome surprise, but unfortunately coincided with the beginning of 'Arturo's illness', and the consequent demise of his income. So now Sofia found herself supporting a family, nursing a sick husband, managing a brothel and, I guessed, sought recreation at Star City.

'Is he going to be all right?' I asked, not daring to ask the exact nature of Arturo's illness.

'God knows, darling. Nex' week he goes in for his fourth operation.'

Sofia's parents looked after Monique when Arturo got too sick, she told me, but she didn't like to depend on them because they were very old.

'Besides, darling, if they fine out where I work, they both die of heart attacks on the spot.'

Sofia usually spoke to the other girls about personal things. About anything. Such small, tentative offerings gave me hope that she was starting to trust me.

'Isn't it cute?' she sang, returning to the outfit. 'If you saw her, Meredith, you would know how much this suits her.'

'What's it made of?' I asked, rolling the material between my fingers.

Suddenly the whole thing was snatched away from my hands.

'I don't know,' she answered abruptly.

I watched helplessly as Sofia folded the outfit and hastily pushed it back in its bag.

'It doesn't matter . . .' I quickly back-pedalled.

'Is polyester or somethin',' she muttered defensively. 'Is juss for fun.'

'Oh, I know,' I assured her, 'half my wardrobe is polyester!'

But it was too late. I'd blown it, and the tiger was back in its cage. We returned to work in an atmosphere of awkwardness, until the demand for girls overtook us and we were too busy landing planes to care. Within an hour Sofia had forgotten all about material that breathes and was abusing me for double-booking Felicity.

The north and south poles of Antoinette

We always described Antoinette as 'mature, affectionate' and 'provides an excellent service'. Unlike the other girls, almost everything on the back of Antoinette's card was ticked. She kissed, she'd see women, couples, paraplegics, the lot. And although she didn't do anal, Antoinette was one of the few girls who performed golden showers. Her card said she was forty-four, and although she was possibly older, we impudently sent her out as 'late thirties'. Antoinette had a wonderful body for her age, slim but curvaceous, with a size 36 bust and double D cup. For some reason, though, Antoinette chose to cover up her figure with one of three conservative black suits that made her look like an usherette. Although they did reveal her ample cleavage, the blazers were bulky, and the skirts were straight, roomy and stopped just above the knees. All she needed was the torch.

When she wasn't smoking by the back door, Antoinette would sit at the kitchen table brushing her straight, thick, shoulder-length blonde hair, and applying mascara and red lipstick to her pale face. When I came downstairs with a booking for her, she'd look up from under the golden fringe with a cautious smile. Antoinette had terrible eyesight but refused to wear glasses, so her large brown eyes would squint as she jutted her head forward, straining to read my deliberately large handwriting. If it was a credit card booking, we bent the rules and read the card numbers back to her when she got to the client, rather than the other way around.

However, my initial, haunting impression of Antoinette was slowly being replaced by something much less disturbing, and much more comforting, if a little eccentric. The more I talked to her, the more I discovered she was friendly, intelligent and had a dry sense of humour, especially when she was being self-deprecating.

But best of all, like me, Antoinette was congenitally curious. In the early days I would ask any girl on her return from a booking how it went, but pretty soon I stopped. It was the look Pandora, Lana and Amber gave me. Maya just smiled with her eyes closed, as if to say, 'I survived.' Heather always shrugged her shoulders. Who cared? It was buxom Marcelle and her baritone friend Trixie who put it most succinctly.

'You don't ask that!'

'Ya burk!'

But Antoinette didn't mind at all. It was as inoffensive to ask Antoinette about a booking as it would have been to ask David Attenborough, on returning from the Gombawii Jungle, if he'd seen anything interesting.

'How was that one, then, Antoinette?' I asked one night.

'Well,' she began in her wavering voice, standing in the middle of the kitchen with her bag still over her shoulder, 'he was quite twisted, actually. Infected … didn't want company so much as a punching bag.'

'Did 'e punch ya?' asked Ronda with sudden interest, looking up from her magazine.

'No,' murmured Antoinette, walking dreamily across the kitchen in perfect turnout, psychological postmortem still in progress.

Ronda looked at me, rolled her eyes and returned to her *Who Weekly*. Like most girls, she didn't get Antoinette, and had given up trying.

Antoinette distractedly opened her bag at the kitchen sink, vaguely aware she had to give someone some money.

'He's a naval architect,' she continued as I nimbly extracted our ninety dollars, 'and carrying a lot of baggage, if you know what I mean …'

I slid into a facing chair at the kitchen table.

'The kids left home a few years ago, and the wife's just become a public relations consultant.'

She sat at the table with poise. 'I should have just shut up. I mean, I know better than that. You know when you're not supposed to have a brain or an opinion …' Antoinette looked up from under her fringe and laughed warily. 'But when they're educated and say such appalling things, I just can't help myself.'

She took out a cigarette with her dainty, manicured hands. I waved away her offer and beckoned her to go on.

'What did he say?'

'Oh,' she sighed, blowing out smoke, 'he was going on about women unsuccessfully trying to compete with men in business, and not coping with the pressure. He said that's why most women still worked in domestic service. He was being deliberately provocative.'

'What did you say?'

'I said crisis management's hardly cleaning toilets.'

'What did he say?'

'He said, "What about you? You're a servant."'

'Bastard. What did you do?'

I just smiled and said I enjoyed my work very much, and that some nights I made as much money as a naval architect.'

'Oh dear.'

'Yeah, stupid.'

We sat for a moment in silence, pondering the consequences.

'Are you okay?' I finally asked.

'I'm a bit sore,' she smiled.

The more Antoinette and I got on, the more my colleagues upstairs disapproved. I still had not witnessed the 'madness' they warned me about and shouldn't encourage a friendship.

'She's on antidepressants, you know,' they hissed ominously, as if one-third of the world wasn't.

'She's sensitive,' I argued, 'and highly intelligent,' only to be rebuked by a chorus of mocking jeers. As if that was of any value in this industry.

'You just wait till she chucks a hissy fit on ya!' warned Raelene, supported by a pitying nod from Maxine.

I had witnessed a flash of anger the night Antoinette had burst out of the room from spanking nervous Gilbert from Tasmania, but that was hardly unreasonable.

An hour later, I'd find myself walking Antoinette to the front door again, sketching any impression her waiting client's voice had

imparted over the phone, and she'd listen with deferential interest.
On her return I'd run downstairs and we'd compare my expecta-
tions with her experience. And rather than agreeing with them,
I was even beginning to take refuge from the girls upstairs in
Antoinette's thoughtful company and her lucid observations. If she
didn't have to work, I could have sat and talked with her all night.

'Light?' I asked when she had returned from another booking,
almost joyful.

'Not light physically. I mean ... unburdened. No shame. He
took total responsibility for what he was doing, and he was very ...
present. Light!'

Weight always featured strongly in Antoinette's descriptions.
A complex character herself, she was intrigued by the complexities
of others and felt the weight of unhappiness easily. I asked her once
if she'd ever wanted to be a psychiatrist. She laughed. Three years
ago, Antoinette told me, she had moved in with one.

'He was a client. A terribly unhappy man. *Terribly*. Married to
another psychiatrist, actually ... Anyway, he kept seeing me for two
years. Became quite dependent ... in fact he frightened both of us.
We tried to stop, but he couldn't let it go. Then he rang to say he'd
left his wife, found us a place ... and so we moved in together. Two
weeks later he had a complete nervous breakdown. I've never seen
anything like it. The wife had to come and collect him.'

Had Antoinette seen or heard from him since?

'Oh, no. Didn't expect to, really. But I always think of him when
I pass his practice in the city.'

And this is where Antoinette got complex.

'He could never accept that this is what I do,' she exclaimed
indignantly. 'And he expected me to just stop. Once we were living
together. Just stop!'

Was I old-fashioned, or did Antoinette's lucid reasoning just
take a sharp detour south?

Then it happened. Trudy had sent Antoinette to Ken in Botany.
Antoinette returned that night in a state I would never forget. It
became a benchmark for all future 'states'. I froze on the stairs,
clutching a booking for Heather as I listened to the volcano
erupting in the kitchen below. A voice was spewing abuse at

anything and everyone in sight with such primal force I barely recognised it. I trembled as I watched the single file of stony-faced girls escaping from their kitchen in fire drill format. Ken in Botany might have been a dud booking, but it sounded more like twenty-five years of mounting despair had let rip. Still clutching Heather's booking, I retreated upstairs and quietly shut the door behind me. When I turned around, I was confronted by two righteous receptionists nodding at me.

'*See?*'

An old pro

It was June, and some time in the last few weeks Valmai had joined the agency as a receptionist, but as we both worked 'downstairs' where only one was needed, we never shared the same shift. Until Sofia told me I was working Tuesday nights 'upstairs'. Didi's orders.

I was becoming immune to these constant shift changes. I'd started off asking for weekend work only, to ensure I was free for any acting work that came my way. But it didn't, so to punish the industry that didn't want me, I started saying yes to any shift going in the industry that did. And I developed a perverse taste for being reckless when I discovered I could go straight from the brothel at five in the morning and be on a television set by six.

'You're tired,' one of the perky young stars had commented during a rehearsal on *Home and Away*.

'Yeah,' I answered, smiling back deliriously, 'I work in a brothel.'

As I wearily climbed the stairs at seven to begin my Tuesday night shift, I wondered which girl had the client with the loud, rasping voice and raucous laugh. It made a nice change from the usual grunting, panting and moaning. Occasionally I heard a girl enjoying herself. If Letitia was in, we were treated to the same shameless array of oohs and aahs no matter who she was with. After one such performance, I was shocked to see her escorting a frail octogenarian to the front door and chastising him all the way in baby talk for being a 'bad, naughty boy'. But as I passed the empty bedrooms, it became clearer to me that the laughing man must be in reception. I opened our door and, through billows of cigarette smoke, he half materialised like a ghost.

'This is Valmai,' Trudy said, introducing me to a mature, dwarfish, blonde woman clutching a big box of Horizon cigarettes.

'Pleased to meet ya!' she greeted me, leaning out of the gloom to shake my hand.

Valmai was at least fifty. She smiled up at me from under her shaggy, layered streaked hair, and winked. Trudy looked very tired. Too tired to notice they were suffocating in the dark.

'Are you new to this business too, Valmai?' I asked, putting down my bag and flinging open the French doors to let in some cold fresh air.

'Nah, bub, I'm an old pro!' And Valmai roared with laughter at her accidental pun, until she thought of another one.

'You could say – I'm an old hand!'

And off she went again, except this time it provoked such a bad coughing fit that for a minute Trudy and I thought she might die right in front of us. Instead, she lit up another cigarette.

Valmai certainly was not new to this business. As the night wore on, we were regaled with one story after another of parlours she had managed in the good old days when all the gents gave tips, the girls wore lingerie and, she lowered her voice, 'got police protection'.

'Perhaps they don't need it, now that it's legal,' I offered, and was deftly ignored.

Yes sir, things were different when Valmai ran her business. By three in the morning it was my least favourite topic of conversation. I had even begun ringing myself on different lines, pretending to take bookings that didn't work out. But it was like trying to ignore a cyclone. Valmai jumped on incoming calls like a bleached hawk on a mouse, her white knuckles gripping the phone as if her very life depended on it. Trudy and I dared not look at each other as our new receptionist touched her chest, dropped an octave and spoke to the man in her poshest voice.

'Hello, Valmai speaking, may I help you? ... Oh yes, sir, we have lovely ladies from Asia, Australia and European ladies from ... well, Europe. Are you calling from a hoh-telle, sir? ... Oh, the

Intercontinental, that's a lovely hoh-telle … May name's Val-mai, what's yours? … Brian? That's a lovely name …'

It was such a relief when the door bell went downstairs. I didn't care that she got on so well with the clients, but I grimaced inside every time I heard her laughing with the girls in the kitchen. My girls. Valmai would return upstairs, panting and shaking her head.

'Oh, that Urszula …' she'd cry, as if she and Sapphire were old friends. 'And that Pandora's a sweetheart, isn't she?' she'd declare of the beautiful, young and silent Pandora, who had steadfastly refused to reveal herself to me. And if it was a group of men she was seeing off at the front door, we could hear Valmai belting out the punch line before the whole house shook with the thunder of laughter.

'See ya next time, Val!' her customers would bawl from the street as they left in stitches.

I muttered to Trudy that I thought we were supposed to be more discreet than that. Trudy just smiled. Trudy had the sad disposition of someone barely able to forgive herself for her own sins. I didn't know what was in Trudy's dark past, but disapproval of others was a luxury she did not believe she could afford.

At midnight, Boris arrived. If Boris had looked uncomfortable when introduced to a receptionist as tall as me, he was positively allergic to the dimensions, age and volume of Valmai. He retreated awkwardly as she barked 'G'day!' at him like a small nervous dog desperate to please its master. Before he could finish his question, Valmai yapped at him that she was having a ball. She'd had a great time with the girls downstairs, and the clients. Yes sir, Boris wasn't married to a fool. Didi knew a 'people's person' when she interviewed one. And she hoped Boris didn't mind, but she'd had a word with all the girls about the importance of wearing good lingerie, which they were all going to rush out and buy the next day, and she'd found Antoinette's missing shoe, so wasn't that great! Boris nodded, retreating from her as if she had leprosy, and Trudy and I knew there would be words with Didi when he got home.

By six in the morning, Trudy, Patrick and I were all packed up and standing in the doorway, waiting for Valmai, who was taking forever to put her coat on. Pretending to play with his computer, Boris was waiting too.

'Where've I seen you before, bub?' Valmai suddenly asked me. Her arms bent like wings before disappearing down their sleeves.

'Don't know,' I replied quickly, sandwiched between Patrick and Trudy. I wished she'd get her coat on before recognising me from *Neighbours* or something.

'Definitely know your face,' she continued, scrutinising me.

'Yeah, I feel that too,' Trudy suddenly piped, looking at me as if she'd been sitting on a pebble for the last four months, and at last someone had told her.

'You haven't worked in this business before, have you?' Valmai enquired.

And for the first time, Boris looked up at me with genuine interest. Even Patrick couldn't help a nervous sideways glance in my direction. I wondered what was worse, them all finding out I'd been on *Play School*, or suspecting I had once been a prostitute. I could feel the blood rushing to my face.

'Ha!' I laughed, clumsily pushing past Patrick.

And my pathetic 'ha' haunted me all the way down the stairs and to the car outside, where I waited in the cold, feeling wretched. I did not like this new receptionist who'd made me blush in front of Boris and Patrick, who roared laughing with clients and girls downstairs and who had already cracked the secret code of Pandora. I didn't like the way she deliberately chose her moment to cast the shadow of suspicion on me, in front of the others. And it augured very badly for both of us if she insisted on calling me 'bub'.

Cracked Sapphire

It was still light when I swung my bag over my shoulder and walked down Arlington Street. As I was an hour early, I took my time, and even bought a small posy from the corner florist on Oxford Street to put in a vase on my desk. As soon as I arrived I would ring Didi and explain to her that one of the new shifts she had assigned me, without any consultation whatsoever, was unfortunately inconvenient. I would be friendly, but firm.

'Oh, Merrediss,' Didi said, laughing, 'you girls do amuse me with your constant complaints about your shifts.'

I laughed too, until Didi interrupted me.

'No. I'm afraid that's impossible. I can't change it. But tell me, how are you settling in?'

I was still struggling to comprehend her swift, uncompromising rebuttal and answer the question when Didi interrupted again. 'You might find you settle in quicker, Merrediss, and not make quite so many mistakes—' She chortled. '—if you did not waste so much time talking to the girls downstairs, yes?'

I found myself chortling too, until outrage finally caught up just as Didi dismissed me and hung up. I stared in disbelief at my sad vase of flowers. Someone had just backed into my garden, waved cheerfully, and driven off.

'It's me, ya sloots!' a voice crackled over the front door intercom. 'Let me in.'

Sapphire was a fearless and frequently in-the-right spokesperson for the girls. She didn't hesitate to roar abuse down the phone at us, or to our faces, over anything from a blown light bulb to her lack of bookings. Such tirades generally took place only when she had a kitchen full of girls, and the more girls, the bigger her performance. But no amount of sound and fury could cover the fact that Sapphire was a sadly constant figure in a changing sea of younger escorts coming and going from bookings. It was especially cruel on the nights she'd dressed up in her best outfit, a long-sleeved black organza top, beautifully cut, embroidered with a fine ropy trail of white flowers, that went over a matching black slip dress. She cut a voguish figure sitting at the table with her straight back, her high cheekbones, high heels and spiked blonde hair, her shapely legs crossed and a perpetual cigarette burning between her elegant fingers. Somehow Sapphire made wearing sunglasses with an evening dress look stylish.

'Did you do ballet?' I asked her one such night.

Sapphire roared laughing. 'I had seven broothers! One of them put me in hospital twice! Do you think I was going to defend myself with a fooking arabesque?'

I muttered something about her good posture as the blood

flowed to my cheeks, but all Sapphire noticed was that she now had everyone's attention. When she was seven, she began with all the theatricality of a Shakespearean prologue, her father saw that unless his little girl learnt how to defend herself, she wouldn't survive the spring. Well, the local judo classes awoke such confidence and bloodlust in the young lass, she not only broke the brother's nose next time he jumped her, she went on to win the North Yorkshire Junior Tae Kwon Do Championship three years running. No, her impressive posture and feline agility were more due to three decades of martial arts than prancing about to 'fooking Tchaikovsky'. This fierce performance may have fooled the new girls, who smiled desperately as their eyes searched for the nearest exit, but not the older ones. They nodded accommodatingly as they flicked through their magazines, except Antoinette, who always feigned complete deafness in Sapphire's company.

As the weeks turned into months, I became more acquainted with the sad woman called Urszula who sat on her own in an empty kitchen at the beginning of each night. She reminded me of an actress mustering courage before getting into her costume and transforming into the dynamic, kick-arse character she'd so appropriately called 'Sapphire'.

Boris allowed Sapphire to park her big, white Land Rover in the back garage, where it was visible from the kitchen window. No one could get the truth out of Sapphire about this expensive 'present' given to her by her last 'employer'. All that mattered, she'd smile, enjoying the intrigue, was that it housed her and her 'boy', Rex. There was something sadly humble in the way she called her car her 'home' and her white bull terrier her 'boy', but it worried me that Sapphire referred fondly to Boris as her 'father'. Upstairs, there was little that was fatherly in the way Boris spoke about Sapphire, or any of the girls.

At the end of the night, when the girls had been paid, the birds had started to sing and the black sky had turned cobalt blue, Sapphire would wash Rex's bowl in the sink, make one last mug of instant coffee, grab her Horizon cigarettes, and bid us a fond and jolly farewell before we locked her out. It was clear she wanted no sympathy with regards to this living arrangement, but nothing

could take away the sting as I double-locked the back door and
waved at the solitary figure through the glass, climbing into her car
with her powerful, stocky white dog. It seemed ridiculous, standing
in the warmth of this large, empty house with all its spare beds
strewn with fake zebra skins and clean sheets.

'Can't we sneak you back in?' I asked her at the door one
bitterly cold night.

'No,' she retorted as she passed me. 'Besides,' she added quietly,
'he turns the alarm on.'

He being her 'father'.

A few hours later, the morning receptionist would arrive at ten
to open up the house. Once the back door was unlocked, Sapphire
would shuffle back in, put the kettle on and, over her first cigarette
of the day, debrief the fresh receptionist about the previous night's
dramas. We turned a blind eye to her sneaking dirty washing in
with the regular laundry. After showering and dressing in the girls'
bathroom, Sapphire would take off with Rex in their mobile
home, windows down, radio blaring, fresh air blowing in their
faces, singing all the way to their 'back yard'.

Sapphire spent her days in Centennial Park, throwing Rex a
ball, reading under the trees, and rollerblading. I didn't believe the
rollerblading until months later, when I went with her.

Although Sapphire was part of the senior core on roster seven
nights a week, she was the only girl who worked the days as well. If
a call came through on her mobile, Sapphire would throw the ball
and Rex in the car, fly back to the house, and turn up twenty
minutes later in some hotel lobby looking a million dollars. Despite
her cramped living arrangements, Sapphire was always clean,
tanned and well dressed. Even if she got one booking a week,
which was not unusual, Sapphire somehow made her hundred and
ten dollars stretch until the next one. Her first priority was to feed
her beloved Rex, and then to feed herself, but I suspect she mainly
lived off toast and coffee from our kitchen. Frugality aside, on a
busy night Sapphire would duck up to her favourite all-night cafe
in the Cross and return with several lattes for anyone who wanted
one. No one had requested her to do so, and any attempt at
reimbursement was greeted with florid abuse.

It was Saturday night. Sapphire hadn't had a booking in three weeks, and that was bad. Even for her. I hurt to see her sitting in the kitchen all dressed up, smoking one cigarette after another. Trudy was worried about her too. Despite all the warnings on the wall about fraternising with the girls, Trudy and Sapphire had a close friendship that went back years. Trudy was constantly in trouble for breaking this rule, but she didn't care, it was her business and if management didn't like it they could sack her. Trudy had a seven-year-old daughter, Molly, who loved Sapphire like a favourite, wicked aunt, ever since she'd had stayed with them while recovering from some mysterious illness. They regularly escaped to Byron Bay with the intention of 'getting healthy'. Packed up in the Land Rover, Trudy, Sapphire, a couple of friends, Molly and Rex would disappear for a whole week, and then beg Boris and Didi for another when they returned, to get over the damage they'd done.

It was due to Trudy's relentless pleas that Boris finally gave in and agreed to let Sapphire work as a second driver, just for the weekend. It was unusually busy, Patrick couldn't be everywhere at once, and at ten dollars a trip for Sapphire, it was cheaper for the girls than getting a taxi. They all took it pretty well, except for Antoinette, who made it very clear in a hushed but articulate petition at the top of the stairs that the kitchen was the only enclosed space she would ever share with Sapphire. Unless, of course, they got a lesbian double booking. After all, she was a professional. Rex took it pretty well. Seeing his mother wasn't upset, he gave up his front passenger seat with noble grace and sat obediently in the back, panting at the mysterious array of beautiful women who climbed in and out of his home till the wee hours.

'As long as Mummy's happy, he's happy,' Sapphire declared.

Although Rex looked like he'd take your head off in a second, he went visibly weak at the knees at Mummy's voice or smile. The only girl Rex barked at was Coral, which was very odd, Sapphire would growl suspiciously. 'It means there's something wrong with her.' From then on, we all looked at Coral differently.

Sapphire enjoyed being second driver and visibly thrived on feeling needed. Any other girl might have found it humiliating, but Sapphire embraced her new job boots and all.

'Come on, Lena, get your arse into my car, we haven't got all fooking night. May-Ling, darling, I'll come back for you in a second. Meredith, don't just stand there, tell me where I'm taking Bridgit, for fook's sake! Antoinette do you want a lift? Didn't think so. Hang on, Amber, my baby's just having a pee, for Christ's sake! Come on all you sloots, move it!'

However, by Tuesday night things were quiet again, and we only needed one driver. Upstairs, we had never worked harder to get Sapphire a booking. Even if the man asked for an eighteen-year-old Asian, we threw Sapphire in as an exciting alternative.

'Why you want a thin Asian girl, Robert?' I heard Sofia imploring. '*This* girl, I'm telling you, Robert, does things you did not know possible! She's sexy – what? . . . Late thirties. She's athletic . . . I dunno, thirty-nine. Blonde . . . oh for Chrissake, darling, does it matter? Is short! . . . No, no I got buckets of Asian, Robert! Jesus, you always eat at the same bloody restaurant?'

Sadly, returning to her post as working girl made little differ-ence to Sapphire's redundancy.

The following Friday night was no better. When I walked into the kitchen the tension was palpable. Sapphire was sitting at the table dealing cards to four girls who looked nervously at each other. The phones were dead. The only sound came from the kitchen clock, a present Boris had given the house – it marked each second with two animated pink pigs fucking. Even through her black sunglasses, Sapphire was looking particularly 'deadly', a word she often used to describe herself. Her angular features looked sharper than ever. Sitting opposite Sapphire was a woman I'd never seen before. The smiling hippy introduced herself to me as Harmony and continued babbling softly to no one in particular about 'chi'. Harmony was either stupid, pissed or suicidal, because it was obvious to everyone else in the room that Sapphire wanted to kill her.

I leant against our door upstairs, panting with relief, and warned my colleagues about the explosion about to erupt downstairs. Shaking her pink-streaked head, Trudy informed me that Harmony was Sapphire's 'Achilles heel'.

'They have a personality clash,' Raelene translated helpfully, in case I thought it was a foot problem.

'Urszula can't stand drunks,' Trudy explained, 'and Harmony keeps a bottle in her locker.'

But why, I asked, did a silly drunk woman so upset her?

'She just rocks Urszula's boat.'

I went downstairs later to find Sapphire's mood had spread like a virus. It was raining outside and the kitchen was now full of angry girls walking mud everywhere, ashing in the sink, and blowing off about bad bookings. Antoinette stood alone at the bench, attacking a piece of toast like an angry child left to fend for herself. Courtenay stood at the back door arguing on her mobile with her boyfriend, getting soaked and demanding he repeat everything. And sitting on her own at the kitchen table surrounded by discarded takeaway containers, overflowing ashtrays and coffee cups was Harmony, pissed to the gills, babbling on about 'cosmic energy'. Instead of holding court in the kitchen as she always did, Sapphire had moved to the lounge, where she sat alone watching television. The whole brothel ecosystem seemed thrown by this break in the chain. It was like in *Macbeth* when the king's been murdered and the owl hunts the falcon and all the horses eat each other.

Troubled by the thought of Boris's sudden appearance, I moved among the disgruntled throng, emptying ashtrays, gathering cups and rubbish.

'Are you okay?' I finally asked, popping my head around the lounge door.

Sapphire sat like Nefertiti watching television in her tomb. Without taking her eyes off the television, one long finger commandingly beckoned me over. Her glasses were off for once, and I was shocked when she looked up at me with her small, pale eyes.

'I'm doing this for her sake, Meredith.'

Before I could answer, Sapphire reached up and yanked me down by my lapel so hard my knees hit the floor with a thud.

'If I stay in that room with that sodden bitch, Meredith,' she growled, 'I won't be responsible for what happens. Do you understand?'

Despite the throbbing of my old knee injury, I nodded fervently until I was released.

Fate was relentlessly cruel that night, as the only two girls who got no bookings were Sapphire and Harmony. Like a restless inmate, Sapphire oscillated between playing patience at the kitchen table and watching television in the lounge. Harmony now sat perched by her locker and bar, and happily continued getting smashed. By two in the morning, Sapphire's wretched mood had permeated upstairs as well.

'Orroight?' announced Boris, smiling in the doorway.

'Orroight,' we chorused back flatly.

As none of us was in the mood for entertainment, he went downstairs in search of a laugh.

Boris couldn't have picked a worse night. If there's one thing Boris hated, it was a kitchen full of girls over thirty-five. It deprived him of a good flirt, and it reflected badly on his business. And maybe their mature faces and bodies reminded him of his own senior years.

'Christ!' he yelled at me when he returned five minutes later. 'Is that the best you could do? That bunch of rejects?'

As downstairs receptionist it was my job to make sure there was always a variety of in-house girls available to meet clients but, as usual, the younger, prettier ones got all the escort bookings, leaving me with the bowling club, including Antoinette, Rita, Maya, Sapphire and now Harmony. I forgot their age when they were cheerful, but tonight their little dresses took on an obscene inappropriateness, and their make-up looked grotesque on their crumpled faces.

'It's like focking Halloveen at a retirement willage!' Boris bawled at me, grabbing his car keys.

'Before you go to the casino, Urszula wants a quick word with you,' Trudy blurted, throwing petrol on the fire.

Boris thrust his arms into his patterned jacket and glowered at me as though I had deliberately peopled his brothel with sagging breasts.

Raelene, Trudy and I huddled like frightened children at the top of the stairs, listening to two voices in combat in the kitchen, one rising like a siren against an obstinate foghorn. In an effort to restore her power in front of the other girls, Sapphire had demanded Boris let her work as second driver for the rest of the night. There would be trouble, she warned ominously, if she stayed in this house one moment longer.

'Then why don't you fock off?' Boris roared.

There was a ghastly silence.

'Go on!' he cried. 'What you vaiting for? Fock off!'

The house had never felt so still.

'I think,' Sapphire began, but her voice sounded strange, 'we need to continue this conversation upstairs, Boris.'

'No! Take your focking dog, and your car, and your useless threats, and get out of my house!'

After a strained pause we heard the screech of a chair and a jangling of keys as Sapphire gathered her things. At first I thought Rex was crying, until I realised the horrible sound was coming from Sapphire herself, because when she opened the back door, we could hear her dog barking hysterically from her car outside. The door slammed and soon the Land Rover roared out of the garage.

Raelene nudged me forward at the top of the stairs. 'You better go down,' she whispered.

I turned to object, but when Trudy smiled with a pitying nod, I knew she was right. Downstairs was my turf. Solemnly I began my descent.

In the kitchen downstairs I found several bodies still hugging the walls in silence, as if Sapphire's departure had left a vacuum. One central figure stooped alone over the dividing bench, squinting over his cigarette like Humphrey Bogart. The silence finally broke when an empty bottle hit the floor, making us all jump, and rolled its way from Harmony's locker to the middle of the room. In a drunken lunge to save it, the hippy fell off her chair and lay giggling helplessly on the floor, like a pile of Indian washing.

'Meredit,' said Boris quietly, not taking his cold eyes off the bottle, 'call this girl a taxi.'

Boris's mistress

It had been a gamble, expanding from escort to in-house, and since the brothel was not doing good business, someone had to take the blame. Didi screamed at Boris, Boris yelled at us, and we tried not to take it out on the girls. Sapphire had been gone two nights, and without its raucous matriach the house in Darlinghurst was not a happy home.

Having left his scary wife and small dog at midnight, both barking orders, propped up by satin pillows on Didi's queen-size bed, Boris arrived in a tortured state. One half of him wanted to tell jokes and be loved, and the other half was a ruthless dictator married to Lady Macbeth, so we never knew if we were getting Hitler or Hancock. One solution for Boris was to alternate personalities upstairs and down. If the kitchen was full of pretty girls, they got the show and upstairs got the drill. If his audience downstairs was pretty enough, and laughed enough, he'd even open a bottle of the good St James Brut, especially reserved for one-hour bookings. But if the kitchen was feeling 'ancient', favour might swing our way and Boris would open a bottle for us, a magnanimous gesture considering he didn't drink himself. I would find out why later. These were the best nights and I swear we made more money. Men were tantalised by the giggling, flirtatious receptionist gushing with unbridled enthusiasm about Heather's bust line, or Celeste's long legs, and 'No, no, no, Warwick, you can't have me! I'm just the recepshnst!'

'I'm on my mobile,' Boris would announce from the doorway an hour later, scrutinising his receptionists through his cigarette smoke.

His pale Bavarian eyes unfortunately lost their mischief when they shifted in my direction. I understood better Boris's suspicion of me when I discovered later exactly what he was up to, but for now I felt relieved to hear the purr of his silver Mercedes gliding towards his favourite place on earth, Star City casino. Despite those parting words, under no circumstances whatsoever were we to call Boris on his mobile unless, Pip decreed, a girl was dead or the house was on fire. Otherwise the office phone bill betrayed Boris's regular sojourns to Darling Harbour when Didi went through it with a fine-tooth comb. It had been so long since I'd seen Didi, she was beginning to take on the nightmarish proportions of a perfumed, teeth-gnashing blonde witch who terrified even her husband.

Around five in the morning Boris would return in a good mood with mysterious wads of cash to a trio of tired and besieged receptionists. Without his cash to pay out credit card bookings, we were being abused by a chorus of understandably tired and literally fucked women downstairs who just wanted to get paid, go home, have a bath and sleep alone. Humming some Dean Martin song, Boris would sit at his desk, turn on his computer and count the night's takings while we described the various botched bookings and tantrums he had missed.

'Ach, tell her to get focked,' he'd scoff. 'No more bookings for that bitch,' he'd decree. 'Why did not Shelby get more bookings?' he would always complain, and no matter what explanations we offered, he'd answer, 'That's not goot enough!'

And all the time, facing the wall at his desk, counting money, Boris was clicking through his favourite website, Asian Sluts.

'Oh Christ,' he'd laugh, 'look at this one!'

And to his childlike delight we'd all look over and groan with abhorrence at the hardcore spectacle on his big colour screen. Boris giggled like a schoolboy. I don't know what he enjoyed more, ogling bored Asian girls spreading their labia for him, or our appalled reaction.

As the months went by, Boris remained a challenge to me. My attempts to be warm and unthreatening just made him even more suspicious. Already at a disadvantage because of my height, I tried being funny instead. God knows we needed a laugh in that office, and everyone else appreciated my jokes, except Sofia. Sofia never knew I was joking in the first place, and by the time I'd explained it to her she looked so tired, it was painful for both of us, and it only served to remind her of figures I hadn't checked or lube containers I should be filling. Boris got my jokes all right, but wasn't taking the bait. Something about me troubled him. Who was this tall, wholesome idiot trying to be funny in his brothel? Besides, comedy was his turf.

'He'll be better when Shan gets back from Singapore,' Pip sighed.

'Who's Shan?' I asked.

'His Asian Slut.'

Shan, from Singapore, was once one of the girls, until Boris took a liking to her and made her an offer she hadn't refused for the last three years. Pip did not think much of Shan.

'She's using him,' she said.

I tried hard not to laugh at the irony of this statement.

'She's been visiting her sick mother in Singapore for the last three months, and keeps asking Boris to send more money.'

I could tell that Pip did not think Shan's mother, if she existed at all, was very sick.

'That's why he's in such a bad mood lately. He knows she's taking him for a ride.'

No wonder Boris and Didi trusted nobody. While Didi's husband was cheating on her, Boris's mistress was ripping him off.

'Does Didi know about Shan?' I asked.

Pip snorted. 'Didi knows everything. So long as Boris manages the business, is a good father to Little Georgie and keeps his Asian Sluts out of her sight, she couldn't give a rat's arse what he does.'

Didi did not know everything, as Pip well knew, but I had not yet proved worthy of induction into the Hall of Brothel Secrets.

Pip was like family to Boris and Didi, having worked for them for nearly six years. It must have required great skill, being so loyal to each of them while juggling their various indiscretions.

'Does Didi have a lover?' I asked.

'She used to,' Pip said, 'but since recovering from cancer last year, she puts all her energy into bringing up Little Georgie.'

I remembered the fair, angelic child in the photo, next to the stuffed moose. A gifted child, Pip sighed. When she wasn't working for his mother at her brothel, Pip was employed as Little Georgie's private tutor. Pip inhaled as if about to relieve herself of a great burden. Although not a qualified teacher, Pip was a member of Mensa. 'You know,' she said, 'for people with abnormally high IQs.' I considered telling Pip that I was a member of Sensa, for the Highly Sensitive, but I didn't want to make her feel inferior.

Boris wasn't a big man, so it was no surprise that he liked most of all the tiny Asian girls. Shrewd, tough businesswomen like his wife and Shelby deserved respect, but no amount of intelligence impressed him so much as a pretty young face and a tiny body. When Boris's jokes fell on deaf but attractive ears, unable to understand or appreciate his wicked humour, it only delighted him more. I watched him salivate like a wolf, aroused by the scent of unworldliness. He'd smile with the bottom half of his face while his eyes remained hungry, fixed on the ingenuous, twitching victim sitting opposite him, giggling in a bewildered stupor.

The rest of us Boris regarded as so many odd socks in a drawer. And nothing annoyed him more than the odd socks getting on with each other. Rather than create a good working environment with a healthy, supportive atmosphere, Boris and Didi preferred one of tyranny and fear. Division and conquest, even among receptionists, encouraged healthy competition. Three times in four months I had witnessed a fellow receptionist tremble on her telephone as Didi interrogated her about some tiny discrepancy in the bookwork, an area, thank God, that no one let me anywhere near. I'd watched Raelene beg for a night off so she could go to a brother's birthday dinner, and then howl like a baby when her request was denied. But worst of all, I gathered from my colleagues' defensive protests to our fragrant despot and their resentful glances in my direction, Didi was blaming them for my poor progress.

'Yes. Meredith knows she should have charged fifty extra, Didi! She just didn't think it was Fantasy.'

It didn't seem fair to me that, as Lance was the one dressed up as a bumble bee, not Tiffany, he should have to pay extra for anything.

And in Sofia, Boris and Didi had the perfect general. Happy to play dirty, there was nothing Sofia enjoyed more than planting little seeds of divisive paranoia.

'That's not what Raelene toll me you said, darling . . .'

With all these dark Machiavellian characters with their thick European accents, I could almost hear the zither music from *The Third Man* swelling in the background.

I smiled. I bounced up and down the stairs. I laughed with the girls. And all the time, Boris watched me. It wasn't until I introduced him to Cordelia, a new girl sitting downstairs, that I learnt how much I displeased him.

'*Boris?*' he yelled at me back upstairs. '*This is Boris?* What the fock does that mean? Is Boris the garbage man? Or is Boris the boss?'

There is nothing so dangerous as a small man, abused by his wife, in a position of power over tall women. As Boris became more aware of my popularity with the girls downstairs, he quietly cultivated his suspicion and dislike of me. He sat with his girls at his kitchen table, silently scrutinising my every move. Night after night he kept us all in suspense as I loaded the dishwasher with a dreadful sense of foreboding.

'Don't worry,' Pip reassured me again, 'Shan will be back soon.'

But Boris had already sucked the spring out of my step, and the smell of my fear had stirred his appetite. Boris was saving something up for me, something very bad.

The importance of remembering where one works

I arrived for work the following Friday night at seven and as usual went straight into the kitchen to see what girls were on and to say hello. Sapphire was the last person I expected to see, but there she stood, wrapped in white towels, emerging from a steamy bathroom like a queen.

'Hello there,' she said, emitting a gentle, vulnerable laugh.

I wanted to hug her, but the way she stiffly leant back stopped me. Sapphire looked beautiful with no make-up on her tanned face.

'Weren't expecting to see me again, were you?'

Trudy had predicted she'd be back, but I didn't believe her.

'No,' I said, 'but I'm very happy to see you, Urszula.'

It was the first time I'd called her Urszula to her face, and it felt almost as good as a hug. She smiled, as if pleased. Leaning on the bench, she took a cigarette from her big box of Horizons, which were never far from reach, and lit up like a movie star.

'I'm not usually like that, Meredith,' she said firmly, re-establishing her character through a thick jet of smoke. 'What you saw the other night is not what you'll see again.'

I nodded. It was a brave performance.

'I don't get in that state too often,' she continued, as if being interviewed on a talk show. 'You see, Meredith, when people make me angry like that, I want to hit them.'

I nodded.

'And I won't hit her out of respect for *him*. It's for Boris that I behave. So when he spoke to me like that, in front of all the girls ... That man's like a father to me.'

Urszula's fierce gaze dared me to deny it.

'He was worried about you afterwards,' I lied, crumbling under the pressure.

Boris was more likely to come in yelling, '*What the fock you doing here?*' any minute, but this was the effect Urszula had on me.

'We all worried about you,' I added.

'Well, that's very sweet of you, Meredith, darling, but I just want you to know, that was not the real Sapphire.'

Urszula and I were still nodding when the front door bell sounded.

'Client!' came Sofia's deep voice through the intercom.

'Are you the only one here?' I asked casually, trying not to sound too alarmed.

Urszula nodded.

Standing at the front door was a tall, fair man in his late thirties with a gentle smile and an open face. I was certainly willing it to be open. Once seated in our waiting room, I handed Andrew our menu. He looked up at me with a disarming smile, as if he knew me and was restraining his laughter out of respect. It was the first time I'd ever felt a sense of rapport with a client, and I was overcome by a desire to be candid and funny.

'Andrew,' I announced, 'there's only one girl available.'

'Oh dear,' Andrew smiled, looking about the room, 'and a moose!'

'Yes,' I said, looking up at the stuffed beast, 'but I'm afraid it's the moose's night off.'

Andrew laughed with delight and I smiled modestly, as if I said funny things like this all the time.

'I'm supposed to leave you now,' I sang, floating to the door, 'watching porn.'

Andrew roared laughing. I bet he had never imagined meeting such a witty, entertaining receptionist.

'Don't be long!' he called after me.

'Unless you'd *like* to watch some porn?' I added, suddenly poking my head back in the door, and Andrew threw back his head and laughed so heartily I wondered if I shouldn't just give him my phone number there and then.

'Oh, all right,' he sighed with a smile, and stretched back with his hands behind his head.

For a moment I wasn't sure if I'd heard him correctly.

'You ... would?' I stammered, blinking, still with my head around the door.

'Yes,' Andrew beamed back at me. 'Why not?'

To cover my shock, I laughed inanely all the way to the bench, turned on the video, and glided back to the door. Andrew was courteous enough to smile back at me and not look at the moaning women on the screen. Mumbling something jolly about fetching girls, I closed the door on Andrew's cheerful face and stood on the other side, mortified.

What was I doing, flirting with a man in a brothel? I'd barely had success with men at parties! Where on earth did I imagine this would go? How could I even fleetingly have entertained the idea of a relationship that not only began in a brothel, but was consummated with someone else?

'How old?' asked Urszula, with uncharacteristic trepidation, not having moved from the kitchen table.

Urszula, Antoinette, Rita and Maya always asked this. If he was under thirty, they wouldn't even bother moving from their seats.

'I dunno ... thirty something? But he's nice. Andrew. Bright and funny.'

Urszula reluctantly shuffled into the girls' lounge to check Andrew out on the monitor. Then, without a word, she sat on one of the big couches, unfolded a compact from one of her dressing gown pockets and quietly began putting on her make-up. I took my cue and busied myself unloading the dishwasher in the kitchen. A few minutes later, Urszula emerged from the bathroom wearing a sexy little black slip and black high heels. They showed off her remarkably toned body and tan. I noticed for the first time that she had a large tattoo on her right shoulder of two black hearts tied by a ribbon inscribed with someone's name, but I couldn't read it. Once her sunglasses were on, Urszula turned to me and, with a little nod, signalled that she was ready.

I introduced Sapphire to Andrew, who stood and greeted her with the same radiant smile that had so impressed me.

I was familiar with Urszula's sexy swagger in and out of that room, her provocative come-on, almost daring the man to take her, the cocky bravado that also shielded her from rejection. But tonight there was no shield or swagger as she shook Andrew's hand. Perhaps Urszula needed those sunglasses, because even with them on, there was something so profoundly accessible about Urszula, I wanted to hug her.

'I'd like to see Sapphire for an hour,' Andrew said when she was barely out of the room.

When I found Urszula, she was back in her robe, watching television.

'He wants to see you for an hour, Urszula.'

Urszula didn't move. She didn't take her eyes off the television. She looked vaguely scared.

'Urszula?' I said gently. 'Andrew said he'd love to see you for one hour.'

Urszula gathered her robe protectively around her throat and glanced from the television up to me. She looked fragile.

'Yeah, okay,' she said quietly. 'Can you just give me a minute?'

I crept out, taking the money upstairs to reception, where I told Trudy and Raelene what had happened. They laughed as I searched the monitor for any sign of movement downstairs. It's true, I was like an anxious mother watching her daughter go out on her first date, even if she was a forty-three-year-old prostitute with a lethal head-butt. Eventually I saw Urszula going in to collect her client, and then leading him upstairs.

Half an hour later, on my way downstairs, I heard both of them laughing.

'It's always been this short,' Urszula cried with her wonderful throaty cackle. 'I was the tomboy of our family, see?'

Sapphire was back.

Much later, I had to call a taxi to drive a drunken Harmony home. She'd only been in the house ten minutes when Urszula, apparently in a very good mood, punched her on her way to the toilet.

Waiting for Marcelle to kill me

It was unusually quiet for a Saturday night, and unusually warm for early July. I even managed to turn the heater off and open the back door without the girls complaining. Pip, Raelene and Maxine were happily devouring pizza upstairs. Downstairs, I stacked the dish-washer, listening to Shelby and Heather comparing push-up bras at the kitchen table while Letitia sat with Maya in the lounge watching television. Letitia had only been with us a month and gave the impression she was just passing through. A tall, dark model from Barbados, Letitia looked pityingly at me and any other plain planet orbiting her beauteous sphere. What Letitia was doing in the sex industry was a mystery to all of us. She could have earned more money keeping her clothes on. But I suspect Letitia enjoyed the sexual affirmation of half-naked men panting in ecstasy at her feet. It certainly sounded that way. And I was fascinated by her inability to settle on one accent for more than a week. Letitia couldn't make up her mind whether she came from Texas, Oxford, New York or the East End. Talking to her was like flicking channels on Foxtel.

Things started to go wrong at eight o'clock, when Raelene came downstairs to swap places with me for half an hour. Apparently Didi was not pleased that I was still unfamiliar with credit card bookings, and had demanded that I complete at least one transaction on my own. I could tell by Raelene's sullen expression that, once again, my colleagues had been hauled over the coals because of a perceived lapse in my training, so I was determined to make it up to them. Now that the brothel was officially running at a loss, Didi's calls had become more frequent, and I lived in morbid fear of being summoned to the phone. I had been taught how to do a credit card transaction a few weeks ago, and felt quite sure that most of it would come back to me. I smiled confidently at Raelene, who sniffed disapprovingly as she plonked herself down at the kitchen table with a magazine. Such was the harmonious working atmosphere Didi liked to create in her brothel.

'Mastercard,' Pip announced flatly, transferring her call to me.

Right. I clapped my hands and swung into action. John and Jane, who'd had a bit to drink, were staying at a Travelodge and wanted a busty girl to service both of them as soon as possible. I knew that the buxom Marcelle was free, and a dab hand at couple bookings, so I rang John back to confirm the booking.

'Okay, John,' I began nervously, 'that will be three hundred and twenty dollars for the hour, plus surcharge, plus taxi.'

'Yeah, yeah,' said John, 'so how much is that, Meredith?'

'Three hundred and – which Travelodge, John?' I asked.

'Parramatta.'

I looked at my colleagues, both busy on other calls. Did we even go as far as Parramatta? But John was in a hurry, Marcelle had her own car, and I wanted to complete a credit card transaction with flying colours.

'Four hundred altogether, John,' I said cheerfully.

'And when will she be here?'

I had no idea but I told John twenty minutes, wished him a good evening, and hung up. Marcelle didn't sound too impressed that she had to drive all the way to Parramatta, and informed me that, as her Concord was in the garage, it would take more like forty minutes than 'fucking twenty'.

The door bell called me away and I couldn't return to my task for another ten minutes.

'You idiot!' Raelene reprimanded me, peering over my shoulder as I hastily punched John's Mastercard numbers into the machine next to her desk. 'You should have approved his card before you sent the girl. What if she gets there only to find out he's exceeded his limit?'

I pressed Enter, and the four of us watched the machine in silence as if it was an undetonated bomb. Not a phone rang. It seemed every man in Sydney had paused to see if John had exceeded his Mastercard limit, and if Marcelle would have to turn back from Ashfield. Maxine took the opportunity to warn me about Marcelle's fiery temper, but Pip disagreed. Marcelle was an alcoholic and suffered mood swings, that was all. No, insisted Raelene, who knew Marcelle better than anyone, she suffered from a hormonal imbalance. As we waited, Maxine enquired where exactly had I sent the bipolar, alcoholic, perimenopausal Marcelle.

'Parramatta,' I muttered.

'PARRAMATTA?' they all shrieked in unison. 'We don't send girls to Parramatta!'

If John hadn't paid his Mastercard bill, Raelene prognosticated, I was dead meat.

Suddenly the grey box whirred into action. As we watched the narrow strip of paper cough and splutter its way into the world saying *Transaction Approved*, I nearly cried with relief. I flopped down at my desk, wrote the invoice number in red pen and cradled my head in my hands. All I had to do now was wait for Marcelle to ring from the room and read back John's credit card numbers to me. Easy.

Almost an hour later, a very disgruntled Marcelle rang from the Parramatta Travelodge. In her own colourful language, Marcelle informed me that traffic had not been good, and she had not enjoyed missing the turn-off, but she was there now.

'Thanks, mate,' she said, as John put a beer in her hand.

Marcelle liked beer, and gulped it down as she read John's numbers back to me.

'Sign there, you idiot,' she ordered him, and I was relieved to hear the three of them having a bit of a laugh.

'Okay, Marcelle,' I said, 'thanks for that, and—'

'Hang on!' she shouted in my ear. 'Don't you want his ID?'

I felt sick. ID. Photo ID. Driver's licence number or passport. To be requested and recorded by receptionist with a green pen when confirming booking. To be read back by girl once in room. To ensure against theft of credit card. To ensure safety of girl. To ensure girl was not in hotel room in Parramatta with criminal and girlfriend celebrating recent mugging and possible murder.

'Um, Marcelle,' I began tremulously, 'I ... er ... I didn't get any ID.'

Pip and Maxine spun around looking horrified. I tried to ignore them as I listened to Marcelle's heavy breathing and Jane's oblivious giggling in the background.

'What?' Marcelle finally demanded in such a way that all giggling ceased immediately.

'We could ask him for it now?' I suggested feebly, wishing I had never, ever met Roy at Jobfinder.

'*You fucking idiot,*' Marcelle hissed at me under her breath.

A pause.

'John, darl,' I heard her ask affably, 'you got any ID on ya, mate?'

I was still shaking half an hour later when Boris surprised us with an early visit. Although Boris had begun with the usual polite greetings, I wondered which one would kill me first, him or Marcelle? Having explained to her angry clients why she could not possibly proceed without photo ID, Marcelle had run out of the room at the Parramatta Travelodge when John threw a glass ashtray at her head. It missed, but Marcelle had rung me from the carpark outside, specifically to request that I not go *anywhere* for at least forty-five minutes.

'What does a man say to a voman with two black eyes?' Boris asked, joining his glittering, lip-glossed entourage sitting around the kitchen table. 'Nothing,' he cried triumphantly, 'she's already been told twice!'

As the girls groaned, Boris giggled like a hyena at his own joke and patted his ears with delight. But the joke made me feel nauseous. I sensed a small grey cloud making its way from the west, gathering momentum as it rumbled closer. Taking three clean mugs from the kitchen cupboard, I set off for sanctuary, upstairs.

'Hey, Meredit!' Boris called after me. 'You come back here, please.'

What did it matter if Boris wanted to humiliate me in front of a few girls? In another ten minutes I'd be dead anyway.

'Heather is sitting here with two hundred dollars for you,' he pointed out cordially when I returned. 'Why is that?'

'I'll take it up now,' I said, reaching for Heather's money.

'But I've just asked you a question,' Boris objected, snatching the cash himself. 'Why do you not answer, Meredit? I asked *why is Heather sitting here with two hundred dollars?*'

Some girls looked at me, others couldn't. Letitia enjoyed a coy smile while Boris, peering at me through his cigarette smoke, waited for an answer.

I told him I did not know that Heather had money for me, and offered to take it again.

'What you mean, you did not know?' he asked, his voice getting louder. 'Why do you not know? Do you not know your own job?'

At last Letitia stopped smiling.

'Yes,' I nodded gravely. 'My job is to take the money upstairs.'

'But Heather is sitting here with two hundred dollars, and you are doing what?'

The girls sought refuge gazing at some safe crumb or stain on the kitchen table.

'Where is your list?' he suddenly demanded, clicking his fingers.

'What list?' I asked.

Boris was appalled.

'Your list for recording every cent that comes in and goes out of this house! *What list?* WHY ARE YOU HERE?' he shouted. 'WHAT ARE WE PAYING YOU FOR?'

'I'll make one now,' I said pathetically, returning the mugs to the bench, where there was paper and a pen.

'Stop,' Boris ordered me again. 'Come back.'

Feeling sick, I walked back to my place and waited while Boris took a leisurely sip of his tea.

'Look at this,' he muttered to his girls, gesturing with a nod at my feet. 'What do you call those?' he asked, and looked up at me.

'Shoes,' I answered, over the thumping of my heart.

A few girls glanced fleetingly at my worn, flat, sensible black shoes. Boris sniggered as he took another sip of his tea, sharing a wry smile with Letitia, sitting beside him in her grey silk dress and strappy silver high heels.

'I don't vont to see these disgusting things ever in my house again,' Boris announced in a low voice before draining his tea. 'Now go upstairs and make your list.'

Feeling too numb to cry, I did as Boris asked.

Ten minutes later, Boris was upstairs, bending over my desk with his head next to mine.

'Who is training you?' he asked quietly.

I could sense my colleagues sitting up straight, absorbing every word through their stiff backs.

'What?' I asked anxiously. 'Everyone. Everyone is teaching me, all the time.'

'WHO?' he yelled in my ear, banging his fist on my desk.

'Just tell me, please, Boris,' I begged him, 'what am I doing that is so wrong?'

'You tell me, Meredit,' Boris answered, so close I felt his hot breath on my cheek, 'what is it you are doing right? Is it that these lazy girls are teaching you nothing? Or are you just stupid?'

We were not allowed to use the clients' bathroom next door, but it was the closest room I could lock myself inside for a moment, to cry. When I finally came out, I could hear Boris shouting at the other receptionists.

'*You are supposed to be training her! Vell then, vy is she so focking useless?*'

I ran downstairs and continued through the kitchen, past the same girls, who all looked up at me. Urszula had joined them.

'Oh, Meredith ...' Shelby cried after me, seeing my puffy red eyes.

I couldn't stop, and had just reached their bathroom door when it suddenly opened from within.

'FUCK!' cried Marcelle, reeling backwards, clutching her heart.

And just as suddenly, she lurched forward and pushed me hard against the wall. Grimacing in pain, I waited for the onslaught of abuse, or a punch. Here it came. But instead, a cold, wet hand touched me lightly on the arm.

'You all right?'

I stopped squinting to see Marcelle searching my face with her large brown eyes. As my tears began to fall, I heard the sound of many chairs moving out from the table, and before I knew it, I was sobbing in Marcelle's open arms, surrounded by six comforting prostitutes. When Shelby got up to the bit about the shoes,

Marcelle clasped me even closer to her pushed-up bosom, where I was rocked like a baby, and soothingly patted on the back. Marcelle even apologised for getting angry over the ID at Parramatta, although I assured her she had every right to.

'No, but you're new, Meredith,' she insisted, 'and you're doing really well, and we all like you. I'm just a bit of a shit sometimes, Meredith, and you've just got to ignore me.'

Marcelle grabbed my face with both her hands. For a moment I thought she was going to kiss me. 'I just get moods, see?' she smiled.

After I'd washed my face, I joined them all at the table. I had no idea where Boris was, but I no longer cared. If he started on me again, I would just collect my things and go.

Urszula tried to cheer me up by telling us about the time she kicked her ex-husband so hard he went through a wall and fell into his sister's kitchen. And how her brothers used to tie her up. And how they whipped her, buried her, tried to drown her and, once, even set fire to her hair. It was a miracle Urszula survived childhood at all. As I sat there laughing at her stories, I hoped that Boris would not come in after all, because now I never wanted to leave.

'Look. See?' Urszula shouted suddenly, punching me in the arm. 'You're sitting with us at table, Meredith! You never do that.'

She was right. I always had to keep moving when I was in the kitchen, I thought because I was busy, but Urszula knew better.

'Because now, Meredith, you've met someone even scarier than me,' she cried gesturing upstairs, and she threw her head back to cackle like a witch.

Urszula was in the middle of another anecdote about being branded with a hot iron when I heard Boris's light tread on the stairs above me, followed by the comforting jangle of keys at the front door. I waited for the purr of his engine before gathering clean mugs for the second time. As soon as Urszula finished her punch line, I discreetly made my exit. Halfway up the stairs, something hissed at me from behind.

'I didn't mean to get you inta any trouble, matey,' Heather whispered urgently from the bottom of the stairs. 'About the money, y'know? He's a miserable old bastard, isn't he?'

I loved the way Heather said 'matey'. Real quickly. *Matey.*

When I reached my post I asked my colleagues upstairs if I was really doing such a bad job.

'Nah,' said Raelene, stretching back in her chair. 'It was just your turn, darl.'

'He's had us all in tears at some time,' sighed Maxine. 'Either him or her. It's just their way, sweetie.'

I looked at Pip. Was she going to say something comforting too?

'Just be glad Marcelle's still alive,' she smiled benevolently. 'And that I reported the stolen credit card for you.'

The reluctant escort

One cold winter night I came into the heated kitchen to find Shelby giving Heather some financial advice. They were both sitting at the table surrounded by paperwork. Shelby's specs were halfway down her nose, her hair was pushed behind her ears, and she was explaining investment loans to the wide-eyed, pert Heather.

'You can't touch this for at least three years,' explained Shelby, pointing at some figure with her pen, 'if ya wanna get anything out of it at all. That twelve per cent per annum, after tax, is really only about eight. Got that?'

Heather nodded.

I began stacking the dishwasher.

Heather was all peroxide and mascara, her tight black dress pushing her small assets up, whereas Shelby was more demure, natural and neat in her red suit.

'What we need to do is put ya profit from this thirteen per cent over here, into ya second installment. See?'

Heather nodded obediently.

Rita and Antoinette hovered quietly at the back door, rugged up and smoking. They always seemed relieved when they saw I was working downstairs. And they'd always ask, a little anxiously, who was working upstairs, to measure their chances of getting bookings.

'Sofia and Raelene,' I answered.

Rita looked pleased but Antoinette rolled her eyes, collapsed in her chair by the door, and lit up another cigarette.

'Meredith,' came Raelene's voice through the intercom, 'booking for Shelby.'

By the time I'd run upstairs, collected Raelene's missive, run back down and handed it to Shelby, the two blondes were packing up their paperwork.

'I've told mine I'm in advertising,' Heather moaned, 'and it's so hard to keep up with all the bloody questions, ya know?'

'Oh, I know,' Shelby laughed. 'My dad is so proud of me, but he keeps asking, "When are they gunna promote you – the bloody hours you put into that place!"'

Shelby perused her booking then removed her glasses, clicked them shut in their case, stood up, brushed her hair, and checked her lipstick in a compact mirror.

'Which Landmark Apartments?' she asked, already breezing down the hall, tossing her bag over her shoulder.

'Um, um . . .' I trotted after her, 'the city.'

Bang. No sooner was Shelby out the door than the bell rang.

'Meredith,' Raelene's voice guffawed over the intercom, 'client!'

Raelene loved it when I had to run up and down the stairs all night, and she knew how much I hated greeting nervous strangers at the door. Some of them were so nervous I don't know how they ever made it to our porch. If ever you see a man making strange, halting progress up your street, with his head down, hands stuffed deep in his pockets, perspiring and muttering to himself as he passes your window for the fifth time in two minutes, you are possibly living very near a brothel.

After struggling with the obstinate video remote control, I swung open the front door to find a tall, scared, black man, with Urszula right behind him.

'Too long, Meredith,' she growled as she pushed past me. 'You left him waiting too fooking long.'

I sat Tesfaye down in the waiting room with the menu, calmed him with a bit of chat, and left him feigning total indifference to the porn show. This behaviour always amused me as a minute later we always caught them on the monitor, riveted to the screen. As

I approached the kitchen I could hear Urszula's harsh voice resonating to a captive audience, so I walked straight into the ring.

'You can't do that, Meredith! You can't leave a client standing out there that long. We'll lose him. He was just about to turn away, but he turned around to the sight of me and that scared the fook out of him so he stayed. But if I hadn't been there, we'd have fooking lost him, sweetheart.'

I was momentarily distracted by the slim, porcelain doll now sitting at the table eating pizza. Where had she come from? I pathetically defended myself to Urszula. It was Boris's rule. I was not allowed to open that front door until I'd made sure the porn video was on, and it always took a minute.

'I don't fooking care, Meredith! Some rules were made to be broken! Use your fooking nut! What are you like?'

'What are you like' was one of Urszula's favourite North Country expressions and, even when she was criticising me, I secretly loved it. Urszula sat at the table with the girl.

'Hi,' said the girl, wiping her hand on a serviette before offering it daintily, with a smile. 'I'm Bree.'

Bree had the clear skin of a teenager and the greenest eyes I'd ever seen.

'Oh, *you're* Bree,' I said shaking her hand, and we both laughed.

Bree's perfectly symmetrical, delicate features were framed by a short brown bob. She was wearing a T-shirt and jeans, and played with half a slice of takeaway pizza as she smoked. I was beginning to wonder if anyone in this business didn't smoke, apart from me and Shelby. I assured Bree I had only heard good things, apart from her recent toast-eating performance for Jocelyn and Graham at three hundred and twenty dollars an hour.

'Oh yeah,' Bree recalled dreamily, looking off into the distance. 'They had a really big screen TV.'

My initial disapproval dissolved with Bree's contrite giggle. She paused as if about to offer a more satisfying explanation, but when nothing came forth, we both laughed.

Bree didn't seem like the sort of girl who would rip people off. She had the charming innocence of a child who means well. She also had a languid, laid-back manner that possibly thwarted those good intentions. I could just imagine her curled up eating toast if she could possibly get away with it. She and Lucy both gave receptionists the occasional headache.

Lucy was only eighteen and lived over on the North Shore with her parents. Lucy was always in trouble for, basically, not providing a service. She'd arrive at the booking, get paid, and then sit with her coat buttoned up and chat away like a virgin. An hour later, the angry client would ring to complain, frustrated with himself more than anyone else for having been such a gentleman. But Lucy had this effect on people, and we often had to ask her to stop it.

Upstairs we described Bree as 'mid twenties—' even though she was thirty '—brunette, part-time model, five foot six, green eyes, 36–25–35, and looks like Kate Moss'.

Raelene had started it, and now we all said it. Just like we all described Antoinette as 'a classy lady'. Although if they could have seen Antoinette at the back door, hunched and scowling over her cigarette with wet hair and no make-up, they would never have rung again. Bree was more beautiful than Kate Moss, but she had a similar girlish look and a cheeky sense of humour that made her a favourite. I asked her if she wanted to check out Tesfaye on the monitor with the other girls.

'Oh,' she said, seeming a little embarrassed, 'I think I'm going out on a booking.'

Bree didn't look like she was going anywhere but home to eat toast and watch more television. I later found out that she did not do in-house. Bree was strictly escort, but had not wanted to offend the other girls who did. So I left her to finish her cigarette and her pizza and introduced the others to Tesfaye.

'And this is Sapphire,' I said as Urszula swaggered in, shook Tesfaye's hand, and looked him up and down before leaning back on one of her high heels.

'Well, my friend,' she declared majestically, 'they don't coom mooch blacker than you, do they?'

Tesfaye very politely declined to see any of the girls and evaporated into the night.

I returned to the kitchen only to be summoned upstairs again to collect an Exclusive booking for Bree at five hundred dollars an hour at the Menzies. Bree read my mind as I handed her the scrap of paper, puffing.

'It's okay, I've got a dress here,' she said with a laugh, covering her mouth full of food. 'Oh, not French again,' she moaned as she glanced at Sofia's handwriting.

For a minute I thought we had a new line that just offered fellatio.

'Why am I always a French model?'

'Do you speak any French at all?' I asked her.

'Oui ... non ... soup de la jour ...' giggled Bree infectiously.

'You know you can send me out as German, Meredith,' Urszula announced loudly, straddling a chair and sitting between us. 'I speak fluent German. Did you not know that, Meredith?'

I shook my head.

'You don't think these Germanic features are just a fooking coincidence,' she shouted in her North Country accent, thrusting her face in front of mine.

Bree and I listened attentively as Urszula informed us of her Germanic ancestry. I was happy to let Urszula distract me from hurrying Bree, who happily let Urszula distract her from going to her booking. You'd never guess we were trying to make money here. The boundaries of plausibility had long been stretched by Urszula's alleged past, but it mattered little to those of us who loved her.

'And are you still living in your car?' Bree asked Urszula.

'It's not a car. It's a fooking Land Rover!' Urszula yelled at me, as though I had asked the offensive question, then she sweetly turned to Bree. 'I was given it.'

'That was a good booking,' I boldly ventured, making Bree almost choke on her pizza.

But Urszula preferred that Bree laugh at something she had said, and so began telling her the story of her latest fight with a carpark attendant who'd refused to park the car with Rex in it.

'And he very foolishly mumbled to his mate "fooking bitch". I can tell you, I was out of that car and in his face before he could think. "Excuse me," I said, "did you just call me a fooking bitch?" And I looked at him so fooking deadly he knew I could take his head off, and the dog wasn't too happy either. Well, he parked the car, dog and all, and has done ever since.'

And having finished, Urszula looked at Bree and roared laughing. I took this as my cue to return to reception.

'Meredith!' Urszula caught me at the door. 'If you're going upstairs, tell those fooking slags I want my money. Twenty for that fooking airport job. And Meredith tell them I want it *now*.'

Bree gave me a sympathetic look. We both knew I would have to get to know her another time.

Upstairs my colleagues told me that Bree worked in the daytime as a freelance make-up artist. And I still wonder what we will say to each other come the day that, on a set somewhere, we find ourselves brush to face in the make-up chair.

$700-an-hour Genevieve

'Call her again!' Boris shouted at me for the second time in five minutes.

I hadn't seen Boris this angry since Valmai put his Tibetan sheepskin foot rug through the spin cycle. The problem had been getting worse ever since Didi had introduced the Exclusive and Cachet lines. Now that Genevieve was making over a thousand dollars a night on just two or three bookings, she didn't need to work a full roster, let alone a full week, and her increasing reluctance to answer her phone for a booking was driving Boris crazy. If he could have done, Boris would have turned up himself in a blonde wig and lain on his back rather than lose Genevieve's big bucks.

'Try her at home!'

I hated ringing girls at four in the morning, especially on their home phones, but if they were 'on roster' we rang them any time, even if it was their first booking for the night at 5 am. While he paced the floor, Pip complained to Boris that recently Genevieve was taking umbrage at being sent even for three hundred and fifty dollar bookings. Pip sighed with disappointment. Her friend Genevieve was definitely developing 'attitude'.

'Focking lazy slut,' Boris railed. 'No bookings for her for a veek!' Possibly just the result Genevieve was after.

Boris commanded me to go downstairs and give the booking to Pandora instead, whether she was pinned or not. Pandora was the only girl on the books who got away with a drug habit. Management turned a blind eye because, with or without the nods, Pandora looked like *The Birth of Venus*, minus the shell, and she brought in a lot of money. Other receptionists gushed about her vast intelligence as well as her beauty, and I wanted to believe them, but as Pandora didn't speak to me, all I saw was the sad picture of a single mother who supported her son and her smack habit by working as a prostitute.

'Thanks, Pandora,' I said at the door as Venus floated past me with total indifference.

'Patrick,' I turned sideways to face my driver an hour later, 'how would you describe Genevieve?'

Patrick glanced at me with vague amusement while I waited for his reply.

'Not my type,' he said at last, with a loaded smile.

And much to Patrick's delight, I couldn't look at him, all the way to Coogee.

For some weeks now, something had been happening between Patrick and me. Whenever we were in the same room, it was like Happy Hour at the Clown House. Just greeting each other had become a gentle comedy routine.

'Hello,' Patrick would sing with delight, flopping against a wall like a drunken puppet.

'Hello,' I'd say with cheeky inference as I stacked the dishwasher.

I had begun collecting data on Patrick from the moment I met him: signs of intelligence, of humour, of possible drug abuse. But in this house brimming with oestrogen, I soon found any nuance or expression of masculinity a welcome and pleasing relief. The lazy way he lit up a Marlboro, or leant in a doorway, or chuckled quietly as he made a cup of tea, the veins protruding from his Portsmouth arms, all made Patrick very attractive, in an aging Rolling Stone kind of way. The fact that no one else saw our driver in the same light mystified me, but then my taste in men has long been a mystery to both friends and family, to the point where I half expect an 'intervention'. I suspect it began with Mary Poppins. I grew up fantasising about chimney sweeps, and then coalminers, or anyone at all with black stuff on his face. In my adult years it broadened to any man up a ladder, with tattoos and possibly a tool belt. Or under a car. I once had a relationship with a mechanic that literally ran on the smell of an oily rag. So whenever Patrick stood on a chair with his sleeves rolled up, putting up a blind or fixing a chandelier for Boris, I kept as far away, and as busy, as possible.

When Genevieve rang the door bell the following night, Boris skulked downstairs growling like a rabid dog wearing a muzzle. He so resented the compromised position she'd put him in. Any other girl would just have been shown the door, but this girl's earnings fattened all our pay packets, and Boris knew he could not afford to lose her. Although I was now busting to clap eyes on this escort queen I'd heard so much about, I dreaded being caught in the kitchen crossfire. I was relieved, therefore, to find Coral sitting in the lounge, along with every other girl in the house. I had a booking for her at the Sofitel. But even as I whispered to Coral with the television blaring, Boris had the senses of a cockroach.

'Meredit?' he called from the kitchen.

All eyes looked up at me as if I'd drawn the short straw to go over the trench.

'Meredit, come in here, please.'

Cheerio then, lads.

I crept into the kitchen to find Boris sitting at the table, glowering at what appeared to be a Bond girl standing on the other side of the bench, playing miserably with a piece of toast.

Genevieve was pretty much how I had described her over the phone. She was tall and busty, with long, thick blonde hair, coiffed by Pasha's, but I would have said early thirties rather than twenties. She wore an expensive ice-blue silk pants suit that matched her pale eyes, but her tanned cleavage promised a calendar girl underneath. Unlike a lot of the other girls, Genevieve showed extraordinary restraint and skill in her choice of make-up. Maybe this was why she'd never left us to work for the exclusive Fleur de Lis, where all the girls had to wear evening dresses and fire-engine red lipstick. And maybe it was Genevieve's sullen, hounded expression and the hype surrounding her that reminded me, just at this moment, of an unhappy Princess Di.

'You were where that you could not answer your phone?' Boris shouted at her. 'These girls rang you all night and you were where?'

'I'm sorry,' Genevieve whimpered, 'I just fell asleep.'

Boris threw himself back in his chair.

'I've never heard such a story. She fell asleep in her car, Meredit!' he shouted at me. 'Last night! When you were all upstairs desperately trying to contact Genevieve for bookings. She was asleep *in her car*. What do you think of that?'

I looked helplessly at Genevieve, who looked glumly at my shoes. My sensible but sad, cheap, stretched suede shoes. Must buy new shoes.

'Meredit!' Boris ordered. 'Tell Genevieve how much you needed her last night.'

I didn't know which one of us felt more wretched.

'We really did need you last night, Genevieve,' I offered pathetically.

'Oh, look,' she suddenly whimpered – at *me*. 'What can I say? I'm really sorry! That's all I can say. I'm sorry!'

I didn't want an apology. I just wanted Genevieve to sit down between bonking businessmen, and eat. And now I wanted her to speak again because, spookily, she also sounded just like Princess Di.

The kitchen phone buzzed and Pip asked me to pick up.

'Is Genevieve with you?' she asked, knowing very well that Genevieve was.

'Mmm,' I answered cautiously.

'Could you tell her she's got a booking at the Marriot?'

'Mmm,' I said.

'It's seven hundred. You gotta pen?'

'Mmm,' I said, taking the pen from behind my ear and writing the booking details on my hand.

When I hung up, Genevieve could not look at me, but Boris could smell a booking.

'What's that?' he asked.

I took a deep breath.

'Genevieve's got a booking at the Marriot,' I said, wishing I'd kicked her in the head instead.

Little pools of pink formed in Genevieve's flawless cheeks. Please don't cry.

'Mr Sindu, um, in Room 2401,' I mumbled, 'and you're a Swedish, er, lingerie model.'

We waited in silence for the Swedish dam to burst.

'Goot,' said Boris as he stood up, then clapped his hands with satisfaction, patted his ears, and left.

I wanted to sigh, or laugh, or apologise to acknowledge that Boris had now left us alone, but Genevieve deliberately avoided any eye contact. Enjoying her martyrdom too much to release me from my forced collaboration with Boris, Genevieve swept, with wounded splendour, into the bathroom. I was still standing there, gormlessly, when she briefly returned for her handbag.

I waited at the front door like a gaoler with my keys to let Genevieve out. Sometimes it was fun to wave the girls goodbye, like Ma Walton on the front step, but if a girl was unhappy with management or reception, it was a thankless post. I always cringed at the way some receptionists told the girls they 'loved' them over the phone, but now I could understand how it happened. Seeing them off, tired and teary, to yet another booking at three in the morning, I found myself struggling to find the right words, any words, that might help. And so when Genevieve steamed down the corridor about to ignore me again, I felt determined to make some kind of amends.

'I'm sorry,' I blurted. 'Genevieve, I don't care if you sleep in your car.'

It didn't come out quite the way I wanted, but Genevieve paused, graciously touched my arm, and at last looked at me. A strange expression came over her beautiful face.

'Do I know you from somewhere?' she less graciously demanded, suddenly gripping my arm.

'No!' I shook my head fervently.

Genevieve released my arm with a vaguely troubled smile before stepping out to where she'd left her white Fiat, double-parked. I could sleep in a car like that, I thought. Like all the other girls who refused to do in-house, Genevieve was not welcome to rest long at the brothel between bookings. As she lived in Mona Vale, she was forced to drive around the city all night instead. I watched her drive off, and remembered Pip saying that Genevieve had grown up on the northern beaches, frolicking with rich, playboy boyfriends. And I wondered, as the Fiat disappeared, was this the fate of wealthy suntanned Avalon girls who didn't marry millionaires?

When I walked back into the kitchen, a deep Germanic voice made me jump.

'Did you find out what happened to Delilah yesterday?'

Boris sat at the kitchen table with a cigarette burning in his fingers.

'I left a note out for all receptionists to chase this up,' he continued menacingly. 'Did not you read the note I left?'

I made it a habit not to read the petty notes left for receptionists about things that were done wrong, and girls who must be punished, and all spelt so badly.

'Delilah, who did not come in for Black Beauties bookings?' his voice rose.

Apparently Boris had spent a lot of money on an ad in the *Telegraph* specifically tailored for Delilah. Various men had come to the front door wanting to see our 'exotic black beauty' and were somewhat disappointed when introduced to Donna, a buxom redhead from Campsie.

I opened my mouth but Boris waved my excuse away.

'Ach! She's in the lounge room. Go in there now and ask her where she voss yesterday.'

I went to the lounge room door, saw Delilah fast asleep on the couch, and returned.

'Boris,' I whispered, 'she's fast asleep.'

'THEN VAKE HER UP!' he boomed.

'Boris,' I implored, 'I have a booking to confirm.'

'THEN GO! What you doing downstairs? Go up! Confirm! Then come back!'

I ran upstairs, sat down, and made a really long paperclip chain.

Trudy had told me about the confirm-a-booking escape route, and it worked for ten minutes, until Pip told me to go downstairs with a booking for Heather.

As I approached the kitchen I was relieved to hear Boris entertaining Shelby at the table. I glided invisibly to Heather, who was standing at the sink, gave her the booking, and almost made it back to the door.

'Go and vake her, please,' Boris shot sideways, barely interrupting the joke he was telling.

Bugger.

I crept into the lounge room where a harem of escorts snored in unison, spread on couches, and dribbling on pillows. The only one vaguely awake was Pandora, nodding from the other side of the room. Tonight she looked more like Millet's watery Ophelia than Botticelli's Venus, with her long thick golden ringlets spread out on a floral pillow behind her head. And it occurred to me that if Shakespeare was writing *Hamlet* today, he might well have sent Ophelia off in Act Four, clutching her herbs and blasted to oblivion by a smack habit. Closest to me was the beautiful, exotic Delilah, fast asleep on the reclining chair, nearly coming out of her dark brown satin bustier top. As I touched her shoulder, she jumped and looked up at me with the now familiar, startled expression of a woman about to be told where to go and have sex with a stranger.

'Delilah,' I whispered, 'Boris wants to know why you didn't come in yesterday for Black Beauties bookings. What will I say?'

Delilah smiled a sleepy, sweet, amused little smile.

'I was seek,' she whispered.

'Thanks,' I said, giving her a thumbs-up sign as I retreated. Delilah always brought out the dag in me.

When I returned to Boris, he waved Shelby to silence and looked at me with resigned disappointment.

'Okay, Meredit, is okay this sad excuse,' he responded, but I knew it was the calm before the storm. 'Delilah's sick because she gets drunk and falls asleep. That's what this girl does now and then.' Now came the storm. 'But Genevieve! This makes me really angry! She voss asleep in her car. What rubbish!'

Boris's hand came crashing down on the table, providing Shelby with the perfect opportunity for a discreet exit.

'Does she think I am focking stupid?' he shouted. 'You know where she voss, Meredit?'

I shook my head.

'I tell you where she voss. She voss in bed with a client! She took private booking!'

I looked appalled.

'That's right! These girls do it all the time! Or sometimes they ring to say they finish and then stay another two focking hours and pocket all my money!'

That's clever, I thought, shaking my head in disgust.

'Do you know *how* I know they do this?' Boris demanded. 'Because I sit in my car outside the hotel vaiting for girl to come out! That's how!' And Boris cackled with frenzied glee, until Pip's voice interrupted on the intercom.

'Meredith?'

'SHE'S BUSY!' Boris shouted at the phone.

Clunk.

'Yes,' he continued feverishly to his hostage, 'I sit there vaiting for the bitch to come out, and—' Boris clapped his hands so hard I jumped. 'CAUGHT! Trying to screw me!'

I nodded frantically, wishing Shelby, or anyone, would return.

'Or I ring the room and say, "Oh, ello, could I just have a quick verd with …" and the dumb bastard hands it over and I got her! HA! The bitch!'

Boris glanced at me nervously as he pulled a perfumed handkerchief from his pocket. 'I tell you, Meredit,' he assured me, dabbing his glistening brow, 'I live for these moments.'

In my second year at NIDA, I was cast as Pompey the pimp in Shakespeare's *Measure for Measure*. I had fun playing him as a lovable cockney, but was fairly criticised by our acting teacher for sacrificing the venal, mercenary side for a more comical Arthur Daly type. Nearly twenty years too late, I meet Boris.

Boris's secret

Little did I know it, but after five months I had passed the test and it was time, Trudy decreed at 2 am on a Tuesday night, for my initiation.

'You're probably wondering why we take your booking sheet from you at the end of the night,' Trudy said.

Did they? I hadn't noticed, but I knew from the serious way she and Raelene were nodding, I'd best pretend I had. The girls looked at each other and took a deep breath.

'Off bookings,' Raelene announced.

'For Boris,' added Trudy.

I looked from one to the other. I had not one clue what they were talking about, and Raelene burst out laughing.

'The look on your face!'

I decided to ignore Raelene. 'Off bookings?' I asked Trudy.

'For Boris,' giggled Trudy.

But Raelene was nearly beside herself. The strain of keeping this secret had obviously been a burden on both of them, and the three of us found ourselves laughing uncontrollably, even though I still had no idea what they were talking about.

'You give my bookings to Boris?' I managed at last.

Raelene was now bent over double, and when the phones started ringing, she shook her head and ran from the room holding her stomach. This was turning out to be the oddest initiation. Poor Trudy had to keep putting clients on hold, not helped by Raelene's frequent attempts to re-enter the room sober.

Finally, wiping away tears, all was explained to me. At the end of the night each receptionist would sacrifice one or two bookings, rewrite her booking sheet without them, and the brothel's cut from these 'unrecorded bookings' went straight into Boris's pocket. The other sixty per cent went to the girl, as usual. For helping Boris steal from his own wife, Boris rewarded his receptionists-in-the-know with a discreet small cash bonus each week. It was an extremely dangerous and complicated task, given the intricate bookwork that recorded every incoming and outgoing cent and Didi's suspicious, meticulous eye. How long had this been going on? Years, apparently. Having been caught out by Didi once already, Boris and Sofia had come up with a Didi-proof system.

'Sofia?' I asked, shocked.

My colleagues nodded.

Surely Little Georgie's tutor Pip wasn't part of it?

Trudy and Raelene nodded. Boris had everyone on this secret payroll, except Valmai, whom he detested, and the two new young receptionists, Leonie and Delia. I was speechless.

'We saw you looking in the receptionists' booking record book last week,' Raelene said, 'and we saw your little frown.'

I didn't have the heart to tell Raelene I frowned at everything in this office. I didn't even know there was a receptionists' booking record book.

'We told Boris you were onto it,' Trudy said, 'and that it was time to tell you.'

I nodded, grateful.

'Where is that booking record book thing?' I asked Raelene casually.

From right above my head Raelene grabbed a blue folder labelled *Receptionists Booking Records* and opened it to the offending page. She had to help me again by pointing to my name on a graph. Sure enough, instead of the six or seven bookings I generally made each shift, only four or five were recorded. All my brilliant bookings that I had so wanted Didi to notice. Even though I was going to get paid more, I felt robbed.

'So from now on, Boris will give you an extra hundred dollars a week,' Trudy cried triumphantly.

That's when I decided that, if Didi wasn't happy with four bookings a night, that was her problem.

Now it all made sense. This was why receptionists stayed on after-hours without pay. This was why receptionists stayed, period. And why no one let me do any bookwork. And maybe this was why Boris had regarded me with such suspicion for so long. Perhaps now he would wink at me too, and slap me on the back and sing Dean Martin songs. But why, I asked, was our millionaire boss stealing from his own wife?

'Where does he go every night?' Trudy asked with a big smile.

Raelene nodded like a loon, suppressing yet another wave of hysteria.

'The casino!' I shouted jubilantly, and we all cheered.

I couldn't wait to tell my parents back in Tasmania. Now I was making money from both prostitution and gambling.

No violins for Valmai

Now that I had been inducted, I thought I'd celebrate my secret promotion by wearing tracksuit pants to work. Not if I was on in-house duty, of course. Downstairs, I kept to my uniform of black skirt, black top, a little make-up and sensible black shoes, which I would replace any day now. But upstairs I was beginning to enjoy the dichotomy of talking to rich businessmen in expensive hotels, while leaning back in my chair with my feet crossed on my desk and casually sucking my pen, in my black tracksuit pants.

Although she never named him, Valmai lived with her boyfriend and her grown-up son Nigel, whom she always said, *sotto voce*, 'had problems'. Valmai also said with a straight face that she was forty-three. The one thing Valmai could be dependably effusive about, however, was her unblemished work record and high standard of professionalism. As a novice to the business, I seemed to be chief recipient of these speeches, and I for one was developing an acute sensitivity to being called 'bub'. Sharing a space with Valmai felt increasingly like being stuck in peak-hour traffic, and I was always relieved when the door bell sent her flying downstairs, clutching her packet of Horizons.

When she wasn't inhaling smoke, Valmai coughed a relentless, emphysemic, hacking cough over everyone and everything. At first I thought it was a smoker's cough until, one by one, we all came down with whatever strain of tuberculosis it was. As the only remaining receptionist not on antibiotics, I mumbled bitterly one night that, if she took a week off instead of being such a 'trooper', we wouldn't all be so sick.

'No, bub, I'm not a "trooper",' Valmai retorted indignantly. 'It's called being a professional. I just don't do that. Take a day off. Never done it in my life. Just not in my make-up. Work till you drop's my ethic. I'm old-fashioned like that. When I ran my business, anyone missed a day, they got the—' hacking cough '—sack! This your red pen, bub?'

Much to the amusement of my colleagues, my reaction to Valmai was getting worse. Sofia especially enjoyed seeing me lose my geniality, a quality she'd always found utterly sickening.

'What's the matter, darling?' she would ask, knowing very well that if Valmai said to me one more time 'Oh, bub, I could have told you that!' I would put a staple through her forehead.

But it wiped the smile off even Sofia's face when Valmai made the fatal mistake of criticising Boris and Didi's business expertise.

'When I had my own business, bub,' she tossed in my direction, 'it was a much smoother, better managed and more successful operation than this one, I can tell you.'

'So what happen?' Sofia asked abruptly. 'Why the fuck you here, darling?'

We all looked at Valmai.

'I just wanted to . . . move on,' she mumbled, with a twitch.

Boris and Didi had fought over Valmai's continued employment, but her popularity downstairs had convinced Didi she was an asset. And it was true. Valmai was like every man's favourite barmaid, and every working girl's favourite auntie. Downstairs, all the bragging, 'bubbing' and laughing went down a treat.

'But she is not to verk upstairs,' railed Boris at us in frustration – it was distressing to see Valmai's effect on Boris, especially when she called him bub – 'unless the phones are really focking busy!'

Despite this, any minor crisis brought Valmai puffing and coughing through our door, covering our office with particles of lung. Boris would immediately bury himself in his Asian Sluts while we busied ourselves seducing potential clients into having sensual massages with Swedish girls from Erskineville. Denied attention, Valmai would stand behind my chair and cough up tedious observations of her client downstairs.

'I could have told you he'd want Greek, bub. I can pick 'em

straightaway. I'm psychotic like that. We got a lot of them at Geishas. Nah, could have told you before that bloke even opened his mouth. Just borrowing your scissors, bub.'

It all came to a head one Sunday night as Boris sat boiling at his desk listening to all our grievances. It was true. The girls downstairs were being unusually hostile towards the receptionists upstairs. I was picking up towels, condoms and vibrators left, right and centre.

'It's because of that dumb cunt downstairs!' Boris finally burst out, referring to Valmai.

'Shh! Don't call her that,' Trudy protested. 'She'll hear you.'

'I don't care if she hears me!' Boris roared. 'She's a dumb cunt!'

'Shh,' Trudy hissed. 'She's old and sick and irritating, but she means well, Boris.'

Boris leapt to his feet. He had obviously been sitting on a volcano. 'You were on a personal call to your mother for half the focking night, I hear, Trudy. Meredit brings alcohol into the office.' He spun around pointing to me. 'Pip tells clients to fock off if she doesn't like the sound of them, and Raelene gives all bookings to Fat Marcelle, her favourite. You vont me to go on? Who do you think tells me all these things, Trudy? If you vont to defend the dumb cunt, Trudy, you're a dumber cunt than she is!'

Boris didn't mess around when he wanted to make a point.

'My daughter was sick,' Trudy muttered, wounded by Valmai's betrayal.

'And,' Boris hadn't finished, 'she tells all those dumb bitches downstairs what bad receptionists you all are. I'm not haffing it! I must haff harmony in this house. Everyone must get on!'

We sat in the deafening irony of Boris's statement, surrounded by all the unharmonious misspelt signs, as my foot nudged an empty bottle of wine a little further under my desk, the bottle shared by three receptionists who spent their weekends locked in a brothel.

From that night on, Valmai was treading water and no one was throwing her a line. It felt cruel, because without the kindness of her colleagues, Valmai stank as a receptionist.

'Oh! I'm sorry, bub. Look! I wrote it down. I write everything down! You learn to do that if you want to run a successful business. But you didn't say anything. So I just assumed you'd done it. Oh, yeah, bub, consider it done.' Hacking cough. 'Oh, you don't have to ask me to do anything twice.'

Sensing her increasing unpopularity in reception, Valmai began dropping into conversations, 'When I had cancer, last year ...', but no one ever asked her to elaborate. It may have been callous, but it just didn't seem an intelligent conversation to have with someone who smoked two packets of cigarettes a night. And I must confess, I felt secretly relieved that this desperate, yapping creature had taken some of the pressure off my unstable tenure in this troubled house.

The manicurist

My agent was telling me not to worry about it, but I still had no idea what she was talking about. I didn't get the job, she repeated quietly. I blinked at her. The Sydney Theatre Company job.

'Oh, didn't I?' I sighed, playing with the paperweight on her desk. 'Ah well.'

I had forgotten all about auditions, wigs, corsets, tours, guest roles and playing nuns in low-budget films, because no script could touch the drama and excitement of the roller-coaster ride I was currently on. And where else would I come across such a cast of colourful, fascinating characters? Besides, every night was opening night at the brothel. I had lost weight with the adrenalin of opening the front door to strangers, sending young girls out into the western suburbs, and being shouted at by tired prostitutes.

'Are you all right?' my concerned agent asked as I sat smiling inanely before her.

I was more than all right. Not having thought about acting for five months was like having a long break from a shaky marriage to a fickle bastard with amnesia.

As my agent's office was five minutes away from the brothel, I decided to pop into the local cafe for a bowl of soup before my shift began. I glanced over at the two young women sitting at the far table, and immediately recognised the tight blonde bun as belonging to Victoria, who had first greeted me at the brothel door. It wasn't surprising she'd lasted less than a month, I thought, considering the effect our door bell had on her. I waved at her, but she pretended she hadn't seen me. And when I walked up to pay for my minestrone, Victoria dived so deep into her handbag, I thought she was going to climb in. So I saved her the embarrassment of pointing at her and yelling that she used to work in a brothel, paid for my meal, and left.

Later that night Trudy and Raelene informed me that, technically, Victoria had never left. She just called herself 'Stephanie' instead. I was gobsmacked. Raelene was once again in hysterics. Stephanie, whom I'd been sending to hotels and private homes all over Sydney for nearly four months, was Victoria? Stephanie, who always deposited her money into the brothel account, and sent her credit card dockets by mail? *Victoria*, who used to have such difficulty answering the door, was now ringing door bells? I hoped it was easier for her, at least, from the other side.

The overpowering smell of acrylic nails and cosmetic adhesive hit me as soon as I opened the front door. Twenty years ago Marilyn's manicure paraphernalia would have brought on one of my asthma attacks. Marilyn had been on the books about three weeks. I opened the kitchen door to find her sitting at the table holding Shelby's delicate paw, both of them elbow deep in bottles, polishes, nail files, buffs and tissues.

Marilyn looked and sounded alarmingly like a younger version of Jeannie Little, but not much younger. She wore incredibly short, tight white skirts with incredibly tiny white tops and called herself 'Marilyn' after Marilyn Monroe.

'Go downstairs and see for yourself,' Raelene had exclaimed the night she first started. 'I mean, she's old, and she's rough, but when she puts that wig on, man, she looks like fuckin' Marilyn Monroe!'

I went down to introduce myself to a scrawny woman with a big smile and big hair already buffing Shelby's nails at the kitchen table. From a great distance, at night, had Marilyn Monroe's life taken an even less fortunate turn, and had there been much harder drugs involved, I could see Raelene's point. Marilyn insisted on shouting, even from small distances, except when she didn't get bookings. Then she spoke in a low, cracked rasp, and if she'd been drinking, sometimes two or three inches away from my face.

Marilyn had decided the second she met me that I was hilarious, and she often roared laughing just because I'd entered the room. Tonight was no exception.

'Hi!' she sang, sounding like Rod Stewart at the end of a concert, and then she laughed so raucously it set Shelby off too.

Marilyn's influence on Shelby was what schoolteachers called 'disturbing'. Usually a well-behaved, good and sensible girl, upright Shelby collapsed into submissive giggles at the mere mention of Marilyn. Her spine dissolved and her very bones seemed to fall out of their sockets as her limbs unfolded like petals at the table.

While the two blondes continued sliding off their chairs, I said hello to Maya, sitting quietly at the back door sewing, and Rita, who was perched on the kitchen bench, applying her make-up.

'Hello, darling,' the Gauguin vision cooed, unruffled by all the hysteria. Once again I noticed that Rita belonged to the school of make-up that believes no amount of dark pencil around the lips can give enough definition.

'Ya sully tart, Shelby!' Marilyn cried, reminding me of our strange first conversation:

'You been in Australia long, Marilyn?'

'What do ya min?'

'Well, I just assumed you were ... from New Zealand?'

'New Zilund?' Barefaced. 'Why would you thunk that?'

Marilyn also swore she was thirty-five, which made her younger than me.

'Why, how old are you, Miredith?'

'Thirty-eight.'

'Fuck no! I thought you were stull in your twinties!'

It was a deal.

But the one thing about Marilyn that was real was how much she loved the job.

'Ya see, Miredith, as much as I love my boyfriend, one man's just not enough.'

'Boyfriend?'

'Yeah. He says I've got the pussy of an eighteen-year-old.'

You never knew what Marilyn was going to say next.

'I've had a hysterectomy 'n all. Ya know, Miredith, it's better after a hysterectomy.'

'And, Marilyn, what does your boyfriend think you do at night?'

'Manicures.'

'Manicures.'

'Yeah. But I thunk he's gitting suspucious.'

'Ow!' Shelby howled suddenly. 'That's my finger you're filing, Marilyn, ya mad bitch!'

'Ya gonna have your hands full tonight, Miredith!' Marilyn hoarsely warned me.

I smiled and nodded my way to the door with my tea, noticing the empty bottle of riesling sitting by the bin. We always knew, by the empty bottle of wine or champagne sitting by the kitchen rubbish bin, that either Marilyn or Delilah was in. It could have been Harmony's, but ever since Urszula punched her, the hippy worked strictly from home. No girl was allowed to drink on the premises, unless Boris himself opened the bottle, so any drinking had to be done very discreetly. But once it was finished, the empty stood by the bin quite indiscreetly for a receptionist to dispose of.

Marilyn and Shelby were waiting for me to say something funny back, and all I could think of was, 'You two ...'

But that's all it took, they were off again. I could still hear them when I opened the office door upstairs to find two very concerned looking receptionists. Had someone died? Almost.

Didi, Raelene informed me mournfully, was waiting for me on line two. I looked from one long face to the other. Trudy tried to offer an encouraging smile, but gave in and returned to sorting out Boris's off bookings instead.

'Yes, Didi?' I asked, already perspiring.

'Merediss,' she began coolly, 'tell me, how can Celeste have had her period last Friday night?'

I explained to Didi that as there was no record of Celeste's periods in the Period Record Book at all, I gave Celeste's period the benefit of the doubt, and let her have the night off. (What did she want? Forensics?)

'I had no idea you were such a stupid girl, Merediss,' Didi replied. 'Did you not think to look in the back of the book to see which girls have had depo-provero injections?'

I had no idea what Didi was talking about, but as soon as I repeated the Italian vaccine out loud, Raelene hastily passed me the Period Record Book and opened it to a page in the back. Apparently five girls had Depro-Provera injections which I gathered, by Trudy's very expressive mime, prevented them from having any periods for three months.

'You can read, can't you? Or are you illiterate as well as stupid?' the heartless Yugoslav interrogator wanted to know.

I assured Didi that I was not either, and that in future I would remember to check any such excuse by looking in the back of the Period Record Book, as well as the front.

'And fine her twenty-five dollars, please.'

Pleasure. I went straight to our fridge, opened a bottle of the good champagne reserved for one-hour bookings, and poured us all a large glass.

It was midnight and, although a busy night, Marilyn had not been out once. I was making a run for the toilet and had only just reached the hallway when I was pinned to the wall by a Brett Whiteley barbed-wire version of Marilyn Monroe with scary hair, lots of fingernails and two large, blue, bloodshot eyes.

'Miredith? What's goin' on?'

'What's up, Marilyn?' I gasped, assaulted by the blast of stale white wine and Alpine cigarettes.

'Ya know, I'm begunning to thunk they've got somethung aginst me up there.'

'No, no one's got—'

'Have they got somethung aginst me up there, Miredith? Cos I'm begunning to get paranoid!'

A combination of age, alcohol and no bookings often sent this small group of mature wallflowers spiralling into a frightening Blanche Dubois despair. By 3 am I could have as many as six anxious women, all smoking at the kitchen table, wearing too much lipstick and looking at me like abandoned animals by the roadside as I passed them to send younger, fluffier things out on bookings.

'It's very quiet, Marilyn—'

'I see girls coming and going, Miredith!'

Young girls, Blanche, young girls!

''Cause, Miredith, I'm good at thus! Ya know? I really am! I fucking love ut. And do you know why, Miredith?'

This would be good.

''Cause I – love – cock!'

Marilyn opened her mouth so wide, I wasn't quite sure if she was having some kind of seizure. Then she let out a laugh so terrifying it would have frightened the devil himself.

At 1 am Heather got cancelled. Mr Banaman, an American staying at the ANA, had asked, along with every other man in Sydney, for a slim, busty blonde in her early twenties, and we had sent him Heather, promising she looked 'just like Heather Locklear'.

Half an hour later, Mr Banaman rang to cancel Heather Locklear.

'I can't believe she did that, Mr Banaman,' Trudy cried down the phone. 'Oh no, she didn't!'

What did Heather do? Raelene and I stopped rewriting our booking sheets to hear.

'I'm so sorry, Mr Banaman ... Of course we will ... No, that's quite unacceptable behaviour, I agree ... yes ... no ... of course ... Heather Locklear! Yes, isn't it uncanny? ... No ... what a pity ... Well, Mr Banaman, how do you feel about Marilyn Monroe? ... Yes we do! ... Oh, she does! ... Oh, she will! ... Yes, all right, twenty minutes.'

Raelene and I watched Trudy like two hungry birds.

'Marilyn,' Trudy called through the intercom.

Raucous laughter and fingernail polish bottles clacked back through the intercom. 'MARILYN, PICK UP!'

Marilyn picked up.

'Room 436 at the ANA,' said Trudy, in no mood for silliness. 'Mr Banaman. Go! Go now!'

We heard Patrick's keys jangling down the hall, followed by hasty goodbyes, a stiletto trot to the front door, and then such a door-slam the whole house shook.

Trudy threw herself back in her chair.

'Boris's got to talk to Heather,' she sighed. 'She's really done it this time.'

Raelene seemed to know whatever it was Heather had done, and shook her head in disgust.

'What's she done?' I asked.

Trudy stood for me, and with one hand on her hip, deftly impersonated the prissy Heather.

'Okay. You can touch me here, here and here,' she said pointing to obscure parts of her body, 'but you're not touching these, and nothing down there, thanks. And no fingers inside either. I don't kiss, I don't do French, and I don't receive it either, thanks very much. Okay then. Where would you like me?'

'Oh, man …' groaned Raelene, like she was singin' the blues, 'someone's gotta tell that girl she's a prostitute!'

Twenty minutes later Marilyn rang to say she was at the ANA with Mr Banaman, who was a 'very cheeky boy' and that she had two hundred dollars cash. Trudy tried to explain to the giggling Marilyn why there was no taxi money due to a cancellation, but soon gave up and put her on speakerphone instead. We listened to Mr Banaman making up for lost time while Marilyn, struggling to hang up the phone, yelped as if repeatedly surprised by something either very cold, or very big.

Shelby's trips to Japan

I didn't walk to work any more. I sprang. I couldn't wait to see the girls. I wanted to know if Maya still had her job as a housemaid at the Hilton, since someone had planted stolen cutlery in her locker. I wanted to hear about Urszula's day in the park with Rex, and if she'd hit anyone. Rita would no doubt fill me in on any squabbles from the previous night, and if I was lucky, Shelby would tell me another story about the strip bars she worked in Japan. I always hoped to find Bree sitting at the table with her bemused, dreamy smile, preferring the company of her entertaining colleagues to the five hundred dollar booking waiting for her at the Westin Hotel. I always hoped it would be one of Antoinette's good nights, and that her lucid mood would produce more sensitive insights into the human psyche from her prostitute's couch. I even looked forward to the possibility of Genevieve subtly ruffling everyone's feathers by deliberately counting her Exclusive cash at the kitchen table in front of girls who hadn't worked for days. And if our Thai lingerie models Song-Lee and May-Ling popped in for one of their fortnightly visits, usually at some ridiculous hour in the morning, the whole house rocked with joy. It was like a scene at the International Terminal, with screaming women kissing and hugging each other like long-lost sisters.

I entered the kitchen to find Rita, Marilyn, Shelby and Marcelle all engrossed in applying Marilyn's dark purple nail polish to their nails.

'I'm good at giving French,' Shelby stated, blowing on her fingers.

I decided to stack the dishwasher straightaway.

'Oh, me too!' trumped Rita in a new, tight silver dress.

The others chorused the same. They were all very good at French. It wasn't a boast. It was just a fact.

'You've got to love cock to guv good French,' Marilyn announced authoritatively in her hoarse voice.

'Mmm,' conceded Shelby, with more professional restraint. 'It helps if he's got a decent cock.'

'There is cock and there is cock,' said Rita philosophically. 'I've seen some shockers.'

They all nodded in agreement before bowing their heads in unison, returning to the task at hand. By the end of the night, every woman in the house, including me, had dark purple fingernails.

When I came down half an hour later, Shelby was telling the same enthralled group how cut-throat it was in Japan, where she'd worked for two years.

'They slip one in your drink if you're not watching. I've seen it.

Girls like this all of a sudden.' Shelby collapsed, dribbling on the table.

'Men slipped mickies in your drink?' I asked, wiping down the bench.

'Not men,' Shelby corrected me, 'the other girls.' And she turned back to her colleagues. 'I've never been offered so many drinks in me life.'

I waited all night to catch Shelby alone so I could ask her more about her trips to Japan.

'It's a much better scene over there,' she began enthusiastically, lifting her weightless frame onto the bench. 'The men are much less aggressive with girls for a start, especially western girls. And you can make a packet of money just dancing or stripping.'

I asked Shelby if that's all she did.

She thought about it. 'A bit of everything, really. I mean, the bar where I worked, I mainly danced, but it's all negotiable. The more they pay, the more ya take off. But if ya take 'em upstairs, that's when ya can make the big bickies.'

What size biscuits were we talking, I had to ask.

'I was making about forty a month.'

'Thousand?'

Shelby nodded.

'Most of that's in Fiji,' she said, hopping down and putting the kettle on. 'I've got a girlfriend over there and she opened an account for me. Ya can't just bring it in, so I'm slowly transferring it. Tea?'

I nodded.

'Slowly, slowly.' Shelby sang like a nursery rhyme. 'That's how ya do it. Don't draw attention to yourself. That's how people mess up. Too much of a hurry.'

'Shelby,' I interrupted her, 'what are you going to do with all your money?'

It was a question Shelby herself never lost sight of.

'By next year, I'll have a Saab, two apartments, and I'll be all set up with me own financial practice. It's time for me to put me legs up.'

Or together, I wanted to say, but didn't.

I asked Shelby if she was tempted at all to keep going, while she still had her looks.

'Nah,' she shook her head. 'When I started in this business, there were three of us at the top, and I was earning top dollar. I never had time to sit around talkin' to the receptionist, Meredith. So it's time to go. Ya know, this is a business ya gotta make serve you, not the other way round. Otherwise,' Shelby lowered her voice, craned her long neck towards the girls' lounge and nodded towards the occupants within, 'ya end up in there.'

A tale of two blondes

I wasn't actually there for the bomb going off, but I felt the fallout. Antoinette and Marilyn, our two 'mature' in-house blondes, were not on speaking terms. No one knew what exactly had happened the night before, except Sofia, who just loved it that way.

'They wen' on a double booking lass night, darling, that's all I can tell you.'

'A lesbian booking?'

'If it was lesbian I would have said lesbian.' Sofia was losing patience with my lack of precision with the terminology. 'I said double, didn't I?'

There was double meaning two men and two women, and double meaning two women and one man but no lesbian, and then there was the rare double of two men and one woman. Urszula was one of the only girls to accept the latter, because she could crack a man's skull between her legs while breaking the other one's nose with her forehead if she had to.

'An' I've taken your two cash bookings, Meredith,' Sofia muttered as I looked down at my booking sheet in horror, 'for Boris, darling.'

My only two bookings for the whole night, with great big red crosses through them.

Whenever I was on with Sofia, I stayed downstairs as much as possible to avoid the stress. But tonight I stayed upstairs, to avoid downstairs, where you could cut the air with a knife. Marilyn and Antoinette tried to camp in the two separate rooms, but it was a vicious circle. The tension that forced them apart also made them crave cigarettes, which forced them to share the kitchen. It's true, I thought as I observed their unhappy, awkward dance, smoking kills.

I had never worked so hard to sell an old blonde in my life. If I could just get one of them out, I knew the other would talk.

'Why you sendin' Marilyn, darling?' Sofia asked, when I hung up from Dimitri in Randwick. 'You got Tabatha sitting down there, you know?'

'He wants bouncy,' I said, pretending to be very busy.

Sofia's unimpressed gaze undermined my performance.

'Marilyn's very bouncy, Sofia.'

Sofia fanned her face with her booking sheet as she scrutinised me warily. She knew I was up to something.

With Marilyn out of the way, I set my trap for Antoinette and began loudly loading the dishwasher. Within minutes, in she shuffled, a brooding cloud in a black suit under a mop of blonde hair, wearing red lipstick and slippers. We exchanged the usual banalities about it being a shocking night, but the air was pregnant with a need to purge.

'Has Marilyn gone on a booking?' she asked tentatively.

'Yeah, some old guy out Woop Woop,' I lied.

Silence.

'I'm amazed they've taken on someone like that,' she ventured, 'you know?'

'She's a bit loud,' I conceded.

Antoinette was unable to restrain herself. 'Trashy, I would have said.' She lit up a cigarette and settled down at the kitchen table. 'I mean, we're supposed to offer an alternative to that kind of trade, aren't we?'

In this mood, Antoinette was dangerous to challenge, so I nodded.

'By the way,' she began, sitting up very straight, 'I've already spoken to Sofia. I don't want to be sent out on any more double bookings with Marilyn.'

'Oh,' I feigned surprise, 'did something happen?'

Antoinette took a deep drag of her cigarette. 'I went on a double booking with her last night,' she began. 'I mean, she was there first.

And he wanted another girl to join, and Marilyn suggested me, which was, you know—'

'Generous,' I said.

'Professional,' Antoinette preferred, 'and so we both shared an hour with him, and then he asked me to stay.'

'Ah,' I nodded.

Now Antoinette looked at me. 'That's not my fault!' she said defensively. 'I can't help it if someone prefers me. You just can't take it personally in this business. She's been around long enough to know that.'

'Meredith?' Sofia's voice came through the intercom.

'Yes?'

'Pick up, darling.'

I picked up the phone.

'Tell Tabatha Patrick's taking her to Randwick. Dimitri just cancelled your bouncy booking.'

Shit.

'What's that?' asked Antoinette.

'Marilyn got cancelled.'

Antoinette managed not to smile, but squinted triumphantly as she took another deep drag of her cigarette.

Although it was a full kitchen, I was glad that neither Antoinette nor Marilyn had arrived when I started work the following night. The large fan heater above the sink was now permanently on high to keep various semi-naked girls in their skimpy dresses warm, and their enclosed lounge room had become a veritable sauna. Even after peeling down to my black thermal underwear, my cheeks still shone like red apples. I'd been brought up to survive Tasmanian winters by adhering to one simple rule: for God's sake, put something warm on! And I wondered what my father would say to Pandora, now smoking by the open back door wearing nothing but a handkerchief. Actually, I don't think he'd utter a word.

As we enjoyed our loaded nightly greeting surrounded by half-dressed women, I always found it ironic that Patrick and I were the only two people in the room not about to have sex.

'And how are you?' Patrick burst out, like a jack in the box.

'Fine!' I shot back, and we both giggled like two happy muppets.

On more than one occasion, the younger girls witnessing this subtle courtship told us we were 'weird' and left the room, but not everyone found our constant mirth so nauseating. If Urszula got a whiff of any kind of flirtation, she'd move in on us like a heat-seeking missile.

'What's going on?' she'd demand with authority, looking suspiciously from one to the other.

Urszula made no secret of the fact that she fancied Patrick, and Patrick made no secret of the fact that he couldn't cope.

'Watch it, sexy,' she'd warn him, running her long fingers down his T-shirt. 'I'm like a cat on a hot tin roof tonight.'

Emitting a giggle, Patrick would hop off like a petrified budgie and hide somewhere till Maggie the Cat was gone.

Now that Patrick had been dispatched to take someone to Dulwich Hill, I reluctantly trudged upstairs, where I was informed by Maxine that Marilyn was no longer allowed in the house, and it wasn't just because of Antoinette. Maxine shrugged. It was nothing to do with her, but ever since Marilyn's arrival, management felt the girls were showing increasing signs of restlessness. A possible mutiny was on its way, or at the very least a mass exodus to Blue Angels. I had never witnessed Marilyn's alleged stirring, and just assumed it was Sofia and Boris being typically paranoid and looking for a scapegoat.

Poor Marilyn sounded so unhappy and isolated on the phone, rostering on from her flat in Hillsdale. Like Urszula, Marilyn needed to be around people, lots of people. But Marilyn also needed lots of sex and lots of drugs. And she was missed. All night long, one girl after another asked me the same question: 'Where's Marilyn?'

Antoinette's eyes darted about the kitchen nervously when she arrived, as if Marilyn might pop out of the toaster.

'She's been asked to stay at home.'

'Oh.'

Antoinette sat at the table with poise.

'She's very gifted, you know,' she offered quietly.

I looked up to see the madness of the past few days had been replaced by a deferential reverie.

'With the nails and the wigs,' she explained quickly. 'I admire that. She really loves what she does. I can't do that for myself.'

It was true. Antoinette spent a lot of money on beauticians and hairdressers out of necessity as much as indulgence. For all her intelligence, I doubt Antoinette was able to boil an egg. And now she sat measuring herself poorly against a woman she'd described only the night before as 'trash'.

The house was quiet without Marilyn. At 2 am the phones were dead and Maxine had another of her headaches. She had a booking at the Millennium for Gabriella, a new girl who'd ducked out for cigarettes an hour earlier and hadn't been seen since. I didn't care. Gabriella sniffed constantly, laughed nervously and smelt funny, but I gladly went on another search of the house just to avoid Maxine's tedious headache updates. I'd actually had nightmares about being left on my own to pay twenty angry women at the end of the night, and Maxine's constant temple-rubbing threats to leave always made me sweat. I crept out of the lounge, trying not to disturb Rita, curled up on a couch.

'Where's Marilyn, darling?'

If one more person asked me where Marilyn was ...

'She's home, Rita. Not coming in any more. Have you seen the new girl?'

Rita shook her head, then looked up at me, sleepily. 'Marilyn upset Antoinette, darling.'

'Yes, yes she did, Rita, that's true. You haven't seen Gabriella anywhere?'

Again she shook her head. 'They silly to fight, those two. But Antoinette should know better.'

I stopped at the door. 'What do you mean?'

'They went on booking together, darling. Antoinette and Marilyn.'

'Last week, yes.'

'Marilyn complained to Sofia—'

'that Antoinette took her booking from her, yes, I know that.'

'No, darling. That Antoinette does not use condoms.'

Rita was babbling on – 'because if one of us does it, the guy expects all girls to do it' – but I was miles away. Antoinette did not use condoms. Was this why Antoinette so often got extended bookings? Because she took such risks with her life? Rita's white legs were like a stuffed doll's, stretched out on the couch, protruding sweetly from one of the tiniest black dresses I had ever seen. I nodded, but I was remembering the night Antoinette called in sick with throat ulcers.

'Off course she has a sore throat,' Boris cried acrimoniously. 'If she lets men stick their tongues in her mouth and God knows what else, off course she is infected with germs and sores. One day,' he divined euphorically, 'she vill catch something *really* disgusting. And then it vill all be over!'

I didn't want my image of Antoinette as a compassionate, skilled and proud expert in bed to be replaced by something so disturbing, and ultimately sad. Perhaps she just risked it this once, I tried to convince myself as I climbed the stairs to get Antoinette more bookings.

Vegan of the Blue Mountains

'Oh go away, you vulgar man!'

Pip was in one of her states. The noise level downstairs had almost drowned out the sound of constantly ringing phones with 'vulgar' requests, and the kitchen was full of girls, all smoking and going through toast like there was no tomorrow. On nights like this I felt I was back working in the theatre, except this time as a stage manager, and happy to be in the wings for a change. From there I conducted a glamorous cast of noisy, talented women from one room to another, calming the nervous, cajoling the bored, and listening to all their grievances. Or else I sent them off 'on tour', where they stayed in up to five hotels in one night. And just as a theatre company prays for a generous, appreciative audience, we also hoped for a smooth run with no drunks or hecklers, please.

I wondered sometimes if I was not vicariously living through prostitutes. If some stage managers are frustrated actors, then what was I? Leaping down four steps at a time to see what sexy new dress Celeste was wearing, or bursting with curiosity about Lucinda's booking, especially if her client had flirted with me on the phone. And as I climbed the stairs again I loved counting the neat wad of twenties and fifties that had made its way from some bedside table into my hands. It wasn't just me, was it? Didn't we all find this game thoroughly titillating? Wasn't this the most exciting job in the world? But did I wish I had the guts to do it too? Or did I just badly need a boyfriend? Hannah would know.

Hannah was a very down-to-earth girl who trickled her way from the mountains every few weeks like a freshwater spring, and I was always pleased to see her. She was a pretty, robust girl, with such a happy and serene disposition it was contagious.

'It's probably just all this sexual energy.' Hannah chuckled at the table, with her full-length, snakeskin print evening dress hoisted up around her thighs as she held one foot in the air and pulled off a Blundstone boot.

I loved watching Hannah transform from Vegan of the Blue Mountains into Lady of the Night as she packed her baggy pants, thermal socks and Blunnies into her faded backpack and threw it in her locker.

'It's potent stuff,' she added, pulling at the messy pile of curly, light brown hair gathered on top of her head.

'Is that what attracts you to do this, Hannah? I mean, apart from the money?' I asked her.

'Not really,' she said, looking pensive. 'What I like about it is how surprisingly accessible men become. And the absence of bullshit can be utterly refreshing. It's amazing what someone will tell a complete stranger just because you've had sex with him. And it's great writing material.'

Hannah was studying creative writing and archetypal psychology. 'And guitar,' she added.

I could imagine a booking for Hannah was an opportunity to take all her clothes off, roll herself a cigarette, have a good rave with a nice bloke and a bit of sex to top it off. If anyone made the crossover to escort work tempting to me, it was this happy, enlightened soul. My parents would panic if they knew what Hannah had me thinking. Yet my parents would really have liked her too. But I think I'll leave my parents out of it ...

Pip got Hannah and Genevieve a dinner booking with an Englishman and his friend, staying at the Intercontinental. And it was funny to see the two of them chatting at the kitchen table, Genevieve luxuriously wrapped in a Prada suit with her smooth hair, and Hannah in her snakeskin dress. Genevieve graciously offered to drive them in her Fiat, as soon as Hannah was ready.

'Oh, okay,' said Hannah, fishing into her purse for her lipstick and mascara.

Genevieve looked at her colleague's crude tools and watched Hannah's brisk makeover with restrained incredulity.

'Let's go.' Hannah smiled, snapping her purse shut.

'Sure!' said Genevieve, who kept a large Louis Vuitton make-up case in the trunk of her car.

After they left I moved through the smoke and noise, collecting rubbish and opening windows, and wondered who would interrupt this party tonight. Pissed office workers, lone labourers, or foreigners whose shaky English still prevented them from being more socially successful: I'd met them all. Asian businessmen were always very polite but disappointed if we didn't have six tall, slim, busty Australian blondes available all at once. Then there were the clients no one wanted; they frequently came in pairs, wearing pendants and jangling large bunches of keys. Keys to what, I always wondered. Newcastle? They'd swagger in, stony-faced and bloated, take a couch each, light up a cigarette and look disdainfully at the menu I handed them, as if it was an imposition. And rather than stand, they'd sit back and peruse the girls with contempt before leaving me at the door with a condescending smirk.

'CLIENT!' an angry voice from upstairs shouted through the intercom, as none of us had heard the front door bell over the din. While the girls carried on obliviously, as if they were at Sexpo, I extricated myself to deal with the intruder.

'Two guys,' I shouted above the throng a minute later. 'TWO MEN ARE HERE!' At last I got their attention.

'Let's have a look,' Pandora said glumly, leading the pack to the monitor in the lounge room. 'Got one I knew the other day,' she mumbled, 'really freaked me out.'

Pandora was not often in-house. She was not often in the kitchen at all. Pandora preferred escort work, and did not socialise with the other girls if possible. But despite her previous aloofness, the others had welcomed her warmly that night, and they all examined the two suits on the screen. I watched as Pandora hastily prepared herself and brushed her hair, unaware of the others around her, who made slower, half-hearted gestures, glancing sheepishly at the Botticelli beauty in their midst.

I did not like the two proud men in expensive suits sitting with their legs crossed in our waiting room. They made me feel like a domestic servant in their home. I had no idea where they were from, but they were tall, dark and cruel-looking men with thick accents.

'We are looking for two,' the leader said, holding up two ringed fingers, 'slim, beautiful, young women. If we like what we see,' he said, with all the regality and pomp of a visiting prince, 'we will book them to come back to the Boulevard.'

Occasionally men called in to look at the girls before ordering a few, like takeaway food to be delivered to their rooms in nearby hotels.

'Two?' I asked, deliberately holding up my two fingers.

'Two,' he repeated, a little peeved at my short memory.

'And what are your names?' I asked politely.

'That will not be necessary.' The prince smiled condescendingly. 'If we see anything we like, we will be paying cash.'

I found the girls so subdued, having witnessed this solemn performance on the monitor, that even Pandora seemed unwilling to face such cold scrutiny. Rita and Antoinette, the eldest, sat completely still. When I looked at Maya, she shook her head with a sad smile.

'No thanks.'

'Shelby?'

'Fuck off!'

'Antoinette?'

Gracious and polite as ever, especially on her good nights: 'No.'

'What's the matter, Delilah?' I asked our African Queen. 'They're not Asian.' If a client was Asian, Delilah would take one look at the monitor then throw herself back in her chair, determined to save herself the rejection.

'Asians regard black as dirty,' Pip had explained to me, along with other folklore. 'Never send a Japanese man Chinese, unless he asks for it, which he won't.'

Delilah looked up at me like a cat being forced to move from its favourite spot by the fire, so I left her there in her body-hugging grey knit dress. I could never, ever understand why anyone, wherever he came from, would not choose to have sex with Delilah.

Pandora stood in front of them and smiled. Neither gentlemen stood, and I watched as they perused her merchandise with not even a visible intake of breath. Using one finger, the prince finally gestured for her to turn around, which she did. With an air of disappointment, the prince looked up at me, and Pandora crept apologetically out of the room. Leanne, a new girl, followed soon after, and fared even worse. She stepped forward to offer her hand to the prince's companion. Without moving a muscle, he looked up at her face, as if to record her embarrassment. What was this? An assessment of the goods, or an exercise in humiliation and subjugation? Apologising for herself also, Leanne withdrew her hand, and even bowed as she backed out the door.

'Is that all you have?' the prince asked quietly when she had gone.

'No,' I said.

'Where are the others, then?' he asked, leaning forward with that condescending smirk.

I looked from one to the other. They seemed so pleased with their trick, having made two beautiful young women disappear before their eyes.

'Netball,' I said. It was the only thing I could think of. Inoffensive, but baffling.

'Net-ball?' the companion finally uttered.

'Every Saturday night,' I said. 'Just to keep fit. They love it.'

'What losers,' remarked a deflated Maya when I returned to the kitchen.

'They know they're losers, darl,' Shelby said breezily, jiggling her tea bag. 'That's why they have to come to parlours, reject a few girls, get their power back, and out they go again, all fixed!'

All in all, it had been a shit of a night. Even the escorts had bounced from crisis to disaster. Abigail got cancelled, Rachel had discovered her client was filming her with his computer, Trixie and Marcelle got into a fight at the Coogee Bay Hotel, and Lottie was still lost somewhere in Epping. But I was most saddened when a disheartened Hannah returned from the city and told us about her ordeal. Apparently when she and Genevieve met Mr Jones and his friend at the Intercontinental bar, he said he would not pay them until after dinner. When Hannah discreetly explained that they would have to be paid in the room before dinner, or else they could be arrested for soliciting, Mr Jones threw a peanut at her forehead.

'Well, as you're hardly able to make a scene without being arrested, I suggest you both shut up, be good girls, and have another cocktail.'

Having wasted an hour, Genevieve went straight on to a booking at the Westin, and Hannah was sent to meet Liam at the Stamford Hotel carpark.

'He didn't make you have sex in a carpark?' Maya yelped in horror.

'He didn't want to have sex at all!' Hannah exclaimed. 'He just wanted to hide behind cars. To run from car to car with an enormous erection, and me!'

I savoured the sight from the doorway, Rita with her heavy make-up, stilettos and glittery top, sitting next to a fresh-faced Hannah, once again in her mountain gear. One had her Silkcuts, the other had her rollies, and both were enjoying a good laugh. I came back downstairs with only ninety dollars change for Hannah, but she seemed happy enough.

'No, Meredith,' she sighed, thrusting the cash into the pouch of her backpack, 'tonight was strictly for the money. Last time I was down, I had such lovely clients, but this weekend I've had nothing but nutcases, and I deserve every cent of this.'

Hannah bid us all a hearty goodnight and strode towards freedom in her Blunnies. Minutes later, I heard the broken muffler of her ute begin its long journey north back to the mountains.

Babes in a brothel

'They sound like horses running in the Cup,' I said. 'Who are they?'

'Downstairs,' Pip sighed with fatigued disapproval.

Shawna and Rochelle had started their roster the night before, much to Boris's chagrin. But since his wife held him personally accountable for the plummeting success of expanding to in-house, Boris's arguments went pretty much ignored these days. Didi had insisted, as Shawna was a blonde, and as both girls were nineteen, that we give them a try for at least a week.

'Boris is disgusted,' Pip said, 'and frankly so am I. I didn't think we employed that kind of girl.'

I was on my way downstairs to see the kind of girl Pip found so offensive.

They looked about sixteen to me, sitting at the kitchen table wearing jeans, T-shirts and no make-up. The Melbourne Cup analogy was not lost completely on one of them, whose long freckled face was framed by lank brown hair. In fact, everything about this girl was long and thin. I introduced myself, and Shawna, the bottle blonde, immediately leapt to her feet.

'G'day, Meredith,' she said, quickly exhaling her cigarette smoke to one side and frantically waving it away. 'I'm Shawna,' she announced with a husky voice, and shook my hand with athletic enthusiasm. 'Pleased to meet ya, Meredith. Now you tell me if I'm doing anything wrong, or what's what, 'cause I don't wanna piss anyone off, okay?'

I wanted to tell Shawna that she could start by releasing my limp paw.

'And this is Rochelle,' she said, gesturing to her friend.

Rochelle scowled like a schoolgirl in detention.

'Chelle!' Shawna reprimanded her horsy friend, with a light cuff to the back of the head.

Rochelle grimaced, then flashed me an unconvincing smile before returning to her ashtray. Shawna hastily compensated by telling me they were both nineteen, had lots of experience in parlours, and were willing to work in-house as well as escort. But something in the way Rochelle stifled a giggle at the mention of the word *parlours* suggested to me that the only experience these girls had was possibly not indoors at all.

I was about to go upstairs when Rochelle called me back, '*Oi!*', as if I was her mother. I poked my head around the door.

'Should I put me stuff on now?'

'Yes, Rochelle,' I said, 'that would be most helpful.'

As I left them there, arguing over who would wear what, I noticed they also shared the same voice, all smoker's rasp and adolescent squeak. I did not like to agree with Pip as a rule, but when she saw my face again, she smiled with smug satisfaction.

I was not upstairs long before the door bell started ringing. There were three consecutive pairs of men, and they all chose Leanne. Leanne, who looked like a friendly bank teller. While downstairs I was pleased to see a major transformation in the appearance of our two young novices. Rochelle had squeezed into a tight-fitting, simple black dress, her perky breasts peeping over the top. And all in white, wound in several gold chains with zips aplenty, Shawna had metamorphosed into ABBA. All four of them. She might have had Agnetha's hair, tied up in a neat ponytail, but it was definitely Benny's strapless shoulders looming above her ample cleavage. When I introduced them to their potential clients, Rochelle loped in, mumbled some inaudible greeting, then loped out, whereas Shawna shook the man's hand as if she'd just bought a sheep off him at the Royal Easter Show.

'Yeah, right,' she shouted with a friendly wink before swaggering out. 'Thanks, Meredith.'

Although Shawna and Rochelle were on their best behaviour, neither of them was shy with the other girls. Instead, they seemed confident in their new surroundings and endeared themselves to their somewhat bemused colleagues, who possibly suspected they would not last long. Shawna told funny anecdotes while Rochelle guffawed at everything anyone said, as if it was all a bit of a joke.

The two girls provided the most entertainment when sitting in front of the monitor, which was obviously a novelty to them. In this situation, our girls usually showed professional restraint. They mainly wanted to check that they did not know the men personally, and only commented if the man was overtly rude, or dangerously large,

or particularly challenging in some other way. But Shawna and
Rochelle embraced the whole ritual as some kind of game show, and
shrieked and giggled at anything from a bald patch to prescription
glasses. And all of us found their naughtiness contagious.

The only time I witnessed somewhat less jovial behaviour was
when two good-looking boys arrived at the door. I wasn't sure if
they had money at all, but we'd soon find out. When I told the girls
in the kitchen how young they were, Antoinette, Rita and Shelby
all smiled and shook their heads. Only Delilah, Leanne, Shawna and
Rochelle would come and meet them. When Rochelle came in
and shook their hands, her sudden bashfulness and twitching smile
revealed a vulnerability that perhaps made the boys overlook her
for Shawna and Leanne. And after the two girls had taken their
clients upstairs, I found Rochelle sitting alone in the lounge,
pretending to watch television. I asked her if she wanted a cup of
tea and, without looking at me, she gave a humiliated shake of her
head, so I left her there.

It was a busy night and by two in the morning almost every girl was
out on a booking. My colleagues upstairs knew never to leave me
a completely empty house, and Rochelle and Shawna schlepped
from room to room like tired children locked inside a school.

We had a large, well-lit door bell, but he chose to knock. A
plump, swaying man with ginger hair and a beard said he was a lost
Irish sailor, and straightaway Jake had me laughing.

'I just want to come in for a glass of Coke,' he insisted. 'And
look, I might have sex as well. But just the Coke for now, okay?'

Jake was affectionate, pissed, and falling in love with me by the
second, so he kept telling me.

'Are you sure you're not availa— Holy Mother of Christ!' Jake
cried, doing a triple-take at our stuffed moose. 'Is that what
happens when you don't pay?'

I apologised for the moose and told Jake I would fetch our two
most beautiful girls.

'Doesn't matter, Meredith,' he said. 'As I keep telling you, a
Coke would be fine. Or you. Bring the ice anyway.'

When I found Shawna and Rochelle convulsing with horrified

giggles at the thought of having sex with our drunken sailor, I reprimanded them for being so mean.

'Well, the two young ones for an hour, I think, Meredith,' Jake said, swaying happily after they'd gone. 'That's if you're not going to have me.'

'Both of them, Jake?'

'Well, I don't want to leave one out now,' he said, pulling a thick wad of fifties from his pocket. 'That would be rude, don't you think?'

Jake didn't flinch when I told him it would be four hundred dollars for the hour, but he seemed to hesitate, and even staggered backwards, when he went to hand me the cash.

'Meredith,' he said, clutching it to his chest, 'will the girls let me do things to them now?'

Do things to them. I hoped that this would not be a request like my client the week before, who'd wanted to 'put things in girl's bottom, and take photo'.

'What sorts of things, Jake?' I asked, carefully.

'I'm that rare breed of man,' he said, lurching dangerously close to me, stifling a burp, 'who likes to put their *mouth* where their money is, if you know what I mean.'

'Ah,' I nodded.

'I like to—'

'Yes!' I interrupted him. 'I'm sure that's fine, Jake, but I'll just have to check with the ladies first.'

'Dams!' I whispered hoarsely to my young charges, huddled over their cigarettes at the back door as if they were about to go to the gallows. 'You put them over ... and then he ... and it's all very hygienic.'

Shawna's eyes bulged as she held her hand over her open mouth. Rochelle bent over, gasping in hysterics.

'That's fine, Jake,' I said, 'but they might insist on using a dental dam.' I took a deep breath. 'It's a small sheet of latex—'

'Oh, Meredith,' Jake reeled backwards, shaking his head, 'you can't eat fois gras through a balloon!'

I was about to return to the summit at the back door when Jake stopped me.

'All right, all right. Whatever they want. Just tell them to come and get me before I pass out.'

I was always impressed when Pip spoke to clients in Cantonese, or Mandarin, or whatever language it was she spoke fluently. And right now I was grateful for any distraction at all from the noises coming from the party room above us. If nothing else, Shawna and Rochelle were having a good laugh with their sailor.

'Bloody May-Ling,' Pip scoffed when she'd hung up.

'What's she done?' I asked, surprised that the dear and sweet May-Ling could have done anything wrong at all.

'Stonie,' Pip sighed.

'Stonie?' I asked.

Pip was surprised that I had not heard the amusing 'stonie' story. Months ago, Patrick had been sent to wake May-Ling, who had not answered her phone, for a very late booking. When May-Ling finally responded to his loud knocking, the door opened to release a fog of smoke and an all too familiar smell to our happy driver.

'Ah, sorry,' May-Ling had giggled at Patrick. 'Stonie!'

And now May-Ling was stonie again. I wanted Pip to keep talking. The laughter upstairs had been replaced by soft moaning.

'Which is fine,' Pip added quickly. 'May-Ling's not even on roster tonight, but he wanted Thai, and—' more moaning, '—you don't hear that too often.'

Pip explained to me that, like it or not, there was a hierarchy when it came to Asian prostitutes and Asian men's preferences. Japanese women were much sought after and at the very top, followed by Chinese, followed by Korean, followed by all the others and Thai were at the bottom.

The moaning was getting louder.

'Why?' I asked Pip urgently.

'Because they are so westernised,' Pip continued over the noise. 'Like girls from Singapore. Most Chinese men prefer someone less affected by western culture.'

Now there were two girls groaning at once. What was Jake doing?

'Tea?' I asked Pip.

'Please,' she nodded gratefully.

Downstairs I filled the kettle to the top with cold water, and cleaned the kitchen from sink to stove. Determined to stay there, once the kettle had boiled I emptied it and filled it again. I was folding the tea towels into small triangles when I heard the unmistakable sound of a drunken, laughing sailor falling down the stairs near the door.

'Are you all right?' I asked, heaving Jake's shaking carcass up off the floor.

Yes, Jake was fine, and calling sweet nothings back to his giggling cohorts, who cooed and waved farewell from the landing. Jake threw an affectionate arm around my shoulders and let me carry him to our front door, where he beamed at me with a look of sheer, post cunnilingus ecstasy.

'Thank you, Kim,' he gushed.

'Meredith,' I said, opening the door.

'Yes! Meredith!' he shouted. 'And, Meredith?' Jake suddenly whispered, and beckoned me to come closer.

I would have stopped him if I'd seen it coming. Jake pushed his face into mine, and gave me a big wet kiss on the lips.

'Thanks for the Coke!' he shouted as I pushed him forward into the night.

It was the closest I ever wanted to come to a lesbian double.

Sprung!

'Oop, here she is,' said Urszula as I came out of the laundry with my arms full of clean towels.

There was a flurry of movement as a dozen or so girls swiftly perched on benches, on the sink, found a spot against the wall, or sat at the kitchen table. I was immediately arrested by a roomful of eyes, all looking at the startled receptionist with her large bundle of burgundy towels and, now a face to match.

'What?' I asked my captive audience.

No one said a word. Even the noisy fan heater stopped for a break. Marcelle and Trixie had always scared me, even after

Marcelle forgave me for sending her all the way to Parramatta without getting her client's photo ID. But now they looked positively terrifying as they swung their legs in unison, perched on the bench, glaring at me. What had I done? I couldn't proceed upstairs until I had found out, otherwise it would be seen as an admission of guilt. Even Shelby leant back against the wall, her arms folded, sentencing me with a sinister nod.

'We're onto you,' Trixie growled at last, like a footballer.

'What have I done?' I asked imploringly.

Only Shawna and Rochelle, who'd been chatting by the back door, looked as bewildered as me. They crept inside to watch my suffering with morbid fascination.

'It's been bugging us for fucking months,' muttered Marcelle.

With a desperate look I appealed to their Godfather, Don Sapphire, for mercy.

'Did you think you could keep it a secret, Meredith?' she asked me sternly. 'Did you honestly think we wouldn't discover sooner or later?'

'Discover what?'

Urszula lazily launched her body from the fridge supporting it and swaggered towards me, her hands placed menacingly on her hips. Hugging my towels close to my chest, I shuffled backwards as she moved in on me, until I felt Marcelle's knees in my lower back. Urszula stopped in front of me, took a deep breath and, in a very low voice, began to sing.

'There's a bear in there, and a chair as well . . .'

For one confusing second I did not recognise the baffling German ditty about a bear, until the whole room erupted in song.

'There are people with games! And stories to tell!'

Almost swooning with relief, I released my towels as the raucous, cheeky choir swayed in unison, nearly deafening me with the chorus. '*Open wide, come inside! It's Play School!*'

An hour later I stood in the middle of the kitchen and gently patted her back as she hugged me tightly. Since realising I was Merri-something from *Play School*, Rochelle could not let me pass her without a hug, which was quite disconcerting as Rochelle was not a demonstrative girl. But some switch within had been flicked, and she could no longer look at me without squirming and blushing, or else flinging her body at mine like a neglected baby octopus. And I was genuinely touched.

'I thought ya might have been a friend of my mum's or something,' Trixie hoarsely whispered to me, hoisting her boobs outside the waiting room before I took her inside to meet Allan from Dubbo. 'It's been really spinnin' me out.'

Marcelle nodded sympathetically. It really had.

'But then I got this image of you barkin' on all fours like a dog, and it all came back to me. Lewis's fuckin' *Play School* video.'

I told Trixie I didn't think she looked old enough to have a son. When Trixie told me Lewis was now fifteen, I felt as ancient as the pyramids.

For the next few hours, the kitchen was alive with a cacophony of animated prostitutes arguing over their favourite presenter, or the hand movements to 'Incy Wincy Spider'. I tried to avoid it as much as possible as I had clients to greet and towels to wash, and they held me up with their questions.

'What's John like?'

'Did you feel like a dickhead, Meredith?'

'Why's she called Hamble? What the fuck kind of a name is that?'

'Did they pay you, darl?'

'Hey, how big's the arched window?'

Urszula just wanted to know one thing.

'How the fook did you end up here, Meredith?'

If Bev asks you for a dance, say no

The first time I heard her powerful voice resonating from downstairs, I waited for Boris to tell me to 'focking go down there and tell that loud bitch to shut the fock up!' but instead, he sat at his desk immersed in some paperwork, and grumbled quietly as if it were a minor irritation.

'Who is that?' I whispered to Raelene.

'Bev,' she answered, and looked at Boris. 'You seen her lately?'

'Yeah, yeah,' he groaned without looking up, 'I seen.'

'Pretty amazing, hey?'

When Raelene could see Boris wasn't going to take the bait, she returned to me.

'Go down there,' she commanded, 'introduce yourself to Bev, then come back up and tell us how old you think she is.'

Raelene giggled like a schoolgirl at the brilliance of her plan. Trudy rolled her eyes. I could tell that Trudy had little time for Bev, but I was going to venture down anyway out of curiosity. Who on earth could be louder than Urszula? And more importantly, who on earth would dare?

The voice grew louder as I approached the kitchen door. 'And I said to her, "You touch one fucking hair on his head, ya fuckin' reptile slag, and I'll pull your heart out your arse!"'

Sensing my presence behind her, the curvaceous, petite platinum blonde turned around. With her leather pants, high heels and frilly white blouse with shoulder pads, Bev was half bikie chick and half Dolly Parton. And Bev liked jewellery. Lots and lots of gold jewellery.

Shelby introduced us. Still chewing her gum, Bev flashed me a perfect set of white teeth as she shook my whole body by the hand.

'Pleased to meet ya, Meredith,' she shouted with a hoarse, smoker's voice. 'I'm Bev, darl.'

Bev was not a person to respect other people's personal space. 'Do I know you, Meredith?' she asked, so close I could smell her lipstick, chewing gum and cigarettes.

'Meredith was on *Play School*,' Shelby piped from behind her, beaming with pride.

'Fuck!' With a sharp intake of breath, Bev stepped back and took me in. 'I think I used to watch you with Jase!' she screeched. 'Yeah! Miss Fuckin' Meredith!'

I smiled. I could never be bothered telling people they were confusing *Play School* with *Romper Room* or *Here's Humphrey*, where they called the presenter Miss Julie, or Miss Helen. On *Play School* I was just plain Fuckin' Meredith.

I ran back upstairs, flopped down in my chair, and then turned to the expectant Raelene.

'Before she opened her mouth I would have said early thirties,' I panted, 'but she's got perfect skin!'

'Forty-six,' Raelene decreed. 'Bev's forty-six!'

'Yeah,' guffawed Trudy, 'and tell her the rest.'

Raelene was ready to explode with the rest. 'Twenty thousand dollars!' she burst out like a dam. 'Bev's had twenty thousand dollars worth of cosmetic surgery done to her face.'

'That's a lot of bookings,' I mumbled.

Now it was Boris's turn to burst. He leapt to his feet.

'Bookings she'll never get!' he shouted as he paced the floor in front of us. 'Focking vaste!' Overcome with agitation, he stopped at Raelene's desk and helped himself to one of her cigarettes. 'What's the focking point? She's too old to verk.'

'Then why keep her on?' I asked Boris.

It was a risky question given his mood, but Boris stood still, looking genuinely perplexed, like a helpless pup, until Raelene broke the silence.

'Bev shot a man.'

I looked at Trudy, who nodded.

'Bev's still here,' Trudy added, looking at our tormented boss, 'because no one has the guts to tell her to go.'

I waited for Boris to object, but instead he just butted out Raelene's cigarette in disgust.

'Focking menthol.'

I knew that Urszula had a gun licence. If anyone had shot a man, it should have been Urszula, and she should have shot one of her brothers. But apparently Bev had connections that made Urszula's look like the Muppets. Which explained why Bev was sitting downstairs with a new face, and not behind bars with a double chin.

Later that night I was treated to pats on the back all round when I got Bev a booking at the Rex. I crept into a kitchen full of smoking, noisy women, where even Urszula struggled to be heard. As I scanned the room for Bev, clutching my piece of paper, Urszula elbowed my arm.

'Who you looking for?' she demanded.

'Bev,' I said.

With one long finger commanding me to follow, Urszula strode towards the girls' lounge. I was right behind her when she stopped at the big chair just inside the door. There, with her legs hanging over the arm, lay the snoring Bev. Her body had sunk into the cushions, leaving her shoulder pads elevated, so that she looked like an emaciated footballer in drag.

'Oi!' Urszula boomed before I could stop her, and I watched in absolute horror as she slapped Bev hard across one of her dormant thighs. 'Wakey-wakey!' she shouted.

I saw my parents weeping over the headline: RECEPTIONIST SHOT IN BOTH SIDES OF HEAD BY TWO PROSTITUTES CARRYING HANDGUNS.

Instead, a miracle happened. Rumbling like Mount Vesuvius, the sleeping volcano only stirred to squint menacingly at the figure at her feet.

'Oh, piss off, Urs,' Bev scowled before turning back into her cushions.

And that was it. No gunfire, stabbings or head-butts. And with a shrug, Urszula left me to give Bev her booking.

'Jus' leave it there, darl,' a muffled voice commanded me through the cushions.

And I did.

Trudy wasn't sure exactly who Bev had shot, or why, or how exactly she'd got away with it, but she was almost certain Bev shot him in a packed nightclub in the city and that he died.

'Can ya dance?' Raelene asked cheekily as she reached for her phone.

I nodded.

'Then you've got nothing to worry about,' Raelene smiled. 'Can I help you?'

A cockroach in the kitchen

The first night I met her, I could not believe she had not walked into the wrong house. Leanne was a polite, incredibly well-groomed young woman who possessed that pleasant, unthreatening, beige quality casting agents search for when casting the mother in a margarine ad. Although she was not tall, Leanne always stooped slightly, and she smiled as if apologising for something. She was the first girl I had met in this house with her natural-coloured hair, which was shoulder length, straight brown, and looked brushed and neat at all times. *I* looked more like a working girl than Leanne, even in my sad black flatties. Must buy new shoes.

Leanne would often wear a dark, skin-tight dress with spaghetti straps, and although it showed off her perfect figure, she still looked like she was about to stamp a deposit slip. But when the girls had paraded, slinked, sashayed and shimmied in and out of the waiting room for their prospective clients, the men always turned back to me with the same request.

'I'll have Leanne, thanks.'

'Leanne for half an hour, thanks.'

'Leanne.'

I'll have the nice, beige girl, please, who's conservative, neat appearance reminds me of all the girls at the bank I can't fuck. Was that it?

It felt so wrong, handing Leanne the plastic soap box with its condom, but she'd stoop and smile, thanking me as if it was a corsage before ushering her client upstairs to show him her needlework. Half an hour later, Leanne would smile all the way to the laundry, carrying the soiled, sticky towel. No one smiled after a booking.

Leanne had only been with us a month when I needed to send a girl on a booking to two men. This didn't happen very often, and not many of the girls would do it.

'Leanne will go, darling,' Sofia said, casually.

I scanned the back of Leanne's card and was shocked to see the bank teller did everything. Couples, B & D, S & M, lesbian double, fantasy, golden showers, and there it was ... two men. So I sent

Leanne to the Rex, still smiling, with her neat hair and a handbag full of condoms and lube.

By eight o'clock the following night, Sofia had me on sheepdog duty. That meant I had to round up all the rostered girls who had still not signed on. As I waited for Leanne to answer her mobile, I remembered her face when she had returned from seeing the two men early that morning, still smiling.

'Hi, Leanne,' I said at last.

'*Who?*' demanded the angry voice on the other end.

Who? It was usually safe to use the girls' working names when we called them on their mobiles, but obviously someone else had answered Leanne's. Someone pissed.

'Nothing,' I said, and hung up.

Sofia looked at me suspiciously as I searched Leanne's card for her real name, which was Anna, and tried ringing her home phone number instead.

'Wha . . . ?' the same voice finally answered.

'Anna?' I asked. 'Is that you?'

'Yeaah? Who's 'is?'

Still not convinced I had the right person, I asked Anna if she was signing on for the night.

'Wha . . . ?' she asked.

So I tried asking if *Leanne* was signing on for the night.

'Noooooo,' she cried at last, 'Leanne drunk.'

Definitely.

'I think you had better all forget about me,' she wailed. 'Wri' me off, Pip! No good.'

'That's okay, Leanne,' I said. 'It's Meredith. You have tonight off. Are you all right?'

Sofia and Raelene were frowning at me, so I did mad drinking gestures.

'Not worth it,' Leanne sobbed. 'Hopeless. Juswanna die.'

'Oh dear,' I said, 'that's no good.'

'You so lovely!' Leanne howled. 'You all so lovely to me! An' I don't deserve it, but thank you soooo much being so lovely. *Who's 'is?*'

By this time Sofia was demanding I put Leanne on hold, so I did. 'Ask her, darling, if she's coming in tomorrow.'

'Leanne?' I said.

'...an' I juss wanna die!' Leanne wailed in my ear.

'And ask her what time,' Sofia persisted.

'Do you think you might be feeling better tomorrow, Leanne?' I asked tentatively.

Silence.

Sofia squinted at me curiously as she dragged on her cigarette.

'Oh, look! Pip!' Leanne's transmission break was over.

'Meredith,' I interjected.

'I can't tomorrow, Pip. I can't,' she howled. 'Because I do this, see? I drink! An' morrow I'll have DTs, an' I won't do that to a client, Pip. I won't!' Leanne sobbed, 'Noprofeshnal.'

The lines were lighting up like a Christmas tree, so I had to let our drunk bank teller go.

Valmai was not having a good night either. Just as we were busy upstairs, so was Valmai, with a dozen girls downstairs. For the second time in ten minutes she burst into our room clutching a fist full of client's money as if it were a hand grenade. And as usual, we ignored her.

'Shit!' Raelene cried, slamming down her phone. 'We're out of blondes!'

'Send Cindy,' sighed Sofia, trying to ignore the flustered, panting Valmai behind her.

'Cindy's at the Intercontinental for another hour,' Raelene objected.

'Doesn't matter,' shrugged Sofia, 'get the driver to pick her up soon as she's finish.'

'You could have Genevieve,' I offered helpfully. 'She's finished in half an hour.'

'Genevieve's doing Exclusive booking, darling!' Sofia shouted at me.

So? Genevieve would be finished before Cindy.

'What if she extend?' yelled Sofia, increasingly horrified at my stupidity.

'I can't make him wait for Cindy for an hour!' Raelene cried.

'Yes, you can, darling,' Sofia insisted. 'Sorry, she couldn't get taxi. Sorry, she went to wrong room. Anything! Send Cindy, darling.'

Raelene rolled her eyes in silent protest.

'Is he pissed', Raelene?' Sofia asked tersely. 'Send him an Asian girl! He won't notice. Just send – WHAT THE FUCK YOU DOING?'

The sprung munchkin froze in terror. Hovering over the open cash box clutching a fist full of twenties was a suspicious-looking activity when Sofia was in the room.

'Oh, bub,' Valmai began disastrously, 'I'm just ' trying to remember if he wanted an hour or half an hour. I've been that busy down there, and—'

One drunk prostitute, a dearth of blondes and two incompetent receptionists were bad enough, but a nervous pensioner calling her 'bub' was the last straw, and Sofia's banks burst. Yes, Valmai nodded, acquiescing to Sofia's tirade, it probably was an hour after all. She snapped shut the cash box and scurried towards the door. Valmai was seconds away from freedom when our door knob came off in her hand.

'Fuck me dead!' shouted Sofia, holding her head in frustration.

I didn't know if it was on account of Patrick, who was supposed to have fixed the loose knob weeks ago, or the thought of being trapped in a room with the quivering Valmai, but Sofia did not hide her despair.

Clutching the knob in her paw, Valmai searched the doorframe, furtively sniffing like a bewildered hamster stuck in a maze with trick exits.

'Get Cockroach, Raelene!' ordered Sofia, who could no longer look at the door, or anyone near it.

Cockroach? Since when did we have a caretaker called Cockroach?

'He's up the Cross, picking up Heather,' protested Raelene.

'Does Patrick know you call him *Cockroach?*' I asked Sofia, a little indignantly on his behalf.

'Cockroach is the new driver, darling,' Sofia snapped. 'Trudy's frien'.'

'Where's Patrick?' I asked, trying not to sound horribly alarmed.

'Holland!' Sofia shouted at me, like I'd missed the meeting.

Some time between Sunday morning, when he'd dropped me off with a cheerful wave, and Friday night, Patrick had apparently gone to Holland. To be with Dutch people. Without saying goodbye. I wanted to crack his skull with a wooden clog.

'How long's he gone for?' I asked.

'Look!' stormed Sofia, who was more concerned with knobs and dwarfs. 'We have a driver! And Cockroach will drive you home, if that's what you worried about!'

Well it wasn't, but now that she mentioned it, I didn't particularly want a man called Cockroach to see where I lived. I wanted Patrick, with his cheerful banter and happy pipes. I wanted to hear Patrick's mellifluous voice on the phone, and to feel hopeful that the long, thin figure bobbing its way up the stairs would materialise into the smiling, carefree Patrick, laughing in our doorway for no reason at all. Not *Cockroach*!

Unable to bear the tension a minute longer, Raelene moved towards the door with ferocious intent, nearly knocking the bleached wretch sideways as she snatched from her hand the rebellious knob and thrust it into its slot. After a few violent rotations the knob finally complied, and at the first sign of light, Valmai scurried out of the room like a sprayed insect.

The only communication I had with the monosyllabic Cockroach for the next few hours did not exactly endear him to me, especially when he kept confusing Coral with Candice and Courtenay with Cindy. And even when I snapped at him for going to the wrong hotel, the response was the same.

'Yeah, right,' he would grunt like a Neanderthal.

I waited for Sofia to tend to Valmai, whose raucous shouting and cackling with the girls downstairs had reached a dangerous new high, before asking Raelene about Cockroach.

'He's a good bloke,' Raelene said through a mouthful of almond nougat. 'He lives above Trude. Helped her boyfriend get off smack. He's a drug and alcohol rehabilitation counsellor.'

'Wow,' I said, feeling a little contrite.

'He just got out,' Raelene added, throwing her wrapper in the bin.

I was still nodding. 'Of ... gaol?' I asked Raelene timidly.

We both waited patiently for her to finish masticating. I wished she didn't put her nougat in the fridge.

'Armed robbery and assault,' Raelene said finally. 'But, you know,' she shrugged, 'he was a junkie. He did his time, straightened himself out, and now he helps other people.'

Raelene felt very strongly that society owed Cockroach a second chance and she, for one, was not going to hold his past against him. And if the girls had a problem with his shagpile-lined panel van, they could all catch taxis.

'Isn't he driving the company Merc?' I asked.

'Are you kidding?' Raelene cried. 'You think Boris is gonna give some guy who held up a 7-Eleven the keys to a Mercedes Benz?'

Leanne was back on the line and, by the sound of things, not in a good way.

'Well that's silly, Leanne,' Raelene chided her. 'What good will you be to anyone dead?'

I had an idea. Perhaps we should get Cockroach, with all his counselling skills, to talk to Leanne. Raelene gave my brilliant idea the thumbs-up.

'What you smiling at?' Sofia accused me, stomping back to her desk and forcing her chair into submission.

I couldn't tell Sofia the truth, but I felt exhilarated. The only other time I could remember being in the midst of such drama and surrounded by so many colourful characters, I was doing a really bad television show in Melbourne. But this was for real.

If I had seen the tattoos, I would never have snapped at him. Cockroach was a powerful, stocky, thickset chap with broad, weightlifter's shoulders and a barrel chest. His thin red hair was gelled back from a receding hairline and his goatee and sideburns had been pruned immaculately. Under his heavy brow, Cockroach's beady blue eyes flicked up at my face then quickly down my body when I walked into the kitchen.

'Yeah, right,' he grunted expressionlessly when I introduced myself, and continued rolling himself a cigarette. 'Sorry if I gave you grief about all the Carols and the Carrots and the Cantaloupes.'

'Oh,' I laughed, perhaps a little too much, 'good grief.'

I had never met someone who'd held up a 7-Eleven before, and I hadn't said 'good grief' since I was about eight, but Cockroach gave me a cheeky wink as he licked his rollie paper. Fascinated, I watched the stranger glance nervously at the various cleavages and bottoms moving about him in our kitchen. I could hear Valmai's unmistakable wheeze complaining to some sympathetic ear in the laundry about being spoken to like a child. Cockroach asked me how long I had worked here, and as I answered him, he seemed to stagger backwards slightly as he blew out a thick jet of smoke. Mine was a short answer, but Cockroach's considered nod lasted for some time. Perhaps he was just very tired, I told myself.

'So, I'll be driving you home,' Cockroach said with a twinkle in his beady bloodshot eye. He staggered forward to collect his tobacco from the table.

'Yes,' I smiled, no longer convinced that Cockroach was tired, or even just a little uncoordinated.

'Well, go down and see for yourself, Raelene,' I whispered to my incredulous colleague upstairs.

'Oh, he is not!' she hissed back at me. 'He's a drug and alcohol rehabilitation counsellor, for God's sake! Ask Trudy.'

'He's not pissed', darling,' Sofia said, turning to me with calm authority. 'You can't drive in all that city traffic pissed'. An' if he was, one of the girls would have noticed.'

Well, maybe I was mistaken, but whatever Cockroach had eaten recently, I wanted a bar. On her way downstairs to give Kimberley a booking, Raelene announced peevishly that Cockroach's counselling services were no longer required anyway. Having forgotten why she rang us at all, Leanne was now weeping over a sad film about a Scottish dog.

At last it was quiet. I looked at Sofia, who sat very still, her face in her hands. She looked so tired sometimes. On weeknights she might stop at the casino on the way home from work, but weekends were for her little girl, Monique, and I suspect Sofia went without any sleep at all. Sometimes I caught her in such sad repose, I felt sure she was wondering where the last forty-six years of her life had gone.

'Why is Patrick in Holland?' I asked, sensing a rare state of surrender.

'I'm not sure, darling,' Sofia sighed. 'I think he has a brother or a sister there.'

'Will he be gone long?' I asked.

'Four weeks,' she said quietly.

I felt as light as a feather. Patrick had not gone for good. I did not even have to think about what his presence must have meant to me in this house. Patrick would be back, and I could worry about it then.

'He's a dear man,' Sofia smiled, looking through the wall beyond me, 'but such a flake.'

Raelene returned from downstairs with a somewhat perturbed expression, and shut the door very slowly behind her.

'What's wrong?' I asked.

Raelene looked confused for a moment, and finally turned to face Sofia. 'I think Cockroach is pissed.'

This time, Sofia was going down to see for herself.

Even though our call had woken her up, Trudy had such a good laugh. Of course Cockroach wasn't drunk, she hooted. Didn't we know? Cockroach was a professional drug and alcohol rehabilitation counsellor! He didn't touch alcohol or drugs. Except occasionally marijuana. Cockroach might be stoned. Did he seem stoned? Yeah well, that was it then.

'He's a really good counsellor, Meredith,' Trudy assured me, sounding terribly serious. 'I shouldn't tell you this, but I asked him to help with one of our new girls. Don't ask me who, but I happen to know she goes on *benders* from time to time, and thanks to Cockroach, she's really making progress.'

'It's not Leanne, is it?' I asked Trudy.

Silence.

But I had to leave it there. Judging by Sofia's booming voice rising from the kitchen, World War III had broken out downstairs.

'Sorry, Trude, gotta go!'

Not for the first time, Raelene and I huddled together on the landing, eavesdropping on the commotion below. Apparently, Valmai had served the complimentary champagne to Letitia and her client in coffee mugs instead of the good crystal. If I had to spend one hour in a room with Letitia, I'd grab the bottle by its neck and skol. But with two chipped orange handles, Valmai had turned our classy boudoir into a cheap tavern. If reprimanded in private, Valmai would have eaten humble pie, but to be so publicly criticised in front of the girls, *her* girls, this old vaudevillian trooper could not bear the humiliation. When we heard her angry hoofs at the bottom of the stairs, Raelene and I nearly flattened each other in our mad scramble to return to our posts. Within seconds, Valmai was behind us, puffing and packing her bag as she muttered about injustice, persecution and a general lack of respect in the workplace. Raelene and I respectfully swivelled around to face her, just as Valmai croaked her final, stoic farewell.

'I'm a human being, Boris!' she yelped.

Raelene and I swivelled back to see the small, foreboding figure in our doorway, holding his briefcase.

'Not a child,' Valmai concluded her somewhat illogical argument.

Boris looked surprised for a moment, but as he fervently followed her signs of vacating, he could hardly suppress his joy. Without having said a thing, Boris had finally won his battle. And if Didi didn't believe him, he had witnesses. A cloud of perfume and cigarettes engulfed us as Valmai dramatically swung her tartan cloak around her shoulders, picked up her bag and, with one last cough, departed.

I was even sitting on it. Shagpile. Was there anything in Cockroach's panel van not covered in thick yellow carpet? So many skulls, feathers and crucifixes bounced and bungied from his rear vision mirror, I could barely see the road when we hit a bump.

'The thing about going out with a trannie,' Cockroach continued, with dangerous attempts to make eye contact with me, 'is that they know how to handle the tackle, if ya know what I mean.'

'Yeah,' I nodded, looking straight ahead.

'Serious!' Cockroach insisted. 'They do! Course they do. They've been there, mate, before they had the snip and tuck, if ya know what I mean.' He chortled.

'Yeah.' I laughed feebly.

'Look, mate,' Cockroach continued, 'I've never been even

remotely interested in other blokes. Not even inside. I fuckin' could have,' he testified earnestly. 'Could have, mate.'

Cockroach was looking at me again, so I nodded back.

'Plenty did. But not me. I just didn't wanna go there.'

Cockroach and I sat in contemplative silence, waiting for the lights to change.

'And are you still with the trannie, Cockroach?' I asked him.

'Nah, mate,' Cockroach said quietly, gazing somewhere beyond the lights, now green. 'Nah. We broke up last year.'

The following night Valmai rang to say she was stuck in traffic and was therefore running a bit late. Pip reminded Valmai that as she had resigned, punctuality was no longer a problem.

Isn't it warm in here!

'And did you miss us, Patrick?' I quizzed the tall, tanned, laughing man leaning in our doorway.

Without taking my eyes off him, I gracefully swung open the other set of French windows, as if welcoming spring itself, even though it was still August.

'I might have,' Patrick sang, with a cheeky smile.

Surely I wasn't the only one to notice that Patrick looked particularly handsome since his return from Holland. I studied his rugged face for some time, searching for the cause of this pleasing transformation, and wished that Trudy was on duty. Trudy had always insisted, especially in my presence, that it was a miracle a man like Patrick was still available at all. Trudy would have gladly discussed Patrick's new haircut with me, but instead I was stuck with Raelene, who'd never liked Patrick since she'd paid him fifty dollars to fix a wonky door in her flat. Although the door no longer jammed, it now opened from the wrong side, completely disrupting Raelene's feng shui.

'Shouldn't you be picking up Abigail in Marrickville?' she asked him, disgusted by our merry reunion.

Smiling graciously at Raelene, Patrick excused himself, winked at me, and left the room.

It was midnight and Anand, in Room 24 at City Central Motel, wanted an Indian girl. We only had one.

'Shanti, ring me back.'

It was a company rule that all working girls with mobile phones had to ring us back for booking details, to keep office phone bills to a minimum.

'Is he Indian or Fijian?' Shanti asked warily.

'How would I know, Shanti?'

'Did he sound like an Indian with an Indian accent, or an Indian with a British accent?'

'Hang on, Shanti.' I was not in the mood for this. I rang Anand on the other line. 'Anand, are you Indian or Fijian? The lady won't have sex with you if you're Indian. Or maybe if you're Fijian. I've forgotten. Would you know, Anand? Who sleeps with who over there?'

Anand said it didn't matter as he was Sri Lankan.

Now we could all get some sleep.

'Shanti, he's Sri Lankan.'

'Is he?'

'Yes.'

'Are you sure?'

'Oh, come on. Do you think I can't tell the difference between a Fijian, an Indian and a Sri Lankan over the phone?'

A pause.

'Okay. Where is he?'

I gave her the details. As the motel's reception was closed, Shanti had to meet Anand downstairs at twelve-thirty, so he could let her in.

Half an hour later Shanti rang me back, breathless. She knew this motel. She was even living there herself until three months ago. Was this true? Raelene nodded with a mouth full of Violet Crumble.

'And it took you half an hour to remember this, Shanti?'

Shanti had been on the phone to Cliff, the doorman at City Central Motel. Cliff said the man who had been in Room 24 checked out this morning. There was no one in Room 24!

'This is very suspicious,' she warned portentously.

'Dangerous,' I added.

Shanti gave me Cliff's number, in case I wanted to ask him myself. Thanks, I said, taking it down, breathless too now at the thought of parts of Shanti being found in various rubbish bags near Central Station. Oh, these girls! The risks they took! I wanted to clutch them all to my breast – though not in a lesbian double kind of way – and keep them indoors watching videos with cups of tea. I wanted to tell Raelene and Sofia, but they were both busy with Asian bookings. Some nights everybody wanted Asian. While I waited, I contemplated Anand and his sinister scheme to lure a young Indian girl to a dark motel where he wasn't staying. I needed advice.

'Su Ling's out,' called Raelene, hanging up.

'No, darling!' Sofia shouted back. 'Su Ling just extended with Gordon in Balmain.'

I couldn't wait for them to finish criticising each other's poor communication skills, so I rang Cliff. Nothing. No sound. No connection whatsoever. Cliffhanger.

'I know you're Sachiko, Sachiko!' Raelene was shouting. 'But for next hour, your name Su Ling!'

'Something a bit funny's going on, Raelene,' I jumped in before her phone rang again. 'To do with Shanti's booking at City Central Motel, a Sri Lankan called Anand, and a guy called Cliff.'

Of course Shanti must not go I was saying as Raelene, nonplussed, punched some numbers on her phone.

'Shanti,' she barked. 'Call me back.'

A little aggressive, I thought, all things considered, especially the rubbish bags.

Shanti rang back.

'Shanti,' began Raelene, 'we got you a booking. You get to that booking right now, please, if you're not there already. And Shanti, if you do not go to that booking, we will be charging you for it ourselves. Thank you.'

Raelene hung up and continued her work. At times I truly admired Raelene. 'Don't shit with me,' she'd often say. And one didn't, if one could possibly help it. Raelene had a big heart, but she was tough. She reminded me of my favourite baby-sitter.

Raelene knew I was looking at her. Without looking up she answered my query: 'I'll let Sofia tell you about Shanti.'

There was Sofia behind us, doing Spanish tangos, puffing on her Winfields and smacking her forehead at everybody's incompetence. 'What about Shanti, darling?'

I told Sofia the story so far. Both women rolled their eyes, and Sofia filled me in on Shanti, a lying, conniving snake who would pretend not to go to a booking on any excuse, then go, take all the money and keep the client forever, thus shafting the agency.

'A booking junkie, darling,' Sofia cried dramatically.

But she had been so convincing! 'Oh, Shanti, you must not go,' I'd cried down her mobile, possibly while she was arriving at Anand's door. I had been such a pushover. As if a receptionless motel near Central Station could afford a doorman called Cliff!

An hour or so later, Shanti finally rang to say she had the cash and was starting.

'Thank you,' I said, fantasising about sending her to some guy in Blacktown who was expecting a blonde.

Then we forgot about her till she rang again to say she'd finished and was ready to be picked up. Now. Shanti was standing outside on the street. I told her Patrick was on his way, and he was bringing her straight to us with our money, thank you very much. Shanti chose this moment to inform me she had traveller's cheques. What?

'Raelene, she's got traveller's cheques.'

'You don't tell us this at the end of the booking!' shouted Raelene.

'Shanti, you don't tell us this at the end of the booking!' I berated her down the phone.

Raelene said to tell her she'd better have his passport details on the back, or they were useless.

'Or they're completely useless, Shanti!' I echoed.

Now the Indian was getting narky with me. 'But it's too late!' she whined. 'I'm locked out on the street. I can't get back to Anand now. You should have told me this before!'

Liar or not, it seemed Shanti was now standing on a seedy street near Central Station clutching two utterly useless traveller's cheques. Until Raelene again took over from me. Sucked in once more.

'Shanti, tell Anand you won't leave till he's given you his passport number, or paid with cash or credit card. Don't waste my time. Get it and call Meredith back.'

How did Raelene know Shanti wasn't locked outside, freezing near a dumpster? How did she know she was still inside? I was so tired of feeling incompetent. Now I was angry. I sat and watched my phone like a cat ready to tear the stuffing out of a small Indian rodent. It rang for one millisecond and I nearly knocked myself out.

'Yes, Shanti!'

Oh, she was cunning. Anand had no passport, so we would just have to take down his details.

'Bullshit!' I shouted. 'If he's got traveller's cheques, he's got a passport, Shanti. I want the full name, and his passport number.'

'And the expiry date,' mumbled Raelene through a Fantale.

'And the expiry date, Shanti.'

I could hear the muffled mutterings of Shanti and her co-conspirator.

No, she said finally, Anand didn't have a passport, but it was okay. She was going to get some other ID off him. I went for the neck.

'No! You're not listening to me, are you, Shanti? If the Sri Lankan wants to pay with traveller's cheques without giving his passport number, you've just been fucked for bugger-all and you owe us ninety dollars. Do you understand me, Shanti?'

If I could just find this side of myself on a more regular basis, life would be so much easier. Raelene was laughing now. I think she was proud of me. And suddenly Shanti had Anand's credit card, she had cash, or the traveller's cheques. Which would we prefer?

'Cash, silly,' Raelene smiled.

'For Boris, you idiot,' Sofia added.

'That'll be cash, thanks, Shanti.'

It wasn't until Shanti was back home in bed that I realised she'd probably spent two hours or more at City Central Motel with Anand, pocketing the extra hour for herself, not to mention giving him her private number for future bookings. No matter how much Sofia slaved over her hot desk, doing cartwheels and backflips to secure a regular clientele for the girls, many of them undermined her efforts privately, with better offers. And although I despised Shanti's elaborate, convoluted deceit, I could not entirely blame the girls for occasionally ripping us off. Not when we woke them up to go to bookings at four in the morning. Not when we demanded to know their menstrual cycles. And not when we fined them so relentlessly.

'We are all a team, darling,' Sofia shouted at me. 'What is good for the girl is good for you and me. We all make money together, darling.'

But not with our bodies, Sofia, yours and mine.

'Ah, Holland,' Boris nodded nostalgically with a hand on his beloved driver's shoulder.

Yes, Patrick nodded in his good-natured way, Holland.

And as Boris looked at me, I nodded too, even though I had never been to Holland.

A wistful pause became an uncomfortable pause as Boris looked from his driver to his receptionist, scrutinising our faces.

'You two are like brother and sister, aren't you?' he said at last.

Embarrassed by this sudden revelation, Patrick and I laughed nervously.

'Yeah,' Boris continued, 'with your funny British accents, floppy faces and crooked English teeth, you two could be tvins!'

A sudden gust of wind slammed my French windows shut. Spring was nowhere near and, thanks to Boris, it would take four shifts for Patrick and I to recover any remnant of intrigue whatsoever.

A mature, busty blonde . . . with a walking frame

As a rule, Patrick was not meant to pick up girls from their homes and bring them in to work. Like keeping herself in condoms and lube for escort bookings, getting herself to work was a girl's responsibility. Most of them caught taxis, some were dropped off by their husbands or boyfriends, but no matter how poor, no girl ever used public transport. For similar reasons, they preferred not to meet clients in public places. Apart from the fact that it could result in an arrest for soliciting, no girl enjoyed the prospect of being scrutinised by leering men outside our waiting room. We rang for so many taxis we had our own pin number, and due to the high number of beautiful women coming and going from this one terraced house in Darlinghurst, the taxi company was in no doubt as to the nature of our business.

'Pin number?'

'Four, nine, six, one.'

'Oh.' Pause. 'And what's the lady's name?'

'Pandora.'

Snigger. 'Pandora?'

'Yes. As in Box.'

Pause.

'And where's *Pandora* going?'

Further than you or I, darling, answering phones at twelve dollars fifty an hour.

On the nights Patrick wasn't working, I had to order myself a cab home. The taxi driver's gaze, so hopeful when I opened his door, always faded to disappointment as my tracksuit pants climbed into his back seat.

'Busy night?' he'd ask doubtfully, scrutinising my reflection in the rear vision mirror.

'I'm the receptionist,' I'd explain, putting him out of his misery.

Until the night I got a Rastafarian driver.

'You too?' he chuckled with amusement as we drove off.

Apparently, all our working girls told the taxi drivers they were 'receptionists'.

'But it's all right,' he continued chuckling when he pulled up outside my house, 'in your case, I believe you.'

The smile froze on my face as I stood, gutted, in my driveway. I never thought I'd feel so hurt, so wounded, that I could not pass for a prostitute.

Antoinette could not drive, which was just as well considering the trouble she had reading out credit card numbers, so she caught cabs everywhere. But no matter how many lesbian doubles she'd had the night before, the money had all but disappeared come the following sunset, and she could not even afford a cab to work. Lately she had developed a worrying habit of ringing us at seven o'clock, all breathy sweetness, to ask if we could possibly spare Patrick to come and pick her up from her flat in Mosman. Although strictly against the rules, if Patrick was free he would bound out the door with unconditional joy. Maybe it had something to do with the half-smoked joint in his shirt pocket, but I preferred to think it was Patrick's generous, benevolent nature.

Although Antoinette was constantly broke and behind in her rent, and regularly depended on me to sneak her condoms and lube from our in-house supply, I noticed there was nary a dark root to be seen on her thick crown of expensively coiffed golden hair. Somehow she always found money for North Sydney beauty parlours. But shit hit the fan when Boris discovered we were lending this aging blonde conundrum his driver. It was easy to dismiss Antoinette as a nutter, if one felt at all threatened by the presence of a higher intelligence. And no one found Antoinette more threatening than Boris himself. He also found her profoundly unattractive, and her success with clients positively baffling. With every 'extended booking' or personal request for her services, Boris shook his head with disgust.

'Focking necrophiliacs.'

Sofia, on the other hand, had no problem understanding Antoinette's appeal, and tolerated her mood swings, having talked the troubled soul down from various ceilings over the years. And I was overwhelmed with relief when I learnt that suspicious Sofia had never for a moment believed Marilyn's story that Antoinette did not use condoms.

'Well, you should know, darling.' Sofia looked up at me from under her heavy eyelids. 'You the one who keeps stealing condoms for her, from our office supply.'

How did she know?

But Sofia never cared to examine any girl too closely. During one of Antoinette's more audible kitchen hissy fits about no money and no bookings, Sofia paused mid credit card transaction, looked at me and sighed. 'Darling, there's nothing worse than an ole prostitute.'

And so, Boris forbade us from ever letting Patrick pick up Antoinette again.

'You know why she has no money for taxis?' he shouted at me. ''Cause she spends it all on the pokies.'

Boris claimed he had often seen Antoinette at six or seven in the morning at his home away from home, Star City casino, perched on a stool, chain-smoking as she desperately fed coin after coin of her hard-earned money into a hungry machine.

'The stupid bitch!'

For a few weeks Antoinette somehow managed to get herself in by seven each night. Boris had his own ideas about how she paid for the taxi, but then Boris would. However she was paying, Antoinette couldn't keep it up, so to speak, and the phone calls were back, now begging us to release Patrick for 'this one last favour'. Patrick hovered in the doorway like a half-stoned monk. As receptionists, we felt like young parents, tortured with guilt about having to teach the baby it will not always be picked up when it cries. But nor should it then resort to alcohol, and spiral into a severe depression.

It all came to a peak one night when a dull thud shook the house. Three nervous receptionists and one stoned driver all looked at the spectre on the monitor. As she charged into frame for her second attempt, we watched our elegant, classy blonde hurling her petite frame against the front door like a thing possessed. Why Antoinette chose to ignore the door bell is still a mystery to this day. Instead, she pressed her face against the intercom and growled for someone to come down immediately and pay the driver. Clutching a twenty dollar note, I ran down to find a pale, frightened man in a cardigan, twitching at a safe distance on the footpath. From that night on, we released Patrick.

It was a Friday night and, due to the howling arctic winds outside, every heater was on high, helping to circulate Maya's cold throughout the entire house.

'You want Patrick to pick you up from *where*?' Leonie cried incredulously down the phone.

Leonie had only been with us a few weeks. A twenty-one-year-old galumphing space cadet in pigtails, Leonie took a ghoulish, adolescent delight in her first-hand experience of the sex industry. Already she had alienated the girls downstairs by circling them with grim fascination, as if they were so many well-dressed cattle with foot and mouth disease. Sensitive to disapproval at the best of times, the girls found being scrutinised by this gawky mass of unsophisticated puppy-fat tiresome to say the least. With her bulky frame often tightly clad in thrift shop retro, and her pale face almost gouged with two Picasso eyebrows and a pair of red lips, Leonie had no right to scrutinise anyone.

'Are we allowed to send Patrick to pick Antoinette up?' she asked.

Yes, I groaned. It was the seventh question in as many minutes.

'She's really old, hey,' Leonie stated with artless candour as she punched in Patrick's speed dial.

'She's *mature*!' Raelene roared. 'And *classy*!'

'Provides an excellent service,' I chimed in.

Leonie goggled from one angry receptionist to the other. She looked startled, but not at all convinced.

'Patrick,' she began cautiously over the phone, 'Antoinette wants you to pick her up at her new address. You gotta pen?'

It was not unusual, I had noticed, for our girls to move house. Perhaps because of their nocturnal activities, domestic harmony proved elusive, and many were asked to find other accommodation. And the girls' phone numbers changed as constantly as the cutlery disappeared from our kitchen drawers downstairs. Boris got so fed up replacing it, he once let them fend for themselves with nothing but a single fork for a whole week.

'Patrick, it's a large building at the bottom of Winkle Crescent in Riverview,' Leonie continued, 'number thirty-two. Hey, and don't beep the horn. She said it's a retirement village.'

No one moved. Even the cockroaches paused.

'That's what she said, Patrick!' Leonie insisted.

One of our more *mature* ladies wanted to be picked up from a retirement village, but neither Raelene nor I was going to so much as glance in each other's direction in front of our new and stupid charge.

'Patrick,' Leonie giggled, 'stop laughing!'

Patrick's apparent mirth may not have posed a serious threat to Raelene's composure, but I was close to cracking. Sheepishly Leonie turned towards me and held out her phone so that I could hear what sounded like a grown man crying. Much to Raelene's disgust, I lost it.

I was on the phone upstairs when Patrick returned with Antoinette before ferrying her straightaway to a booking at the Menzies.

And I thought I had heard them all. 'Girl must have two feeh!' Mr Kurasaki at the Furama barked at me.

'Girl must have *two feet*, Mr Kurasaki?' I repeated calmly, just to be sure.

'TWO FEEH!' he barked again.

For the second time in an hour, Leonie was beside herself.

'Yes, Mr Kurasaki,' I humoured him, 'they do tend to have the better balance, don't they? Although no one quite *hops into bed* like our Janelle . . .'

Raelene commanded Leonie to get a grip while shooting me a warning look. But it got worse. Mr Kurasaki's girl with two feet should also have two toes.

'One toe per foot, Mr Kurasaki?' I enquired calmly, 'or two on each?'

By now I was wondering if this wasn't another of my housemate Peter's practical jokes. The previous week an angry Hamish MacTavish had rung and, despite an outrageous Scottish accent, had us all madly searching our booking sheets for a 'wee, plump Dutch lassie' he'd ordered hours ago. Again 'resting' between various mini-series, Peter had a lot of time on his hands. I apologised to Mr Kurasaki before hanging up and wished him good luck with his feet.

Finally, after two one-hour extensions, Antoinette returned from her booking at the Menzies, and I could tell by the tone of her calm voice over the front door intercom that it had been a good one. With an insatiable urge to talk to a forty-four-year-old prostitute now living in a retirement village, I ran downstairs.

I had barely grabbed her money and sat down with Antoinette and two cups of disgustingly weak tea (due to my impatience) when Patrick arrived. Patrick always entered a room with a look of 'Really? I had no idea!', and tonight was no exception. After he'd made his cup of tea, he gingerly joined us at the table. Antoinette knew very well her new accommodation had aroused great curiosity, and she smiled coyly as she withdrew a packet of cigarettes from her handbag and placed them on the table in front of her. Patrick and I sat staring at the table, smiling in anticipation. A few hours ago, this would have been impossible, but such was the wonderful and unpredictable madness of Antoinette.

I felt happy, because the three of us had proved a winning combination on previous occasions, perhaps because each of us was a quiet observer in his or her own way. Even Urszula left us alone. Although Antoinette was usually happy to sit by the back door and let Urszula rule the kitchen, it was not out of deference, and Urszula knew it. She also knew not to seek any confrontation with the articulate and volatile blonde. As the two eldest women on our books, there was a silent stand-off between them. No doubt neither of them imagined she'd still be sitting in a brothel in her mid forties, and possibly didn't appreciate the weary reflection of the other she caught through the kitchen traffic on a busy night.

'I've been kicked out of my flat,' Antoinette smiled at last.

'Oh dear!' I protested.

'Dear oh dear!' added Patrick, gilding the lily.

'And I've moved into my mother's retirement village at Riverview.'

'Ah!' I said.

'Oh!' said Patrick. And after a pause: 'With your mother?'

'And fifty other octogenarians,' she said, 'yes.'

Antoinette's broad smile gave us permission to laugh.

'Do you get on with your mother?' I asked.

'No!' Antoinette smiled, signalling yet another catastrophe in her life. 'She doesn't approve of me.'

Patrick and I nodded to cover a multitude of questions.

'Of . . . what you do?' I finally asked.

'Oh, she doesn't know,' Antoinette said. 'It would kill her!' And with that she released a deep, guttural laugh, suggesting that hers, perhaps, had not been a happy childhood. 'She thinks I'm a secretary.'

I wondered what kind of secretary Antoinette's mother believed worked till five in the morning with that much cleavage.

'We're completely different,' she mused, 'yet, you know, both of us feel utterly repulsed by the inevitable similarities.'

Patrick lit her cigarette.

'She's Irish,' Antoinette added, and Patrick nodded, as if that explained something.

I would never know what because at that point Raelene's angry voice broke into our congenial atmosphere ordering me to return upstairs. Mr Kurasaki had called again, and wanted to speak to me.

Back at my post I listened carefully and repeated out loud the same baffling request for a girl with two feet and two toes. Although Leonie, now in foetal position on the floor, found my foot dilemma terribly amusing, Raelene did not. She sat huffing with a mouth full of Rocky Road until she could bear it no more.

'Hand it over!' she demanded, nearly broadsiding me with the same plump arm that had flattened various sisters-in-law.

I had cringed before at Raelene's habit of shouting at foreigners, as if their bad English was a deliberate ploy to piss her off, but I had no choice but to surrender my client.

'*You want what?*' she roared down my phone at him. '*Well, that cost you extra!*'

Leonie and I looked at each other. Perhaps Raelene knew a girl who knew a girl . . .

'Here.' Raelene thrust the phone back at me. '*Tattooed* feet, you fucking idiot! He wants *tattooed* feet, and *tattooed* toes.' And with that she grumpily returned to her confectionery and *New Idea*, mumbling flat-vowelled profanities about a general lack of competence in the workplace.

When a meeker, more compliant Mr Kurasaki said he didn't care how much extra it cost, I knew straightaway what Sofia would do. Sofia would charge Mr Kurasaki seven hundred dollars for the hour, and throw the nearest barefoot girl into a corner with a ballpoint pen. So having agreed on seven hundred and ninety-five for the hour, including ten per cent credit card fee plus taxi, I madly phoned any girl with tattoos ticked on the back of her card. And as luck would have it, one of my favourite girls had just finished at Quay Grand, with surprising good news on the foot front.

'Darling, you're not going to believe this,' Lucinda fluted, 'but I have butterflies on my ankles and little flowers on all my Terry-toes!'

Lucinda was a vivacious, tall, laughing, jolly–hockey-sticks English girl who had all the cheer and bounce of a Jane Austen heroine. And just like a Jane Austen heroine, Lucinda worked strictly escort-only. If Hugh Grant was in town, I'd have sent him Lucinda. Or perhaps Delilah.

'But, Meredith, darling, I have the biggest bunions the dear man's ever seen. Dancer's feet, darling. If he can get past the bunions, literally, he can party with my tootsies to his heart's delight.'

Lucinda and I consoled each other on the ugly legacy of feet forced into ballet pointes too early. Many times I have begged my GP, any GP, to fix my unsightly hoofs.

'It's a terribly painful operation, Miss Eastman. First, they break the foot, saw off the offending bunion, and then reset it. Would you like me to refer you to an orthopaedic surgeon?'

And end up like Flaubert's hapless club-foot at the mercy of some butcher called Bovary? Poor man never skipped again. I bounded downstairs like a ballerina.

'So, how old is your mum?' I asked Antoinette before my bum hit the seat.

'Eighty-six,' she said. 'She's a sturdy thing. Wilful. My poor father didn't stand a chance.' Antoinette chuckled to herself. 'She even told him when to die.'

Patrick and I looked at her.

'It's true!' she insisted. 'One day she just said to him, "Harold, I can't look after you any more. It'd be better for us both if you'd just die." So he did.' Antoinette smiled. 'He was obedient like that.'

We weren't sure whether to laugh or not.

'But when all the quotes came in for the funeral,' Antoinette continued, 'my mother was so appalled, she probably wished he hadn't. So she decided on the cheapest of absolutely everything.'

'The plain pine coffin?' Patrick asked merrily.

Antoinette nodded. 'She'd say to people, shamelessly, "It's what he would have wanted." And yet there she was decked out in the most expensive new dress and hat, stepping out of a limo, but again, "It's what he would have wanted." '

This job was so much better than nannying.

'But she was quite upstaged by him in the end,' Antoinette said and smiled. 'My father was a florist, and everyone sent the most extraordinary wreaths and bouquets until the church almost exploded with elaborate flower arrangements.'

'How did your mother react?' I asked.

'Oh, she was disgusted. Found the whole thing excessive and vulgar.'

I could have sat there all night listening to Antoinette fill in the funny and tragic details of her background, but I was once again called upstairs to confirm Lucinda's happy arrival at the Furama, with tattoos and two harmless bunions for seven hundred dollars an hour.

It came as no surprise that Antoinette had been brought up by a malleable florist and his disapproving wife, who spared no expense on their daughter's education. But I could not stop wondering all night what unhappy chain of events had led this bright young girl from the North Shore to end up a struggling prostitute at forty-four, now living in a retirement village with her disgruntled mother.

'You're an actress?' Antoinette said to me late one night, having seen me in an ad on telly.

'Yes,' I answered.

'Do you know X?' she asked, of a well-known television actress.

'Yes!' I said. 'Yes, I worked with her once. Why? Do you know her?'

'You could say that,' Antoinette smiled. 'She was my brides-maid.'

The unhappiness of the high-class escort

'What's the difference?' asked Cyril.

So I told Cyril that the difference between a two hundred and eighty, three hundred and fifty and a five hundred dollar girl was that some were 'university students', others were 'lingerie models' and the more expensive were 'part-time models'. This was the spiel, if a man rang on the Cachet or Exclusive lines.

'Yes,' Cyril said, 'that's what they do, I understand that, but if I'm paying for their sexual services, what is the difference between these women?'

I was tempted to tell Cyril that some were simply a better root. I could hardly tell him the truth, which was that we sent pretty much the same girls to all these bookings, whether it was two hundred dollars an hour or seven hundred. Obviously we sent the most beautiful girl available to the more expensive booking, but there had been nights when the only Cachet Australian blonde available to send to Mr Yakimoto at the Wentworth was Shawna. Shawna who walked and talked like a truckie in high heels. Shawna who loved Rochelle, and cuddled her protectively on the couch downstairs.

Usually we sent Genevieve, Lucinda, Pandora or Kimberley, and maybe three or four others that we could comfortably send out at these high prices and still sleep at night. Lucinda was thirty but could pass for twenty-five, and she was a pleasure to describe over the phone as a five-foot-eight, leggy, strawberry-blonde, very busty but slim, with measurements 37D–28–35.

Kimberley was an immaculately groomed and incredibly slim brunette with green eyes who Blue Angels must have been sorry to lose. As with any defecting Blue Angels, when Kimberley came to play on our team Boris gyrated about the office and sang Dean Martin songs all night long. Although she had an unfortunately nasal monotone voice, Kimberley could smile, walk and chat with flawless poise in very high heels, and was so David Jones you could almost shop in her. Kimberley always looked as if she was about to spray something on your wrist or ask you to return your seat to its upright position. None of us knew what on earth it was Kimberley did with her clients, but they always, without fail, requested another hour when the first one was up, and at Kimberley's rate of two hundred dollars for the extra hour, not ours of a hundred and fifty. We let her do it as she'd been honest enough to tell us in the first place, and her clients certainly never objected. With respect and admiration, we liked to refer to Kimberley as 'the machine'.

In a business in which the most popular request was for tall, slim, busty blondes, Genevieve was in high demand, whatever price she commanded, and this created multiple problems for her, making her very tired for one. Tonight Genevieve stood with her arms crossed over her ample bosom and gazed into the middle of the kitchen floor looking miserable as Urszula whispered some words of encouragement in her ear. Even though she made more money than anyone else, it seemed that struggling girls were always whispering words of support, and caressing this sad, tanned princess, who now barely registered my presence as I stood at her side, holding her booking details.

Apparently, when she wasn't working nights or surfing on the northern beaches, Genevieve was studying. What, I had no idea. Nothing funny, that's for sure. Since our last meeting, when Boris had reprimanded her for not answering her phone, I had avoided Genevieve, because I didn't want to upset her with yet another booking. Although most girls would have celebrated such financial success and popularity, it was obvious that Genevieve found it nothing but a burden. It saddened me to see how unhappy she was, but I found it difficult to sympathise with someone who turned up her nose at a standard booking in front of girls who had not worked in days, girls who cleaned toilets, and girls who lived in their cars.

Genevieve kept me waiting until the end of Urszula's sermon before turning to me with regal tolerance to accept her booking details. Suppressing the urge to walk backwards out of the room bowing, I reached the door only to hear Genevieve burst into tears. What was the problem? It was a five hundred dollar booking!

'I'm not a fucking robot!' she cried, and collapsed dramatically in Urszula's open arms.

I moved towards Genevieve with a helpless gesture, sending her diving further into Urszula's bosom as though I was about to strike her with my pen. In front of all the girls, Urszula shooed me away as she patted her sobbing charge's naked back. Genevieve was wearing a halterneck cream dress that looked suspiciously like pure silk. Urszula nodded at me to let me know she had the situation under control. But Urszula didn't have the situation under control at all. Cyril at the Ibis had paid five hundred and seventy-five dollars with his American Express card, including surcharge and taxi, and was expecting Genevieve in twenty minutes.

'Well, is she going?' I whispered anxiously to Urszula, 'or should I send someone else?'

You'd think I'd snatched Toto from Dorothy, for all the howling that followed.

'I'll send someone else,' I sighed with defeat, and turned to leave.

'No,' a little voice whimpered from behind me.

And with her trembling chin held high, Genevieve extricated herself from Urszula's protective embrace, sniffed and, with a brave little nod of assent, picked up her handbag and pashmina wrap, and marched towards the door as if she was walking to the block. All the girls who had come out from the lounge looked at Urszula, who nodded authoritatively.

'She'll be all right,' she declared.

And they all returned to their posts. Except Maya, who had not moved from the kitchen table where she silently flicked through her magazine, waiting for her first booking in almost four days.

Much later that night I was folding towels in the laundry when Antoinette, having returned from a booking, came in to use the toilet. She told me with a delightful, girlish smile that Mr Abdullah at the Regis had turned out to be an eighteen-year-old Arabian crown prince.

'I thought you didn't like young boys,' I teased her.

'Oh, you know, if he's a prince . . .'

We laughed, and Antoinette thanked me for the booking but did not want me to leave straightaway.

'Genevieve's actually a lovely person,' Antoinette said quietly. 'She's just unhappy. I don't think the money is doing what she thought it would. And she feels ripped off.'

I trusted Antoinette's knack of unravelling people because, more than anyone I've ever met, she possessed the gift of listening. I'd watch her sitting in her corner by the door, taking in the other girls, their conversation, the way they moved, and no doubt she absorbed her clients' every nuance with the same delicate, sensitive receptors. Antoinette explained that, despite the thousands of dollars and beautiful hotels and clothes and beauticians, Genevieve still felt cheap, and didn't understand why. I understood, but suggested Genevieve take some responsibility for her situation and get another job if she couldn't accept the harsh reality of her profession.

'Well, you never know the parameters of that reality,' Antoinette said softly. 'And one thing to remember with Genevieve, it's not always the guys with the most money who treat you with the most respect. In fact, they're frequently the worst.'

I could forget Antoinette's off-peak madness when she was like this. I now saw that, the more we disliked Genevieve, the more we helped her blame us for the unhappiness she felt.

Later that night I knew Genevieve was sleeping in the lounge room, and thought I'd look in on her before returning upstairs. If she was awake, I might surprise her with my more sensitive perspective, and perhaps even ask how she was. Unseen, I stopped in the doorway and witnessed an unexpected and tender moment in progress. There Genevieve sat, looking sadly at the sleeping Maya next to her. Poor Maya, who'd not had one booking all night, looked utterly exhausted from cleaning hotel rooms all day, and dribbled onto her pillow. I watched in silence as Genevieve gently reached over and put a hand on Maya's shoulder.

'Maya!' she shouted, shaking the sleeping woman awake. 'Wake up, Maya. You're snoring!'

There I was, surrounded by lesbians

Lesbian double: When two women may or may not be required to service the man, but are definitely required to service each other in front of the man.

There had been a lot written in The Bible about lesbian double bookings. Who would do it with whom, and who, under no circumstances whatsoever, would do it with anyone. I was surprised to see a lot of girls would do lesbian bookings with their buddies. I would have thought it would be easier with a stranger, but Marcelle would do them with Trixie; Shawna, of course, would do them with Rochelle; Antoinette had been extremely impressed with Pandora's professionalism; Coral would always do them with Antoinette; Zora would do them only with Genevieve, but under no circumstances whatsoever was Genevieve to be sent on a lesbian booking with Zora. This was in capital letters, highlighted and underlined three times. I felt sorry for Zora. She was a great girl, but quite plain, and her chunky frame looked all wrong in a dress. Zora was our resident B & D mistress. She was Mexican, had big boobs, wore thick-lensed glasses and, all dressed up, looked like an accountant at Halloween.

Looking up from The Bible, I asked the other receptionists if Zora had 'a thing' for Genevieve. Oh yes, Pip told me. Zora had had such a thing the previous year. Genevieve had moved house, and now had an unlisted number.

Had Zora stalked her?

'Yes,' Pip nodded, 'just for a while, after they broke up.'

Genevieve was gay?

'Oh, yeah,' sighed Raelene. 'She and Zora were together for a couple of years.'

Genevieve and Zora had been together?

'Who else is a lesbian?' I asked.

'Zora, Genevieve,' began Raelene, sucking her pen and leaning back in her chair, 'Shawna and Rochelle.'

'Bree,' added Pip.

Bree was a lesbian?

'Kaz, Hester, Celeste,' continued Raelene, nonchalantly.

'Celeste?'

Noel Coward would have loved porcelain, long-necked Celeste. Even her two male flatmates, Giles and Hugo, sounded on the phone as if they were waiting for her on stage somewhere in their smoking jackets.

'A rampant lesbian,' Pip declared fervently, 'and heavily into drugs.'

'Song-Lee,' added Raelene.

Song-Lee?

Song-Lee was a tall, stunning, bright, affectionate, Buddhist … lesbian from Thailand. It wasn't that I didn't know that lesbians could be beautiful, or Buddhists for that matter, but you just didn't get much more of a heterosexual context than a brothel.

'May-Ling's bi,' Pip continued, 'Marcelle's bi. Sapphire's bi. Coral … Cindy …'

'And Patrick?' I laughed a little hysterically. 'Is Patrick a cross-dresser?'

I would witness Genevieve's affectionate nature, Pip assured me, the next time she hit the bottle. Which was fine. But Pip still hadn't answered my question, and now I was worried that Patrick actually was a cross-dresser.

Why were so many working girls lesbians? Were lesbians drawn to the sex industry because it was easier to separate their private lives from their professional? Or did the meaninglessness of paid sex prompt heterosexual women to seek real intimacy with other women instead of men? Which came first? The authentic lesbian egg? Or the straight, hardworking chicken, who just wanted to cross to the other side?

Dr Darius Slade

I was in the city. It was late. I needed a new prescription for Inderal, and I was looking for the nearest surgery. There were no patients in the medical centre near my bus stop, just two pretty, laughing receptionists in tight, white uniforms, like rejects from Dr Edelsten's days. *The Simpsons* was on the television. I was told to take a seat, and it wasn't until I looked up from last February's *New Idea* that my eyes caught three words that sent my heart leaping to my throat.

Dr Darius Slade.

How many times had I read 'PANDORA WILL NOT SEA DARIUS SLADE!' stuck on our computer screen at the brothel?

'DO NOT SEND HANNAH TO DARIUS SLADE!' was stuck on the wall next to the fire extinguisher.

'DO NOT SENT NEW GIRLS TO DARIUS SLADE!' had been plastered above Leonie's desk ever since she sent new girl Tracy, who never showed up again.

And also, 'WE DO NOT AXCEPT CHEQEUS! ECCEPT FROM DARIUS SLADE.'

'Who's Darius Slade?' I'd asked Raelene months ago.

'He's depraved,' she answered without looking up. And that was it.

'What does he do?' I asked.

'What doesn't he do?' Raelene guffawed. She loved holding all the cards.

On Dr Slade's computer record was the longest list of girls sent to one man I had ever seen. Miao-Jing, twenty-two, Chinese; Carmelina, thirty, Danish; Song-Lee, Shelby, Lola, Shanti, Sapphire, Zora, May-Ling, Odette, Coral, Cindy, Charnelle, Tracy, Mandy, Jasmin, Beula . . . girls I'd never heard of. Beula?

'Tell me, Raelene!'

Raelene finally turned her chair to face me. 'He lives across the road, in the Arlington Apartments. He brings us a lot of business, not just for himself. Quite a few of our clients are friends of his. So if he rings, no matter how off his face, you have to send him a girl. Usually two. You'll know it's him. He'll say he wants to play.'

'Why won't Pandora or Hannah see him?'

Raelene sighed. 'He likes to fuck boys in front of the girls. Or he might want a lesbian double with his wife. Sometimes he likes to just watch.'

Wife?

'Yeah. But she's not always there.' Raelene saved the best for last. 'And he's into bestiality.'

No one had too much information about this. To my knowledge there had never been a goat or a dog present at a booking, but the good doctor apparently boasted of tapes he'd made of his wife copulating with various four-legged friends, or pets. The girls generally put up with him because, apart from being pretty harmless, the doctor was a generous supplier of copious amounts of cocaine and ecstasy.

I had to wonder how many oblivious women sat in this surgery flicking through *Woman's Day* before routinely unbuttoning their blouses for this raving, debauched coke-fiend they trusted with their ovaries. The thought of him doing a pap smear sent me into a complete panic. I just wanted Inderal, I reminded myself. A harmless beta-blocker used by half the Sydney Symphony Orchestra, as well as actors, my last doctor informed me, to stop opening night nerves and screen test tremors. Nothing to do with breasts, or vaginas. Legs, even, were safe. I'd let Dr Slade take my pulse. That was it.

I tried to absorb Don Burke's *New Idea* gardening tips for the fourth time, but it was useless. Not two nights ago I had answered a call on the Sensual Companions line.

'Can I help you?'

A pause, heavy breathing, and then a deep hissing.

'Yyyeeesss.'

Enunciating slowly and lasciviously, the deep voice continued, 'I want to playyyy.'

It sounded like it was already inside something.

'Darius Slade?' I boldly ventured.

'Very gooood,' he slithered. 'Who's this?'

'Meredith,' I answered, crossing my legs under my desk.

'Ahhh . . . And who have you got for me tonight, Mmmeredith?'

I felt like the greenhorn, forced to confront the insatiable swamp creature that terrorised our small village and had to be appeased with a sacrificial offering. A virgin? A prostitute? Hamster?

'Can you just hold my mind – the line, please, Dr Slade?'

I asked Sofia for help.

'Send Marilyn, darling. She loves a party. Say she's mature, but she'll play. Tell him I said so. Oh fuck, give it to me.'

Before I could transfer her, Sofia swooped over, plucking the phone from my hand.

'Darius? She looks like a hooker, but she's what you want, darling.'

Raelene and I gasped. Had Sofia actually described one of our girls as a hooker? I mean, Marilyn didn't exactly dress like a librarian, but this was shocking. Sofia chuckled wickedly with the doctor before handing him back to me.

'Yes, Dr Slade,' I stammered before hanging up, 'a cheque would be fine.'

Suddenly *I* felt like a cigarette. I was about to ring Marilyn when Sofia informed me she was sitting downstairs, having just dropped off a credit card booking.

'Should I warn Marilyn?' I asked Sofia, who looked back at me blankly. 'Are you kiddin', darling? Juss tell her cocaine!'

Downstairs, Marilyn flew out the door before I could say 'and possibly a wombat!'

'Is she goin' to Darius Slade?' asked Shelby, leaning against the sink with a knowing smile.

Shelby! Good old chatty Shelby. I immediately bombarded her with a million questions about Dr Slade. Yes, Shelby nodded, she had once been a regular. 'But once he knows he can't shock a girl any more, he moves on.'

Dr Slade, according to Shelby, was about fifty and 'a complete pisshead' who always had lines of cocaine ready for the girls on a glass table, or ecstasy, if that's what they preferred. His wife was often there, but Shelby wasn't convinced her heart was always in it. I was yet to come across one woman in these 'menages' whose heart was.

'He generally likes to play with two girls at once, and he's got to have it all goin' on. Vibrators, videos, music, drugs, champers, the lot.'

What about the rent boys?

'He didn't try that with me, thank God.' Shelby looked off into the distance, momentarily lost in nostalgic reverie. 'But he did want me ta bugger 'im with a strap-on once. And he likes to talk dirty.' She laughed throatily. '*Real* dirty.'

Back in Dr Slade's surgery, the two receptionists in snug white uniforms giggled and whispered on the other side of their bench. Behind that surgery door was the voice attached to the body frequently attached to anything else with a pulse. I had a pulse. I could hear it. And in a minute Dr Slade, who'd asked Shelby to bugger him with a strap-on, would be taking that pulse. Could I actually sit in this man's office, facing him, knowing what I knew, without blushing, shaking, stuttering or fainting? Faint? Mustn't faint, I chanted. Dr Slade might interpret that as some kind of unconscious craving from a sexually deprived, single, peri-menopausal receptionist who'd wandered in off the street secretly harbouring fantasies of being ravaged by an insatiable, bodice-ripping, reprobate doctor dressed in nothing but a stethoscope and a strap-on. No, I would be wearing the strap-on. He already had a penis. I'd have killed for an Inderal.

As my brain struggled with Don Burke's gardening tips for the eighth time, I remembered the sound of the front door slamming, signifying Marilyn's return from her first booking with Dr Slade, and how I flew down those stairs to get her money, and hear her story, not necessarily in that order.

'He's outrageous!' she was shrieking at Shelby when I arrived at the kitchen doorway. Marilyn tossed her bag so hard across the table, all three of us marked its rapid flight with surprise as it hit the wall beyond. She was coked to the eyeballs.

'He wanted to do anal!' Marilyn continued shrieking. 'And I said, "No, Darius, I don't do anal! They should have told you at the office I don't do anal!" But do you know what, Shel? He didn't want to use a condom! He wanted to stick his dick up there! Without a condom! And he's a bloody doctor!'

Shelby nodded and smiled knowingly, but insatiable, outrageous Marilyn had more than met her match, and it had thrown her.

And so the weeks had passed, and we sent Darius more girls, and they usually came back speeding, if a little subdued, sometimes a tad perplexed, occasionally bewildered, but consistently trashed. I had this shocking urge to go and see him on any pretence, just to put a face to the snake on the phone, but of course I wouldn't. Not consciously.

Back in the medical centre, I sat breathing heavily over Margaret Fulton's tofu recipes when suddenly his door swung open. The two men within laughed, but no one came out. Just to scare the life out of me, one strong, hairy arm reached around and played teasingly with the door knob while its baritone-voiced owner continued chuckling on the other side. The hand had second thoughts about coming out and suddenly withdrew, shutting the door again. More muffled laughter. I was about to do a runner when the hairy arm appeared again, this time attached to a young, wholesome-looking man who glanced at me indifferently before disappearing into his room next door. It hadn't occurred to me I might be seen by another doctor, but instead of decreasing the tension, it just added an element of Russian roulette to my torment.

I had read about the 'flight or fight' response in a crisis, but had never experienced it with such intensity as I did when Dr Slade's door swung open for the third time. I peered over my trembling magazine to see a tall, handsome, silver-haired man stretch and yawn in his doorway. Oblivious to his solitary, twitching patient, my doctor moved in a leisurely fashion towards his two tightly wrapped receptionists. On reaching them he leant against their counter, uttered something inaudible and, as if kicked in the back of the knees, they instantly fell about laughing. Basking in glory, the doctor picked up my card, strutted back to his doorway and, smiling more at himself than at me, called forth his next patient.

'The faaammmousss Mmmerridy Eastmannn!'

When I finished gathering the contents of my bag which had somehow spilt all over the floor as I stood, I looked up to see Dr Slade waiting for me, holding his door open with a smile that reminded me of a hungry reptile. Definitely not a fluffy, warm animal. As I got closer to him, Dr Slade's smiling grey eyes shamelessly dropped to measure my dimensions. This made me negotiate such a ridiculously wide berth as I passed him that my left shoulder crashed violently into the doorframe, propelling me backwards right into his open arms. At the shock of his hand on my shoulder, I hurled myself forward and, with my legs already crossed, collapsed sideways onto a moving chair. Something else was bothering me, apart from a broken collarbone and imminent debauchery. Why had Dr Slade said 'famous'? Did he recognise me from *Play School*? Had he already seen me on all fours barking like a dog? Had he taped it for his wife? I felt so ashamed.

I was in there for one hour. If a good bedside manner is a combination of medical professionalism and intimate pillow-talk, Dr Slade had it in spades.

'Who cares?' he cried when I told him I'd been taking Inderal for over ten years. 'If it makes you feel calm,' he leant forward, 'take it!'

Did he think I could take Inderal with Hyperiforte when I suffered from PMT?

'Of course! Why not? Go for it!'

Was it okay to be on Inderal, Hyperiforte, and take the occasional sleeping tablet?

'Sure!'

'Alcohol?'

'Drink!'

Now that I was feeling bolder, and Dr Slade had taken my pulse without incident, I wanted to steer the conversation to more dangerous territory. I guess I wanted to hear from a doctor who had unprotected sex with prostitutes and rent boys, and the occasional dog, how he advised his patients on the issue of safe sex. I created a boyfriend who preferred not to use condoms, not too difficult a leap for my imagination, and asked how concerned I should be about catching a sexually transmitted disease.

'Have an AIDS test!' he said, throwing up his hands as if he'd just performed a magic trick.

'Yes, but what about things like ... herpes, or warts, or—'

'Oh, for God's sake!' he cried. 'So someone's got a sore on his dick, or you get one on your vulva, so what? It's not going to kill you.'

As we could hear every word of *The Simpsons* from outside, I very much hoped that Dr Slade would lower his voice, but before I could assure him my vulva was fine, he resumed shouting.

'You're carrying millions of diseases and viruses anyway, darling! We've all got chlamydia! We've all got herpes! It's just inactive in some of us. Christ!'

This was a bigger reaction than I think I deserved, and of course I wondered if Dr Slade had any of these STDs himself, until I remembered Marilyn's experience. Then I wondered what diseases could possibly have missed him. But the initial boisterous, subversive charm had developed an unsettling crack and I was beginning to feel like Eve having a consultation with a somewhat pissed-off serpent: 'It's only an apple, Eve! You'll just feel a bit of shame now and then. We all feel ashamed now and then, Eve! It's just inactive in some of us! Want some ecstasy, Eve? Here, strap this on.'

Dr Slade never recovered his initial good humour, and I left him in a funk, as if suddenly bored with his own performance. Letting myself out, and clutching my Inderal prescription, I turned to find the empty waiting room now full of sick people, sick people who all looked up at me with a certain air of disapproval. It wasn't until I was out on the street with a takeaway coffee, that I felt the indelible impression Dr Slade had left on me, and I wondered how such a dark and disturbingly restless spirit could ever be satisfied.

I couldn't wait to see the shocked expressions on the faces of my fellow receptionists when I went into work the following night and told them of my bold adventure. I went in deliberately early so I could enjoy telling Pip before she left for the day. Pip had a prudish contempt for clients at the best of times.

'Guess who I went and saw yesterday?' I beamed.

Pip and Raelene were all ears.

'Darius Slade.'

The look of horror on Raelene's face made me realise how appalling it sounded out of context.

'As a patient!' I added quickly.

Both girls looked vaguely amused for a moment, then told me how each of them had done the same, ages ago.

'I had food poisoning,' Pip said casually.

'I had a sore throat,' Raelene added without missing a beat.

'Sofia's seen him too,' Pip went on.

I was speechless.

'He's very professional,' Raelene said to Pip.

'Oh, I was very, very sick,' Pip said to Raelene, 'and very impressed with him.'

I'd never seen such earnestness. Until Maxine came in.

'He's good, is he?' she asked the sages, as if she'd take her sick mother there tomorrow.

Profound nods all round.

Half an hour later, after the day shift girls had gone, Sofia listened to my adventure like a patient but exhausted mother, occasionally nodding and puffing on her Winfield blue. When I'd finished, she leant back in her chair, looked at me, and I almost detected a smile.

'Well, darling, is funny you should mention Darius, because I want you to ring him.'

Maxine looked up too.

'The cheque he gave Felicity lass week,' Sofia continued, 'is no good.'

I begged Sofia to let Maxine ring him, but this was Sofia's entertainment for the night, to replace my bravado with sheer terror at the prospect of being recognised by Dr Darius Slade.

'Why me?'

'Ring him at the surgery,' she smiled, 'he works late.'

I found things to do for an hour or so, hoping Sofia would forget, but like a big Spanish elephant, Sofia never forgot.

'How did you go with Darius, darling?'

'Yes, yes. Just ringing him now.'

Surely he would be gone by eight.

'Hello?'

'Darius!'

'Yes?'

'It's ... Meredith from the escort agency.'

'Oh, hello, Meredith. What can I do for you?'

It was the same question he'd asked yesterday before I spilt my entire medical history.

'Look, Darius,' I began in a deeper voice, 'it's about Felicity's cheque.'

'Oh! God, I'm sorry, I meant to transfer some money into that account today.'

'That's okay, we just wanted to let you know she's having trouble cashing it. Can we tell her it will be there tomorrow?'

'Yes! God, I'm so sorry. It's all the wife's bloody shopping, you see?'

I laughed, just the way I had the day before, so I stopped.

'She's a lovely girl, Felicity,' he said, as if maybe considering another booking.

'Isn't she?' I gushed. 'Oh, well. Just wanted. Darius. Good.'

I was sweating when I hung up. Someone was singing. It was Sofia.

The Hollywood star and the lesbian

Genevieve was getting worse.

'And if a girl is unhappy with the job, or with the receptionists,' Pip stated finally, 'it is a management problem, Boris.'

Boris had listened to Pip's lengthy protest, nodding with grave concern.

'Yah, yah,' he repeated, his shifty eyes darting from receptionist to receptionist, until he realised Pip had finished and we were all waiting for his decision.

'Well, she can go fock herself,' he declared, sticking his thumbs in his belt. 'I'm sick of it! She vonts special treatment, she can have it. No more bookings. Ha!'

But Pip wasn't going to let him get away with it.

'You have to talk to her, Boris,' she argued. 'Genevieve is not only rude to us, but she's refusing bookings, and she's accusing us of abusing her by sending her out at all.'

I thought I'd pinch a dash of Antoinette's anthropological observation to throw into the pot.

'Perhaps Genevieve has unreal expectations of the job, and she's just not coping with the disappointment.'

They all looked at me.

'She can go fock herself!' Boris repeated.

Genevieve could not help but notice that we were no longer

sending her on bookings, and she had heard that Boris wanted to talk to her. After two days of silence, she began ringing in very late, sounding drunk and teary, begging to speak with Boris.

'Boris's gonna sack me, isn't he, Meredith?'

I assured Genevieve I had no idea.

'Where is he, Mereth?'

I would look at Boris and once again he would shake his head. For all Boris's vitriol he was hopeless at confrontation with the girls. Oh yes, Genevieve could go fock herself, but she'd have to guess it first. There was something quite sad about a beautiful, statuesque blonde beauty who could command five hundred dollars an hour when she walked into a room at the Sheraton now sitting alone in her flat in Mona Vale, pissed and crying to me on the phone at two in the morning. I wished Genevieve had a girlfriend or someone to hold her. More than anything, I wished she would work it out, or stop working altogether, because if I heard one more time that we treated her like a robot, I was going to scream. I couldn't accept blame for someone's decision to be a prostitute! It was just too much. I had been on *Play School* for Christ's sake!

I was not expecting to find Genevieve perched on the kitchen bench and smiling from ear to ear when I arrived at seven the next night.

'What?' I asked straightaway. 'You and Boris have talked?'

Genevieve playfully recollected someone called Boris, and then gave a mischievous giggle.

'Nope,' she smiled, and swung her legs teasingly.

I was obviously meant to guess her good news, but Genevieve couldn't wait.

'I've just come back from seeing Charlie Sheen,' she squealed triumphantly.

Genevieve and I grabbed each other's arms and screamed like two schoolgirls.

Charlie Sheen! Who was here for the Fox Studios Opening tonight. Who'd slept with all those prostitutes in America!

'Oh, Genevieve,' I cried, throwing my arms around her. 'How wonderful!'

Apparently Mr Sheen's personal assistant had made the booking that afternoon, and Genevieve, who was not even on roster, was immediately found and dispatched to the presidential suite at the Sheraton on the Park for one hour.

'Was it a seven hundred dollar booking?' I asked, sure that Charlie would have ordered top shelf.

'No,' Genevieve replied, disappointed, 'he rang on a two hundred dollar line.'

I didn't know what to say. Genevieve never worked for anything under three hundred and fifty.

'But I got a massive tip!' she squeaked.

And we both screamed all over again.

Genevieve told me that Charlie Sheen was very short, but that he had a great body, 'for a guy', and lots of tatts. He was a real gentleman, she said, and a wonderful lover, but he had to let her go early so he could get into his tux and hit the red carpet.

'What's the time?' Genevieve asked suddenly, looking at her Bulgari watch.

Seconds later we were standing in the girls' lounge watching television, surrounded by several other excited escorts, and Leonie all screaming at the Hollywood actor in the live telecast.

'Oh my God!' yelled Leonie. 'Wouldn't it be amazing if he booked one of our girls.'

Everyone looked at the new receptionist in utter disbelief before shouting her to the ground. 'HE JUST DID, YOU FUCKING IDIOT!'

A sharp cry grabbed our attention. And there in close-up was Charlie Sheen, on the red carpet in his tux, fresh from bouncing around with our Genevieve at the Sheraton, with a rose in his lapel, and his arm around . . . a slim brunette?

'Who the fuck's she?' asked Genevieve accusingly.

The room fell silent as we all examined Charlie's date. She was all right. A bit skinny. But Genevieve was definitely more beautiful, and we told her so, until she confessed that Charlie certainly had seemed happy with her service.

For the rest of the night Genevieve was besieged by screaming prostitutes, much to Raelene's annoyance, who hugged the body and held the hands of the woman who'd had sex with Charlie

Sheen. She seemed to enjoy her new star status, surrounded by a bevy of girls who broke into wild applause at every little detail of her booking with the notorious Hollywood star.

When Boris appeared in our doorway at midnight, he looked baffled. He had come prepared for a showdown with his sullen leading lady, and wasn't expecting such an enthusiastically happy response to his strict new demands that she work longer shifts and be much kinder to receptionists.

'Who the fock is Charlie Shine?' he asked.

When we explained who Charlie Sheen was, Boris still seemed unimpressed.

'What films has he been in?' he asked suspiciously.

Oh, we all protested and guffawed, what films *hadn't* Charlie Sheen been in? But the three of us had some trouble recalling the name of even one of them, though Leonie thought he might have been in *Dead Poet's Society*. I was relieved when Raelene finally came to the rescue.

'*Hot Shots!*' she shouted triumphantly.

'Yes! *Hot Shots*,' we all shouted at Boris.

Boris stood in the doorway looking at his three smiling receptionists.

'I'll be on my mobile,' he said, and left.

When a booking turns into a deposit on a relationship

The new girl was sitting at the kitchen table. Mia was a petite, quietly spoken Malaysian girl, twenty-two years old and quite beautiful, with long black hair down to her waist. She had a sweet, serious face, with large almond-shaped eyes that remained sad even when she smiled.

'Are you coming in?' I asked Mia for the third time that evening.

Every time the girls filed out of the lounge to meet a new client in the waiting room, Mia sat very still at the kitchen table, hoping she was invisible.

'Yes.' Mia smiled at me as she stood, pretending she had every intention of joining the others.

And every time the client made his choice, I had to give Mia the same bad news, once I had found her almost buried behind cushions in the darkest corner of the lounge.

'Sorry, Mia,' I'd say to the almond eyes peeping over her knees. 'Half an hour.'

Avoiding the gaze of her more willing colleagues quietly filing their nails, Mia quickly collected her condom from me at the door before she took her client upstairs.

I sat at my desk counting Mia's money, and told Pip and Raelene about the mysterious, reluctant novice downstairs. As usual, Patrick sat on the other side of my desk, studying the crossword as he sipped his tea and pretended not to be listening.

Suddenly, the door swung open.

'Ach, why don't you ask her out, Patrick, instead of just hanging around her desk?'

I don't know what he'd heard, but Boris was obviously no longer of the opinion that Patrick and I were like brother and sister after all. And in this mood, he was like a bull in a china shop.

'Ha! Haff I embarrassed you, Patrick?' Boris laughed as Patrick folded his newspaper and quietly rose to his feet. 'Haff I made you go red in front of your *English girlfriend?*'

Without looking up from rewriting her booking sheet, Raelene humphed in disgust at the very thought, while Pip chose to ignore. To save the blushing Patrick any more suffering, I distracted Boris with the problem downstairs, and at the mere mention of a petite Asian girl, Boris dropped his tortured driver like a hot rock.

'If Mia doesn't vont to do in-house, then get her out of here!' Boris shouted at me. 'Get her an escort booking. Now! Or we lose her to focking Blue Angels!'

Boris looked so ferocious that as soon as a phone rang, I pounced on it.

'Yes, this girl really is beautiful,' I assured Ben in Coogee.

I wanted to tell Ben about Mia's sad eyes, and her delicate, vulnerable disposition, but something about Ben's young voice reassured me Mia would be in good hands. And sure enough, when

Mia rang to say she had arrived in Coogee twenty minutes later, Ben requested to speak to me in person.

'Thank you, Meredith,' he gushed. 'Thank you so much. I can't believe it. She is *sooo* beautiful!'

Two hours later, Mia was still with Ben, the girls were asleep in the lounge, Shelby was having a shower and I was seeing her happy client out the front door. I was just about to return upstairs when a bony, cold hand pulled me into the waiting room.

'Don't do it!' a skinny receptionist hissed at me in the half darkness.

The porn video was still on, and several women moaned and writhed behind Pip's head as she continued her urgent petition.

'You can do so much better than him!'

'Who?'

'Patrick!'

'Right!'

It was difficult to match Pip's earnestness, with Moaning Monica so close to orgasm.

'What are you talking about, Pip?'

Apparently a rumour was going around that Patrick and I were enjoying some kind of forbidden liaison, and Pip found this 'vulgar speculation' about a possible communion between me and the driver terribly upsetting.

'You have so much going for you,' she cried. 'You're educated, cultured, artistic. You have a strong career as an actress ahead of you.'

I wondered if Pip had noticed we were both working in a brothel. Still, her faith in me was touching, given that she'd only seen me in a mayonnaise commercial. I looked at the gyrating harem on the television behind her and wondered if that's where Pip thought I'd end up if I went out on a date with Patrick. Had Moaning Monica been at similar crossroads, forced to choose between a promising career as a Chekhovian actress, or mud-wrestling in a G-string? I thanked Pip for her concern and assured her I had no serious intentions of dating a man who wore a Matraville RSL jacket and sneakers.

I was ashamed to admit it, but with all her 'anti-vulgarian' talk, Pip had unearthed some prejudices of my own, and it was time for me to think before acting irresponsibly. I felt sure that Patrick was on the verge of asking me out, if Boris hadn't scared him off forever, and the Matraville RSL jacket was a concern. Could I really go on a date with a man who socialised in a room full of pokies and ate from a buffet? Was Patrick really an old Rolling Stone in his faded jeans and worn runners? Or was he just stoned and old? I stood in the waiting room on my own watching the credits roll off the screen. Monica had come, and I'd missed it again.

The following week I was back on downstairs duty, and for the first hour, Mia was the only girl in the house. She sat quietly reading at the kitchen table as I stacked the dishwasher.

'You know that man you sent me to last week?' she suddenly piped in her little voice. 'The one who said such nice things?'

When I said Coogee Ben, Mia's sweet face lit up.

'I'm seeing him now.'

I stopped stacking dishes and looked at her. She was wearing a crisp lilac slip of a dress and looked like a fragile doll. With a sense of urgency, Mia confessed to me that Coogee Ben had invited her to move in straightaway with the promise of supporting her.

'Do you like him, Mia?' I asked.

Mia shrugged and looked wistful. She thought so, but the question seemed a little overwhelming so she told me about young Ben's successful pool-cleaning business instead. I was trying to imagine Mia ever looking happy when we were interrupted by a large crash as Leonie fell through the door like a load of loose timber.

'My God!' she shouted, picking up her tray and doing a double-take at Mia. 'Haven't you got long hair!'

I introduced Mia to Leonie, who had been off sick all week due to a bad eccie, and promised her I would bring her and Trudy a cup of tea in a minute. But now Leonie wanted to tell us about someone else with long hair, her friend Simone, whose extensions got caught in the escalators at Central Station.

'Her hair was that long?' Mia asked, laughing.

'No!' Leonie objected, 'Simone was sitting down, hey.'

Only a friend of Leonie's, I thought, would be sitting on the escalator at Central, no doubt at five in the morning, with hair extensions, holding a shoe. To get rid of her, Mia and I conveyed our deepest sympathy for Simone, who would have lost an ear had it not been for a bag lady who heard the screams and hit the red button just in time. Satisfied that her story had stunned us into a contemplative silence, Leonie returned upstairs.

I resumed our conversation by asking Mia how long she had been working in this industry, and was alarmed to hear this was only her third night. With her visa about to run out, Mia explained, she had only a few weeks to quickly make her fare back to London, where she lived. Hoping not to distress her further, I asked Mia if she had told Coogee Ben about her situation.

'He put the cash for my airfare on the table,' she almost wailed. 'He said, "There. There it is. You don't have to do this. Stay with me. I will look after you. And when you need to go back, the money's there."'

I stared at the furrowed little brow and sad eyes. What on earth was Mia doing here?

'I need more than just an airfare,' Mia muttered, playing with the material of her lilac dress. 'I have a little girl, you see? Back in London.'

It didn't seem possible that such a little girl could have a little girl, but I gathered that Coogee Ben had yet to be told too.

'Where does Ben think you are tonight?' I asked her.

'He thinks I'm out with friends,' she said, so burdened with remorse I thought she was going to cry.

Leonie interrupted us again, but this time with a booking for Mia at a house in Leichhardt. I wouldn't see Mia again until after five in the morning, when she asked me to call her a cab for Coogee. But this time Mia didn't smile. She couldn't even look at me as she handed me the money from her bookings. And so I left her there, sitting in the kitchen, with the birds singing and Ben waiting.

There was only one other girl I knew to be involved with a client. A month earlier, I'd witnessed Heather saying goodbye to her tall, dark, handsome young client in the hallway. And I could tell by Heather's body language that this had not been one of her 'you can't touch me here, here or here' bookings.

'Ring me,' she cooed after him as she shut the door.

Heather used to make the bathroom smell like vomit. Not all the time, but occasionally. No one else thought it smelt like vomit, but I did, and I should know. Before Heather made the bathroom smell like vomit, she would fill the kitchen tidy with chocolate bar and ice cream wrappers. But now the kitchen tidy was just full of cigarette butts again, and the word upstairs was that we'd lost Heather to Blue Angels.

'For God's sake,' Pip railed, 'a leggy, busty blonde should never be sitting down there waiting for a booking. No wonder she left us!'

But Pip was forgetting that Heather was also profoundly stupid, no spring chicken and most clients didn't appreciate her rules. And that she wore push-up bras.

'She'll be back,' said Boris, sounding very much like Arnold Schwarzenegger. 'You hear, Meredit? She's shacked up with a focking client. She met him here, for fock's sake. Ha! And now she's verking her arse off at Blue Angels to keep them both. Ach!'

Boris paced the room in agitation, and I wondered which girl he got his information from.

'I haff seen it all before,' he continued, 'it's pathetic. What bastard lets his girl go out and verk to keep him? Hmm?'

Boris stopped in front of my desk, and waited for an answer, so I shrugged. And then he left before I could ask him how he met Didi.

How many stockbrokers can you stuff in a condom dispenser?

I liked Sunday nights because it was Sofia's night off, and therefore Leonie and I got home while it was still dark. It was my only downstairs shift, and although I hated answering the front door, I preferred the company of the girls in the kitchen to that of my colleagues upstairs. And tonight, the combination of Pip's delicate airs and Leonie's bong-happy recklessness was combustible, to say the least. I had barely put my bag down when they began arguing over the new girl downstairs.

'Her name's Consuela,' Pip informed me, 'and she's a very impressive and bright young lady.'

Leonie snorted, giggled and muttered something about 'a psycho'.

'She is not a *psycho*,' Pip turned on her. 'She's a stockbroker.'

Only Pip could draw a line between the mentally deranged and people who worked in finance.

'What about the Spanish dancing?' Leonie protested.

That was all I needed to hear. I was on my way down.

The kitchen was unusually empty, except for a petite young woman, extremely beautiful, with long locks of velvet brown hair, who leant against the sink. As soon as I introduced myself, her Bardot lips parted in a smile, revealing her even, white teeth, and she twirled around in her tight red dress, giggled and paraded across the floor towards me. Pip was right. Consuela was a very impressive, bright, popular, incredibly desirable young woman. I knew because she told me so.

'And I'm not doing this because I have to,' she continued her monologue. 'I just want to make a whole lot of money, and retire young.' Consuela finished with a click of her fingers.

Could this be the Spanish dancing Leonie had mentioned? And where were the other girls?

'I'm a stockbroker, you know,' Consuela stated. 'It's true, I am!' and she giggled and twirled for me, just like a stockbroker. 'So, I might need to plug my computer in here, if that's all right.'

Consuela flounced over to the kitchen table and, with a magician's assistant's flourish, proudly presented to me her very smooth, compact, laptop computer. I told her she could plug it in wherever she wanted, but that it would be stolen the second she turned her back.

'No one would have stolen it at Blue Angels,' Consuela pouted.

'Then perhaps you should never have left,' I smiled.

Consuela paused for a moment, then giggled again. I'd seen enough.

'Tell them I'm Spanish!' Consuela called as I reached the doorway.

I turned around.

'Although I'm not really,' she smiled coquettishly. 'Can you guess where I'm from?'

'Loch Ness?' I suggested.

Consuela laughed and laughed.

'Mattel?' I asked.

No, she was not from Loch Ness! Or . . . or that other place. And to make a difference to my otherwise mundane night, Consuela suggested, with a teasing wave of her finger, that I keep trying.

'Can we all have a go?' I asked, trying to contain my excitement.

'Sure!' she nodded.

I smiled, crinkled my nose at her, and shut the door.

Leonie was in hysterics.

'What's a *gorgon*?' she shrieked.

Pip was much less amused, and covered her disappointment in me by aggressively stapling anything in sight, but Leonie was delighted that I had sided with her for once. Fortunately, I was saved any more office tension by the door bell.

'Coming!' I shouted down the intercom, ignoring the flinching Pip.

Having left blond Mike the builder in the waiting room, I found the missing girls watching television. How could they bear to be in such an airless room with such a powerful heater? Shelby, Delilah, Rita and Maya all seemed rather more subdued than usual, slumped in various couches and chairs. In sharp contrast, Consuela perched on the edge of a pouf, riveted to the client on the screen.

'He's cute,' she squealed.

The others did not agree or disagree, but one by one they looked up at me, smiled and shook their heads. I was used to this reaction if the client was a teenager and they just wanted to be saved the humiliation of feeling so ancient, but Mike the builder was in his forties.

'Come on,' I implored them. 'You know Boris will hit the roof if he finds out none of you went in.'

But the girls knew very well that Boris would never find out, and they were not moving.

'I'll meet him,' Consuela announced, leaping to her feet and pulling her tight dress down over her young, curvaceous torso.

Yes, we knew *she'd* meet him. That was just the problem. But maybe Mike, too, would find Consuela unbearable. Maybe our builder was a sweet, discerning man with taste, and intelligence.

'I'll have her for half an hour,' the big oaf grunted.

Half an hour later, there was a timid knock on our office door. I opened it to find the dishevelled Consuela in a robe, smiling up at me like the cat who'd just given a canary the full service. As in-house receptionist it was my job to show any new girl how to remake her room.

'Stay,' I ordered Consuela, and ran downstairs with my keys to let her builder out.

I asked the obligatory question as he stepped out onto the porch: 'And did you enjoy the service, Mike?'

'Yeah. She's a real little—'

I shut the door.

When I returned, Consuela was waiting for me in the bedroom, coyly smiling on the other side of the bed, as if we were going to play a game together.

'So,' I began like a *Play School* presenter, 'first, we smooth out the covers, and then we plump up the pillows.'

As Consuela smiled, flounced, pouted and patted her way around the bed, I wondered why she bothered. I wasn't a man.

'And then we pick up the towels, and take them down to the laundry,' I said.

Consuela looked at me. Her tail stopped wagging.

'I thought *you* washed the towels,' she said.

'I do,' I smiled graciously, 'but not until *you've* picked them up and transported them to the laundry.'

'And what about the condom?' she asked.

Ooh yes, I felt like saying, give that to me, that goes on our condom tree!

'You take the used condom, Consuela, put it in a tissue, and then place it in the condom dispenser at the bottom of the stairs.'

'Okay,' she said dubiously, and then pointed next door. 'Can I just have a shower first?'

'Not in there, Consuela,' I said on my way out. 'That's the clients' shower. You use the one in the laundry, like all the other girls.'

I left Consuela feeling a little less cute, and gingerly searching the carpet for a used condom.

As I stacked the dishwasher, I wished that the girls would come out from the television room, but by now they were all miserably engrossed in *Mrs Doubtfire*. Consuela sat at the kitchen table giggling at some text message on her mobile phone, while sweet Yvonne, single mother from Mascot, sat opposite, smiling at her. Yvonne only worked one night a month, and none of us really understood why. Only Leonie passed through on her way to the toilet, muttering something about Pip having a vegetable lodged up her nether regions, although she didn't quite put it like that.

'That's where I know you from!' Yvonne suddenly cried, snapping her fingers at me. 'You were on *Home and Away*!'

And she was off. What a wonderful show it was. What good values it taught children. She and her son watched it every night. How sad, I thought as I looked into Yvonne's small, kind eyes, imagining them fill with tears when Gipsy had indigestion.

'Were you on *Home and Away*?' Consuela asked scornfully.

I played it down, which wasn't far enough considering how bad my performance was. Besides, I knew that Leonie, who'd mentioned her budding career as an actress, was just in the laundry. Too late.

'It's hard when you haven't got a good script to work with, hey!' Leonie burst out, her hands dripping water on the floor. 'I remember when I had to do this scene on *Crimestop*—'

'Hey, what are you doing?' I shouted at Consuela, who had picked up the kitchen phone.

Consuela pouted. She just wanted to ask them upstairs if anyone had a black felt-tipped pen.

'Pip's probably answering ten calls at once,' I lectured her, 'and when you pick up that phone, it beeps *very loudly* up there, Consuela, until someone has a spare second to deal with your *emergency*. Do you understand what I'm saying?'

Consuela stuck her tongue out at me and I didn't know which one of us I hated more, her, or the person I'd become since meeting her an hour ago. All I knew was that I belonged upstairs, with kindred sufferers of misplaced carrots.

Finding Pip in a state of high anxiety over a lack of Asians, and not one cash booking for Boris, I quickly answered the next call. Mr George at the Wentworth was looking for a 'more mature lady' who kissed, and preferably a blonde. I immediately told him about one such candidate on our books, 36DD–29–35, who was extremely affectionate and provided an excellent service. Mr George thought Antoinette sounded perfect, and eagerly awaited my call to confirm.

'She's downstairs,' Pip emitted, with an anguished flick of her hand. 'I just let her in.'

I rang Mr George with the good news, and then, leaving Pip clutching her distraught face in her hands, I skipped down to the lounge room to find my mature blonde.

Antoinette was looking particularly beautiful tonight, I thought, when I knelt down beside her in the lounge room. As I whispered about Mr George and his gentle manner and cultivated voice, Antoinette looked up at me with a bemused expression from under a flop of blonde hair.

'Yeah ... he sounds impressive on the phone,' she said in her quiet, calm way, 'but he's an abuser.'

'Mr George?' I cried, interrupting *Mrs Doubtfire*.

A restless ripple went through the room.

'You know him?' I whispered.

Antoinette nodded.

'And he's violent?' I asked.

'No,' Antoinette smiled, 'he's passive aggressive. I saw him for a few hours last week, and he *played games*.'

We all watched Mrs Doubtfire's breasts catch fire in silence.

'I can send someone else,' I offered, and three girls instantly glanced our way.

'No,' Antoinette said firmly. 'I'll go. Tell Patrick I'm ready when he is.'

Mr George had certainly played one game with me tonight, by making me describe in absolute detail the same woman we'd sent him last week, and not letting on. Bloody passive aggressives, I thought, as I went in search of passive Patrick.

'No, silly!' cried Consuela, pouring her cleavage over the kitchen bench. 'Gemini?'

Opposite Consuela, giggling like a loon at the kitchen table, sat our driver, who wasn't so much sitting as Open for Inspection. Patrick's arms were stretched out on each flanking chair, his bum had all but slid off his seat, and his bent knees pointed as far east and west as they could possibly go. In fact, I could not recall, ever, having seen Patrick's limbs placed in such inviting repose. Apparently invisible, I turned the kettle on.

'Come on,' Consuela pleaded.

'I don't know,' Patrick laughed pathetically.

'Could you please take Antoinette to a booking at the Wentworth, Patrick?' I interrupted them.

With a vague nod in my direction, Patrick returned his attention to Spain.

'Libra?' he asked.

'No!' she squealed.

I noisily emptied an ashtray into the bin.

'Sagittarius?' Patrick tried again.

'*Sagittarius?*' Consuela cried in disgust.

I was Sagittarius.

'Think more sensual, more exciting, more ... *sexy*!' she said.

I reached into the bin to extract my ashtray. When I looked up, Patrick and Consuela were regarding me with the same air of repugnant disapproval.

'Antoinette's booking?' I reminded Patrick, flicking some pineapple off my sleeve.

'Yes, of course,' Patrick mumbled, gathering his keys and heading for the lounge.

'Scorpio!' she shouted after him.

Consuela waited for the front door to shut, then turned to me and squealed with delight. 'He's cute!'

The door bell kept me busy all night. Men arrived and departed. The girls reluctantly shuffled in and out of the waiting room, but the only one to ever make it upstairs was Consuela. If only she'd been more gracious. As the girls congregated outside the waiting room and checked their make-up in the hall mirror, yanking their breasts up as high as they would go, Consuela pranced and giggled before them, like the birthday girl about to open all her presents at once.

'*What are you on?*' Shelby finally asked, towering over her.

It was a warning, but Consuela took it as a compliment, and tittered. 'Why, you want some?'

For a second I thought we might see a financial consultant deck a stockbroker. Alas, Shelby was too professional for that. Although she did warn me once, 'Meredith, I grew up in the western suburbs with five brothers. You don't want to fuck with me.' Even without the brothers, I didn't want to fuck with Shelby.

Five minutes later the door bell rang again, just as Consuela was taking her latest prize upstairs, so I waited for them to begin their ascent before herding in the next lot.

'Hello, come in,' I greeted two hirsute young men on the porch, both wearing caps and both jangling.

Here were the keys again. Big bunches hanging from their belts. *Keys to what?* I had to step back for the second one to pass me, so huge was his girth, and then I looked behind me to see what vision had momentarily paralysed them. Posing on the stairs, all teeth and legs, Consuela delicately waved her fingers at our guests with a coy giggle before pushing her embarrassed client up to the landing. Any other girl caught in this situation would have scampered, not just to protect her client's anonymity, but also to avoid any confusion about her own availability. But as we knew, this wasn't any other girl.

The caps sat down opposite each other. The large one's couch made such a long hissing noise under his great weight, I didn't know whether to wait until it had finished before speaking, but life was too short.

'So,' I began cheerfully, 'been here before?'

'Nuh,' grunted the slimmer and more articulate of the two as he lit his cigarette.

'So,' I continued, searching for an ashtray, 'have you had a good night?'

'Who's she?' grunted the large one over his still-hissing couch, pointing back towards the stairs.

'She's unavailable,' I said, passing him a menu instead.

'What do the others look like?' the smoker asked, ashing into our potted fern.

'I'll go and get them, shall I?' I smiled. 'Oh, and what are your names?'

The caps looked at each other uneasily.

'You can make names up,' I suggested helpfully, 'if you're worried about being stalked.'

They looked at me expressionlessly.

'Joe,' the fat one said at last.

'Fred,' said the smoker.

And they nearly smiled, so amused were they by their hilarious new identities.

I found the women huddled around the monitor, biting their nails, all seriously concerned about the possibility of being crushed by Big Joe, so I decided not to tell them about his body odour.

'Don't forget,' I reminded them heartily, 'the camera puts on ten pounds!'

'Yeah, but how d'ya explain the other two hundred?' muttered Shelby, her eyes fixed on the screen.

As the ladies filed in, introduced themselves and filed out, Fred and Big Joe did not move from their seats, and their faces remained so utterly expressionless, I was not surprised they had to pay for sex.

'When will the girl on the stairs be finished?' Fred asked.

'In an hour,' I sighed.

'We might come back,' Fred said, and they both got up without looking at me.

'Please do,' I smiled as I let them out, not caring that they could hear a chorus of cheers coming from the girls' lounge room.

'Can't you send Consuela out?' I pleaded with Pip in the doorway of our office upstairs. 'Someone's going to kill her if she stays.'

'Who?' asked Leonie hungrily, looking up from her magazine.

'If someone rings,' Pip answered flatly, 'I will.'

Just then a phone did ring. But it was only Antoinette, extending for another hour with Mr George at the Wentworth.

By the time Laurel and Hardy returned, Consuela had joined the others watching television.

'Have those two come back to see me?' she enquired gleefully as I entered the room.

'No,' I lied, 'they've come back to see everyone.'

But of course no one moved. And as Consuela swept past me with a superior smile, I looked at Shelby, Rita, Delilah and Maya. It was a voiceless vote. We hated her.

I could not bear to watch, and so I waited outside in the hall while Consuela flirted with Fred in the waiting room. Despite his granite expression, Fred was quite attractive, in a thuggish kind of a way. When she was done, Consuela closed the door behind her and, like Carmen, clicked her fingers over her head.

'They're all yours, darling.'

I wanted to stick her in the condom dispenser.

Once again, I returned to the caps.

'You want to see Consuela?' I sighed, looking at Fred.

There was a pause. An awkward pause. A wonderful pause.

The two of them sat on opposite sofas, looking at each other in a silent challenge. Oh my God. Could it be possible that Spain was up for grabs?

'Tell you what,' I said, clapping my hands together, 'why don't I just leave you to talk about it?'

I hovered in the hallway, listening to their voices, low and monosyllabic, and prayed to God to give the fat guy a break. Fat guys never get a break. Unless they've got a really good sense of humour. Then they can play romantic leads in movies opposite supermodels. As the grunting had stopped, I went back in.

Fred and Big Joe sat looking at each other like two snakes in a stand-off.

'So,' I clapped my hands again, 'have we come to any decision?'

After an unbearable silence, Fred slowly lifted a finger and pointed to his large friend.

'He'll have her.'

I looked at the happy winner. His chest was moving, so I knew he was alive.

'For how long, Joe?' I asked, grinning from ear to ear.

'How much is half an hour?' he grunted.

'Nothing at all,' I wanted to sing, and hug him to my breast.

'A hundred and twenty,' I said, slapping the bench heartily. 'I'll just go and get Consuela.' I stopped at the door. 'She's Spanish, you know.'

They looked at me in cataleptic unison.

'She'll even dance for you, if you like!'

I opened the door to the girls' room. No one could be bothered looking up from *Entertainment Tonight*, except the gloating, ever-smiling Consuela.

'Half an hour, Consuela,' I said, handing her the condom with restrained ecstasy.

Consuela smiled and bounced her way down the corridor, with me doing cartwheels close behind until I leapt past to open the waiting room door for her. Once she was inside, I did a little Spanish dance of my own. When the door opened again, a somewhat subdued Consuela shuffled past me as if she was on death row.

'They want to see you,' she said mournfully, collapsing at the bottom of the stairs.

Again? Why?

I walked back into the waiting room to find my lads in heavy discussion.

'Okay,' Big Joe grunted, as if conceding.

'You *sure*?' asked Fred.

'Yeah, yeah,' Big Joe nodded.

'You sure?' asked Fred again, getting his wallet out.

No, Big Joe! Not sure at all! Fred, put wallet back!

'How much for the whole hour?' Fred asked me.

'Two hundred,' I said, biting my lip.

'He'll have her for an hour then,' Fred said, offering me a wad of twenties.

An audible gasp could be heard from the bottom of the stairs.

I took Fred's money and clasped it to my heart. 'Consuela?' I called softly.

Hours later, while Consuela still sat in shock at the kitchen table, I was summoned to reception. Mr George at the Wentworth had requested to speak to me personally.

'Yes, Mr George? I hope everything's okay with Antoinette.'

'Oh, yes,' Mr George assured me, 'but the lovely lady has just left without her purse.'

I profusely thanked Mr George for his honesty, and rang Antoinette straightaway. Antoinette could be terribly vague, and was also as blind as a bat. She was probably at that very moment standing in a broom cupboard at the Wentworth Hotel, waiting for it to take her to the ground floor, asking the mop for a cigarette. I rang her mobile.

'Thanks,' Antoinette gushed, with a breathy, apologetic laugh. And I could have sworn I heard the clatter of buckets.

Half an hour later, I found Antoinette in our kitchen, counting her money.

'How was he?' I asked, waiting patiently for our cut.

'He was actually quite lovely.' She smiled. 'I think that the last time I saw him,' she confessed with a chuckle, 'I might have been having one of my *mad* nights!'

It was refreshing to hear Antoinette could laugh at herself, but by the time she had counted her cash a third time, all jocularity had ceased.

'FUCK!' Antoinette yelled, her hands crashing down on the bench with such force I was surprised it didn't crack. 'FUCKING BASTARD!'

Girls stopped chatting, looked up from their magazines, nail files suspended in mid air.

'HE'S *FUCKED* ME AGAIN!'

No one dared make the obvious joke.

'Him and his FUCKING GAMES!'

I did not know if Antoinette's madness was getting the better of her, or if Mr George had played yet another round. Whatever it was, she was terrifying.

'What's wrong?' I asked timidly.

'He's taken half of it OUT!'

'Are you sure?' I asked.

'YES I'M FUCKING SURE!'

'Let's count it again,' I said, leaping out of my trench, holding a banana.

'CUNT!' she fired.

And for one frightening second, I wasn't absolutely sure whether Antoinette was referring to Mr George or me.

'Well, your money is your responsibility, sweetheart,' came a lone, saccharine voice from behind us.

Everyone looked with disbelief towards its source, sitting at the kitchen table.

'Your responsibility, and nobody else's,' continued the smug Spanish ingénue, felt-tipped pen poised over Filofax. 'You can't blame other people if you don't keep an eye on it.'

As Antoinette squinted threateningly at the brunette blur at the table, there was a chorus of magazines down and compacts snapping shut as girls briskly evacuated the room. If Big Joe hadn't crushed Consuela, Antoinette surely would. I too remembered some urgent paperwork I'd left unfinished upstairs, and bolted. And as I shut our office door behind me, the whole house shook with the unmistakable rumble of a black hole, about to swallow a new star.

'AND WHO THE FUCK ARE YOU?'

Don't judge a book by its jacket

We were almost at Coogee, and Patrick had asked me a series of questions about my unadventurous social life. Now, at last, it was my turn.

'So, you go to the Matraville RSL often, Patrick? Or do you collect these?' I laughed, giving the embroidered lapel on his jacket a jovial flick.

'No.' Patrick smiled. 'RSL clubs are not my scene, really.'

Of course they weren't! Patrick hung out at noisy, friendly pubs with bands and played pool with women.

'Except Wednesday nights,' Patrick added. 'You'll always find me at the Matraville RSL on a Wednesday night.'

'Why's that?' cried a little voice.

'Competition darts night.'

Patrick played darts, and was proud of it. I felt so depressed. He may as well have said he went bowling. What was the difference?

One was overarm, the other was underarm, but they were both just a stone's throw from a regular seat at bingo. This was a world of Sport and Leisure I wanted to remain as ignorant of as possible. Like Tupperware. But it got worse.

'We're fifth in the state.'

I wanted the conversation to end before Patrick invited me line dancing.

'Better he throws darts at a wall than sticks needles up his arm,' Trudy declared later.

Trudy, always devil's advocate, was very fond of Patrick. She'd also gone out with more than her share of junkies.

'And better he smokes dope than crack,' she cried.

Maybe Trudy's parents should be even more anxious than mine.

'And better he hangs around in RSLs than in public toilets.'

By the time Trudy had finished comparing our driver with every bisexual, low-life, thieving, drug-fiend ex-boyfriend on welfare who'd stolen money from her purse, I suggested *she* go out with Patrick, just for the break.

'No,' Trudy sighed mournfully, and looked out the window. 'He's not my type.'

So I decided to expand my social boundaries, let go of my middle class prejudices, take Trudy's advice, and go for it. After all, hadn't my new-found happiness working in a brothel with all its fascinating inhabitants taught me not to judge a book by its cover? And hadn't dating actors who used more Clarins products than me been an absolute disaster? Why stop exploring new worlds now? I was going to take a risk. I was going to take some initiative. Spring was here! Whole trees burst into colour right in front of me. I felt sure sparrows and butterflies danced about my head from the bus stop to our brothel door. If Patrick asked me out, I was going to say yes!

Weeks passed. Cells died. Bryce Courtenay wrote two more books. I changed the colour of my hair, and still waited to say yes.

Maxine was having another one of her bad nights. She was too good for this job. She was overqualified. Shelby had read her palm and told her she should start her own business. Shelby? Read palms?

'I could just go now, Meredith. Seriously!'

I gave her a nod.

'I'm a very giving person, Meredith. You know that.'

Nod.

'I'll always give a person the benefit of the doubt. Even if I know they're lying.'

I had absolutely no idea what she was talking about, but to avoid any explanation, I nodded.

'Meredith, look at me.'

I did.

'I'm not well. I shouldn't be here, should I?'

That, of course, required a shake, not a nod.

Maxine's performance alternated nightly between playing the consummate and unappreciated professional on the verge of quitting, and the naughty drug-fucked party girl. I preferred the latter, as it was more honest.

'Meredith sweetheart, just between you and I . . .' she would lean forward and whisper carnivorously to me after one of her big nights, 'I am completely out of it! Ripped – off – my – tits!'

Or behind the other receptionist's back, she'd mime like a tripping crocodile, 'I – have – not – slept!'

I'd oblige by feigning shock and admiration, which sent her smiling like a satiated, dope-blasted reptile back to work. Just a few minutes later, I'd hear Maxine repeating the same performance behind my back for the other receptionist.

'You didn't tell me you're an actor, dollface,' Maxine cried as I stood in the doorway holding cups of tea for her and Leonie.

The whole house had now seen me in an ad for a new bread product, in which, coincidentally, I played a nervous receptionist, but at a bakery. I did not feel comfortable with the way Maxine and Leonie were now leering at me.

'I'm an actor too!' Leonie squealed.

'This is amazing,' Maxine went on. 'All my friends tell me, "Maxine, you are such an actress!" I mean, not a professional actress like you, Meredith, but I just love to entertain. I'm up on tables at parties. I perform all the time. You haven't seen that side of me yet. But I'm mad!'

With half a bucket of cocaine up her nose, I bet she was.

'I'm an actor too!' squealed Leonie again, to no one.

'I just love to make people laugh,' Maxine mused whimsically, 'you know?'

For the next hour or so, I was assailed by questions from both directions. What had I done? Did I go to NIDA? Had I worked with anyone famous? Did I have an agent? I quite enjoyed all the attention, until Leonie screwed up her face at Robyn Gardiner Management. No, she shook her big head, she hadn't heard of her. Was she new?

'What should I do?' demanded Maxine, the undiscovered talent competing for my attention.

'Hey, don't you hate having to wear all that make-up?' Leonie said cheerfully, as if we now had something in common.

I looked despairingly from one to the other, not knowing which conversation was worse. And I'd expected just a little more glory before being demoted to career adviser. But then I *could* just imagine Maxine, with her big teeth, stiff teased hair and her size four body clad in tight blue jeans, whining to some anorexic in a flimsy coffee shop set, 'Why don't you just tell him you love him, Charmaine?' Leonie, on the other hand, possibly wanted to be surrounded by actors in the same way she just wanted to be surrounded by prostitutes. Leonie was an extra on set and off.

Despite my best intentions, by midnight I was advising both of them to at least take classes at the Actors' Centre in Surry Hills, before auditioning for NIDA the following summer.

'You know, Meredith,' Maxine sighed, 'I was going to do that last year. If I'd pulled my finger out, I'd be halfway through NIDA by now.'

That was the most difficult nod ever summoned.

'Is it true they make you take your clothes off?' Leonie asked.

I gradually managed to disengage by burying myself in paper-work, but this didn't stop them from wildly speculating together on their respective acting careers.

'I don't want to do theatre, hey,' avowed Leonie, ''cause it's just so pretentious, you know?'

Maxine likewise disapproved. 'Theatre? Ugh, no! Television or films. But not theatre.'

'Theatre's fucked,' Leonie proclaimed. 'I've got friends who've done theatre heaps, and not even been paid, hey.'

I sharpened pencils until they were stubs, listening to two brothel receptionists discard the last fifteen years of my life.

'Although I liked *Buddy*,' Maxine sighed.

'Well then,' I remonstrated finally, 'you'd better both forget about NIDA. At NIDA it's theatre, theatre, theatre. Shakespeare, Shaw, Brecht and Chekhov. Taught by skilled theatre practitioners. Like Geoffrey Rush. He does a bit of theatre, Leonie, but unlike your friends, he gets paid.'

Maxine and Leonie looked at me like two naughty schoolgirls who weren't quite sure what they'd done wrong.

The door bell rang and, thankfully, a wave of boys with no necks who just wanted to look kept me downstairs for a while.

Although I left Maxine and Leonie bonding over show business, when I walked back to my desk an hour later, I sensed the honeymoon was over.

'I don't know, Leonie. Do whatever you want!' Maxine snapped at her, and rolled her big eyes at me. At the very least, Maxine had pantomime potential.

After a strained pause, a timorous Leonie turned to me. 'Um, Meredith? Would you send a girl to a guy who was, like, staying at a friend's place? But he didn't know the friend's name? And he only had a mobile phone?'

I looked at my dangerously crack-brained colleague and was tempted to say, 'Well, that depends, Leonie. Did he sound nice?' But Leonie would have given it too serious consideration.

'No,' I said instead, irritated that Maxine was willing to play games with a girl's safety.

I asked Leonie if she had ever stayed at someone's place and not known their name.

It was a stupid question.

On Sunday nights we closed at four, which meant we usually got away by five. This night, however, Maxine was determined to get away at four o'clock on the dot. At three-thirty she placed the fat blue envelope full of the night's takings, which came to nearly two thousand dollars, on Boris's desk and announced she was ready to go. But a few girls had yet to be paid, and therefore the bookwork had yet to be finished, and then there was Patrick's driving money which always took twenty painstaking minutes. I reminded Maxine that Patrick was still sitting in his car out at Duffy's Creek, an hour away, waiting for Yoko, a new girl, who wasn't due to finish for another ten minutes.

'Fuck!' Maxine held her head in her hands. A moment later she surfaced. 'Well, let's just go before he gets back. I'll say we forgot.'

Leonie and I looked at her, gobsmacked.

'We can't go before he gets back,' I protested. 'For a start we have to pay him, and then he drives me and Leonie home.'

Maxine didn't care. Maxine had her own car, which was as big as she was little. For a frightening moment it always looked as if it was being driven by nothing but two sets of white knuckles. I surmised that tonight Maxine had places to go, drugs to snort, and people to entertain on tables. So we waited in silence for Patrick to return, which he did in half the time we expected.

The sight of Patrick hovering in our doorway, balancing on one leg with his usual lopsided smile, filled me with happiness. As we both grinned at absolutely nothing, I knew one of us had to leave, and so on the pretence of meeting the new girl, I passed him at the door.

'Is she nice?' I asked, standing close enough to inhale him.

'Yoko?' he laughed, taking me in. 'Why, she's lovely!'

It was cryptic, but I nearly burst.

'But you should know,' Patrick added on a more sober note, 'Antoinette's down there too.'

After yet another fight with her mother, Antoinette had finally been thrown out of her mother's unit and was now sitting downstairs with her suitcases packed, waiting for me to collect her money and call her a taxi. I felt relieved. The nightly jokes about picking up Antoinette from a retirement village were irresistible but cruel.

'Where's she going to live?'

'Boris's house,' Patrick said with restrained mirth, 'in Redfern.'

Boris and Didi's three-storey investment in Redfern housed a motley bunch of homeless working girls, including our young lesbian couple, Rochelle and Shawna, as well as the exotic Delilah and, now that she'd returned to us, the bulimic Heather. The thought of Antoinette shuffling among them stretched absurdity to the absolute limit.

A plump, pretty Malaysian girl with long black hair sat upright at the kitchen table in a shiny green dress with plunging neckline, smiling guilelessly at no one. Yoko laughed as she gave me two credit card dockets to take upstairs, and reassured me that she'd had a 'really lovey nigh'.

'Could you call me a taxi, please?' a dangerously wavering voice rose through the cloud of smoke at the back door.

There sat Antoinette, surrounded by suitcases, hunched in her crumpled black suit that looked more than ever like an usherette's uniform. On hearing Antoinette was going to Redfern, the gentle Yoko kindly offered to drive her there as it was on her way.

'Phil wasn't too drunk, then?' I asked Yoko from the doorway.

'Oh yes,' Yoko laughed and nodded. 'Mr Phil very, very drun!'

'Could you just get Yoko's money *now*, please,' requested Antoinette with strangled urgency, 'so we can get the hell out of here?'

Within minutes I returned with the grateful Yoko's cash. But when Yoko's smooth brow creased with uncertainty over the amount, Antoinette began contorting and moaning in her seat, her eyes rolling back in her head. Yoko watched this alarming spectre with startled apprehension, and I left them again, Yoko possibly regretting her offer of a lift.

Upstairs I interrupted Maxine and Patrick, who were arguing over twenty dollars, to ask for help with Yoko's pay. Maxine calculated Yoko's money again, but came up with exactly the same amount. Patrick looked at us helplessly while Leonie giggled in the corner as she coloured her nails with yellow highlighter. Suddenly

214 All the world's a stage and all its receptionists are actors

Godzilla was booming from the phone downstairs: if we couldn't fix up Yoko's money *now*, could someone call her a taxi? I couldn't bear the thought of the mild Yoko being subjected to this madness on her first night.

'Leonie,' I ordered the office idiot. 'Go downstairs, get Yoko, and bring her up here.'

When Yoko arrived upstairs, the four of us stood in a huddle going over and over credit card surcharges, agency cuts and Patrick's driving money. We all kept smiling, because Yoko was a darling and we each understood some part of her finances, but not the whole. Our congeniality was interrupted by Leonie, who beeped us from the phone downstairs.

'Um, can we like call Antoinette a taxi?'

Antoinette could be heard fitting in the background.

'Like right *now*?' Leonie's voice quavered.

In unison we all shouted at Leonie to do it herself. Did the stupid girl not have a phone in her hand?

Ten minutes later, exhausted and laughing less, we were counting Yoko's money for the third time when Leonie beeped again.

'Meredith, did you know there's a box of *in-house* tissues on the kitchen table?'

The four of us squinted incredulously at the phone.

'So?' I cried, exasperated.

'Well, it's just that Boris always chucks a hissy fit if any tissues are taken out of the bedrooms and—'

'LEONIE, FUCK OFF!'

Silence.

'Oh,' Patrick began timidly. 'Antoinette owes me ten dollars.'

It was a receptionist's job to get any driving money owed from the girls.

'Well, why didn't you get it off her before?' I implored him. 'When she was sane?'

We had to laugh, especially Yoko, who needed the relief more than anyone.

Feeling bad that I'd yelled at her, I went downstairs to help Leonie deal with mad Antoinette. Why she had stayed down there given the effect she always had on Antoinette was proof of Leonie's bizarre proclivity for war zones. She often volunteered to deal with Antoinette or Urszula, the only two women who never hid the fact they found her unworldly disposition utterly intolerable.

'What did you say to upset Urszula?' I asked Leonie on her very first night.

'I just told her she should wear a bra,' she retorted innocently.

'And what did you say to Antoinette?' I asked, less than an hour later.

'She's wearing too much make-up! She looks like Witchy-poo.'

As I approached the kitchen, I could hear Leonie wailing to Witchy-poo, 'Sorry, Antoinette, but I honestly don't know!'

'WHAT DO YOU MEAN YOU DON'T KNOW?' the frightening voice demanded.

'I'm sorry!' Leonie cried helplessly. 'Maybe Meredith knows.'

'HOW CAN I CALL A TAXI IF I DON'T KNOW WHERE IT'S GOING?' the crazed harpy bawled.

'I know it's in Redfern.'

'WHERE THE FUCK DO I LIVE?'

Patrick could get his own ten dollars. This was too insane for me.

Now that she understood her pay, Yoko bid us goodnight, and Patrick offered to drive Antoinette home himself. He knew where she lived, even if she didn't.

'Right,' Maxine snapped as soon as he was out the door. 'Let's go.'

For the second time, Maxine was determined to deprive us of our lift home, and have Patrick return to an empty house. What was the big hurry? Rather than fight with her, I escaped downstairs to clean up. Halfway down I passed Leonie coming up. I apologised for yelling at her about the tissues, explaining that we had been dealing with a crisis.

'Hey, what about my crisis?' she laughed. 'Antoinette nearly killed me 'cause I don't know where she lives!'

When the front door slammed, the whole house seemed to sigh with relief. Maxine, at last, had taken her purse and her nose, and gone. I bounded up the stairs to find Leonie cheerfully spraying my desk and lovingly straightening my pens for me, and I wished I'd never apologised to her. Patrick rang to sing he was one minute away, and Leonie and I ran down those stairs like two giggling girls on their last day of school. We checked the back door was locked, then locked the front door behind us, and dropped the key through the letterbox, as usual.

The silver Mercedes welcomed us like a warm, upholstered womb, and the three of us sang to the radio all the way to Leonie's strange graffiti-covered flat in Randwick. Once she was out, Patrick and I slipped into our familiar, awkward, silent intimacy all the way to Coogee. Trudy was right. We were both cowards. Only when I was out of the car could I think of something funny to say.

'I still didn't get your ten dollars off Antoinette!' I called out from the front gate.

Patrick eagerly wound down his window.

'Ah, yes,' he gurgled merrily, 'but I know where she lives!'

I laughed all the way to bed, and dreamt of having Patrick's children, who would all be carpenters and possibly not drive prostitutes anywhere but just fix things around the house, singing.

The next afternoon I woke up to about ten messages from Sofia. My housemate Peter looked worried, and when I heard Sofia's several urgent requests that I call her at home, I was worried too. What had I done? Was a girl missing? Had we left a heater on? Was it the tissues?

'Yes, Meredith,' Sofia answered with profound gravity, 'we have a big problem.'

'Oh dear, Sofia, what have I done now?'

A pause.

'Two thousan' dollars, my dear. Lass night's takings. Where is it?'

The Spanish inquisition

Sofia allowed me a quick gasp before she continued breathlessly.

'Now, I'm sorry, my dear, but it has to have been one of you. One of the receptionists.'

Why?

'Because when Boris arrived at six this morning, it was gone. Now, what I need to know from you is if any of you were alone in the office, and for how long?'

I felt like the Winslow boy.

Sofia continued. 'Maxine has been helping us all day. We rang her at ten this morning, so she has not slept, and you can imagine the state she is in.'

The thought of Maxine in an authentic state was actually refreshing.

'Have you called Leonie?' I asked.

A pause.

'Meredith, do you know what that fucking idiot said to me? "Hang on, Sofia. I'll juss go and check my bag."' It was good to hear Sofia laugh. 'Can you believe that?'

Sadly, I could. Sofia resumed her solemn tone and asked if there was anything whatsoever unusual about last night. I could think of nothing apart from Maxine's obsession with leaving early, even though Patrick hadn't been paid.

'Were there any girls upstairs at any time?'

After thoroughly blasting me for having Yoko in reception, because I knew the rules, Sofia gave me the bad news.

'I'm sorry, my dear,' she sighed, 'but as the three of you were on lass night, Didi says all three of you are responsible for the money going missing.'

Flushed with an unusual, euphoric sense of propriety and calm, I silently dared Sofia to continue.

'So unless it is returned immediately, my dear, it will be coming out of all your pay packets.'

'Sofia,' I began, a clear fountain of serenity, 'I am not responsible for any money that is missing from anywhere. And I would like to make it very clear to you, to Boris and to Didi that if one cent comes out of my pay, I'm not coming back at all.'

I had been paid for the week, and it was a good call.

'Okay, my dear,' Sofia said, sounding unusually respectful.

'By the way,' she added, just before hanging up, 'you know you left one of Boris's off bookings on your sheet last week?'

My fountain spluttered to a trickle.

'Yes, my dear.' Sofia guffawed. 'Holy shit hit the fan when Didi saw. She's been yelling at Boris all week. He wants to fucking kill you.'

'Oh.'

An hour later Sofia rang again, just wanting to go over a few details, and to ask me if I would come in at seven that night with the other two, to talk to Boris.

'And Boris wants you to know, Meredith, of course he knows you did not take it, and nothing will come out of your pay, okay?'

I arrived early and sat around his desk with Boris and Sofia for a few minutes. Pip and Raelene were on duty, both skilfully pretending they weren't pleased as punch to be witnessing the scandal unfold before them. When Boris offered me a Minty, I took one.

Boris's face was soft, and his eyes were clear, and there was a genuine alpine beauty radiating from him. In the light of this crime, I guessed he'd forgotten to kill me. Maybe it was his very genuine need to communicate, or his decision to approach this as a forgiving boss, not a fear-mongering one, but whatever it was, he smiled at me for the very first time. While we waited for the other two, I savoured the suspense. Which girl took the money? Both blew their pay on expensive drugs. Perhaps Boris, due to his gambling addiction, had framed his employees and taken the money himself. And who, if anyone, suspected me?

At five past seven, Maxine burst in dramatically. As there were no chairs left, she knelt at our feet, and pushed her face into mine.

Wasn't this awful? She hadn't slept! Nothing like this had ever happened to her before.

'In all my years in this business, and I've held tens of thousands of dollars in my hands, Meredith—' To prove it, Maxine showed me her hands. ' nothing like this has ever happened. And I'm embarrassed! I'm embarrassed, Boris!'

Boris nodded graciously.

'And I can't believe I'm going to lose my job because of some fucking stupid—' and here Maxine broke down crying.

What a show. Although it was being played to me, it was obviously for Boris's benefit. I let Maxine have the stage and enjoyed my Minty.

As usual, Leonie was late. Even for this. So Boris and Sofia began without her. But before I could answer any of their questions, Maxine jumped in, with tears running down her face, looking desperately up at me for support, as if I held her life in my hands. I honestly couldn't remember her counting the money, or what time she put it on Boris's desk, and her talons were digging into my knees as she cried, 'Oh, please, Meredith, say you remember! You saw me do that!'

Boris and Sofia had to shoosh her constantly as she became more and more shrill.

When Leonie joined us, she too knelt on the floor and looked up at us.

'Hey, I know it looks like I did it,' she smiled, 'but I didn't take that money. No way. I know you all think like I probably did. But I didn't.'

Leonie looked good tonight. She had clear skin and clear eyes and she looked like a fresh-faced kid. But they came down on her hard, asking a million questions, revealing a million discrepancies. Leonie could barely recall what she'd had for breakfast, and it seemed unfair to read such culpability into her usual witless disposition. And then we came to Exhibit A, my bit of paper.

Ever since the night Boris so horribly humiliated me in front of the girls in the kitchen for my poor business skills and my appalling footwear, I had religiously recorded on a piece of paper all cash transactions between me and the girls downstairs, and ran around in socks. At the end of my shift, I always deposited my paperwork on Boris's desk for post-casino perusal. But Boris had found my piece of paper this morning, not on his desk where I always left it, but on Maxine's. Who had put it there? And why? Not me. Not Maxine. Not Leonie.

'No way.'

Boris was in full Sherlock forensic investigative mode as he asked Sofia to place the evidence, carefully using a tissue to pick it up, exactly where he had found it. Whoever had stood at his desk stealing the money, Boris deducted, had been interrupted, and had quickly feigned legitimate activity by moving some paperwork from his desk to Maxine's. It didn't look good for Maxine, who suddenly turned to Leonie.

'Leonie, darling, I'm not accusing you of taking the money, okay?' Maxine whined. 'Okay, Leonie? But, darling, just think, really think hard for us now, did you touch that piece of paper at all?'

Now it was Leonie's turn to get upset. 'No! No! No!' she cried.

'The only people who touched this paper,' Boris continued, 'are myself and Meredit, so we vill let the police check it for fingerprints.'

Was he serious?

'I'm serious. I do not vont to do this, but if the money is not returned . . .'

That was fine with me, and fine with Maxine. Leonie looked a little confused and troubled, but then Leonie always did. Maxine got up and shared a look with Pip, who discreetly pointed to Leonie and mouthed, 'Boris – knows – it's – her.'

Sofia was searching for a plastic bag to place the evidence in when Maxine let out a cry.

'Oh, no!'

As she stood up, Maxine had accidentally placed her hand on the very evidence, still lying on her desk.

'Oh, Sofia, I'm so sorry! I put my hand on it, I didn't think. I didn't see it there!'

'Is okay,' said Sofia flatly, 'it juss got your palm, darling.'

That's when I felt sure it was Maxine.

'I think Maxine did it,' Trudy said to me on the phone a few days later.

Apparently, Maxine had thrown various turns at work during the shifts that followed. Although no one had said a thing to her, Maxine felt victimised, accused, persecuted, and she wasn't going to take it any more. She came in crying, having not slept, having lost weight, if that was possible, and still no one had said a word to provoke her. Finally, Maxine announced, it was all just too much! She'd had enough! She was leaving!

When Didi told Maxine that leaving would be interpreted as an admission of guilt, Maxine tied herself to the stake and stayed. But the damage was done. Her histrionics had cleared Leonie of all suspicion, and now even Pip suspected the Egyptian Smurf.

As soon as I arrived on Friday night, I was dragged into

bedroom one by Sofia, who sat me on the leopard-skin bed cover for a 'serious chat'. Although surrounded by vibrators and lubricants, I knew not to joke with Sofia unless she'd had a scotch. Then she found the funny side to everything.

'No one believes for one moment you touched that money, Meredith. This is why we're not taking money out of your pay. But if either of the other girls ask, you must say your pay is being docked too. This is from Didi. Okay?'

Amen.

I was sad to hear both girls were allowing their pay to be docked. That meant one was admitting guilt, and the other was plain stupid. No prizes for guessing.

When Maxine sensed the pressure was off Leonie, somewhat predictably she pointed the finger at me, so my colleagues informed me.

'And do you know why no one suspects you?' chirped Pip.

'Because I didn't take it?' I asked, weakly.

'Because you were on *Play School*!' Pip piped cheerfully, and gave me a big bear hug.

Extraordinary rumours circulated over the next two weeks. Although he never mentioned the fingerprints again, Boris took the trouble to ring Sam, Maxine's previous employer at Blue Angels. Boris began by asking the ex-cop if they'd had any problems with Maxine while she worked there. Well yes, Sam said, if you counted the time they caught Maxine on surveillance video passing money through the window to her boyfriend outside, who was now in jail. Was that the kind of problem Boris meant?

'But that could be bullshit,' Boris said standing at our door and shaking his head at two in the morning. 'People in this business lie all the time. I sack Maxine, Sam takes her back, and finds out how we run things here. Don't believe everything you hear, Meredit.'

He tapped his nose, winked, and left. I loved Boris when he was like this, our Bavarian Humphrey Bogart in his rose-scented suit.

I got the distinct impression Maxine was avoiding me. For three Sunday nights in a row she was too ill to come in and work our shift together. But one day, out of the blue, she rang me at home.

I listened nauseously to the little voice on our answering machine. I always feel suspicious of people who only give their mobile number. Before returning her call, I rang Sofia to check what my story should be.

'Tell her your pay is being docked, darling. That's what Didi said. Get any information out of her you can. Then ring me straight back.'

'Yes, Maxine, they are docking my pay too!'

'Are they? Because Didi told me they weren't.'

Terrific.

'Meredith, they're already taking eight hundred dollars from me, and eight hundred from Leonie, so if they are taking eight hundred from you too, darl, that means they're making a profit.'

She had a point. Now I had not only to feign outrage that all our pays were being docked, I had to discuss our employers' shocking lack of moral ethics with a lying, felonious coke addict who had, not twenty-four hours ago, pointed her thieving finger at *me*. And I'd been on *Play School*!

I rang Sofia, Sofia rang Didi, then Didi rang me.

'Merediss,' Didi cooed sweetly, 'I have told Maxine and Leonie that as you were on downstairs duty that night, the money was more their responsibility than yours, and that I'm not docking your pay, all right?'

When I turned up for my next shift, I found I no longer cared about criminal records, witch-hunts or docked pays any more. I wasn't going to lie for anyone, or even return a call. The dirty towels on the laundry floor were cleaner than the office politics in this place, and despite all the notices warning us not to socialise with the working girls, I just wanted to hang out with my favourite prostitutes.

Playing hard to get

I don't remember what we were laughing about as Patrick turned
into my street at sunrise. Whatever it was, we both had to hit
something. Patrick chose the steering wheel, and I chose Patrick.
I had been hitting him a lot lately. I don't know if he noticed, but
he didn't seem to mind.

'Would you like to go for a drink some time?' Patrick asked
suddenly.

'Yes!' I practically shouted.

And then we both sat in silence. No car had ever taken so long
to pass three houses and pull into one driveway, and no woman had
ever sounded so desperate.

'Next week then?' he suggested as I attempted a graceful exit.

'Sure,' I said, not quite clearing my head.

The following Thursday night, Patrick would pick me up at
eight.

A romantic dinner, a moonlit walk and a pole-dancer
from Belfast

On Sunday night at work, Patrick informed me he couldn't pick
me up on Thursday after all, as he wouldn't have the car.

'It's not your car?' I asked.

'No,' he said, 'it's Limpy's.'

I had no right to be disappointed that Patrick had no car, or that
he lived with a man called Limpy. After all, I had made it to thirty-
eight with not so much as a licence. But when Patrick also told me
we might have to postpone our date till he had 'more dosh', I felt
sad. I didn't necessarily want to date an architect or a gynaecologist,
but I did want someone who could afford half a bottle of wine and
a bowl of pasta. And so did all my friends.

'After all,' whined Libby, my disappointed housemate, 'he's got
money for hooch.'

And Libby was right. I'd played second fiddle to hooch before.

Whenever my ex had rolled up a number, I always felt somewhat inadequate, as if my company wasn't interesting, funny or stimulating enough. And as he sat there sprinkling his tobacco with chopped green heads and leaf, I prattled on about anything, desperate to engage him on any topic of conversation before he went under and I lost all contact. I'd climb over him, abandoning all dignity, only to have him look at me as if he were taking in the vast plains of the Nullarbor from a window seat on a Greyhound bus. Once or twice, out of sheer desperation, I took a drag of his joint, hoping it would transport me to the same benign twilight zone, but instead it ripped a hole in my chest, blew my head off, and convinced me our dog was the devil.

Each to his own. The following Thursday night, I poured myself a double vodka as I waited to see if Patrick would arrive. At eight I found him on my front doorstep, smiling dreamily with heavy eyelids and dilated pupils. As we were both so nervous, I suggested a quick tour of the house. When we got to my bedroom Patrick and I moved around each other like two blind square dancers in a barn, so it was a relief when I got him outside, into our courtyard.

'My God,' he cried, 'you've got a pool!'

Patrick laughed so much at the sight of our swimming pool, I found myself wondering if this date was such a good idea after all.

'I'm sorry,' he managed at last.

As neither of us had cars and it was an unusually mild September night, I suggested we walk down to the Aquarium Bar in Coogee and enjoy the view with a drink on the balcony before going somewhere for dinner.

'Righty-ho,' sang my stoned date, still struggling to overcome his mirth at our pool.

Worried that our large house had made Patrick feel socially or economically inadequate, I madly explained that I paid very little rent, but I need not have worried. Patrick was oblivious to anything I said as we walked to the beach. He just ambled along smiling, hands stuffed in his pockets, only breaking his silence once, to ask if I liked *The Simpsons*.

We were on the escalator on our way up to the Aquarium Bar when Patrick turned to me, still smiling. It was powerful dope.

'Um, I might have to borrow something off you tonight, after all,' he said.

'What?' I asked.

I wondered if I'd hit an all-time low as I handed a man fifty dollars to have a date with me. Could there be two sadder people on an escalator outside a Paul Cox film?

'Better he borrows fifty dollars than a hundred,' Trudy would say.

And I would smack her in the head.

'It's my no-hoper housemates,' Patrick explained, placing a Guinness and a chardonnay, which wasn't so much cheeky as abusive, on our wet table.

We were surrounded by so many backpackers, I had to wonder who was left in Ireland.

'We've got a sweet old landlady,' Patrick continued, 'and as the only one with a job, I'm always covering the rent. They promised to fix me up by tonight, but as usual . . .'

Patrick said he lived in a ramshackle old house in Matraville with Limpy, a Vietnam Vet on a pension, and Den, a 'crusty old bastard' on the dole. According to Patrick, what Limpy and Den lacked in financial independence and hygiene, they more than made up for in character.

'We laugh a lot,' Patrick said, chuckling as he shook his head, 'at just about anything.'

Wait till he tells them about our pool, I thought.

'Are you near the bay in Matraville?' I asked hopefully.

'Yeah,' Patrick answered, 'right next to Botany cemetery.'

And the more Patrick told me about his life, the more I drank.

Although Patrick was polite enough to ask me about my family and my acting work, with every answer I could feel him drifting further away, as he nodded with sad defeat and gazed into his ashtray.

'Sorry?' he asked with a jolt.

'My mum,' I repeated. 'She just got her MA. At seventy-two.'

'Oh.'

I ended up condensing my acting career, minimising my eccentric family, and made my life sound as ordinary as possible.

At midnight, with stomachs full of chips and alcohol, and muttering something about cabs, Patrick and I stumbled out into the rain. Escaping the downpour, Patrick pulled me into the bus shelter on Arden Street, where we huddled like two drowned rats on the dry bench and waited hopelessly for a Streetcar Named Forget It. We watched the backpackers stagger past us and into McDonald's across the road. One straggler, precariously lurching from pillar to post, made her way towards us, flattening the occasional bush. With one final lurch she flung her body around our bus stop like a deranged pole-dancer, and then threw up at our feet. I hoped that Patrick was not like my friend Sal, who spontaneously retched at the mere smell of vomit. Sal once took her sick husband to a Thai restaurant for their wedding anniversary, and the night ended before it ever began, over a basket of prawn crackers.

''Scuse me,' our sick, drunk Irish friend emitted mid heave, 'but were you on *Neighbours*?'

'No,' I mumbled, trying not to breath through my nose.

'You sure? You look just like her.'

Smiling politely, I shook my head.

'Juss as well,' she groaned, 'she was shite.'

At which point Patrick thoughtfully suggested we walk back to my place and call him a taxi from there.

As we strode across the park in the rain, I was explaining to Patrick how vulnerable good actors are to bad storylines, and how difficult it was to seduce a teenage boy while dressed as a golf fanatic, when he stopped suddenly.

'What?' I asked, turning.

And Patrick kissed me. No warning. Just collected an unhappy actress and kissed her in the rain. For a moment I forgot about darts and the Matraville RSL. I forgot about the fifty dollars, and Limpy and Den. I even got the swimming pool joke. All I wanted was for Patrick to come back to my place, put up a blind or two, and then go quietly before we remembered we had absolutely nothing in common.

It shouldn't be called a 'one night stand', I thought, as I lay next to the snoring Patrick in my bed and wished he wasn't. It should be called a 'hit and run'. Because that's what it felt like, knowing

Patrick would wake up in his new surroundings and wonder how welcome he was to stay. And knowing that he wasn't. I lay there, planning my afternoon with military precision. After a hearty breakfast and a cheerful goodbye, I was going to empty the ashtray that had made its way to my bedroom, open the windows, wash the sheets, have a bath, burn incense, and get some sleep.

'Thanks for the big brekkie,' Patrick said at the front door as he kissed me. 'And see you tonight!'

'Well,' I cautioned, 'hang on—'

'At work,' he added, grinning.

'Yes!' I cheered.

That's right. At work. Patrick and I worked together. Three nights a week. Every week. It all came back to me.

The big booking

I would be friendly, but not intimate. Present but not promising. Warm but not *warm*. And I would be sober. Patrick and I would work together as two mature adults who, one rainy night in Coogee, downed tools, had sex, then picked them up again and paid back any money owing.

It had not stopped raining since the previous night, and I was soaking wet when I trudged into the warm kitchen. The usual girls sat at their usual posts, and there stood Patrick, halfway up a ladder, nail in mouth, tool belt on, hammering in a shelf. Brilliant. I concentrated hard on architects and gynaecologists who'd be interested in my mother's MA, and made a B-line for the laundry.

'Hello,' Patrick sang.

'Hi,' I said, striding towards the laundry, muttering something about a towel.

Once inside, a head popped up from behind the dryer door.

'I saw your bread commercial this afternoon, Meredith,' Leonie piped. 'They played it all through *Jerry Springer*.'

Snatching a towel from Leonie's pile, I turned to brave the kitchen once more.

'How are you?' Patrick asked.

'Fine,' I answered from under the towel, manically drying my hair.

'Look!' he said.

I came out from hiding.

'I'm putting up shelves,' Patrick gloated provocatively, his hammer poised, and winked at me, 'like a *good tradesman*.'

I left Patrick grinning at me like Malvolio, resplendent in his yellow, cross-gartered stockings, and fled upstairs. What stupid drunken things had I said about carpenters last night?

I gathered from the four girls' names on the board that it was going to be a hectic night. Raelene was already sweating over her desk, telling some guy from Star City to calm down.

'Fuck me dead,' Sofia grunted, stomping through the door like a cold, wet, angry bull. 'Give me that towel, darling,' she said, pointing with one hand, and answering a phone with the other.

While I put a blitz of callers on hold, Sofia frantically searched for a lighter and argued with Manuel at the Sofitel, in Spanish.

'Sofia,' Raelene interrupted her. 'I've got Felix on Asian Fantasy and he *insists* he speaks with you.'

'Who the fuck is Felix?' Sofia cried angrily, and then pushed a button. 'Ello, Felix? Is Sofia! How you been, my love?'

While Sofia juggled Felix and Manuel, I sent Antoinette to a couple in Balmain, and Raelene returned to her caller from Star City.

'Okay, okay. Hang on, Bruce,' Raelene said. 'I think I'd better hand you over to my manager.'

Sofia, who could eavesdrop on three calls while speaking in Spanish, looked at Raelene in a way that made us both nervous.

'What, Raelene?' she demanded.

'Sofia,' Raelene began timorously, 'this guy at Star City has just won sixty thousand dollars, and, what he's thinking, um, is that he'd like to treat his friends . . .'

'Oh, fuck me dead,' Sofia groaned, clawing a free hand through her wet hair. 'How many?'

'Fifteen,' Raelene squeaked, trying hard not to laugh. 'There are fifteen of them. And they would like fifteen girls.' Pause. 'Now.'

Sofia shook her head at me as if to say 'Typical!' or 'My luck!' and I, too, struggled not to laugh.

'Oh, fuck me dead,' she groaned again.

Although there were more than twenty girls on roster on any given night, half of them were soon booked, sometimes for hours, and the rest called in sick or just didn't answer their phones. Sofia got rid of Manuel, sent Lottie to Felix, and immediately swung into action.

Bruce at Star City didn't know he wanted to book fifteen women for a four-hour dinner booking. He hadn't even thought about food, but Sofia had. This way it was going to be at least six hundred dollars for each girl before she'd even sat down. Six hundred dollar dinner bookings were very popular with the girls. Although they could earn more than that over four hours, back-to-back bookings were very rare. And this way they spent most of their time being wined and dined, instead of being mauled and clawed, and by one man instead of three. Plus, the dinner booking rate charged a whopping three hundred and fifty dollars for any extending hour.

'You got to feed the ladies, darling,' Sofia berated the reluctant Bruce. 'You want to celebrate this night, don't you? An' drink champagne with your friends?'

When Sofia finally closed the deal for nearly ten thousand dollars, including taxis, she threw her damp body back in her chair, lit up a cigarette, and looked over at me.

'A coronator's nightmare,' she uttered dismally, like Brando in the cave.

She meant coordinator, but I let it go.

'How the fuck I am going to get fifteen girls to Star City at the same time?' She looked from Raelene to me, measuring our combined uselessness with contempt.

'Perhaps we could build a large wooden horse,' I said quietly, 'and put all the girls inside ...'

I had always been the clown in our family.

At that moment Leonie maundered into our office, slouching with exhaustion from putting three large towels in the washing machine, and collapsed into a chair. The three of us watched in silent disbelief as she picked up a magazine and began to flick through it listlessly.

'WHAT THE FUCK YOU DOING?' Sofia exploded, as the magazine flew through the air. 'GO DOWNSTAIRS AND WASH SOME TOWELS FOR CHRISSAKE!'

Only Leonie would be stupid enough to protest she had just done so.

'OH FOR CHRISSAKE, JUST GO!'

And Leonie did, very quickly.

'All right,' Sofia thumped her desk, making us jump. 'I gotta ring Min. We need all Min's girls.'

'Do they want Asian?' I sensibly asked, as often men didn't.

'Look!' Sofia yelled, head-butting me right in the sensibilities. 'They want fifteen women, darling. If they don't say, don't ask! They get Asian whether they want or not!'

She was still possibly angry about the horse, but I made a note anyway.

'Meredith, get me Lucinda, Kimberley, Delilah, oh fuck, Pandora! Raelene, get Patrick! I don't care what he's doing. He's gotta – that you, Lan?' she suddenly yelled down the phone. 'Get Min, Lan. Ring me back!'

Like all of our girls on mobiles, Lan and Min had to ring us back on theirs, even in a crisis.

'Raelene, tell Patrick he's gotta pick up Pandora from Marrickville,' Sofia barked. 'I don't care when she's finishing! Ah forget it, I'm doing it. Meredith, get Min again, I can't wait!'

There was such pandemonium, I half expected George Clooney to wheel in a bleeding patient any moment, yelling, '*Stat!*'

As Sofia kept getting girls' message banks, her blood pressure rose, and Raelene and I feared for our safety. Leonie crept into the room with another problem.

'FUCK ME DEAD!' Sofia yelled, slamming down her phone.

Leonie turned around and left.

'You see, darling?' Sofia spoke to me in a deceptively calm voice as she tried to ring Min again. 'You see why we have to punish these girls? See why we have to lie? Because when we need them, when the shit really hits de fan, THEY FUCK OFF!'

I nodded. It always amazed me how, in the midst of chaos, Sofia could still think of my training. I almost considered going to Star City myself, such was the loyalty my general inspired.

'This is why we send Min's girls,' she continued, still waiting for Min to answer. 'At least they are reliable! And I tell you something else, darling. Whether these men want Asian or Australian, is the Asians who'll get the extensions. You see. Not the Australians.'

At last someone answered her call.

'LAN, WHERE THE FUCK IS MIN? I GOT A FUCKING EMERGENCY HERE!'

I had noticed Raelene's several furtive glances in my direction, waiting until Sofia was distracted before sharing some guilty secret.

'I've got this guy,' she whispered to me finally, 'a real sweetie, never done it before. Who do you think I should send?'

'Hang on, Min,' Sofia interrupted her call. 'RAELENE! SEND HIM AN UGLY GIRL! SEND HIM A PIECE OF FRUIT! WHO CARES? WE GOTTA FUCKING CRISIS HERE!'

Raelene and I got the giggles. A piece of fruit.

While Sofia rounded up the girls, Raelene and I took turns at answering Bruce's increasingly pissed queries from Star City.

'On their way, Bruce, any minute now ... Yes, fifteen Bruce, all beautiful ... No, they can't meet you in the restaurant, Bruce. Just wait for them in your room ... because you can't pay them in the restaurant, Bruce ... well, because they could get arrested for soliciting, Bruce, and then they'd have to spend the night in jail ... That's right, Bruce, no good to anyone ...'

'Wait for the others in the foyer,' Sofia repeated the command down her hot phone. 'I want you all to go up together! *Together!*'

She was right, it was a coronator's nightmare. And a driver's. Patrick had never worked so hard for a cup of tea in his life. Communicating with him was proving almost impossible as he could never hear us over the excited chatter of so many women in his car.

'Patrick, where are you?'

'I've got her!'

'*Where?*'

'Who?'

It took nearly an hour, but we gradually assembled a small battalion of fourteen women, armed with condoms and lube, in the foyer of Star City casino. I had Shelby on the phone and, judging from the wolf whistling in the background, the sight of so many attractive young women standing outside one lift was creating a bit of a commotion.

'SUCK YOUR OWN FAT ONE, FATBOY!' Shelby bellowed in my ear. 'Sorry, Meredith, go on.'

'Sofia wants you to wait till Pandora gets there, Shelby.'

Pandora, our youngest and most beautiful, was somewhere between a booking at Marrickville and Star City.

'Nah, Meredith,' Shelby responded to my request. 'We're not waitin' round here. We're goin' up.'

And she hung up. Such was my authority with the girls.

How we would confirm payment for so many girls was anyone's guess, but for now, we just had to wait for a call. Anyone's call. Sofia crouched over her phone like a deranged cat, ready to pounce. Finally, Trixie rang, but we could barely hear her over the loud, boisterous, boozy cheers that welcomed each girl as she came through Bruce's door.

'Trixie!' Sofia cried in vain. 'TRIXIE!'

But Trixie and her colleagues were too busy flirting to secure their stay, and money was the last thing on the men's minds, so Sofia hung up.

'You see?' she smiled in sad surrender. 'Until Pandora gets there, is useless. She the only one with a brain.'

Really? Silent Pandora who sat downstairs like a pinned Botticelli angel with the nods? Ten minutes later, Pandora rang from Star City and did a roll call, insisting every man pick his girl then and there.

'I told you,' Sofia quipped in my direction.

It must have been like choosing teams for basketball, and just as humiliating and painful for poor Maya and Rita, who were both cancelled on the spot. But we didn't have time to worry about that. We had to find their replacements urgently.

'Oh, fuck me dead ...' Sofia groaned.

I don't know which house in Parramatta Min raided, but within twenty minutes Lan was driving two new Vietnamese girls to Star City.

Half an hour later Patrick shuffled into our office, carefully placed his cup of tea on Raelene's desk, and then collapsed in the chair opposite, as if he had transported each girl to Star City on his back.

'Sofia,' he said quietly, 'Lucinda said to tell you, after this one, she can't possibly take another booking tonight.'

'Why?' Sofia asked him the dreaded question.

'Ah,' began Patrick awkwardly, 'because she's been working since three o'clock this afternoon,' he blushed from head to sandshoe, 'and she can tell you the rest herself.'

Despite her cool Jane Austen charm and aristocratic grace, Lucinda could swear like a trooper and was prone, on a busy night, to describe in florid detail the ravaged state of her vaginal walls. Even to Patrick. I always found Lucinda's graphic descriptions at two in the morning refreshingly honest, and a welcome comic relief. But my colleagues did not share this opinion. Unable to get past her Sloane accent, they regarded this incredibly down-to-earth girl as 'stuck up'.

'Tell her to use more lube,' muttered Sofia, returning to her paperwork.

Patrick pretended not to hear and quietly sipped his tea.

Due to the unusual amount of cash to be collected from one booking, Sofia insisted the troops return to the house as soon as they'd finished. From around four in the morning the door bell chimed repeatedly, like a broken record. As downstairs receptionist, it was Leonie's job to collect all the money and bring it upstairs.

'Should I go down and help her?' I asked Sofia.

'Go! Run!' she shouted.

The kitchen was noisy with laughter and corks popping as a dozen beautiful women, draped in satin or silk, or wrapped in Lycra and good old spandex, celebrated their combined victory. It was like being backstage at an international beauty pageant, without the Americans. I walked through the sea of hothouse flowers, carried along by the scent of their delicate perfumes, and let their petals caress me, as Lucinda, May-Ling and Genevieve planted

234 The big booking

kisses on my cheeks, and Shelby poured me a glass of champagne. I too ignored Leonie's futile pleas for money and immersed myself in their reverie. After ten minutes of hearing stories of four-course meals, French champagne, penthouse suites, room service and tips, I wondered what change Bruce had, if any, from sixty thousand dollars. He would certainly be in for a hefty bill in the morning, and a hefty hangover. The only time the girls' celebratory mood sagged was when I enquired about the Asian girls who still had not returned. Once again, Sofia was right.

Clutching a thick wad of cash, I quickly popped my head into the lounge to see who was boycotting this party. Usually its reclining inhabitants would look up from the television and smile at me, but not tonight. Maya and Rita looked straight ahead and continued watching a demonstration of a thing called the 'ab buster' with as much dignity as they could muster. A cancellation was a miserable experience for any girl, but to be rejected so publicly, in front of their peers, and by such a large group of men, must have been crushing, to say the least. Unable to think of anything to say, I quietly closed the door and continued upstairs.

Halfway up, I met Patrick coming down.

'Hello!' he sang. 'Do you want to do dinner next week?'

'Look,' I said, biting the bullet, 'Patrick, about the other night—'

'Yes!' He cut me off. 'Yes, I know.'

'You know?'

'I owe you fifty!' He nodded gravely.

'No,' I began again, 'no, it's—'

'Yes!' Patrick almost shouted. 'I insist! I owe you fifty dollars.'

Not wanting the whole house to hear me discussing money owed in a brothel with the driver on the stairs, I shooshed him.

'And I'll get it back to you next week,' he whispered, 'promise.'

'Patrick—'

But Patrick just touched his nose, smiled and nodded assuringly as he continued down the stairs and out the front door. I watched him go and dared to recall, at last, our recent intimacy. Maybe it was because of the late hour, or maybe it was this familiar context where Patrick's presence was so precious, but I did not mind the memory as much as I'd anticipated. For a second I even enjoyed it, and wondered if we shouldn't go out for dinner next week. Then I remembered why we shouldn't go out for dinner next week. The thought of Patrick asking me for another fifty when the bill came was more than I could bear.

'Not the crystal, darling, Jesus.' Sofia berated Leonie, who hovered awkwardly in our doorway carrying a tray with two bottles of the good St James, reserved for one-hour bookings, and four glasses. 'Boris will have a heart attack! Oh fuck me dead, gimme a glass.'

Now that Sofia had counted over ten thousand dollars for the agency she wanted to celebrate.

'But I was going to put strawberries in!' Leonie cried, unloading her cargo on my desk.

'Sure, darling. Put strawberries in,' Sofia told her, 'just put the fucking things in now before I die!'

Sofia giggled at Raelene and me to see if we were as close to hysteria as she was, and to show our loyalty we laughed like a pair of demented kookaburras.

Boris stood in the doorway with his legs apart, like something out of *Gunsmoke*, observing a hens' party taking place in his saloon. The last time Boris arrived in the early hours to find us drinking his St James, it had not been pretty. He slowly scanned the debris, the opened bottles, the strawberries and his four dishevelled, giggling, drunken receptionists.

'This had better be goot,' he warned us, nodding.

And we fell apart, as if Boris was funnier than the Marx Brothers.

While Sofia boasted to him about our extraordinary achievement and her coronator's nightmare, like a nervous child to her disapproving father, Boris peered over her shoulder.

'Thirty thousand, three hundred and seventy-five dollars!' he shrieked, interrupting her.

'And that's not counting the four Asians still in there, Boris!' Sofia shouted at him.

'Ah yes,' nodded Boris and turned to me. 'You know, Meredit, it's always the Asians who get the extensions. You votch. Not the Australians. The Asians.'

I nodded.

Smiling and swivelling on his throne, Boris ordered Leonie to open another bottle of the good stuff. Although he didn't drink himself, the big booking seemed to have made him tipsy, and Boris was in an entertaining mood. He told us funny stories about Bim, a receptionist who'd worked for them during the good old days at North Sydney. Bim was a born-again Christian from Papua New Guinea who once told a man who enquired if the girls did 'French', 'It doesn't matter where you come from, sir, they do anyone.' Needless to say, Bim didn't last long, but she provided much material for funny anecdotes for years to come.

'Dim Bim,' Boris shook his head and chuckled.

Grabbing his keys and standing suddenly, Boris congratulated us once more, bid us a fond farewell, and returned to his beloved casino, his wallet fat with off bookings.

As usual, the 5 am drunks were calling from the Furama, or the Cross. It was always two Asian girls for two drunk men, but this time it was us who were pissed.

'Sure they're beautiful,' I boasted effusively to Mr Chan.

'Because if they not, we kick them out!' Mr Chan warned me.

'No, no, you pay girls cancellation fee, Misser Shan,' I sang.

What an arrogant prick.

'No. I not pay anything if girl not up to scrat!' he insisted.

'Scratch.'

'What?'

'Mr Shan. You pay fifty dollar cancellation fee, whatever you think of girls. I'm not negotiating, Mr Shan, I'm telling you. Now, you want girls or not?'

Reluctantly, Mr Chan agreed to let me ring him back with suggestions. But the truth was, I had no girls to send Mr Chan, or his friend. All our Asians were still extending at Star City. And although it was a long shot, Candice and Glenda would not be finished at the Marriot for at least another hour.

'Morning, Misser Shan!' I sang. 'Me again! Just letting you know, girls are on their way, but not Asian. Two *stunning* Aussralian models. In a taxi.'

'Not Asian? Australian?'

'S'right, Misser Shan. Reeeeeally beautiful Aussralian girls. Blondes. All of them.'

'Oh ...'

'Same price. Four hundred and fifty cash. Won't be long!'

I hung up.

Two blondes on their way in a taxi seemed to have stunned him. I let Leonie pour me another champagne, vaguely aware that I should perhaps find two blonde Australian sex workers some time soonish, to send Mr Thingy at the Whatsit.

5.30 am and it was Mr Chan again.

'Missershan!'

'Where are girls? You said in taxi half an hour ago!'

'S'right.'

'Well? Where are they?'

'No idea! Hang on, just put a hold on you.'

I looked at Raelene and Sofia, who found my dilemma very amusing.

'Missershan?' I said. 'Candice and Glenda there any minute now.'

But when Candice finally did ring at six, she didn't want to go to the Furama. She was going straight home to a hot bath. And Glenda got a one-hour extension. I made myself a really strong cup of coffee.

'Cho-cho and Yin will finish in 'alf hour at Star City, darling.' Sofia chortled over her drink.

'Sofia! He's already waited an hour.'

'So?'

'He's expecting two blondes!'

'Well, he get a nice surprise!' she roared laughing. 'Now you got the hang of it, darling!'

I rang Min.

'When Cho-cho and Yin finish at Star City, Min, could they go see rude man and his friend at Furama?'

'Sure, dali,' Min croaked.

Sorting Patrick's pay always wiped the smiles off everyone's face. Sofia looked a fright, surrounded by paperwork and adding machines, with her hair sticking up in tufts. Raelene rubbed her eyes, Leonie ate everyone's strawberries, and Patrick and I held our heads in our hands as we listened to the birds singing outside.

'I can't do this,' Sofia announced finally, 'my brain's gone.'

Once again, she and Patrick tried to add up his lifts for the night, and finally agreed on a hundred and eighty dollars. It was seven o'clock and the Saturday morning traffic outside was already intruding. We patted each other's backs as we cleaned up, sprayed down our desks with disinfectant, closed our folders and turned off our lamps. As we drained our glasses of stale champagne, one lonely phone rang. Sofia answered, then looked at me and smiled as she spoke. 'Hi, Cho-cho and Yin at the Furama. You got four hundred and fifty cash? You happy? We happy too.'

Driving home with Patrick was a pretty silent affair. I had no feelings at all on the subject of his proposed date. All I could think of was that, in less than twelve hours, I'd be back at work, doing it all over again. I even forgot we were carrying an extra passenger.

'Hey, Meredith,' came the familiar whine from the back seat.

'Yes, Leonie.'

'Do you think I took that money?'

'No, Leonie,' I droned, gazing out my window, 'no one thinks you took that money.'

Suddenly, Leonie's large, pale, childish face loomed next to mine.

'Really?'

I nodded. 'Not even Sofia.'

Leonie looked ahead at the horizon, as if mesmerised by some wondrous apparition.

Crossing to the other side

Pronouncing Leonie too artless to be a criminal was, to Leonie, the greatest compliment possible. Her euphoria and gratitude was pitiful to watch, until she used this affirmation as a catalyst for a complete transformation. Our paltry token of faith was absorbed like moisturiser on dry skin, and Leonie resolved to reward us all by becoming the most efficient, hard-working receptionist in any brothel, ever. It was as if she'd heard voices in a field, or a nightclub. When she wasn't answering phones, Leonie was on her knees scrubbing something, or making us cups of tea. Overnight she'd become computer literate, much to Computer-Pip's annoyance. And like a magician, Leonie had become an authority on who did golden showers, B & D and lesbian doubles without looking at their cards. She answered any query with gushy enthusiasm, only too pleased to help. Sofia hated it. She could no longer vent all her anger on Leonie's uselessness.

'What are you doing?' Sofia yelled at her.

'I'm cleaning under your desk!' Leonie's innocent head popped up between Sofia's knees.

'Well ... go an' ... fucking do something else!'

So she fixed the photocopy machine that had sat broken for weeks.

Sofia watched the new Leonie, tortured with conflicting emotions, and smoked even more than usual.

Instead of saying incredibly stupid things in an attempt to be noticed, Leonie now came up with the odd sensible comment. Not all the time, but occasionally. And as she lost weight, she mysteriously gained intelligence and poise. She'd given up dairy, and it was as if her stupidity had fed off her fat cells. She stopped wearing her Mickey Mouse retro pieces and now favoured long, sexy dresses that revealed a slimmer body and more than a little cleavage. And Leonie was laughing more. I found myself feeling quite proud of her. She responded to any measure of warmth like a thirsty plant does to water, and I wondered if the plague of weaknesses she'd cultivated was just in want of a little love. Leonie had always cut a lonely, neglected figure whose obsession with anything second-hand stretched from clothes to opinions.

One night she looked at me with her big round eyes in her big round face, and told me what a good friend she had in Delia, who'd started as a receptionist at the same time as her. I was happy for her, because Delia was a bright, young, beautiful girl from a good home who enjoyed Leonie's wacky perversity and tolerated her alarming naivety and tactlessness with fond amusement. They confided in each other and pawed over magazines together, passionately arguing about Britney Spears' wardrobe mistakes and Brad Pitt's sex appeal, as if they knew any minute they'd be too old for this.

'Do you have many other friends?' I asked Leonie.

'No. None,' she smiled.

'None?' I was shocked.

Visibly moved by my disappointment, Leonie blinked at me gratefully, which made me want to hit her. I thought she would at least know an eclectic, motley bunch of drug addicts and other miscellaneous misfits.

'What about the guy you live with? Isn't he a friend?'

'No way!' she retorted, repulsed at the suggestion. 'We've got a seven hundred dollar phone bill. Phone sex! Disgusting, hey?'

There had been a boyfriend. She had broken up with Corrie six months earlier. He'd gone to live in the States but they kept in touch and still loved each other. Hey.

'I love my cat. And Delia,' Leonie said, until she remembered she really 'dug' her parents, who lived up north and ran a nursery.

'They're cool. They dig that I'm working in a brothel. They used to know everyone on the Sydney nightclub scene, and they took heaps of drugs ...'

I asked Leonie if that was why they'd moved away.

'Hey, yeah. Probably.'

I don't know how it happened. Maybe we didn't reward Leonie's efforts with enough praise. Most of the time we found her born again receptionist too irritating to bear. And I suspect it shamed us, having treated her so badly in the past, all of us except Trudy, who'd always been sweet to her. I came in on a Friday night as Sofia was bitching to Raelene about Leonie's laziness. Had she fallen off the wagon, I asked. Sofia's contemptuous gaze slowly travelled towards me as she blew out a thick cloud of smoke.

'I don't know what bloody wagon you talking about, darling,' she said. 'You may have been sucked in by that performance—' Sofia sniggered, looking at Raelene, who obediently smiled back. '—but I fucking wasn't!'

Leonie's recent behaviour had embarrassed Sofia, who was now making up for lost ground.

'You should have seen her in here lass night, darling. She sat there and did fuck-all. Is her lass week, so she think she can juss—'

Her last week? Was Leonie leaving us?

Again Sofia enjoyed making me feel like a complete imbecile for my ignorance. 'Not completely, darling. Leonie crossing to the other side.'

Crossing to the other side meant only one thing to a receptionist working in a brothel. I looked at Raelene who, having watched my face with delight, now roared laughing. Sofia was not so amused. I couldn't tell what irritated her more, Leonie's liberation or Raelene's merriment, until she snapped.

'Raelene, shuddup!'

I had such mixed feelings. Horror, initially. Leonie was all of twenty-one, terribly naive, and possibly stupid. However, a small part of me felt happy for her. She was free! Free from Sofia, and all the persecution and unpopularity that accompanied her former inadequacies as a receptionist. And maybe Leonie's thick skin and buoyant resilience might be suitable for such a career choice. What did her friend Delia think? Suddenly Delia was in the room.

'What do you think of Leonie's decision to be a prostitute, Delia?'

Delia was miserable.

'I think she's making a big mistake. She's excited because she thinks she's going to make a whole lot of money. She compares herself to Song-Lee and Genevieve, like it's going to be all Exclusive bookings at the Sheraton.'

That did it. The room was suddenly full of shouting receptionists, those finishing the day shift and those of us starting the night. Everyone had a violent response to the concept of mixing Exclusive with Leonie. She was nowhere near attractive enough or experienced enough to carry off an Exclusive booking! And there was no paucity of indignation at Leonie daring to harbour such delusions. Genevieve was a goddess! Song-Lee was Buddha! Victoria had crossed to the other side and we now sent her out as Stephanie, but Victoria was beautiful! Raelene took this opportunity to remind us that Glenda could now go as Exclusive, having lost more weight. But Leonie had fat calves! Bad head. Too white. Puffy. Weird.

'Hi, Leonie!'

Leonie knew we had been talking about her but she interpreted it, with some accuracy, as jealousy. Leonie knew that every one of us had secretly entertained the possibility of crossing over, even if just for a moment. From her beaming face I could see she already fancied herself standing in mirrored lifts, wearing a teddy under a coat, with pockets stuffed full of cash and condoms.

'Have you heard?' she asked me excitedly as soon as we were alone.

'Yes,' I answered, giving nothing away.

Leonie searched my face with her sparkly eyes. You'd think she'd won a raffle.

'You've decided to become a prostitute,' I said at last.

Leonie collapsed in a peel of giggles. 'You are so *funny*!'

Not quite the response I was looking for.

'Are you sure about this?' I asked.

'Yeah,' she retorted defensively. 'I know what I'm doing. I've thought about it heaps, hey? I can do it.'

I studied Leonie hard, trying to imagine her just having a conversation with a man in a bar. I remembered the early morning after work when she had come with me and Trudy to some bar in the Cross. All she could talk about were the 'lecherous creeps perving on us'. I assured Leonie I wasn't doubting her ability, which was a lie, and I reminded her of that night with Trudy. Could she imagine herself, I asked, stuck in a dark hotel room for an hour with one of those lecherous creeps' penises in her mouth?

'With a condom on, hey!'

I didn't laugh, so Leonie pondered the question.

'Yeah,' she said, finally, a little disappointed by my negativity.

And she was going to work for us?

'Yeah! Hey!'

In-house?

'No way!' Leonie was disgusted.

Strictly escort?

'Yeah!'

Had she told her parents?

'No, but I'll tell Mum. She'll think it's cool.'

'Your mother will think it's cool?' I asked.

Leonie thought about it. 'I might wait till I've saved ten thousand dollars, and then I'll tell her how I did it.' She glowed with the brilliance of her plan.

Delia shuffled into the room and sat sadly at her desk.

'My mother has never hit anyone in her life,' she said quietly, 'but if I told her I'd become a prostitute, I think she'd punch me in the face.'

I wondered for a second what mine would do. It only took a second.

'Have you told Corrie?' I asked Leonie, trying to catch her out. 'Your ex-boyfriend?'

'He thinks it's great!' She nodded excitedly. 'Reckons I'll be really good at it.'

Something in my expression made Leonie fall about laughing again.

'You should see your face. You are so *funny*!'

'What about lesbian doubles?' I asked.

'Yeah ...' she responded nonchalantly. 'You can just fake it anyway.'

Could you? I wondered how you faked being a lesbian in bed with another 'lesbian' and the client, who'd paid to watch two lesbians having sex with each other. But more than anything, I wondered how I was going to describe this large, simple, eccentric girl to businessmen staying at the Hyatt.

Best actress in a brothel drama

It was the first night I'd seen Maxine since the money had gone missing three weeks previously. She'd been away with various illnesses, panic attacks and boyfriend trouble. Troy was out of jail, and I think that was the trouble. Personally, if I were being accused of stealing, I would not be confessing to 'panic attacks'. And so I turned up this Sunday night to find her, tiny little stick-thing with broken tufts of bleached hair, bent over my desk, crying her eyes out. Pip was there too, but busy on a call. Maxine looked up at me, as if ready for her close-up. I hated to give her credit as an actress but, I had to admit, she performed like a trooper.

'What's wrong?' I dutifully asked.

Maxine opened and shut her mouth, demonstrating she was lost for words. 'I . . . I thought you were my friends.'

I never felt so unmoved in my life.

With her little girl's body dressed up in pretty little girlie tops and cardies, her traumatised white hair gathered on top in a cute tuft over black roots, and her pretty cartoon mouth and eyes set in the grey complexion of a junkie, Maxine looked like Bambi on smack. I felt exhausted just anticipating the effort the night would require. Even without a crisis Maxine took ten minutes just to say she was tired. And she had an excruciatingly tedious habit of backing up every sentence with, 'you know what I mean?'

Yes. You mean you're tired. Please die.

To cut a long story short, Maxine had heard we all believed she had stolen the money. Which was absolutely true, but who had told her?

'Sofia told me,' she said. 'She said you all talk about me behind my back.'

Although I loved Sofia's tough Colombian bad cop persona, and enjoyed her high blood pressured, chain-smoking, forehead-slapping antics at work, and marvelled that she supported a seriously ill husband and a four-year-old child, I was beginning to notice that Sofia also had a dangerously reckless predilection for flinging shit at passing fans.

I was relieved to be given a break from Maxine's performance by Leonie ringing back for her booking details. Never had we known a girl to take so long settling on a working name. Leonie had gone through all the names of all the supermodels, but when she got to 'Iman' the week before, Sofia lost it.

'If the man is expecting Elle and he open the door to you, darling, all he sees is a porpoise in a tight dress.'

It was cruel, but effective. Until Leonie rang the following night.

'Calista?' Sofia wailed. 'Oh, fuck me dead.'

And tonight it was my turn.

'It's French!' Leonie cried, defending her latest suggestion.

'No, Leonie,' I corrected her, '*Carnelle* is not a French name, and even people who *don't* speak French will laugh at you.'

Leonie insisted she had read a book in which the French heroine was called Carnelle, but I suspected Leonie had only read books given to her in the street, either by the Hare Krishnas or the Church of Scientology. And after a long and tedious argument with Leonie, Reg from Bexley North was expecting Gigi.

At least Maxine's boyfriend troubles were over. A lot had happened in three weeks. Now Maxine was with Craig. And to prove the seriousness of their new relationship, Maxine proudly displayed a framed key-ring with a photo of their smiling faces pressed together. Craig's head was twice as big as her's, but then anyone's was. I marvelled that a grown man could have sex with Maxine without killing her. Anyway, now that the tears were over, the tedious conversations were back.

'I haven't slept for two days.'

Hadn't she?

'No. I've been out partying!'

Goodness.

'I haven't taken anything though.'

Terrific.

'Do I look like I have?'

This was a difficult question. To me, Maxine always looked like she got out of bed that afternoon, put half a bottle of bleach through her hair, and then drank the rest.

'No. You look fine.'

'Do I?'

'Yes.'

'I don't feel fine. I feel shocking. I don't want to be here, that's for sure!'

And Maxine would chortle as if she had just said the most outrageous, wickedly funny thing.

'I just love to make people laugh, Meredith, you know?'

Maxine was back.

'You haven't seen that side of me yet.'

Maxine was back, and she had sides.

What visions I have seen! Methought I was enamoured
of the driver

When I was eight years old, my sister and I played fairies to my
father's Bottom in the Rockhampton Little Theatre's production
of *A Midsummer Night's Dream*. It was a magical experience for a
child with a lively imagination, to leap about the stage with other
goblins and fairies all night in a cardboard forest full of lovers,
casting spells and singing lullabies about spotted snakes, thorny
hedgehogs and newts. Twenty years later, when I found myself
leaping about a real forest, doing Shakespeare in the Park, the play
had lost none of its magic and charm for me. I'm sure Shakespeare
did not mean to write an analogy of the sex industry, but
sometimes, late at night, pairing up lovers and sending diaphanous
creatures out all over Sydney, I felt caught up in those same ethereal
spirits' midnight sport. Once inside our brothel, it was as if I had left
Athens behind me and entered the forest full of strange, nocturnal
creatures who took me with them on another journey beyond the
comfortable boundaries I knew.

The line between my two worlds was clearly drawn by the
rising of the sun. If the sun was already up when Patrick dropped
me at my front gate, I saw our recent indiscretion but as *a dream and
fruitless vision*. Not that I rejected the memory like Titania, with
repulsion, or regarded Patrick as a donkey I'd once bonked when
pissed, but as far as any fruitful future was concerned, ours was
cactus. I was not normally attracted to older men who played darts
at the Matraville RSL with Den and Limpy. But if, on the other
hand, it was still dark when Patrick drove me through the glittering, dormant streets of Sydney, I was still intoxicated by some
little western flower . . . now purple with love's wound. And by the time
we got to Coogee, I felt compelled to lead Patrick to my bower.

'Do you want to come in then, Patrick?'

'Yes, that would be lovely.'

Patrick and I never had that second 'date'. We never even saw a
film together. We somehow knew that, whatever it was we had, it
could not survive in sunlight, or in public. So instead, Patrick
would occasionally come in from the early morning cold, where

we'd warm ourselves with a glass of scotch and laugh about the night's dramas before racing to bed before sunrise. When I ventured further to invite Patrick over for the occasional dinner, even my two housemates remained an invisible reminder of my real world. Libby was now working nights on *Moulin Rouge*, and Peter was filming a television series in London, but Patrick never asked about them, not even when I shamelessly pointed out the birthday flowers sent to Libby from Nicole Kidman.

'You do know who she is, don't you?' I asked him, with haughty incredulity.

'Yes,' Patrick humoured me, 'she's your housemate. Shall we have a Black Velvet?'

Patrick had arrived with a bottle of champagne and four cans of Guinness. How anyone can cheerfully mix Guinness with champagne and call it a 'black velvet' instead of 'barman's revenge' I will never know.

Patrick never asked to see my 'show reel', and I never asked him about his pipes. He never invited me back to Matraville, and for that I was eternally grateful. I still had no idea who he was, other than a gentle, cheerful soul who treated the girls with respect and drank me up with joy. And the more my cheerful lover found delight in me, outside my usual context of artistic endeavours and cafe brunches, the more liberated I felt.

'What *are* his politics?' asked my concerned Labor Party friend, Sara.

'Wouldn't have a clue.'

'Well, what do you two talk about?'

'Anything. Nothing.'

Frustratingly, the only subject I could never discuss with Patrick was the girls. When I pressed him to name his favourite passenger, he curled up on the couch like a distressed caterpillar.

'Oh, I don't know,' he squirmed. 'Let's not talk about them.'

But I was pleased to extract from him, over some weeks, that he did find Antoinette highly sensitive and intelligent, Lucinda refreshing, Yoko endearing, and Sapphire hilarious. I learnt, with Patrick, to keep things positive.

And so our cosy refuge continued.

What, wilt thou hear some music, my sweet love?

'Chrissie Hinde? Patsy Cline? Nirvana?' I'd ask.

Patrick would giggle and shrug. Patrick didn't care, and neither did I. I didn't even mind that he filled my bedroom with cigarette smoke, and coughed his lungs up in the morning.

Oh say, sweet love, what thou desirest to eat.

'Muesli? Rice bubbles? Raisin toast?'

And a happy, careless banter would ensue over copious cups of tea before breakfast, followed by more tea afterwards. But come Patrick's second post-breakfast cigarette, the magic waned and I wished him to repair back to Matraville, *and think no more of this night's accidents, but as the fierce vexation of a dream.*

As if poked in the back by some mischievous fairy, Patrick would suddenly leap to his feet.

'I'd better go and—'

'Yes, thanks for—'

'Catch you—'

'Absolutely.'

Our complicity was made all the more enjoyable back at work, where we kept our secret from our disapproving colleagues, except Trudy, who played devil's advocate to my increasingly unsettled conscience.

'Of course you're not using him. It's your house, your food, your bed, your hospitality he's enjoying. I hope he at least turns up with a bottle of wine.'

I nodded. I couldn't tell anyone about the black velvets, not even Trudy.

'Has he paid you back the fifty dollars he owes you?' she asked me.

Good old Trudy. I felt much better. The bastard still owed me fifty.

A man in a bungalow

I arrived at seven to find our short-sighted Mexican B & D mistress, Zora, an accountant from Hurstville, sitting at the kitchen table, wrapped in a white sheet tied above one shoulder, with a crown of leaves on her head. As Zora squinted up at me through Coke-bottle lenses that distorted her heavily made-up eyes, I noticed her face, shoulders and arms seemed to glow a dull shade of gold. Urszula roared laughing from the other side of the bench.

'That's right, boys and girls,' she boomed, 'it's dress-up day on *Play School!*'

Zora bravely weathered Urszula's scorn and continued beaming at me like a shy child in fancy dress.

'Drugs?' I asked Zora.

She guffawed. Zora may have been a lesbian dominatrix, but she didn't even smoke. I could never imagine Zora doing B & D, and sometimes wondered if she hadn't got Bondage and Discipline mixed up with something less sinister, like Bed and Breakfast.

'A rehearsal for this year's accountants' Christmas party?'

Zora emitted a childish giggle.

'The Hurstville Rep's production of *Julius Caesar?*' I asked her.

Zora shook her head. 'Think Greek gods,' she suggested quietly, like a librarian.

Ignoring Urszula's suggestions that Zora was Herpes, God of Nightclubs, or perhaps one of the Gorgons at Happy Hour, I noticed my goddess was clutching a brown paper bag full of grapes.

'Aphrodite!' I cheered, slapping my forehead. 'Goddess of beauty!'

'Close,' she smiled demurely. 'I'm Hera, and Mr Little at the Swiss Grand is Zeus. He's expecting me at ten.'

I congratulated Zora on her fantasy booking, and most inspired preparation, albeit much earlier than necessary.

'I wouldn't get too carried away,' warned Urszula scornfully, 'she'll be dead by then.'

Zora rolled her eyes and dived into her bag for a grape.

'I've told her, Meredith,' Urszula harped on, 'the silly tart's been slapping on some fooking toxic rubbish in there—'

'It's not metal-based,' insisted Zora.

'It's got fooking gold in it!' interrupted Urszula. 'How are your pores supposed to breathe, you idiot? And what about him? One lick and he'll die of lead poisoning.'

Zora calmly explained to me that she had seen Mr Little the night before, and there was no licking, no undressing, and not even any sex.

I looked at her.

'We just sit on Mount Olympus,' she mumbled, 'drink some wine, and feed each other a few grapes.'

Suddenly the kitchen door swung open and Antoinette paused for a moment to take in the bespectacled gold accountant sitting at the table in front of her. With her messy blonde hair, full lips and turned-out feet, Antoinette looked like Daffy Duck at the end of duck-shooting season. She had recently moved back in with her mother at the retirement village in Riverview, and I wondered if things were going well. Antoinette turned and shuffled to her locker by the back door, and I knew by the way she crouched on her haunches, looking more like a gargoyle than an escort, it was going to be a bumpy night.

'Who's on?' she demanded, looking up at me.

'Um, I think it's Pip.' Then I prayed she would not ask who else.

Antoinette was convinced that Raelene, under Boris's instructions, conspired to kill her with a lack of bookings. On her more paranoid nights, she believed we held meetings about it.

'Who else?' she shot.

'*Meredith?*' Raelene's voice crackled over the kitchen intercom. '*Come up, darl, or you'll miss out on the sultana cake I made!*'

I smiled helplessly at Antoinette. Why couldn't Raelene sound angry with me, as usual? And since when had we started making fruitcakes for each other?

To show my allegiance was not necessarily with the big girls upstairs who had cake, I postponed my departure as long as possible, wiping benches, drying cups, folding tea towels, but I don't think it helped. Antoinette plonked herself almost violently next to Zora at the kitchen table, and lit up a cigarette.

'What are you supposed to be?' she finally quipped with a sideways glance at the accountant.

'Hera,' Zora smiled timidly. 'Zeus's wife.'

Antoinette snorted, as if she'd been fucked around by one too many Greek gods that day as well.

I was relieved when the door bell rang.

Four Japanese businessmen in suits stood huddled in a circle. None of them spoke English, but it was obvious from the tone of their discussion that they were a little disappointed by my offering of two mature blondes, one of whom seemed particularly unfriendly. The only other girl available had covered herself in gold paint two hours before she was due at Mount Olympus.

'Sorry,' I smiled as I held the waiting room door open for them to leave.

But the tallest of them seemed struck by an idea, and spoke animatedly with his friends, who listened to him attentively and then looked at me.

'He want know,' said the leader, pointing at his happy, tall friend, and then at me, 'you?'

'*Me?*' I yelped, pointing at myself in disbelief.

The delegation nodded and giggled.

I was not up there with Delia, who had been offered a thousand dollars to have sex with an Arab on her very first night, but still, I was touched.

'No!' I shook my head, madly gesticulating with my hands. 'Me receptionist. Not girl.'

But as his friends passed me, the tall, happy chap continued beaming at me with such undeterred enthusiasm, I had to leave the room without him.

With a flurry of happy nodding and much laughter, I let my Japanese friends out, only to find two black men waiting on our doorstep. Ten minutes later, as my African party departed, shaking their heads, Louis from Chile arrived. What was this, Womad? It never rained but it poured, but did it have to pour when I had only two girls available, both over forty, and one about as friendly as a python? As downstairs receptionist, it was my responsibility to round up any missing in-house girls, or else Bavaria would invade at midnight with all cannons firing. So as soon as Nathan from Tempe left, I tore upstairs to make some hasty calls.

'We can't find Patrick!' Pip announced dramatically as I entered the office.

Had they rung him?

'Yes, of course we have,' she huffed, 'but they've never heard of him on that number. He must have moved and not told us. Didi is livid,' Pip stated dramatically, 'and Patrick's in big trouble.'

An hour later we knew that something was definitely wrong. In two years, Raelene swore, Patrick had never been late. While Pip looked up the Matraville RSL in the book, I decided to try Patrick's old phone number myself.

'Could I speak to Patrick please?'

'Here we go again,' grumbled a gruff voice. 'No!'

'May I ask why not?'

'Well, mainly because there is no Patrick here,' he answered emphatically.

'Has he moved?'

'I daresay he has, from time to time,' the gruff voice replied. 'Haven't we all?'

I could hear another man's high-pitched giggle in the background.

'Who am I speaking to?' I asked the comedian.

'You are speaking to Den.'

'*Den?*'

Pause.

'Is there a Limpy there, Den?'

'That is correct,' Den answered. 'Would you like me to put him on?'

'No.'

'Suit yourself.'

'Does a third person live in that house, Den?'

'He does.'

'Would you mind telling me his name?'

'His name is Mort.'

'Mort?'

'That is correct.'

'And Mort is from Portsmouth?'

'That too is correct.'

'Could I speak to Mort then, please, Den?'

'Mort's out.'

'Well then, would you mind telling Mort, Den, when Mort gets in, that Mort was supposed to start his night shift two hours ago, and that he is in *big trouble*.'

'Who shall I say called?'

'Bathsheba.'

'Bathsheba,' repeated Den. 'Big trouble.'

I was angry. All this time I thought I'd been having an intimate relationship with Patrick, I'd been sleeping with some guy called Mort. You don't have sex with someone and lie about your name! You lie about your marital status, your age, and your allergy to the rubber in condoms, but you at least have the decency to use your real name! Who the hell was Mort? And if Mort was Mort and not Patrick, what else was Mort that Patrick wasn't? Did Mort vote One Nation?

'Off course I know he's Mort,' boasted Boris as he strolled in, taking us by surprise with an early ambush. 'I could haff told you stupid girls to ask for Mort, but you're too stupid to ring me, and now no one can find the dumb prick. And who is receptionist downstairs, please?'

Boris had no doubt already assessed the paltry ensemble slumped around his kitchen table.

'Ur,' I began, reminding myself that I could always waitress, or sell Amway.

'Well, speak of the devil,' Raelene interrupted as Mort practically fell into the room.

Patrick's 'Really? I had no idea!' expression was magnified almost to cartoon proportions as he breathlessly stumbled about our office, addressing no one in particular, with arms flailing.

'I'm so sorry,' he kept repeating, facing Boris, then Raelene, then Pip.

I gathered by my exclusion from Patrick's epileptic apology that one relinquishes any professional accountability to the colleague one is sleeping with.

Patrick's excuse could have won Best Original Excuse in the Short Excuse Category at the Annual Excuse Awards.

'I've been up since five this morning looking after a sick friend. She took so crook, I had to drive her to St Vinnies this afternoon. And I'm sorry, but I fell asleep in Casualty.'

Boris nodded with weighty consideration, Pip gave Patrick a hug, and I wondered who 'she' was. Only Raelene dared respond to Patrick's heroics with palpable indifference.

'Can you take Antoinette to a booking in Kensington, after you've dropped off Zora at the Swiss Grand?'

Raelene still hadn't forgiven Patrick for her door.

'And you'd better warn Antoinette, Meredith,' Raelene said, tearing off a piece of paper for me with the booking details, 'it's a bungalow out the back.'

'Bungalow?' I gulped, trying to decipher the death sentence Raelene had handed me as I felt my way to the door.

'It's okay,' Raelene assured me flatly, 'he's in the book.'

We always preferred a private home to be in our computer records, but apparently Mikey had never used our services before. It got worse. Antoinette had to walk down the side of a house in the dark, turn the corner, and then knock on the door of Mikey's 'bungalow', otherwise known as a 'small shed'. But it was all right. Mikey was in the book and, as we all knew, murderers and rapists had silent numbers.

Downstairs in the kitchen, Antoinette accepted her booking with numb resignation. I tried to explain about the bungalow, but it could have been a paddock in Bosnia for all she cared. I don't know what misfortunes Antoinette had already suffered that day, but one more wasn't going to surprise her. Even Zora registered concern about a bungalow, until she stood too quickly and almost strangled herself in her own sheet. As I let the three of them out, Patrick brushed past me with his usual cheeky smile. He even gave me a wink.

'See you later, Mort,' I quipped.

How apt, I thought as I swung the door shut, just in time to catch a glimpse of his face as he spun around. Patrick looked mortified.

Halfway up the stairs I met Boris coming down on his way to the casino. I knew by now that the best way to survive one of

Boris's tirades was to agree, apologise, and look even more distressed by my own incompetence than he could ever be. Promising to fill his house with nubile sex workers immediately, I had continued to the top of the stairs when he called me back, and I had to shout down from the landing why Zora was covered in gold paint. Boris slammed the door behind him in disgust.

Who was *she*? Patrick had been looking after a woman since five o'clock this morning, he said. And did *she* call him Patrick? Or Mort?

'Well, congratulations, Lucinda,' Raelene sang down her phone as I entered our office in a cloud of insecurity. 'Here, I'll put her on.'

I could tell by Raelene's and Pip's animated faces that Lucinda had a surprise for me.

'And how pregnant are you, Lucinda?' I asked, trying not to sound alarmed.

'Three months, darling,' Lucinda cried with delight. 'So I might have to disappear for a while, you understand,' she added in a conspiratorial whisper.

'Of course!' I agreed, unconditionally. 'Was it ... er ... planned, Lucinda?'

'God no!' she retorted. 'But you never plan these things, do you, darling?'

Well no, not if you're a sex worker living with two queens in Paddington.

'Are you going to be all right?' I asked Lucinda, who had never mentioned any partner. 'I mean, how are you going to support yourself if you're not working?'

'Ah, well, darling,' Lucinda chortled, 'that's where *you* come in.'

But I didn't want to come in to a prostitute's pregnancy at all. 'How?' I squeaked.

Lucinda asked, very sweetly, if I would put in a good word for her with Boris, in regards to working as a receptionist for the next six months or so.

'Of course I will!' I promised, and then gushed about what a great receptionist Lucinda would make, until I was distracted by the disapproving looks coming from my colleagues.

Prompted by Pip's frantic charades, I promised Lucinda I would ring her back as soon as I had discussed her proposition with Sofia the following night.

'Sofia won't have a bar of her,' Pip sniffed when I'd hung up the phone.

'Neither will Boris,' snorted Raelene.

This was the second time in a fortnight that one of our girls had suddenly announced she was pregnant. Cindy, also single, and living in a flat in Petersham, had sounded just as delighted the preceding week. It was a baffling response, to say the least. Almost as baffling as Patrick's sick friend, who was with him at five o'clock this morning.

Of course, now that I had rounded up Rita, Maya and Shelby, not one man knocked on the front door but the pizza boy. I felt like the girl who cried 'Client!' But we were not short on in-house drama, as usual, thanks to Urszula. And I was grateful for any distraction from my growing jealousy over Patrick's sick friend, or girlfriend, or wife. I entered the kitchen to find Urszula sitting in her robe, still wet from her shower, as the other girls ran around her with cups of tea and warm towels.

'I didn't want to worry you, Meredith,' Urszula announced in a commanding voice from within her throng, like Queen Elizabeth, 'but we've had a wee crisis here.'

Apparently, on hearing strange noises coming from the laundry, Rita had gone in to find a naked Urszula in foetal position on the shower floor, with the shower curtain pulled down around her.

'I just couldn't fooking breathe!' Urszula exclaimed as Maya rubbed her back soothingly.

'You hyperventilated, darling,' Rita the nurse cooed.

Urszula had had a similar scare only a few weeks ago, at Hester's flat, and had laughed at me when I begged her then to give up her Horizon cigarettes. But judging from the shower curtain I found ripped beyond repair in the laundry, this experience had really frightened her. I was just about to fetch my Ventolin from upstairs when the front door slammed with such force that I found myself retreating back into the safe cocoon of four prostitutes. As the stomping grew louder, the five of us watched the kitchen door in fear until it was finally kicked wide open. There stood Antoinette, hair sticking up, eyes blazing and frothing at the mouth like a demented harpy.

'FUCK YOU ALL!'

Now we all had breathing problems.

'Sending us out to fucking psychopaths in the middle of nowhere! FUCK YOU ALL!'

I gathered the bungalow booking had not gone well, and knew from the creaking floorboards above that my frightened colleagues had tiptoed out to the top of the landing to eavesdrop. Moving only a foot away from my quivering fold, I struggled to sound calm as I asked Antoinette what had happened.

'WHAT DO YOU CARE?' she yelled at me, lurching dangerously close. 'What do you, or any of them up there, care what happens to any of us? As long as you get your FUCKING MONEY.'

Taking my life in my own hands, I gingerly ventured forward another foot and again asked Antoinette what, exactly, had happened. But Antoinette ignored me, choosing instead to crouch on the floor, where she struggled to open her locker. Once it had opened, Antoinette continued a florid stream of general abuse as she threw hairspray, teddies and empty lube tubes all over the place.

'I'm not working here another minute,' she spat, violently shoving a blonde hairpiece, which got caught on her bracelet, into her bag. 'Why should I waste my talent working for these fucking low-life criminals?'

Antoinette jerked her wrist in the air until she'd finally ripped the wig from its trap and shoved it into her bag. But the tuft of hair still caught in her bracelet now resembled some gruesome piece of forensic evidence, and I implored Antoinette to tell me if she had been hurt by Mikey at Kensington.

'CRIMINALS!' she roared, waving one stray diamante shoe in my face.

We had been minding the other one for weeks upstairs, but I did not think now was the time to tell her.

'Are they waiting for one of us to get killed?' she continued. 'IS THAT WHAT IT'S GOING TO TAKE?'

'Calm down, Antoinette,' came an insane command from behind me.

I followed Antoinette's crazed gaze to see Urszula, sitting like a
queen, still flanked by her entourage. Was she mad? Didn't we all
remember what happened to Consuela, who now took escort
bookings from home and sent any money owing by post.

'Don't you fucking tell me to calm down!' Antoinette spat,
leaping to her feet like a rabid cat, threatening to pounce if
contradicted.

Urszula and Antoinette had never liked each other but had
always kept a professional distance – until now. Witnessing Urszula
concede with a curt nod was like catching a total eclipse of the sun.
Later Urszula would explain to us that it would have been a
different story had she not been having breathing difficulties.

Antoinette's large black bag, the one that had always seemed as
bottomless and mysterious as the Tardis, now bulged with bottles,
brushes, underwear, one shoe heel, and a handful of curly blonde
hair. At a glance it looked as if she'd killed a blonde contortionist
and stuffed the body inside.

'Tell them,' she commanded me with a quavering voice, 'tell that
low-life cunt and his wife that I left before I let them kill me!'

'You have to tell me what he did, Antoinette,' I implored her.
'Are you hurt? Should we call the police?'

When she finally turned to face me from the kitchen door,
Antoinette was shaking as she fought back tears.

'Can't she tell on the phone,' she said, pointing upstairs, 'when
they don't even have a basic command of language, that something's seriously fucking *wrong* with them?'

I turned to the girls, who looked back at me feeling equally
hopeless.

'FUCK!' roared the voice from the front door. 'WILL
SOMEONE LET ME OUT?'

Fumbling for my keys, I stumbled down the hall and released
Antoinette into the black night.

Visibly shaken by Antoinette's accusation, Raelene swore to Pip
and me that the man who had made the booking sounded perfectly
normal over the phone, even when she had rung him back to
confirm, and we believed her. While Raelene rang Mikey's
number over and over again without success, Patrick drove back to
Kensington and knocked on the bungalow door, and then tried the

house as well, both to no avail. We were in a quandary. Boris had turned his mobile phone off, and although we knew never to wake her unless it was an emergency, one of her girls had left for good under traumatic circumstances. And so against my trepidatious colleagues' advice, I rang Didi.

Didi listened in glacial silence as I described Antoinette's upsetting experience and distressed departure.

'Let me get this straight, Merediss,' Didi interrupted me in a tone quite bereft of the sweetness she displayed at our initial interview. 'You let a girl go before she paid us the money she owed?'

I was speechless.

'Get her card for me, will you?' Didi commanded.

Raelene immediately presented me with the requested card.

'How much money does it say she owes us?' Didi demanded.

'Um,' I stuttered, straining to follow the tiny rows of red, green and blue hieroglyphics written by various receptionists. 'Twenty-five dollars for last night's taxi, I think.'

'And it was a standard booking tonight?' she asked flatly.

'Yes.'

'So you let a girl go, Merediss, who owes us one hundred and fifteen dollars?'

'I let Antoinette go, Didi,' I began, astonished by her heart-lessness, 'because she was terribly upset, having been through a traumatic experience, because we sent her to see a man who was perhaps not the full quid.'

'What do you mean?' Didi snapped.

'Didi, he lived in a shed, and Antoinette said he could hardly speak—'

'Merediss,' she interrupted me, 'I do not know about your privileged background, but in this profession we don't discriminate between the lower classes and the highly educated. Do you honestly expect me to screen clients for a level of elocution that pleases both you and Antoinette?'

'Didi, I'm not talking about a lack of sophistic—'

'The fact that the girl has gone is not important to me, actually, Merediss,' Didi steamrolled over me. 'This girl is somewhat psychologically challenged herself, something you and your critical powers of observation failed to detect as you let her out of our house with money that is not hers to take. When is she coming back, please?'

'She's not coming back, Didi!' I cried. 'That's why I'm ringing you! And I think she may have been—'

'I'm glad you rang,' Didi interrupted again, 'because this is a problem for you, Merediss. Due to your negligence and stupidity, we are now missing one hundred and fifteen dollars, and therefore I will have to take it out of your next pay, you understand?'

I felt poleaxed. I had rung my employer to report a possible assault on a girl and it had ended up costing me a hundred and fifteen dollars.

'I hate her,' I fumed as Patrick pulled up at the lights. 'She's evil.'

Patrick nodded accommodatingly.

'Tomorrow,' I stated, 'I'm going to look for another job.'

Patrick sighed. 'Antoinette'll be back. She's left before, you know.'

I looked enviously at some nurses laughing in the car next to us, and I remembered something. 'Who's your sick friend?'

Patrick earnestly explained to me that his next door neighbour, an Indian woman whose husband works nights as a security guard, woke in extreme pain due to a twisted bowel.

'They said at the hospital she could have died,' he said, which reminded me of something else.

'Mort?' I asked incredulously. '*Mort?*'

'Boris asked me, on my very first shift, did I want to use another name,' Patrick gabbled, with anxious sideways glances. 'Well, what would you do if your real name was Mortimer?'

I looked back at the nurses who were now in hysterics. Mortimer. He had a point.

Five days later, after I decided I could not possibly work for two orthodontists in Edgecliff, I was back at my Friday night shift. Antoinette had returned to work and paid back the money she owed. Patrick understood that I could never call him anything else, and promised me he had never voted for One Nation. And although I would stay in her employment, I felt strangely liberated. I was no longer scared of Didi. I hated her. It's a fine line between fear and hatred. Just ask any gay man living in Tasmania.

Moulin Rouge

It's a small world, as they say.

'Hey, Meredith,' Leonie shouted down the phone. 'Guess what I'm doing from tomorrow!'

Since Leonie's last newsflash, I didn't dare.

'I'll give you a clue.' Leonie giggled with excitement. 'I'll be working with your housemate, on a certain film, about a French circus.'

French circus? Oh God. What on earth Leonie could be doing on *Moulin Rouge* was anyone's guess. She couldn't be singing or dancing. And certainly not acting. Unless she was an extra, playing a patron in the audience. Or perhaps—? Oh no, surely not.

'I'm a prostitute!' Leonie shouted with jubilation.

'Well, that's a bit of irony, isn't it?' I said, laughing with her.

'What?' Leonie gasped suddenly. 'Don't tell me you're playing one too?'

I tried to speak, but no words would come.

'Oh, Meredith!' Leonie exclaimed. 'Does this mean we're finally going to work together?'

Must warn Libby. If on set, stay away from Whore Section.

And what does Patrick do?

It was wonderful telling my friends that, at the very least, I was 'seeing someone' again. Their faces lit up like it was the Second Coming. The one we thought never would. And then the inevitable questions began. 'What does he do?' And my favourite. 'Where did you two meet?'

I could never answer either question without using the word *prostitutes* or *brothel.*

Strained smiles lingered their faces as they continued nodding inanely, fingers twitching in search of a phone. I never wanted to apologise for Patrick, or justify what he did for a living, but seldom could I bear the pregnant pause that followed my answers. And all my attempts just made it worse.

'The girls just love him,' I said to Barbara, an actress friend.

We were sipping chardonnays on the picturesque wharf balcony of the Sydney Theatre Company, having just auditioned for the new David Williamson play. Although she was now married to a Qantas pilot and bringing up their baby in leafy Rose Bay, Barbara and I had shared several years of off-stage debauchery after graduating from drama school, but motherhood seemed to have given Barbara amnesia.

'Goodness!' she said, holding her smile as if it was a used tissue in search of a bin.

There was another actress sitting with us at the time.

'The driver!' Beatrice exclaimed getting up. 'Oh, Merridy.' And she left in disgust. At least it was a more honest response.

When I told my parents, I realised just how desperate they were to see their single thirty-eight year old daughter find a partner.

'I'm seeing someone,' I said.

'Wonderful!' they chorused.

'His name's Patrick.'

'He sounds lovely!' my mother gushed.

I told my parents that Patrick was the driver at the brothel and that he was a kind man and respected the girls and was intelligent and had a wonderful sense of humour and smoked and drank and had no prospects or even direction in life and laughed all the time and it wasn't serious, but I was happy. There was a silence.

'Terrific,' my father said at last.

'Isn't that lovely!' my mother declared.

I love my parents.

Trickier was the family reunion to celebrate my aunt and uncle's fiftieth wedding anniversary in Punchbowl one warm October Sunday morning. My father's cheerful brood of Baptist brothers, sisters, cousins, aunts and uncles always welcomed me, and loved me unconditionally, but since *Play School*, I'd also acquired an embarrassing kind of star status. At eleven o'clock in the morning, we congregated in my Aunty Dot's immaculate lounge room. They had all come straight from church, and I had come straight from the brothel, after breakfast, due to a particularly busy night. And there I stood, surrounded by balloons and lamingtons, holding a fistful of gerberas and being adored and celebrated for my latest toilet paper commercial.

'And is there a boyfriend, may we ask?' my Uncle Roy enquired cheekily.

A sudden hush filled the room. All I could hear was my gerberas shaking.

'Funny you should ask, Uncle Roy.' I laughed nervously.

And they all cheered.

When I told them he drove taxis, they all cheered again, because Uncle Barry drove taxis. So it was Uncle Barry who asked what was the lucky fellow's name.

'Patrick.'

'Patrick who?'

'Patrick ... Dart!'

And they all nodded approvingly. Patrick Dart. Bull's-eye.

Antoinette in Lebanon

I now worked in Redfern. It had all happened very quickly.

'We're moving,' Pip announced one Friday night. 'We're packing up the office on Sunday. Did you know?'

I was sitting in Boris's big leather chair at the time, dutifully reading The Bible so as to be completely briefed and up to date with every new development since my last shift. I knew Trudy had bought extra paperclips, that Donatella now had a forty-inch bust, and that yet another of Dr Slade's cheques had bounced, but there was no mention of completely relocating the business to new premises at all.

'Yes,' Pip sighed as she struck a pose of elegant indifference and lit up one of her long white cigarettes. 'Didi's fed up with Boris's incompetence. The brothel has been a total financial disaster, and she blames him.'

I swallowed hard. This meant Boris would blame us. Pip continued.

'So we're going back to doing strictly escort-only, which suits me fine. I never agreed to work in a brothel. I found the whole thing unspeakably vulgar.'

I don't know why Pip found the whole thing so 'unspeakably vulgar'. She'd steadfastly refused to work downstairs, and had never so much as clapped eyes on a vulgarian at the front door, let alone picked up a damp towel. But I was fascinated by Pip's persistent use of this word *vulgar*. I always found Pip's social airs in such an unlikely environment very entertaining, unless I was tired. Then I wanted to deck her with the full vulgar thrust of my right fist.

Pip explained to me that Boris and Didi had already placed Arlington House on the market, and on Sunday they were moving everything within it to their other house in Redfern. The only house in Redfern I knew of was the one that accommodated various girls, like Shawna, Rochelle, Delilah, and sometimes Antoinette, if she'd fought with her mother.

'But isn't that where some of the girls are living?' I asked.

Pip closed her eyes and smiled as she took a long drag from her cigarette. 'It's not a refuge. They've got to stand on their own two feet sometime.'

It certainly wasn't a refuge. I knew only too well the healthy amount Boris charged them for rent because I frequently had to dock it from their pays. And as far as I was concerned, any girl who paid her rent by working on her back, or on her knees, was more than standing on her own two feet.

It was true that I would not miss opening the front door with a knot in my stomach, lest it be cousin Al on the other side. I had never enjoyed picking up sticky towels and the odd dildo – sometimes very odd. But despite my friends' predictions, my brothel experience had given me more rather than less respect for the man who chooses safe sex with a prostitute over a drunken one night stand, possibly with one of my friends. And I knew better than anyone that it takes guts to walk into a brothel. Although I would miss not being closer to the front line, I was most anxious that I could still sit in a kitchen full of chatting perfumed girls, and one laughing, gentle driver. This was terribly important. Otherwise, they were taking the wonderful womb out of my brave new world. Did this other house even have a womb?

'Yes, there's a kitchen,' Pip prattled on, 'but the girls won't be encouraged to sit in it. Boris wants them to just drop off or pick up their money at the front door, then go.'

On she went, her words like tanks, blindly squashing my happy village.

'Boris doesn't want them coming upstairs, lying all over the furniture, making a mess everywhere, and gossiping. So you'll be glad to know, we no longer have to clean up after them.'.

Would I never see a collage of tired, recovering bodies curled up in corners and draped over couches like Klimt maidens again? Had I gathered my last armful of forgotten nail polish bottles, used cotton buds and soiled serviettes, and emptied my last ashtray overflowing with lipstick-covered cigarette butts? These tawdry scraps now seemed like precious keepsakes to me, and life without such refuse dull and empty.

I had an hour to kill, so on my way to my new office, I popped in on my agent to pick up a script. For the next three weeks, between brothel shifts, I would be playing Marion Mahoney, married to Walter Burly Griffin, in a documentary film about the husband and wife architects who designed Canberra, among other things, where I was born. But just as I was about to leave, my agent called me back again. She was in the middle of a phone call, so put her hand over the mouthpiece and asked if I was interested in a small role in *Moulin Rouge*.

'How small?' I whispered, extremely interested.

'Small,' she nodded enthusiastically.

'How many scenes?' I asked eagerly.

My agent asked the person on the other end, then came back to me. 'One,' she said.

'How many lines?' I asked.

Another prolonged exchange between the two of them, surely a good sign.

'None,' she said at last.

'I'll do it,' I said.

'Hang on,' my agent commanded, holding up a warning hand as new information was coming down the wire.

More lines perhaps? One to Ewan MacGregor?

'Really?' she asked. 'Oh! Okay,' and hung up. 'They've cancelled.'

Once again, my film career took off like a comet without any passengers. Ah well, we both smiled, farewell Paris. I still had Canberra.

I sat on my script up the back of the bus so my legs wouldn't stick to the hot vinyl seat. I hadn't worn a short dress in months for fear of being mistaken for a sex worker. But now that summer was here and my in-house duties had disappeared with the condom dispenser, the string section look was a thing of the past. The house in Redfern was in the very heart of one of Sydney's Lebanese food havens. Twenty years ago I'd discovered these restaurants and their wonderfully filling fare as I sat with my NIDA colleagues quaffing cheap wine and planning our glorious theatrical careers, before pairing off into the night for yet another disastrous sexual experiment.

As I walked past Fatima's and Baba's on Friday night, I found that nothing had changed. There were still the same fluorescent-lit rooms full of noisy NIDA students who had no idea they'd end up working in a brothel. And there, next to Moustafa's grocery shop, was the same old Lebanese coffee house full of big, burly Lebanese men playing backgammon.

As a naive eighteen-year-old drama student, I had gone in there once and sat at a table before realising there was no counter to speak of, no menus and not even a sugar shaker in sight, just a dozen or so Lebanese men with big moustaches regarding me with vague disapproval. I felt like I had wandered into a paddock full of grazing bulls. With every passing second, the opportunity to flee diminished, until I resigned myself to seeing out a spectacularly humiliating experience instead. When the smallest man with the biggest moustache approached cautiously and asked if I would like a coffee, I nodded in a crimson flurry. It was the quickest cup of coffee I ever skolled. And as I left, the big moustache kindly waved my money away with a smile, as if the entertainment I had provided was more than enough.

Ten years later, on a trip to Turkey, I had observed similar tea houses full of Turkish men playing backgammon all day. The only women I ever saw in the villages were those working out in the fields, or packed in dusty trucks like so many cattle being transported back home at sunset. My boyfriend at the time thought this was a brilliant division of labour, and we broke up on the Greek islands a week later.

I walked past Moustafa's, past the Lebanese coffee house, and crossed at the lights to my new workplace, a solid, three-storey house standing on one corner of the main road and a narrow alleyway. Finding no entrance at the front, I walked down the little alley to a solitary door set in a vast, graffiti-covered brick wall.

'Come on up, baby!' sang a very cheerful Raelene over the intercom.

The door automatically opened, and I was immediately confronted by my old friend Moose, and its cousin, Facing Moose Two, hanging on the walls of a majestic foyer. The room was full of the familiar leather couches, lamps and coffee tables, but this was an even grander house than the other. The door to the right opened up to a spacious office where Boris's large leather chair sat at his antique mahogany desk, opposite a bar. This separation from Boris alone could explain Raelene's cheerful tone.

I continued up the polished stairs to find two identical sparkling clean bathrooms at the top, side by side, burgundy towels hanging in place. To their right was a large kitchen containing our inviting old table and several chairs. And beyond that was a lounge, with the same couches, tasselled pillows, glass coffee tables and television unit I knew from the girls' resting room. I returned to the bathrooms and continued in the other direction, climbing six stairs to a raised level. On my right was one large, and now spare, bedroom, cluttered with several redundant mattresses. Straight ahead, overlooking the street, were two large bedrooms that had been made into 'offices'. The one on the left was occupied by our puffing Spanish bull, hunched over her desk.

'Yes, Didi,' she grimaced with pain, as if trying to pull the phone away from her ear, '*I toll you that!*'

So I quickly ducked into the office on the right. Raelene and I laughed at each other as I flung my bag on a spare desk before continuing my exploration up the last flight of stairs.

At the top were three more bedrooms, one cluttered with bed bases, another hosting a king-size bed, and one tiny bedroom with a single bed. Sofia later told me the big bedroom was for Boris, and that a girl was only allowed to sleep in the tiny bedroom, on its tiny single bed, if she was critically tired between bookings and too far from her own home to sleep.

I began my shift feeling excited by my new surroundings and liberated from the nightly chore of dealing with men face to face. As the night grew busy, my happiness soared with the familiar noisy chorus of women's voices rising from the kitchen below, and Urszula's unmistakable rich cackle cutting through the rest. On the pretence of a toilet break, I skipped down to greet them. There they sat, same old cast, different set. Antoinette was squinting as she held Rita's new lingerie up to the light. Bree, Trixie and Marcelle were almost in hysterics at one of Urszula's stories, and dear Patrick sat hugging his mug of tea, chuckling away in a corner. Even though it had only been two days since I'd last seen them, we greeted each other with all the excitement and affection of long-lost friends. The reunion continued when I entered the lounge room and got hugs from Maya, Shelby and Yoko.

'You wearing a little dress, darling?' Rita cooed, stepping back from me.

'Yes!'

'You crossing to the other side?' she laughed teasingly, and Maya joined her, waving a wicked finger at me.

'Meredith?' Urszula cried out from the kitchen next door. 'Crossing to the other side?'

Rita, Maya and Shelby all smiled comfortingly as the walls around us shook with Urszula's laughter.

A week later and chaos still reigned supreme, despite all the new rules. The door bell rang constantly, high heels clacked up and down the wooden stairs, the kitchen was full of noise and toast, and the lounge once again resembled Klimt's painting. Antoinette now almost resided in the tiny bedroom upstairs, and I was back to emptying ashtrays, picking up bathroom towels, and moving among my favourite girls. Even Boris found it difficult to play by his new rules. He'd forgotten how fond he was of sitting like a king at his kitchen table, with a court of accommodating beauties laughing at his shocking jokes, and humiliating any passing receptionist. Sofia huffed and puffed alone in her office like a frustrated Goering, while her commander kept slipping into the concentration camp for a game of cards with the prisoners.

Now that we had moved to this neighbourhood full of Middle Eastern culinary delights, we constantly had to remind the girls to gargle with Listerine as we'd had a few complaints of escorts reeking of garlic. The fridge was a morgue for half-eaten congealed kebabs, stiff pita bread and baklava cakes. And as the girls became more and more familiar with their new locale and diet, the neighbours became more and more curious about the constant stream of arriving and departing girls. The man at the pub bottle shop was almost beside himself.

'You girls having a party tonight?'

'Not with just one bottle, no.'

'Nah. You'd need a case, wouldn't you? There's that many of you.'

'Yes, there is.'

'So many girls! In one house!' I'd never known a person take so long to put a bottle of wine in a brown paper bag. 'And all pretty good lookin' too,' he cried.

'Aren't they?'

'Not a bad apple in the bunch. Except for a coupla Granny Smiths ...' he sniggered.

I never knew what to say to an ugly man who made derogatory remarks about the unattractiveness of women.

But it was my old friends at the coffee house across the road whose response was most noticeable. Baffled by this sudden influx of well-dressed, attractive women clacking past their glass window, they slowly ventured from their tables to their doorway, and from their doorway they boldly ventured right out onto the footpath, peering across the road to the mouth of the breeding nest down the alley. Whatever they concluded, they were visibly excited, and now greeted us with approving nods and cheeky smiles on the street. Since Urszula and a Rastafarian taxi driver had expressed grave doubts about my chances of being mistaken for a sex worker, I was pleased to see that at least one small Lebanese community were of the opinion that men might actually pay to have sex with me.

We had been operating from the new house for only two weeks when Boris realised Antoinette had moved in upstairs and hit the roof. With nowhere else to go, and working full rosters, Antoinette decided the most practical and cheap thing to do was move into the pub on the corner. It was a dirty building on a noisy corner, and no doubt a miserable room, but at least she wouldn't have to worry about money for cabs to work. Then something strange happened. At first we thought Antoinette might have had something done to her face. But even her gait was more youthful. She still shuffled, but more like a girlish geisha than a sedated housewife.

'Maybe she's taking her pills, darling,' Sofia offered, nonplussed by my observation.

'Maybe she finally got her period,' Raelene grumbled.

'No,' said Maxine, on her way home, casually throwing her bag over her shoulder, 'she's got a new boyfriend.'

Who?

'One of the Greeks across the road.'

Having stunned us with this news, Maxine departed. I tried to imagine Antoinette playing backgammon in the Lebanese coffee house. Even Sofia's face contorted with the effort of trying to visualise such an unlikely merger. I wanted to believe, however unlikely, that this extraordinary union could somehow work.

'I give it a week,' snorted Raelene.

Spandex and the QC

I passed the Lebanese fraternity drinking their coffees. They waved and smiled because they thought I was a prostitute, and I waved back anyway. I crossed the road at the lights and, as it was Sunday, there was Craig, parked in the alley, kissing Maxine goodbye in their car. Craig often had no shirt on, and I'm ashamed at the conclusions I jumped to about him, just because he had a missing tooth. I knew from drama school days that no amount of make-up tricks, accents or limps could make up for the good old missing tooth. Black out a tooth and you've instantly forfeited an education, regular meals and kind parents. But Craig was friendly, and I liked him for being good to Maxine. We all liked him for not being Maxine's ex. Her crazy drug-taking days were over, and Maxine was calm. She'd even given up smoking. Craig would drop her off, ring for chats during the night, then pick her up at five in the morning. What more could a girl want? Well, food apparently.

Maxine and Pip often stood side by side comparing their skinniness, encouraging us all to marvel at this tribute to fast metabolisms, because no eating disorders or liposuction had been used to achieve these tiny bodies. Pip was skinny, it was true, but Maxine was positively bonsai. I would look from her tiny frame to Craig's footballer's body and wonder how on earth it was possible, without crushing her little pelvis or without her spindly legs snapping off at the hip. Pip ate pizzas and smoked, whereas Maxine ate half of anything, all night. I didn't become suspicious until she began obsessing about putting on weight.

'Oh my God,' she'd say, rubbing her concave stomach, 'look how fat I am!'

Maybe Maxine had lost too many brain cells through starvation to realise how insulting it was to whinge about her obesity to a woman at least three sizes bigger. On this particular Sunday night, though, Maxine was especially preoccupied with her weight.

'Look at this roll!' she exclaimed with horror, pulling at her flat, tanned stomach.

I pretty much ignored her until she finally asked me, 'Meredith, seriously, do you think I've put on weight?'

Of course the temptation was to say, 'Either that or your head's shrunk.'

Luckily, I was interrupted by a call from our favourite QC. Bernard was a regular of ours who had a proclivity for girls wearing spandex. Anything spandex: bicycle shorts, aerobics tops, but unequivocally a spandex G-string. And foot jewellery. A strange combination, I always thought. And he was possibly the one client we allowed to see girls in his office in the city. The girl had to arrive barefoot, toe-bejewelled and spandex-clad. Bernard would always ring several times before confirming a booking.

'Hi. It's Bernard,' he'd say with unceremonious brevity, and let me do all the talking.

This night Bernard listened attentively as I described our two new girls, both young and blonde, qualities he liked.

'And the spandex?' he asked promptly.

'Call you back in five?' I shot back.

'Fine.'

Click.

I liked to think I understood Bernard. He didn't feel comfortable that we were all so familiar with the kinky preferences of a man in his position, so when I called him back, I kept it as brief and to-the-point as he did.

'Hi Bernard. Meredith. It's a green light on the spandex. Just waiting on feet.'

'She hasn't got any?'

'She's borrowing from a friend.'

It sounded bizarre, but Bernard and I understood our shorthand. I was madly rummaging through our drawer of emergency lingerie and jewellery, preparing for Cathy, who was going to swing by the office on her way to his, when Bernard rang again.

'It's not the foot jewellery from the office, is it?' he asked.

Damn.

'No. It's from a friend, Bernard.'

But you can't lie to a QC.

'I'll call you back.'

Click.

Without looking up from her *Who Weekly* and her half-eaten baklava, Maxine smiled knowingly. 'He hates the office stuff, darl.'

She then stretched out like a cat, made some comment about her obesity, and asked if I'd wake Antoinette for a booking while she went to the toilet. Please go. Cathy and I had bigger problems.

Cathy now thought she could make creative adjustments to her own jewellery. I rang Bernard back and left a message on his machine.

'It's Meredith. Just ringing to let you know that Cathy's got foot jewellery you've never seen. She's got her spandex G-string on and anytime you say, she's ready to pop up to your office, barefoot, okay? Call me back.'

But something was wrong. Why did Bernard's machine say to leave a message for Brian? I rang the number again and got Bernard straightaway. Oh dear. Poor Brian. Please get home before your wife.

When I found Antoinette resting in the tiny bedroom upstairs, she confessed to me in the half light that she was, indeed, quite in love with her dark, brooding Lebanese boyfriend next door.

'It's a bit volatile,' she croaked, smiling girlishly from under a mop of bed hair. 'He's quite fiery. And it's all just below the surface. I like that. He's a bit like me.'

The only thing she didn't like, she said, was staying at his place. Antoinette was North Shore through and through, and she was finding it difficult adjusting to the occasional weekend in Lakemba. But that was nothing compared to the adjustment required from Lakemba, where all hell had broken loose.

'They keep telling him he must stop seeing me. That I'm a *whore*.'

'They know what you do?' I asked.

'Yes, of course,' she replied indignantly, then groaned. 'Oh, but it's such a problem.'

I could imagine it was. If Abdul's family had been expecting him to bring home a nice Muslim girl, veiled from head to foot, it must have been quite a shock when Antoinette walked through the beads.

'You've got a booking at the Mercure, by the way,' I remembered.

'Oh good,' she smiled. 'I'll just get ready and come down.'

Maxine was back, fatter than ever, and with a headache to match. And wasn't it cold? It couldn't have been hotter, but she was already shutting the windows, cheerfully distracting me by asking questions about my current acting job. So I told her I was working on a documentary film about the Burly Griffins, the husband and wife team of architects from Chicago who came to Australia in 1912 bringing a revolutionary love of landscape and incorporating an expression of philosophical principles into their design of Canberra, among other things.

Oh that's nice, Maxine sighed. She liked Canberra.

Patrick came in with a cup of tea and sat down. It was always good to see Patrick, but now it was positively exhilarating. Antoinette was getting ready downstairs, he said, but could someone please give her some condoms, and weren't we hot in here? While Maxine reluctantly saw to Antoinette I resisted the urge to leap on Patrick, and opened some windows instead.

'How are you?' I asked the man who'd just left my bedroom that morning.

'I'm very well! And how are you?' he asked cheerfully.

Once we both came in to work so badly sunburnt from having spent all morning in my swimming pool, we thought they'd guess for sure. But they still didn't. I noticed, however, that we weren't the only ones affected by the extra warmth in the office on these occasions. Receptionists giggled, played with their buttons, and for no reason felt compelled to share intimate stories of first sexual encounters.

'I'm fine.' I smiled down at him, opening a window to let in the summer breeze.

I felt the brutish presence even before I caught the silhouette in the light of the phone box on the corner. There stood Antoinette's pining, tortured paramour, sweating in the moonlight, poor unhappy beast. Any second I expected him to break into an agonised howl.

'STELLA!'

He was even wearing the Brando singlet.

'STELLLLAAAAAAA!!!'

'I really don't feel well at all, you know?' Maxine was back. 'I've got this really funny feeling . . . thumping headache . . . weird in the tummy . . . you know?'

Patrick gave me a quick guilty smile as he left me with the thumping tummy. When the phone rang I let her answer it just to have some peace, but soon wished I hadn't.

'Hi, Bernard, darling, it's Maxine, sweetheart. What can I do for you, gorgeous?'

No, no, no! You didn't talk to *Bernard* like that!

'You sure, precious?'

Precious?

'All right, honey, you get some sleep and call us tomorrow, darling.'

Men didn't ring to let us know they'd changed their minds! Bernard was like a wild animal you had to coax gently, without making any sudden movements. You had to be Virginia McKenna, not Pamela Anderson. In a sulk I rubbed Cathy's name off the board, but as I passed Maxine on my way back to my desk, I got an unmistakable whiff of regurgitated food.

'Just going to the loo,' I said.

There's nothing worse than the pious reformed addict. They can be the most irritating, self-righteous, suspicious, twelve-step bores. I used to go out with a recovering alcoholic who loved nothing more than to sit with all his AA buddies facing the drinks table at a party, where they'd smugly entertain themselves by measuring the alcoholic propensity of all my friends. Maybe that's why I chose a psychiatrist over a meeting to face my own demon, years later, with bulimia. I have to say that I too have shamefully rejoiced in recognising the symptoms of bulimia in others, although not in ex-bulimic packs opposite the supper table. But the night I smelt vomit on Maxine, and in the toilet afterwards, I wondered why I hadn't put the pieces together sooner. The baklavas, the trips to the bathroom, the headaches, the obsession with her stomach, her complexion, her moods, her tiredness, feeling cold all the time. One night she'd returned from the toilet in a cloud of tiger balm. Now that I knew, I had to stop myself from congratulating her. All bulimics know how difficult it is to cover the smell of vomit after a purge. It's like Lady Macbeth trying to get rid of the blood.

'Sorry about the smell of tiger balm, everybody,' she whined, 'but I've done something to my neck.'

Inspired.

It was sad, but sadly not surprising, when Antoinette came into work some days later wearing dark glasses to cover her bruised face.

No one needed to ask what had happened. We gathered from her silence that it wasn't from a booking, and just hoped it was over. But of course it wasn't. From the tiny room upstairs we could hear her mobile phone ringing till five in the morning, and after brief but intense and heated discussions, she'd disappear across the road for an hour or so. And so it continued for weeks. Patrick told me he drove past one night to see them fighting on the street, and pulled up to let her in.

Had the boyfriend hit her again?

'No,' Patrick said in his quiet, bemused way, 'it actually looked more like she was giving it to him.'

Hilary, born in the Year of the Monkey, and the rat

Inevitably, shit hit the fan. I walked into the kitchen to find a circle of concerned girls in a huddle around Antoinette.

'They're threatening to do something,' she said in a low voice. 'If I don't leave him alone, they say they will hurt me, or do something to the house even.'

When I suggested that Antoinette just keep away from her paramour, she snapped at me. 'Of course I keep away from him. Do you think I want to antagonise them? It's *him* who won't keep away from *me*!'

I had only just passed her foe on the footpath cheering, 'Hey, beautiful!' – but then again I wasn't sleeping with one of them. The contradictions made my head spin.

When I entered the office upstairs I looked on the board to see only one girl was out. Hilary was at the ANA. I had not a clue who Hilary was. She had only been with us a week and I still hadn't met her, but no matter which receptionist I spoke to, I got the same response.

'Hilary?' Pip paused on her way out the door. 'Oh, she's lovely.'

Even Sofia lit up at the mention of her name. 'Hilary is lovely, darling. Could you get that?'

I answered the ringing phone.

'Oh hello, it's Roger from Room 1103 at the ANA. I just wanted to say what a delight Hilary was. Thank you so much for sending her. Hilary is lovely.'

'She'll be dropping off a credit card booking, darling,' Sofia said to me. 'You wait.'

I couldn't.

It was going to be a bumpy night, Sofia warned me, as Maxine had called in sick at the last minute, 'with one of her heads'. Sofia had a throbbing ovarian cyst to contend with, but that didn't stop her from coming in. I tried to change the subject. How was her husband, Arturo?

'Fingers cross, darling,' she groaned, 'they think they got it all.'

Now I felt sick too. Sofia and I had never been alone in the office before, which made me feel a little awkward, until I remembered that she now had her own office next door.

'So I'll be working in here with you, Meredith.'

'Great!'

I smiled at Sofia, who tried to smile back, but it was my fault for starting it.

'Hilary?' Sofia cried when the door bell rang. 'Come on up, darling, and meet Meredith.'

Seconds later a short woman in a blue floral dress hovered in our doorway. Hilary had an attractive face with a large mouth and kind eyes, but she was more mature and somewhat rounder than I was expecting. She also had a magnificent head of thick, shiny red hair with swing in it, and a smile that could defrost a fridge.

'Hello, Meredith,' she said with a soothing voice, and her kind eyes twinkled as she leant forward to reach for my hand.

I began by asking Hilary how she was settling in.

'Oh, I'm not new to the game,' she said, 'but, you know, it's been a few years.' And then she laughed. 'I hope I'm not too rusty.'

We laughed too, assuring Hilary she was not. Probably. And then I remembered Roger.

'Roger rang, singing your praises.'

'Oh how sweet.' She smiled warmly. 'He just needed a bit of TLC, that one.'

'And a GF!' Sofia roared laughing.

Out of politeness, Hilary laughed too.

'Yes, I've been so lucky,' she said. 'My first few bookings have all been really delightful.'

Sofia and I looked at each other. You didn't hear that too often.

While Sofia lied about the 'delightful clientele' we attracted, I quickly scanned Hilary's card, which said she was a part-time nurse, a single mum, and went by no other working name.

'Oh, I just like to be Hilary,' she told me, then hesitated. 'If that's okay?'

Of course it was, we chorused. As long as she didn't mind the clients knowing her real name.

'Well, that's who I am,' Hilary shrugged. 'If I call myself something else, it would all feel a bit ... pretend.'

Sofia and I nodded, as if this was a common problem for all the girls.

I was not surprised that Hilary was a nurse. She reminded me of Rita, who regarded her night shifts as a kind of extension of nursing. And considering the easygoing, warm yet professional nature of both these women, it wasn't difficult to see how they might see themselves as carers in either career. But I wondered, as I did with many of the girls, why such an attractive, 'lovely' woman like Hilary did not have a partner, and why she worked in this profession at all. So instead of asking her about her past, I complimented Hilary on her fantastic hair. Hilary was touched, and we were bonding quite enthusiastically when the phones started going silly. While Sofia put three callers on hold, Hilary politely excused herself and said she'd be in the kitchen with the other girls if we needed her. I smiled back until she disappeared out the door. It was true. Hilary was lovely.

Unfortunately, all the men who usually wanted redheads seemed to have gone to some out of town Redhead Convention. Tonight there seemed to be a special on tiny Asians, or busty blondes. I had one guy who specifically asked for anything *but* a redhead. Clive sounded like he would be sick at the very thought.

'But she's a very beautiful girl, Clive.'

'NO!' Clive screamed. 'NOT WITH RED HAIR!'

So I sent him Lottie. That would teach him.

At ten o'clock they all settled in front of the footy, went down the pub or went to bed, because not one man in Sydney required the services of almost any escort agency in the Yellow Pages. Until one in the morning, when they all had the same urgent impulse and the phones went berserk again. What was going on? It was Wednesday! Why did everyone suddenly want sex at 1.30 am on a Wednesday? I can honestly say, after working in the sex industry for a year, that men's sexual urges are frequently, miraculously and unconsciously synchronised.

Sofia was on the phone for ages to a Godfrey in Ermington. We thought we'd heard them all. Godfrey wanted us to send him a girl, any girl, who was born in the Year of the Dragon. And for some reason, instead of getting rid of him Sofia kept putting him on hold, even ignoring my offers to deal with him. Meanwhile I was going crazy with a very charming and terribly English Derek, staying at the Airport Hilton. Derek was ringing on all the different lines, shopping around, and no matter what vocal register I used, or which accent, including Welsh, he kept recognising me.

'Thee provade the full sarvice, inclooding a sensual bordy massage—'

'Is that you again, Meredith?'

'Er—'

'Is every one of these ads in the Yellow Pages *you*?'

'Er ... nooh ...'

'Meredith, I'm going to ring the time in a minute,' Derek said, 'just to see if you answer.'

And we both enjoyed a good laugh.

'Don't bother, Derek,' I finally told him, 'it's twenty past two.'

Occasionally, just occasionally, I wanted to put down the phone and go to the booking myself.

While I frantically answered eight lines at once, Sofia sat, girlishly coiling strands of black hair around her plump fingers.

'And that makes me a Horse, does it?' she mused softly, swinging on her chair with her legs crossed.

With six red lights flashing on her phone, Sofia was still dealing with Godfrey at Ermington.

'Yeah,' she said with sudden gravity, 'yeah, I can be pretty aggressive . . . tha's true. Hang on, Godfrey, I gotta take another call.'

I had a crisis. Yoko was halfway out to a booking in French's Forest and I'd just heard from the credit card authority that both her client's credit cards were registered as stolen. I tried to get Sofia's attention, but it was too late.

'WHAT?' Sofia barked down her phone. 'No, this is not *Meredith*. This is *Sofia*!'

I halted my frenzied waving for a moment.

'Well, I have a Spanish accent, my friend, because I am from Madrid! . . . Don't fucking believe me. See if I give a fuck!'

After Sofia had hung up on my poor friend Derek, she went straight back to her Chinese horoscope lesson.

'And that's a Pig, is it, Godfrey? Yeah, that's him all right . . .'

When I finally got Sofia's attention and told her what I'd done to Yoko, she shook her head at me as if I was born in the Year of the Idiot.

'You juss have to tell her, darling. She has to turn around and come back.'

I knew that, but I didn't have Yoko's new mobile phone number. Sofia rolled her eyes at me – it was a new phone, but the same old number – and returned to her call.

'Go on, Godfrey. The Pig.'

It was the first and only time Yoko had ever arrived anywhere on time.

'No,' Yoko giggled. 'Man okay. Man very nice.'

'No, Yoko,' I said, feeling terribly anxious that for the second time in almost a year I'd sent a girl to see a wanted criminal. 'Man not okay at all. Man very bad. Man has stolen credit cards.'

'Oh,' she said in a sad little voice. 'You sure?'

'Yes, Yoko. I'm sure. Now, Yoko, I want you to say you left something in your car, and just get out of there as quickly as possible, all right?'

'All right,' Yoko sighed with disappointment. 'I have to go,' I heard her apologise to the thief. 'Boss says you have stolen credit cards.'

While I vainly yelled out, 'Yoko! Yoko!', I could hear the voice of the accused rising with indignation in the background.

'Man says he has passport to prove they are his cards,' she returned to me brightly.

'YOU LEFT SOMETHING IN THE CAR!' I shouted at her.

'What?'

'GET OUT OF THERE RIGHT NOW!' I bellowed.

Click. She was gone.

For one tense moment, all was quiet, except for Sofia.

'So I should really be with a Ox,' she mused, still on the line to Godfrey, 'not a Pig.'

Finally, Yoko rang back from the street. She was fine, but wanted to know what she had left in her car.

Sofia had arranged to send Godfrey the lovely Hilary.

'He loves redheads, darling,' Sofia shouted down the phone to Hilary in the kitchen, 'and you are twenty-seven.'

Suddenly Hilary was panting in our doorway.

'Twenty-seven?' she asked, looking very alarmed.

'Yes,' Sofia said, a little defensively. 'You could be twenty-seven, darling. Couldn't she be twenty-seven, Meredith?'

I nodded. If Antoinette could be thirty-nine, Hilary could definitely be twenty-seven.

'But my *daughter* is twenty-seven!' Hilary exclaimed, gawking at both of us. 'I'm forty-four!'

I stole another glance at Hilary's card, still in front of me, and there it was. Born in 1956. Wow. What a refreshing change from the television industry, which wants women in their mid thirties to play mothers to teenage heart-throbs. And here we were, sending a woman out as the same age as her daughter. This was much better.

The craziness continued, and over the next hour or so, when she wasn't on a call or organising Boris's off bookings, Sofia tinkered with the computer, lazily looking up clients she'd already sent girls to see. She also had a niggling feeling that she had dealt with a Chinese astrologer before, and wanted to look up Godfrey. But now I had another problem.

'This girl will not let you do that without a dental dam, Mr Omasuka ... No, not a condom ... Den-tal dam ... Latex sheet ... Small sheet ... No, much smaller than bed sheet.'

Suddenly, Sofia let out a cry. 'OH! Fuck me dead! Fuck me dead fuck me dead fuck me dead!'

I left Mr Omasuka expecting Penny armed with armfuls of latex bedding, and turned to Sofia, who sat with her face in her hands, nervously laughing in front of the computer screen.

'You know this Godfrey I sent Hilary to?' she said, her red face peeping through her fingers.

I nodded. Hilary had rung to start the booking half an hour ago.

'Listen,' Sofia began with a timid smile, and tremulously read from the screen. 'Godfrey. Ermington. Has seen Bree, May-Ling, Coral. Cleo will not see again. Heather will not see again. Rita will see, but check first. Comments: Girls should be warned. Man has two amputated legs. And mechanical penis.'

For some time Sofia and I looked at each other, mouths open, speechless. How could we have sent a new girl to such a booking without warning her? And what on earth was a mechanical penis? Without a word, Sofia reached under her table for the Black Douglas, and poured us both a glass. We sat in silence, each cradling a large glass of scotch, pondering this extraordinary phenomenon, until Sofia's shoulders started to shake and she turned to me with eyes full of tears.

'Do you think it can come?' she shook with laughter. 'Mechanically?'

We slapped our knees, rocking backwards and forwards in silence.

'Perhaps his last girlfriend left him—' I could barely go on, '—because he was too mechanical in bed!'

If only my colleagues could see us now, me and our tyrannical supervisor, with tears streaming down our faces, bent over our knees, banging our fists on our tables, and quaffing Sofia's best scotch. Just then the phone rang.

It was Hilary, calling from Godfrey's, to finish.

Sofia struggled to speak.

'How did you go, darling?' she asked, brushing away her tears.

Sofia listened intently for some time, deliberately avoiding my eyes.

'Frustrating?' she repeated tremulously, and had to turn away from me.

Laughing out loud with relief at something Hilary had said, Sofia swung back to me to share the joke. As Hilary had to lie about her age, Sofia explained, Godfrey's Chinese horoscope reading was most comprehensive, but also totally useless, as Hilary was actually a Monkey, not a Rat.

'All right my darling—' Sofia said, trying to wind her up.

But Hilary also thought we should know, just for the record, and for the other girls' information, that Godfrey had absolutely no legs whatsoever, and a mechanical penis.

'Oh well, there you go!' cried Sofia, as if it was our fourth one tonight. 'Well, thank you for that, my darling. And goodnight!'

Hilary really was lovely.

As Patrick and I were leaving at five o'clock that morning, we saw them, two tortured souls arguing in the phone booth under the streetlight. Antoinette stood inside like a trapped animal, while her brutish lover leant against the doorframe. He was a frighteningly large, dark, thickset man, and despite an extra chin and protruding gut, he was handsome, in a primal kind of way. At the sight of us he sprang back a few feet, to demonstrate his tiny blonde hostage was free to escape if she so chose. But Antoinette did not choose. Instead, she smiled at us awkwardly and waved us away. We waited for a moment until she finally came out of the booth and, somewhat less courteously, waved us off. Reluctantly, we left her there.

Patrick and I drove home in silence, and I wondered if it was because he too was struck by the similarity between our situation and Antoinette's. Patrick and I never discussed our different backgrounds, our unlikely relationship and its inevitably short life span. I did not know Patrick's reasons, but I guessed at my own and felt plagued by shame. Although Patrick was self-educated, bright, funny and sensitive, I did not want to see him outside our dark cocoon. Or more to the point, I did not want to be seen with him. I felt proud that I worked with prostitutes, but I did not want to own in public my relationship with their gentle driver, who played darts and mixed Guinness with champagne.

Urszula had a predilection for mobs. Not only had she worked for the Mob in Kings Cross, Urszula had also served the Mob in America, where she was now wanted by the FBI.

'That's why I have a slight American accent,' she said, in thick Geordie.

I never questioned the truth of Urszula's stories because to me, her very existence was miracle enough. Besides, I just loved listening to the rich timbre of her distinctive voice with its North Country vowels and theatrical inflections.

'I don't exist!' she boasted.

Urszula had no tax file number, and no Medicare card.

'And let me tell you, Meredith, that cost me a lot of money.'

Whether I believed her or not, no one else had captured my imagination so strongly since Uncle Tom told ghost stories after card tricks at Christmas.

Urszula had been missing for four days. On Monday morning she had picked up Sofia from the hospital, as a favour, and driven her into work. Only Sofia would do a whole day shift on her way home from having an ovarian cyst, 'as big as a grapefruit, darling', removed. Urszula promised to drive Sofia home at the end of the day as well, but an hour into my night shift, Sofia was still waiting, pale and sweating, for her lift to arrive.

'Come on,' Sofia wailed down her phone every time Urszula's mobile almost rang out, until she got the message bank. 'Where the fuck are you, my love? I got a belly full of stitches here, and a sick husband and a little girl waiting for me at home.'

It wasn't like Urszula to go missing, especially in a crisis. When Urszula felt needed, she shone. Something was wrong.

Friday came, and still no word. Trudy called yet again, asking Sofia or me to ring her if we heard anything at all. In the back of all our minds was Urszula's problem with her breathing, but none of us dared mention it. At nine o'clock, Sofia asked me to confirm her bookings while she rang every other girl on the books who might have any idea of Urszula's whereabouts. She began with Urszula's best friend, Hester.

Sofia had been avoiding Hester lately. Hester had done nothing wrong, except perhaps get too many things pierced.

'But they can all come out,' she gushed in her cockney accent, referring to the stud through her tongue, the ring through her nose, and the diamond in her belly button.

The truth of the matter was, Boris just didn't want Hester on his books any more. 'Because she goes woof woof!' he yelled at me for asking. 'And I am not the bloody RSPCA!'

Hester was not a pretty girl, it was true. Somewhere around forty, with short, thick brown hair and a deep melodic voice, Hester was a wired, witty and wily bisexual from East London who steadfastly refused to wear a dress. I could only ever take Hester in small doses as she found too many things amusing, and spoke too inaudibly to be able to share the joke properly, having had one line too many. Hester loved four things in life: speed, sex, her dog and Urszula, possibly in that order. On the rare nights when Hester did come to the house, she and Urszula entertained us with their hilarious double act of abusive banter, cackling like two deranged witches in a British sitcom.

'Ah, shoot it, you fooking slag!'

'Oh, fuck off, you poxy slut!'

Hester and I got off to a bad start. I had only just begun working at the brothel when Raelene promised me that Hester, who lived nearby at Clovelly, would give us both a lift home. She got it half right. At half past four in the morning, Hester dropped me off in the back streets of Bondi Junction, sang cheerio, and sped off into the darkness with her apologetic passenger waving pathetically out the back window. A foolish move, I always thought, considering I got her bookings. Occasionally, however, we really did require Hester's services. She was the only girl with everything, absolutely everything, ticked on the back of her card.

'Of course I do golden showers, darling,' she laughed like a machine gun. 'I'd piss on the bastards for nothing!'

There were things Hester did that we hadn't even thought of and, frankly, preferred not to.

'So you haven't heard from her since Monday either?' Sofia repeated on the phone to Hester.

Urszula had crashed at Hester's place last Sunday night, and left in the morning to pick up Sofia from the hospital.

'All right, my dear.' Sofia smiled, then frowned. 'What? Yes, your name is always on roster, Hester, but is very quiet, my dear,' Sofia lied. 'What can we do?'

For all their bark, Sofia and Boris adopted a somewhat cowardly method of culling girls from their books. Rather than put her out of her misery, they preferred to let an unwanted girl die slowly of confusion and neglect.

The Saturday night receptionists had rung Urszula's mobile and left messages that went unanswered as well, but by Sunday night the phone was just ringing out, and now Hester was as concerned as we were. Trudy was talking about ringing hospitals, and even Boris was doing his best to pretend he wasn't worried. He hovered uncomfortably at my desk asking about the most trivial things, until he could stall no more.

'And haff we heard from bloody Urszula yet?'

I knew Urszula would be so happy to hear of her 'father's' begrudging concern. And decided to tell her in person. Tomorrow I would go to Centennial Park myself, and look for the lady with the bull terrier.

Chinese New Year

'Oh, come on, Rodney! Admit it, you're horny,' her strong voice boomed from our office above.

As I climbed to the landing, all I could see was a *Star Trek* cap peeping over a large collection of grotesque latex dolls assembled on her desk, and the soles of two black army boots resting beside them. Leslie, our new receptionist, seemed to be settling in just fine. With a grin that could take passengers, the jolly blonde giant winked at me as I passed circumspectly on my way to my desk. I bristled at the premature familiarity she had with her new surroundings, with me, and even with Rodney, but as Leslie had the shoulders of a gridiron player and the neck of a boxer, I decided to get over it.

It was seven o'clock on Chinese New Year, and only five girls had rung to sign on, not including Urszula. I told Sofia about my fruitless search of the park, but she was too anxious about ten missing girls to worry about one. I could have killed Maxine for her constant bad heads. It meant that Sofia sat with us, shortening all our lives, instead of next door in a cage of her own. With nostrils flaring she stamped her hoof, snorted angrily and began hunting the others down, relentlessly begging, bullying or shaming them into work. But even this proved ineffectual, as one after the other insisted she was sick, or her boyfriend had suddenly arrived, or her mother, or her period, or she'd had an accident, a panic attack, or had been arrested for speeding. With every call Sofia was closer to having a coronary. When stalwart Maya rang, I knew I could not be the messenger and survive.

'Just putting you on hold, Maya.'

'No, Meredith! Please don't put Sof—'

Too late.

'No, Maya! What you mean you're celebrating Chinese New Year?' Sofia shouted, smacking her forehead. 'You're fucking Thai, Maya! ... I don't care where your father's from, let's think about your mother.'

Poor Maya was too honest to have made up an accident, and so she reluctantly agreed to sign on at eleven, after she had celebrated with friends.

'How can she celebrate the new year only until eleven o'clock?' I protested feebly.

'Oh, give me a break!' barked Sofia. 'Don't tell me the Chinese stayed at home on first of January. How many new years do they need, for fuck's sake?'

While Sofia fought with reluctant sex workers, I glumly watched our confident new receptionist score three bookings within ten minutes. Blue Angels must have been sorry to lose Leslie. She had a likeable larrikin charm and an effortlessly persuasive manner on the phone. Leslie could call men 'sweetheart' and sound like she meant it. And she had an old soul for a twenty-four-year-old. When things went from bad to worse this hideous night, and Leslie commanded us to 'take a deep breath' and get a hold of ourselves, even Sofia obeyed.

'How did you get into this business?' I asked her when she stopped for a cigarette break.

'My dad.' Leslie grinned. 'It was his idea I study business and admin at college. He reckons I'd make a great madam.'

Had I understood her correctly? Leslie's father had encouraged her to get into the sex industry?

'Yeah!' she beamed back at me.

'Do you mind me asking why, Leslie ?'

'He's a retired cop.'

Having heard that both Blue Angels and Raquel's were run by ex-policemen, this was not such a surprise. Everyone knows the days of illegal parlours made the sex industry and the police strange bedfellows, in more ways than one. Apparently, the lucrative possibilities of running a brothel had made such an impression on Leslie's dad during his days on the force, it would have broken his heart had his little girl chosen any other career path. I like to think he might have hesitated had Leslie looked less like a bouncer.

An hour later, slumped on my desk, I listened to our new receptionist confirm her sixth booking in a row.

'What a card,' Leslie chortled, shaking her head as she hung up on Neville in Cronulla.

Tony, Stavros, Gary and Mandrake had all been cards too. Soon Leslie would have the whole pack, and I still hadn't put pen to paper. I waited for Sofia to berate me for my lethargic perform-ance, but it was so mute on the Spanish front, I had to look over to see if she was even in the room. Sofia sat very quietly at Maxine's desk, cradling her head in her hands. Since having her ovarian cyst removed the week before, Sofia had worked one day and three nights, smoking two packets of Winfield each shift. While Leslie flirted with Aldo, I asked Sofia if she was okay.

'What?' she barked. 'Oh. Still bleeding like a stuck pig, darling, but I'm fine. Juss worried.'

'About Urszula?'

'About Boris.'

Boris?

'Chinese New Year.'

I looked at Sofia, and my ignorance clearly exhausted her.

'Shan is Chinese, darling.'

Yes, Shan, Boris's Asian Slut, as we liked to call her, was Chinese ...

'So Boris will be out celebrating Chinese New Year with her,' Sofia said.

And that was bad because Boris was Bavarian?

'Is bad, darling, because Boris is drinking again!'

'Ah,' I sighed. 'He's fallen off the wagon to celebrate the dragon!'

'You should have been here lass night, darling,' Sofia said flatly. 'That wasn't funny either.'

Boris was already a frightening and unpredictable man, and the thought of him drunk was sobering. We sat in silence, hoping our Bavarian dictator and his Chinese floozy would stay out all night.

I'd heard many stories of the good old days at North Sydney, interrupted by the occasional bad old day, when Boris was in his cups. The receptionists, who worked in an office downstairs just under Didi and Boris's penthouse suite, often had to sneak out to get him alcohol. Unable to escape his wife's sharp eye, Boris would include cryptic notes with his paperwork. Raelene had told me that '2C/2B' meant two bottles of champagne and two bottles of beer. Not leaving his room might have fooled Didi at first, but crashing into furniture while singing Schubert for the next five hours, surely that was a bit of a giveaway?

The phones were dead and the streets were empty. We could hear the not too distant sounds of fireworks and festivities going on in Chinatown. A few of the girls sat in the kitchen, reading magazines, eating toast, filing nails. Even Patrick had nothing to do, so he sat with us, sipping tea, smoking his Marlboros and politely chuckling as our new receptionist entertained us with more colourful stories of her past. As a child, Leslie was taught to play poker by off-duty policemen while her mum prepared supper in the kitchen. While other little girls had bedtime stories, young Leslie hungrily absorbed parley about illegal boudoirs and protection deals.

'Oh yeah, they knew all the girls, where the houses were, which cars not to book. They were even invited to the brothel parties.'

I asked Leslie how her mum felt about her dad partying with prostitutes.

'Oh, Mum always controlled the purse strings,' Leslie winked at me reassuringly, 'and she only ever let Dad have twenty dollars, in case he was tempted.'

Yes, I smiled back at her, that would have done it.

Leslie told us that she and her brother Jimmy ran a security company.

'Well, it's Dad's company, really, but as a cop that's illegal, so it's in our names instead.'

I wondered which actor played Leslie's dad on *Blue Murder*.

'So if any client gives a girl a hard time,' Leslie boasted, 'Jimmy could send some boys over in a jiffy.'

I had a bizarre image of four burly men pulling up in a giant slipper.

'I've got a gun licence!' Leslie trumped, looking at Patrick.

Patrick gulped down his mouthful of tea. 'Really?' he asked quietly. And as she prattled on, Patrick obligingly smiled, nodded, laughed, drank his tea and smoked his Marlboros. Dear Patrick.

At three in the morning, the mood was not so cheerful. The phones were going ballistic and we still had no girls. While Sofia was having a heart attack, I was having an argument with our new receptionist, who was about to send Antoinette to see Gregory in a private home. He wanted to watch her having sex with a young male prostitute.

'Have you even checked with Antoinette that she'll do that, Leslie?' I asked.

'Why wouldn't she?' Leslie objected. 'It's fifty extra for the old guy to watch!'

'Have you asked Antoinette if she will have sex with a male prostitute?' I cried.

'It's one of Brad's Boys!' Leslie exclaimed.

'*So?*'

'Ah, Meredit,' a deep voice boomed over the top of us. 'I arrive just in time for another of your moral dilemmas.'

We all looked up to see Boris swaying dangerously in our doorway. I had barely opened my mouth when the cannons started.

'I don't focking care who it is, or where she's going!' he said, dismissing my protest with a giant wave. 'Send her, Leslie! Send the girl!'

As Leslie flew into action, Boris turned his disapproving bloodshot eyes towards me. 'What is your problem, Meredit?'

I was dead.

'Antoinette?' he sneered, with such contempt he nearly lost his balance. 'Goot!' he said, clutching the wall behind him. 'And if the focking bitch don't vont to go, tell her to fock off!' Boris paused to burp. 'And why is Maya sitting out there sulking?'

Sofia explained to him why Maya had wanted the night off.

'She's fucking Thai!' Boris cried, throwing his hands in the air.

'I know that!' Sofia yelled, throwing her hands up too.

'Who else is on roster?' Boris demanded.

This was the moment we had all been dreading. Sofia buried her head in her hands as I passed Boris the roster sheet, now covered with red absentee crosses. For a moment I thought he was going to vomit on it.

'Jesus the fock Christ!' he shouted, flicking the paper. 'What is this shit? Shut up!' he interrupted Sofia before she could explain.

Boris hovered for a moment in the doorway, regarding his three useless receptionists with snake eyes.

'I'm taking Patrick,' he growled, and left.

Nearly choking on his tea, Patrick leapt to his feet and followed his sozzled master out the door, madly checking his pockets for cigarettes, lighter and keys.

Even the girls in the kitchen were irritable. It seemed everyone was in a foul mood, except the Chinese, and Leslie.

'Dad always said—' she was off again, '—"to be a good cop, you have to be a fucking good criminal".'

I'd had enough of the cops and the guns and the brothers in jiffies, and could have stuck pins in her Smurfs for being so unbearably proficient, but I didn't want to end up face down in a pond in Centennial Park. I just wanted Urszula to ring, or walk through the door, or call out '*Oi, where's my booking, you fooking slag?*' from the kitchen below. Which reminded me, I had a booking for Celeste at the Stamford.

'Celeste?' I rang through to the kitchen. 'Would you pick up, please?'

It was hard to believe that the loud groan below, followed by heavy, petulant stomping, came from the tall, elegant Celeste, who smoked long cigarettes in a tortoiseshell holder.

'What?' she demanded at last.

'I've got you a booking, Celeste,' I said, very nicely.

Silence.

'Celeste?'

'*Yes? So?*'

'So are you ready?' I asked, not so nicely.

'Well I have been for the last seven fucking hours,' Celeste replied, and slammed the phone down in my ear.

I commanded Leslie to call Celeste a cab, and then did some stomping of my own. As I passed her, Sofia looked up from her paperwork and smiled, vaguely pleased that someone else was going to yell at a girl for a change.

There, perched on a crimson leather sofa in the downstairs waiting foyer, I found Celeste looking straight ahead, like the sphinx. On the opposite sofa sat a gently bemused Antoinette, waiting for the details of her booking with a male prostitute.

'Here you are, Celeste,' I said, handing her the booking. 'Happy Chinese New Year.'

'Have I got a driver?' she snapped.

'No,' I answered calmly, 'you're going by cab.'

'Well have you bothered to *call* me one?' she asked spitefully.

I'd had enough.

'Look!' I shouted. 'What's the matter with you? I've got you a booking in a clean hotel and the cab is on its way!'

While Celeste attacked me for her lack of bookings, and I berated her for her rude manner, Antoinette watched us as if she was at a ping pong match, until suddenly, from behind, Boris's office door swung wide open.

'WHAT THE FOCK IS GOING ON?' the pickled Bavarian roared.

My heart jumped. Why wasn't Boris in Chinatown? My heart jumped again. Cowering behind him, wishing he was in Chinatown, was Patrick.

'Hi, Mehe-he ...' Shan waved weakly, perched like a kewpie doll on Boris's mahogany desk. Shan could never remember my name.

'Hi, Shan.'

It got worse. On a small television monitor in the corner of Boris's office, I recognised myself, and an angry escort sitting on a couch. I looked up to my right, and there was the camera. I looked from Boris to the camera, to Celeste, to Antoinette, to Patrick, to the monitor, like a frightened deer. A frightened deer caught yelling at a weeping prostitute. Weeping? Oh great. The one time Celeste showed any sign of being human, it had to be now.

'Get upstairs, Meredit!' Boris shouted, pointing the way.

I told Sofia not to ask as I threw my body into my chair. Boris would be here any minute and they'd soon know everything.

'Now, Meredit,' Boris began, striding through our doorway, 'I won't haff it. Tears, Sofia! Meredit had poor Celeste in tears!'

Boris looked at me as though, even growing up in Germany during the war, he had never seen such cruelty. And when did he get so sober?

'A girl just about to go to a booking, Meredit! How could you be so stupid?'

And while Boris and I shouted at each other, Sofia and Leslie tried to follow the score, until his voice rose like a siren with a sentence that froze me in my tracks.

'AND IF CELESTE GETS CANCELLED IT VILL BE ALL YOUR FAULT!'

Boris had said the C word. Even on a busy night the word *cancellation* sent a shocked ripple through the house. And whatever the reason for a cancellation, it had better not be the receptionist's fault. Now I was nervous. Celeste had been cancelled for turning up late, turning up stoned, turning up with bad skin and, just last week, for turning up and falling asleep. Now she might be cancelled for turning up in tears.

'I'm on my mobile,' Boris scowled at the door. 'Come on, Patrick.'

'Righteo!' sang his lapdog, lurking somewhere in the shadows.

No doubt Boris would give Patrick a sermon all the way to Chinatown about my incompetence, bad judgement and stupidity.

And the ever-friendly, pusillanimous, over-accommodating Patrick would nod, laugh and sigh. Spineless man. I hated Patrick.

Twenty minutes later, Celeste was cancelled.

'What's the problem, Lawrence?' I asked anxiously.

'Girl has skin disease!'

I could hear Celeste scoffing in the background, '*Skin* disease? Oh, for God's sake!'

'I'm terribly sorry if you think the girl has a skin disease, Lawrence,' I said soothingly. 'That's no good at all, is it? Could you just pop her on the phone for a moment?'

'Hello, darling,' Celeste purred down the phone to me. 'Isn't this unfortunate?'

It did not surprise me that Celeste was already over our recent spat. All differences were swiftly put aside once the girls were out there, in the battlefield, sometimes facing brutal and candid rejection by ugly men. And as a seasoned actress, I found Celeste's Cowardish tone irresistibly contagious.

'Celeste, I'm terribly sorry but this ridiculous man is having a problem with your luminous skin.'

'Darling, you know I suffer with a little eczema around my neck in humid weather,' she purred. 'That's all.'

'Of course I know, darling,' I said. 'Come back and I'll get you another booking.'

'All right, darling.'

In the face of the Lawrences of this world, Celeste and I joined forces once again, and I was happy to get her, and her bad skin, two more bookings.

It was nearly closing time. Even the Chinese had gone home, except for half-Thai Maya, who'd not had one booking all night and was curled up asleep in the tiny bedroom upstairs. She smiled sleepily when I woke her, and nodded when I apologised for ruining her night, as if used to disappointment. I left her to change out of her good black evening dress with the little diamante stars. As she descended the stairs in her black and white uniform, Maya waved her fingers at me. The sad irony was not lost on either of us that at a quarter to six in the morning, Maya was finally on her way to a hotel, this time as a housemaid. Within half an hour, Maya would commence her morning shift at the Hilton, and possibly have to clean the very rooms in which her more fortunate colleagues had just entertained.

On my way back to the office, I was delighted to find a relaxed and amused Antoinette sitting at the kitchen table.

'Don't take Celeste personally,' she said quietly. 'Despite the performance, I think she feels painfully invisible most of the time.'

Ah, Antoinette. Explain all the girls to me, and how on earth you came to be here in the first place.

'What about you?' I suddenly remembered. 'How did you go with Brad's Boy, and old man Gregory?'

Antoinette said it was fun as both men were too tired to do anything, having spent most of the day together already, so they just sat around talking, and drinking some of Father Gregory's fine wine.

'*Father* Gregory?' I asked.

Antoinette nodded. 'Sometimes I wish I could take my puritanical mother along to these bookings.'

As I wearily climbed the stairs to our office, I could hear Sofia arguing with someone on the phone, but not with her usual formidable force. I leant in the doorway, watching her push wet strands of hair from her damp forehead as she released a series of defeated grunts. When Sofia finally hung up on her caller, Leslie and I waited patiently for orders.

'Boris says we cannot have the driver,' Sofia groaned as she pushed herself up and out of her chair. 'Patrick is teaching him how to play pool.'

As she waddled towards the bathroom once more, Sofia told me to order three cabs, one for Central Station.

'Don't call one for me,' sang the ever cheerful Leslie, swinging her backpack over her broad shoulders, and donning her *Star Trek* cap.

Sofia turned as if about to protest, but at the sight of the hulking blonde putting her earphones in, she continued on her way instead. I begged Sofia to get a cab all the way to her home in Burwood, but as usual she ignored me. Leslie lived just ten minutes down the road and swore that, once in her heavy metal nirvana, she felt quite safe to walk anywhere. Admittedly, if I saw Leslie's silhouette approaching me on a dark and stormy night, I'd cross to the other side pretty smartly.

The next day Arturo rang the office to say that his wife would not be coming in to work. Sofia had been admitted to hospital that afternoon, suffering haemorrhaging and a secondary infection, due no doubt to a poor diet, no rest, and a lack of available girls.

Learning not to give a shit

It was after ten on Friday night and I was on the phone to Kimberley, who wanted us to know that if ever clients requested a 'man and a woman' booking, her husband, Scott, was more than willing to help out.

'And has Scott had any experience, Kimberley?' I asked.

'Oh yes, Meredith,' Kimberley said through her nose. 'Scott has danced all over the world.'

It was an unusual analogy. Baryshnikov had danced all over the world, but I'm sure it didn't lead to couple bookings at the Kiev Hilton. What sort of dancing qualified one as a sex worker, I wondered. Certainly not Irish dancing. 'Scott provides a wonderful service, but will be keeping both arms by his sides at all times.' I was about to inquire if Scott had been a male pole-dancer when I heard the wonderful and unmistakable Northern caterwaul coming from the kitchen.

'Gotta go, Kimberley! Girl in trouble.'

I dropped the phone and leapt down the stairs in two strides.

There she stood, leaning against the sink, dressed to the nines in her tight black leathers, and entertaining her court. As I ran towards her, she held her hand up to stop me.

'Don't you fooking tooch me!' Urszula commanded angrily.

So I didn't.

'What are ya like?'

I always loved the way Urszula said this, but tonight it wasn't so funny.

'It's good to see you too,' I said, still panting from my sprint.

She was giving me her *deadly* look, and for her sake, I was dying.

'Seventy-two fooking messages for fook's sake!' she shouted at me.

'We were worried about you!' I shouted back.

'Well don't!' she bellowed, ashing in the sink. 'I don't like people worrying about me. Makes me feel claustrophobic.'

'We thought maybe something had happened to you—'

'Something had happened! But it's no one's fooking business but mine. I'll call in when I'm good and ready!'

Urszula moved towards the table and the girls parted like the red sea, giving their queen a throne.

'I don't like it, Meredith, all this fuss. And you can tell those other bloody slags up there to leave off too.'

What was she like?

'Seriously!' she commanded.

Urszula may not have been able to scare me any more, but she could surely hurt.

'Okay,' I said, turning at the doorway. 'I'll tell them. From now on, if anything happens to Sapphire, no one's to give a shit.'

'Thank you!' she called after me.

I was stomping up the stairs when I nearly crashed into Antoinette, stomping down.

'I'm sorry,' she began haughtily, 'but I'd rather you gave my lesbian booking to somebody else.'

Apparently Antoinette was no longer speaking to Yoko, who had flirted with Abdul when Antoinette introduced them the previous week.

'Are you sure?' I asked her. 'Yoko's a ridiculously friendly girl, Antoinette, forever bringing us chocolates and cigarettes—'

'Yes, but I'm suspicious of all that too,' she scowled miserably. 'I think she's convoluted.'

With a mutual nod, we continued stomping past each other.

Maxine and Delia were not expecting such curt replies to their eager questions about Urszula when I threw myself back into my chair, and neither were Trudy, Sofia and Hester when I rang each of them at home to give them the news.

'And yes, Hester,' I lied, 'it's really, really, very quiet.'

I got out my dictionary and looked up *convoluted*. Antoinette thought Yoko was coiled, twisted.

If we'd managed to get her one booking, I might have been able to stay angry with Urszula, but as girls came and went, she was forced to share the kitchen with Zora. Dressed like a Greek goddess again, Zora had been sitting for hours clutching her bag full of grapes, and I couldn't bring myself to tell her that Mr Little had called and booked Marcelle instead.

Around four in the morning, when there was nothing left in the kitchen but a brown paper bag full of grape pips, Urszula rang from her Land Rover outside to say goodnight.

'I'm sorry if I sounded ungrateful, Meredith,' she growled affectionately. 'I know you and Trudy were genuinely concerned. If you like, I'll tell you all about it over that coffee you keep saying we're going to have.'

Feeling slightly appeased, I suggested I ring her tomorrow, when we'd both had a good sleep.

'How long do you need?' she asked me.

'Eight hours. You?'

'I only need four, darling, but you just call me when you're up. We'll be in the park, waiting for you.'

Four hours' sleep in a car with a dog. I could never stay angry with Urszula.

I rang Urszula at two the next afternoon, and she sounded very upbeat.

'And are you coming to play with us in our park?'

It was a beautiful, sunny day and Urszula had been throwing the ball to her 'boy', as she liked to call Rex, and was preparing to do a few laps on her rollerblades.

'I've got rollerblades!' I cried, stupidly. 'But I'm not very—'

'Well fooking bring them, child,' she shouted, nearly deafening me with enthusiasm.

When I arrived, I could see Urszula's white hair glinting in the sun as she glided towards me, barking commands to a confused albino bull terrier who pulled in the opposite direction. People turned to look at this spectre on rollerblades, struggling with a large white beast and cackling madly. If only she'd tried acting, I thought as she skated towards me, looking like one of the replicas from *Blade Runner*. Urszula's looks and voice alone assured her of a good run of screen baddies, and she could even have done her own stunts. But here again was another baffling contradiction. When Trudy's casting agent aunt got Urszula a role in a Jackie Chan film being made in Australia, she never turned up on set and disappeared underground instead, until everyone knew not to ask why.

Urszula skated straight into me, laughing loudly as she gave me a big bear hug. It was strange seeing each other in daylight, surrounded by nature, instead of make-up and fluorescent lights. Urszula had the strongest and fittest body I'd ever seen on a woman in her mid forties, but out of our usual context, she looked tiny. And I could tell by something vulnerable in her smile, it meant a lot to her that I had come.

Once Rex was locked up in the Land Rover, Urszula turned all her attention to her student and the task at hand. She obviously relished her role of teacher as she grabbed my arms and led me forward. We skated around Centennial Park and Urszula held my hand tightly, warning me of every little approaching incline or bump in the road. Occasionally she would look up at me and roar laughing at the sight of my bright red, sweat-drenched face.

'I'm the one who's supposed to be fooking sick!' she cried.

Somehow I knew not to ask Urszula if this was the cause of her recent absence. She'd tell me that soon enough. So I continued, puffing and stumbling beside her like Frankenstein on wheels while she glided at my shoulder, chatting away without a trace of perspiration. She was right. It didn't make sense. I was the one who ran eight kilometres a day, and she was the chain-smoker with respiratory problems.

'Can we stop now?' I panted hopefully as her white Land Rover came into view again, parked by the large pond.

'Now?' she retorted. 'You've only done one lap. I do five of these a day!'

I didn't mind Urszula gloating over her athletic prowess and laughing in my face, so long as we stopped before I died.

Upon his release, the grateful bull terrier obediently stepped down from the passenger's seat, stretched his legs and sniffed at the grass.

'Do you want some of this?' Urszula asked as she filled a little pipe with weed.

'No,' I said, collapsing in the grass at her feet.

When I'd caught my breath I rose on my elbows to see her silhouetted in the sunlight, leaning against her car, pipe in hand, smiling down at me.

'So what do you think of my place, Meredith?' she asked, beaming.

'It's beautiful, Urszula,' I said, taking in our lush green surroundings. 'And it's good of you to share it with so many people.'

Chortling with glee at my complicity, Urszula sat down beside me and described in detail her daily routine. It began in the morning on the far hill, throwing the ball to Rex, and was followed by a takeaway coffee from Oxford Street, before returning to the park, where she sat in the shade under this tree or by that pond, and read, or talked on the phone, or slept. Sometimes she'd skate for another hour or two before showering at Hester's, or at the house, and starting work for the night.

'What do you eat?' I asked. 'And when?'

'Oh, I eat when I feel like it,' she dismissed my question with a wave.

I suspected not often enough or healthily enough, but I also knew not to give a shit.

'So, is there someone in your life, Meredith?' Urszula asked cautiously.

'Yes, there is someone,' I answered guiltily, 'but it's not serious.'

Urszula nodded, pretending that Trudy hadn't already told her about Patrick.

'What about you?' I asked.

'God no,' she scoffed. 'I don't want relationships, Meredith, and they don't want me.'

I was never convinced when people said this, any more than I had been when I used to say it.

'I'm too independent, too headstrong,' Urszula stated. 'It's the fooking German in me!'

I waited to hear exactly where the German came from, but it passed.

'Oh sure I get offers, but once men realise what they're dealing with,' she growled, 'they run for the hills.'

On another occasion Urszula had told me it was she who ran for the hills, and that men woke up to find her gone. Whatever the truth was, there were a lot of people up in the hills, and not many left on the dance floor.

Urszula said the longest she'd ever been with a man was one weekend, except for her marriage, which lasted a few months. It was the second time I'd heard Urszula mention a marriage.

'How did that end?' I asked.

'I broke his nose,' she said. 'We were fooling around in bed, and he wanted a bit of rough and tumble. I couldn't resist.'

She looked at me, and we both laughed. Rex looked up to see if he was needed, and returned to his patch of grass with a look of forlorn neglect.

'Some people take me for a dyke,' she exclaimed suddenly.

'Really?' I asked innocently.

'Yes!'

And we nodded in cheerful unison.

'I'm not,' she stated emphatically. 'Although I love my girl-friends with a passion.'

I badly wanted to ask Urszula how doing a lesbian double with Hester affected their friendship, but decided not to.

'I get taken for a dyke too,' I told her, sitting up. 'I guess because I'm tall, I have short hair, and I dress like Sporty Spice.'

'Is she gay?' Urszula asked, sitting up too.

'I don't know.'

We watched Rex cock his leg on a tree, and pondered the sexuality of Spice Girls.

'That probably doesn't help, you know, Urszula,' I said, pointing to the large black tattoo on her tanned bicep.

'What?' she asked with a smile, her hand immediately covering the inky inscription of a woman's name wrapped around the two hearts.

'Who's Miranda then?' I asked cheekily.

Urszula threw her head back and laughed so hard, I had to join her even before I knew the punch line.

'That's my baby, you idiot!' she shouted.

'Your baby?' I cried.

'My daughter, Miranda.'

'I didn't know you had a daughter, Urszula!'

Urszula shook her head as her laughter subsided.

'Where does she live?' I asked.

'Well,' Urszula began and stood up, tugging her jeans above her hips. 'Miranda *used* to live with her grandpa, in Morpeth.'

I watched for any signs of discomfort as Urszula searched the ground for a stick, and then, with a quick whistle to get Rex's attention, she threw one high in the air.

'Miranda died when she was nine,' Urszula announced, following the stick's journey and her dog's hot pursuit.

Then she turned to me and smiled.

'She was born with muscular dystrophy.'

Urszula put Rex back in the car and, against my pathetic protests, dragged me off for a second lap of the park. My legs were still shaking from the last turn, but I could refuse her nothing. Once we were mobile again, Urszula cleverly took my mind off my pain, and possibly her own, by unravelling the mystery at last.

'Do you want to know where I've been for the last two weeks?' she asked with a wicked smile.

Holding my hand, Urszula told me how she had picked Sofia up from the hospital on Monday morning and dropped her off at the office before returning to the park for an hour or so. It was a difficult time for her, she said, grabbing my elbow as I stumbled over a twig, as she wasn't well. Not only was there a problem with Urszula's lungs, but she had now been bleeding for three weeks nonstop. I knew from Trudy that Urszula had only recently survived cervical cancer but did not want anyone to know because she was worried it would affect bookings. When it was time to pick up Sofia from the office, Urszula packed up the car and was driving slowly towards the park exit when a red Mazda closed in behind her, almost touching her rear bumper bar. Urszula signalled its two male occupants to overtake if they were in such a hurry, but they were having too much fun annoying her, she said. Big mistake.

'I mean, what were they thinking, Meredith?' Urszula shouted. 'A fooking Land Rover!' She stopped skating to face me. 'Let alone this crazy bitch at the wheel.'

Unable to stop, I drifted past.

Urszula continued when she'd caught up with me. Without warning, she had hit the brakes, and of course the inevitable happened. Doors were flung open, angry words were exchanged and, before she knew it, Urszula was being physically restrained by one of the local park rangers. All the rangers knew Urszula by now – they hadn't much choice, really – but only one of them had taken an instant dislike to this tough 'spiky-haired dyke' with her fearsome looking dog. And sure enough it was this ranger whose arms now trapped her with unnecessary force.

'I'm not stupid, Meredith,' she told me calmly. 'Head-butting him would have been like head-butting my landlord. But you would have been proud. I told him very quietly, to take his *fooking arms* off me, or *lose* them.'

Urszula wasn't sure if it was the tone of her voice or the presence of a pink-eyed bull terrier growling through foaming yellow teeth, but the ranger swiftly cooperated. No charges would be pressed, he decreed, as Urszula had clearly been provoked, but all parties must leave the park immediately. All agreed, and as the ranger drove away, Urszula ran to her car to answer her ringing mobile. When she heard the screeching wheels, Urszula turned to see the red Mazda swerving dangerously close to Rex on its way out. And that's when she lost the plot.

'It's a blur, Meredith,' she stated as we hit a bump, and she helped me back to my feet. 'Within seconds,' she continued, 'I'd overtaken them at the main gate. And as Dickless frantically tried to wind his window up, I got my arm in, opened his door and pulled him from his seat.'

By the time Urszula had punched one and knocked the other out with one of her famous head-butts, a crowd had gathered, including the ranger, Rex, and finally two policemen and one policewoman from Paddington Police Station across the road. Urszula spent the night in the lock-up, and Rex spent the night locked up in the Land Rover outside, with a mobile phone ringing every five minutes.

'He must have been so fooking glad when that battery ran out,' she said.

So where was she for the rest of the time?

'At Hester's,' Urszula answered nonchalantly, 'nursing a very nasty bump on the forehead.'

Hester's.

'I'd nutted him all wrong, Meredith,' she grumbled. 'Off centre, which means I'm losing my form.'

I didn't care about bumps or form, all I could think about was what a lying cow Hester was. All those phone calls asking if we'd heard from Urszula. The next time she rang, I was going to tell her it was terribly busy, and that we hadn't had a quiet night since the Gulf War.

'Are you listening to me, Meredith?' Urszula asked accusingly. 'I'm telling you the two reasons I cannot be charged.'

I apologised and Urszula continued.

'One, I don't exist, and two, I'm wanted.'

Still nodding, I wondered how a person who did not exist in the first place could be wanted.

'I'm going to have to ask for help, Meredith,' Urszula continued gravely, 'from people I'd rather not be asking for anything. People I used to work for.'

'What did you do for them?' I asked breathlessly.

'Security mainly. You know, bouncer, bodyguard,' she lowered her voice, 'deliveries.'

'Drugs?' I panted.

'No. I told them I wanted none of that. My job was to walk from one hotel in King's Cross to another, with millions of dollars worth of illegal diamonds and a handgun stuffed in my purse.'

I wondered what my friend Colin, at Centrelink, would make of Urszula's CV.

To get off all charges and disappear from police records, Urszula declared, it was going to cost her twenty-five thousand dollars.

'It used to be five,' she said, skating ahead of me. 'Shows how long I've been out of it.'

My legs visibly shaking with fatigue, I pleaded skate distress to my indomitable partner, who kindly let me collapse on the dirt track while she finished the lap to get the car. Despite my pathetic protests, Urszula insisted she was going to drive me home.

'But don't lie there, Meredith,' she sang over her shoulder as she glided off. 'That's the horse track, darling.'

I didn't care. A swift hoof to the head and instant unconsciousness would be a welcome relief from this agony. As I surrendered my limp body to the dirt, my head spun with visions of Urszula head-butting Colin at Centrelink, and Hester doing a lesbian double with Sporty Spice.

Urszula parked in our driveway and smiled as she shook her head. No, she would not come in for a cup of tea, she said, patting my knee affectionately. She had people to visit, places to go and dogs to feed. But I sensed by her sudden vulnerability that it was perhaps the thought of meeting my two housemates that made Urszula falter with such uncharacteristic shyness. And as I stepped out of her tiny mobile home in front of our large house with a pool, I felt ashamed.

'So will we do this again?' she asked as she lit a cigarette.

'Of course we will,' I assured her.

'Tomorrow?' she suggested.

I opened my mouth, and Urszula laughed at my feeble attempt at enthusiasm.

'Oh, Meredith,' she guffawed. 'Don't even try!'

It was my legs, I insisted as she threw her car into reverse. As soon as my legs were better, I'd love to go rollerblading again.

But Urszula just laughed as she swung her car backwards into our street.

'You on tomorrow night?' she hollered over her engine.

I nodded enthusiastically.

'All right, my darling,' she called, grinning. 'I guess I can wait till then.'

And I waved goodbye until the Land Rover disappeared out of sight.

It was my legs! It wasn't that I did not want to see her socially, or that our two worlds were so different, or that my friends could not cope with a prostitute who lived in her car, or the unbelievable stories she told of her past. It wasn't all the men who'd run for the hills, or the hidden sadness and loneliness in her life, or a father in Morpeth who had buried her child.

I stood in my driveway, feeling angry with myself. After all, was it such a daunting responsibility if this unusual woman, who was perhaps very ill and in trouble, was in need of a friend?

Standing in my kitchen the following morning, I remembered Trudy's warning as I waited for my toast to pop up. It was true. Loving Urszula breaks your heart.

How much do we charge for kidnapping?

It was about three in the morning and I picked up the International line. A woman's voice, a smoker's voice, very friendly and possibly on speed, asked if I could tell her about our escorts. I was halfway through my usual spiel when she interrupted me.

'Is that you, Meredith?'

It's quite disconcerting when someone ringing a brothel recognises your voice.

'Yes?' I timidly replied.

'It's me, Meredith. Bev!'

'Bev?'

'Bev, darl!'

As usual, Bev assumed an easy familiarity, despite her absence for the past four months. If any other girl had gone missing for four months, she certainly wouldn't have been welcome back, but there was a different set of rules for Bev. If Bev wanted to leave, she was free to go. If Bev wanted to return, she was always welcome back. Everyone pretty much let Bev do whatever she wanted. Bev shot a man.

Bev was calling from a private apartment at the Quay Grand. She was with an old client.

'Well, he's not that old,' she said, cackling for his benefit, 'but I've been seeing the old bastard for twenty years.'

A deep voice muttered something in the background, sending

Bev into a frenzy of more wheezy cackling, cut short by a coughing fit.

'Anyway, darl,' she continued after recovering, 'me and Gerry are lookin' for a bit of fun tonight, so I told him I'd get us an escort. Is Abigail still there?'

The last I heard of Abigail, she'd left the business altogether and was now living in Surfer's Paradise with a plumber. When I told Bev this, she sighed.

'Oh, what a pity ...'

By now Sofia had realised who I was speaking to and was demanding I transfer the call.

'Ello, stranger,' Sofia boomed down the phone. 'Where the fuck you been?'

I sat eavesdropping while Sofia asked Bev all the questions I wanted her to.

'Still working? ... That's good. Coming back to us then? ... Good! Divorce come through? ... Good. You got custody? ... Oh no, fuck me dead!'

If there was one thing that visibly shook Sofia, it was any talk with any mother about any child.

'Oh Jesus, no.'

Once again, Bev had lost custody of Jason. Not surprising, as the last time I saw her, she told me she'd kidnapped him and 'stashed him' with friends in Byron Bay.

'They weren't feedin' 'im, love,' she said at the time.

They being her sister, who'd run off with Bev's husband.

'Why don't you go to the police, Bev?' I asked.

Bev stopped chewing, leant back on one stiletto, and took me in with a contemptuous sneer. 'Darl,' she snarled, 'he *is* the police!'

I was the last to know, but before he ran off with her sister, Bev's police officer husband had been on the news in relation to an illegal gambling ring, and no small amount of cocaine.

With twenty years service to the sex industry, a failed marriage to a bad cop and one charge of manslaughter behind her, Bev and her twenty thousand dollar face were in for a big night at the Quay Grand with her old friend Gerald. After cursing the Family Law Court, all men and especially backstabbing sisters, Sofia and Bev decided that Bree might be the girl for the job at hand, so to speak. Bev couldn't remember Bree, possibly because of the way Sofia now described her.

'Oh, she's your girl, darling. Bree's always up for fun. Always laughing, darling. Meredith's ringing her now. Yes, a real joker, our Bree.'

'You're lots of fun, and up for a laugh,' I told Bree quietly.

'No I'm not!' she whined.

'And Sofia got you five hundred an hour.'

'Oh, well in that case,' Bree chortled, 'three prostitutes walk into a bar ...'

Bree was always grateful for the more highly paid bookings, unlike Genevieve, who barely yawned for three fifty.

'Okay, then,' Bree finally sighed with dreamy resignation, 'I ... guess I'm on my way.'

And we both laughed. Bree never got to a booking in under an hour.

While Sofia processed Gerald's credit card, I looked him up on our computer. Gerald had sampled as many hotels as girls, I noticed, before recently purchasing an apartment at the Quay Grand. Like all our married regulars, he insisted we only contact him on his mobile, unless he was calling from his new premises, which I noticed was in his company's name, as was his credit card. I wondered if Mrs Gerald had a clue about the apartment, or even cared, while she had her weekly pedicure in Double Bay. Sofia told me that, although Gerald owned property all over the world, he was notoriously stingy with girls' taxi money.

'Like all our millionaires, darling. You wait till you get Max Deverish. He thinks the girl should pay for the pleasure of fucking such a rich bastard.'

However stingy he was, I said, I liked Gerald for his loyalty to Bev for twenty years.

'Yes,' murmured Sofia, a little less impressed than I was, 'I did not know Bev had been seeing him privately all this time. That's poaching a client, you know, darling,' she warned ominously. 'We throw girls off the book for that.'

But Sofia knew as well as I did that Bev could poach to her heart's content.

'Who's Bev?' asked Leslie, taking a breather from making her mountain of bookings.

Maybe it was because she was so efficient, or maybe it was the hilarious repartee she seemed to establish with every male caller, or maybe it was her recent habit of flirting outrageously with Patrick, but for some weeks now Leslie had been pissing me off.

'He's a funny guy, that Patrick,' she'd sigh, returning from the kitchen where she'd been enjoying a good laugh with our driver. 'He just cracks me up.'

Leslie was sure she and Patrick shared some kind of *simpatico*.

'Sometimes we just look at each other and crack up,' she'd grin at me, 'for no reason.'

Well sometimes, I felt like grinning back, we have sex all night long for no reason whatsoever, and then laugh our heads off for days.

I was not alone. Sofia's tolerance of our new receptionist's vigorous enthusiasm was also running on empty. Leslie had made so many suggestions about improving the running of the office lately, she had even called a meeting with Boris. Sofia's reaction to this was to lie very low, watch very carefully, and smoke many, many cigarettes. Sofia could smell a Machiavellian streak camouflaged by a relentlessly cheerful demeanour, in army fatigues and a *Star Trek* cap at fifty paces. I had a horrible feeling that within a year this jolly, large giant would be my new manager, and I actually felt sentimental about losing my Spanish general, until I remembered that I wouldn't be staying that long.

I enjoyed the fact that Leslie, who knew all, didn't know who Bev was.

'Bev shot a man!' I bragged shamelessly.

'Don't say things like that, Meredith.' Sofia came down on me like a ton of bricks. 'This is what pisses me off! All the lies and gossip that gets spread because everyone hears only half a story, and makes up the rest.'

'So she *didn't* shoot a man,' Leslie quipped, as if it suddenly made Bev ordinary.

Sofia took a second to register the blow, then exploded. 'SHE FUCKING DID SHOOT A MAN!' she shouted, going red in the face.

'In a nightclub,' I piped.

'She shot him and killed him, and got off with self-defence because he had raped her!'

I looked at Sofia. So that's what had happened. I quickly returned my knowing gaze to Leslie. 'Your father would know Bev,' I said, deliberately trespassing on forbidden territory.

'Oh Chrise yes,' Sofia said. 'Every cop in Sydney would know Bev.'

Leslie glowered at me with silent malice as she stubbed out her cigarette.

Ten minutes later Bev phoned again wanting to speak to Sofia. She was busy on another call, so I asked if I could help.

'Meredith, love, can you tell . . . er . . . Betty? Beula?'

'Bree?'

'Whatever,' Bev continued. 'Tell her we're playing a bit of a game here tonight, darl. Ya know? Me an' Gerry are up for a bit of fun. And what we're gonna do is pretend we're kidnapping her, and tie her up and stuff, just for a laugh, okay?'

Pause.

'Hang on, Bev, I'll just get Sofia.'

For a few minutes Bev and Sofia discussed different strategies of how to trap a young girl in a pretend kidnapping with a millionaire and a mature prostitute without giving her any prior warning. Sofia took the opportunity to mention the extra fifty dollar charge for 'fantasy'. Finally they decided that Bev should meet Bree downstairs in the lobby and break it to her gently in the lift, giving the trapped animal less chance to bolt.

Half an hour later, Bree rang to start the booking. With a concentrated effort not to laugh, she read out Gerald's credit card numbers to me, very slowly.

'Are you all right?' I asked.

'Yes,' she whispered, 'I think so.'

'Okay,' I said quietly, 'but we're just a phone call away if you need us.'

'Okay,' she giggled, and hung up.

At 5 am Leslie stretched and yawned. She had confirmed twice as many bookings as me and Sofia, and now she just wanted to go home, roll a fat joint and chat on the Net, or get into bed with her drag-queen flatmate, Lorenzo, have a cuddle and a good rave.

I always dreaded the moment when Sofia left the room because Leslie saw this as a green light to continue telling me the tedious saga of her life. Or worse, she would open her wallet and extract more photos: photos of Leslie hugging a large man with a green mohawk; Leslie hugging a skinny bald girl wearing a garbage bag; Leslie hugging a man or a woman so pierced I could not make out his or her face for jewellery. Although she obviously had strong friendships and no lack of street culture in her life, I found Leslie's endless anecdotes about her miscellaneous tripping friends and their outrageous antics as depressing as the state of their teeth. But worst of all was her superior, boastful delivery, as if her unconditional love for this motley crew which transcended theft and infidelity was something I'd suffered without in my life. Leslie was laughing as she described the hilarious magic mushroom experience that had put her and Lorenzo in Intensive Care for a week, when I became quite distracted by the glints of light from the silver stud that pierced her tongue.

'Does that thing hurt?' I interrupted her.

'No.' She grinned, immediately exposing her tongue and pushing the stud out through her teeth. 'And it's good for blow jobs.'

This sort of comment would not usually have embarrassed me, but I was suddenly terribly aware of Patrick's presence. He had been sitting quietly in a corner, sipping tea, and out of sheer boredom had picked up a *Cosmopolitan* magazine.

'Terrific,' I smiled.

'It's true!' Leslie promised, winking at Patrick. 'You should try it.'

I answered my phone instead.

It was Bree, extending for another hour.

'How are you going there, Bree?' I asked.

'Um, I'm a little tied up at the moment,' she whispered, 'can't really chat.'

'Is it on the same Amex card, Bree?'

A bearish voice took over.

'*That's enough!*' Bev barked down the phone, and hung up.

While Sofia put another hour through on Gerald's card, Leslie and I began wiping down our desks, turning on the answering machines and turning off the lights. It felt wrong leaving a girl tied up in an extended 'kidnapping', but such was the industry I now worked in.

The crew wrapped and went home, leaving the actors on set, halfway through a scene, often having to perform their own stunts without a double, or even a safety officer.

The first duty of the day shift receptionist when she arrived at ten was to check the board to see if any girls were still out, and then listen to the private line answering machine to note their finishing times. This meant it could be five hours before we knew if a girl was missing or had been in any kind of trouble. For this reason, I was glad I never worked day shifts. Although no girl had ever gone missing during my tenure, there had been a few false alarms when girls had simply forgotten to ring in. Usually it was Marilyn, suffering another of her drug-induced memory lapses, or Antoinette, who sometimes literally *slept* with her client. Although it seemed terribly irresponsible to leave the girls stranded with nothing but an answering machine to protect them, we knew that many took advantage of the situation, and even profited from it. If a client paid in cash, a girl was free to extend without telling us, thereby pocketing a full hour's pay, or more. The very thought of it drove Boris crazy and kept him up all day, like a restless Bavarian vampire.

I'm sorry, all our girls are on a float just now

Sydney couldn't have wished for a more perfect summer evening to celebrate Mardi Gras. And as I walked to work through the colourful crowd gathering at Taylor Square, it was impossible not to be affected by the euphoric and moving demonstration of solidarity. Tottering drag queens in platform shoes and big hair chatted eye to eye with policemen on horseback, while tanned boys in sequinned hotpants hooted and squawked as they greeted each other. Spunky girls dressed as warriors in leather underwear fastened each other's straps as they prepared for the parade, and glittering trannies leant out of windows, waving iridescent feather boas at the crowd below.

As I wove my way through smiling bikies and some rather dubious-looking nuns, I wondered how this festive event might affect our business tonight. Would straight men be too distracted by the parade to think about straight sex? Would they perhaps abstain out of respect? Or would the phones go silly as the homophobic retaliated in a heterosexual frenzy? As I stopped to take one last, lingering look, a little girl in butterfly wings and a tiara, perched high on her mother's shoulders, smiled down at me like an angel. I smiled back, just as her little arm brought a perspex wand crashing down on my head.

'Gently, Tammy!' her mother chided, giving me an apologetic smile.

Half concussed, I staggered off towards Redfern.

Sofia and I were relieved to see the day shift receptionist had reported Bree's finishing time of 6 am, but not so relieved to see the meagre number of girls on roster for the night. Song-Lee, Kaz, Zora and all our other lesbians had made it quite clear they'd sooner work Christmas Day than Mardi Gras night. Especially Celeste and Genevieve, who wanted to celebrate their recent unlikely but blossoming union. Instead of our usual twenty, we had only eight girls to choose from, not counting Lottie. But the phones were so dead, even Sofia was reluctant to recruit more.

I no longer minded working with Sofia on my own. Sending Hilary to a man with a mechanical penis had somehow brought us closer together.

At eight o'clock we got our first call for the night. Gerald at the Quay Grand wanted to know if Bree was all right after her ordeal. Gerald assured us the kidnapping had gone very smoothly but he was concerned – Bev had played bad cop with a little too much enthusiasm for his liking. So while Sofia continued spinning her web to trap a millionaire in another booking, I rang my favourite lesbian. As I waited for Bree to answer, I remembered that this was the night Bev had promised to return to us. Bev had told us to roster her on every night from seven till dawn but, Sofia had sighed at the time, we might also never see her again. It was difficult to hear Bree over the thumping bass and exuberant crowd in the background. Yes, Bree shouted, she was fine, although she still had one wrist handcuffed, as Bev had thrown away the key.

'It's okay, though,' Bree yelled over the music, 'it goes with my cossie!'

I quickly passed the information on to my supervisor.

'She's fine, darling,' Sofia assured Gerald, 'so, who can we send you tonight?'

And before he knew it, Gerald was expecting our very own Gigi, who had been playing a prostitute all day on the set of *Moulin Rouge*.

At nine o'clock my phone rang for the second time that night. Malcolm, staying at Kirribilli Mansions, required the services of an escort in her thirties. I liked this quietly jovial and well-spoken man immediately, especially when he explained that he was a regular but had been studying at Cambridge for the last six months.

'Do you mean Cambridge University, Malcolm?' I asked.

'That's just what I mean,' Malcolm answered.

'Do you mind me asking what you study?'

'Well, it's very boring, I'm afraid,' Malcolm laughed. 'It's a PhD in Tudor architecture.'

'That's not boring at all,' I exclaimed.

I don't know if Malcolm was just being polite, but he seemed very impressed that I could recite not only the names of Henry VIII's six wives but all the actresses who'd ever played them. And so we continued chatting about Anne Boleyn, Hampton Court, Malcolm's PhD, my mother's MA, the four-hundred-year history of

Malcolm's surname and his Welsh ancestry, until I remembered the reason Malcolm had rung in the first place.

'So what sort of lady can I send you, Malcolm?' I asked.

'Well, I'm rather partial to a lady with a French or Italian accent, if that's at all possible, Meredith?'

'I'll see what I can do, Malcolm.'

'And could she masturbate in front of me, Meredith?'

'Of course she could, Malcolm,' I promised.

'Most kind of you, Meredith.'

I looked through the girls on roster, vaguely envious that one of them was about to earn two hundred dollars just for masturbating in front of an academic for an hour. The new girl sounded too good to be true. Mignon from Paris was thirty-five, taught French at a private school and was quite, quite beautiful, according to Sofia.

'And Mignon,' I asked her over the phone, 'you don't have a problem masturbating in front of the man, do you?'

'Mais non!' Mignon exclaimed, as if the French had thought of it first.

'So what's she look like, this French girl?' Patrick sang from his car phone, on his way to Mignon's flat.

Dear old Patrick, whom I'd spent the entire day in bed with, laughing, having cups of tea ... I scanned Mignon's card.

'Um ... petite ... brunette ... great figure ...'

'Stunning!' Sofia called out.

'And quite attractive, Patrick, okay?' I snapped.

Sometimes I wished more girls caught cabs.

At ten o'clock Boris arrived in a bad mood due to all the Mardi Gras road blocks, and his homophobia was at an all-time high. He stood over my desk raving about the immorality of parents who let their children watch a parade full of 'sick fuck poofters' and 'hairy butch dykes' until Sofia interrupted him.

'Where the fuck is Patrick?' she asked me. 'He should have dropped off Mignon by now, and picked up Hannah from Manly Pacific.'

As I waited for Patrick to answer his car phone, I asked Boris if he'd not noticed that half his girls were lesbians.

'Ach! Lesbians?' Boris scoffed. 'Prostitutes can't keep boyfriends, you dumb idiot,' he laughed almost maniacally, 'so they fock each other instead!'

Ah, so much to learn, so little time.

'Ello?' a French voice finally answered Patrick's car phone.

'Patrick?' I asked, incredulously.

'Patreek cannot talk just now,' the voice informed me, ''ang on ...'

And Mignon hung up on me!

Sofia's response could not have been worse. 'What the fuck are they doing in that car?'

With a wicked smile that was meant for me, Boris tossed a cigarette in the air, caught it in his mouth, and left for the casino.

I was in no mood for Thomas Vomeitz. I hated Thomas Vomeitz. I hated dealing with him even when Patrick wasn't missing with a stunning French prostitute in a Mercedes somewhere in the back streets of Kirribilli. Thomas was a pedantic, sententious Austrian bore who always lectured us about sending him the wrong type of girl. Thomas was in his seventies, he kept reminding us, and a gentleman, he kept reminding us, so he did not want 'young trash'. Thomas wanted a more mature lady, someone he could talk to, someone refined, and someone who had not been in the business for too long. What angered me about Thomas was not so much his lofty, critical appraisal of our girls, but the hypocrisy of a man who actively sought the services of a prostitute and yet was repulsed by anyone vaguely resembling one. Sofia had a theory that Thomas Vomeitz was a Nazi, not just because of his superiority complex, but because he'd spent a number of years living in South America after the war.

'That's where all the Nazis went, darling,' she'd warned me. 'South America. Look it up.'

And Thomas also had an annoying habit of trying to recruit loyalty from one receptionist by bitching about the incompetence of another. He often bemoaned the fact that we could not all be as 'intelligent' and as 'discerning' as Pip, who always sent him someone appropriate, or was at least honest enough to send him no one at all. This comparison hardly motivated me to please him.

Thomas was mid tirade against Sofia, who had recently sent him Bunny. It exemplified Sofia's blatant, mercenary exploitation of his purse and patronage, and Thomas had not forgiven her for it. Bunny had only been with us a month. A statuesque six-foot eighteen-year-old blonde from the western suburbs, Bunny kept complaining about clients being violent, until we discovered she had a boyfriend who followed her from booking to booking and waited by her car to punch her when she got out.

'So, what do you like in an escort, Thomas?' I asked him. 'Enlighten me, so I too can please you, like Pip.'

For all his appreciation of others' intelligence, Thomas himself was oblivious to sarcasm.

'She should not be a robot, Meredith,' he began with ceremonial pomp, 'and certainly not money-conscious. She should be friendly, Meredith, but not familiar. I do not mind a lack of sophistication. That can even be endearing, so long as she has manners, and a natural smile. I have an intense dislike of tattoos, if you have not already heard, and I prefer a lady in her thirties. But no older, Meredith,' Thomas said with a chuckle, 'as one geriatric is enough.'

But contrary to all his preferences, over the years Thomas had developed quite an obsession, I had been told, with Marguerita, our tough, streetwise, dark-eyed Argentinian who never smiled.

'Is Marguerita still in Spain?' he asked despondently.

Marguerita, or Kaz, as she now called herself, was at this very moment dancing in a spiky dog collar and a leather G-string on a Mardi Gras float with her girlfriend, Frank.

'Still in Spain, Thomas,' I sighed. 'Her mother is no better, I'm afraid.'

'Chrise, Niko!' Sofia suddenly cried down her phone. 'How many periods do you get each month?'

'I don't like girls who can't speak properly, Meredith,' the Austrian continued as I passed Sofia the girls' Period Record Book. 'I prefer someone with education.'

'You're a very articulate man yourself, Thomas,' I said. 'Do you mind me asking what it is you do?'

Sofia had already told me what Thomas did for a living.

'I drive taxis, Meredith,' Thomas answered peevishly, 'but you might be surprised how highly educated some taxi drivers are.'

'Oh, tell me about it, Thomas,' I gushed. 'Our books are full of overqualified girls too, as you would know. Girls with BAs, MAs, even PhDs. I'm constantly amazed by the high level of education they have.'

'Well, Meredith,' Thomas snickered, 'I have not met too many of them through your agency, I can tell you that.'

'Oh, that's a pity, Thomas,' I said. 'I thought Pip would have sent a few your way.'

And at last the Nazi hung up on me, which was just as well as our switchboard had lit up like a Christmas tree.

Mardi Gras had indeed made a big difference to our night. Apart from a millionaire, an academic and a Nazi, hardly a phone had rung. But now, at midnight, every man and his dog not on Oxford Street suddenly wanted Asian. What did it mean?

'Min!' Sofia was shouting, with three calls on hold. 'I need all your girls, Min! Ring me back.'

And for the next few hours Lan and Patrick tackled road blocks and dodged tottering drag queens as they ferried Asian girls all over Sydney. I was glad that Maya was so in demand for a change. She even risked bumping into her fellow house staff and accepted a booking at the Hilton. Patrick had to drop her off at the more discreet back entrance, so that she could use the stairs before prowling the corridors like a cat burglar. Maya found it so exhilarating, she even accepted another booking two floors up when it was over.

It was time to go home. While Sofia took one more call, I went in search of my driver. I poked my head into the girls' lounge and there in a corner, hunched over a magazine and looking perplexed, sat Patrick.

'Who do you think brought this in?' he asked me, holding up a *Time* magazine.

'How come Mignon answered your car phone?' I asked.

Patrick looked at me for a second with dumb incognizance.

'Oh!' he said, jolting with the recollection. 'Petrol stop. I told her not to answer but, well, she's French, isn't she?'

Sensing I was tired, Patrick stopped giggling, put down his

magazine and grabbed his keys. But before we could get going, Sofia's booming voice shook the house.

'WHAT THE FUCK YOU DOING HERE?'

Patrick and I ran out to the landing, expecting to find Sofia confronting some intrepid intruder on the stairs below, and timidly peeped over her shoulder.

'It's all right,' Leonie whimpered, looking up like a baby seal about to be clubbed, 'he's asleep.'

'WHAT?' Sofia looked at her watch in horror. 'HE'S PAID FOR YOU TILL SIX O'CLOCK! WHAT IF HE WAKES UP?'

It was painful to watch Leonie as she babbled on, promising that Gerald was 'completely out of it, hey' and that she was 'really tired, you know, and just thought—'

'HE'S A MILLIONAIRE, YOU FUCKING IDIOT!' Sofia interrupted her, and pointed down to the front door. 'Go!'

As Leonie quickly scuttled down the stairs, I was reminded of Sofia's porpoise in a tight dress analogy.

'COME BACK!' Sofia roared again, and turned to Patrick. 'Take this idiot back to the Quay Grand, will you?'

Rolling her eyes, Sofia trudged wearily up the stairs to her office with me not far behind her.

'And Malcolm juss wants you to masturbate in front of him, darling, okay?'

I spun around in shock and was relieved to see that Sofia was not speaking to me at all, but finishing an interrupted call to one of our girls.

'Thank you, Lucy,' she said, and hung up.

Without looking at me, Sofia reluctantly answered my silent protest.

'Yes, darling,' she sighed, 'after your professor saw Mignon, he book Coral, then Candice. And now he wants Lucy.'

It was not unheard of for men to go on booking benders. One night the same man rang on five different lines for five consecutive girls. I would have sent Donald his sixth, but his card ran out of credit.

Patrick was unusually quiet on the way home, and I wondered if my irrational jealousy over Mignon had actually displeased him.

Or maybe he felt flattered by my jealousy, and disappointed that we still had not gone public as a couple. Not that we were a couple. Were we? I didn't think so. Did Patrick think so? And so I sat beside Patrick, struggling to find a comfortable context for our bizarre, off-peak relationship. But I needn't have bothered.

'Which girl do you think brought in a *Time* magazine?' he asked finally.

And an hour later, in bed, just as I was drifting off to sleep.

'I mean, what girl would read *Time*?'

She knows!

I had barely said hello when three receptionists threw me into a chair, held me down and forced me to watch a mad Bavarian leap about the room in a bizarre game of charades. Boris only came in this early when there was a crisis, so whatever his book, film or stage play was, I'd better get it right. First word. Explosion? Huge explosion! Second word. Next door? Wall! My desk?

'There's a bomb behind my desk?' I cried.

Suddenly everyone was leaping up and down in front of me, frantically miming Shoosh! Shut up! Third word. Idiot. You fucking idiot! Shut up, you fucking idiot! Pip shook her hands in the air and winced in pain, as if the sound of my voice had hurt her ears, and I wanted very much to hit her. Maxine shook her head at me with disappointment, something Maxine should never do at anyone, and Boris imploringly conducted us to be more *pianissimo*. I'd never seen them all in such a state. The house was empty! Who were we hiding from, and why were we whispering?

'Here,' Raelene hissed, scribbling something on a piece of paper and shoving it in my hand.

I squinted over Raelene's hasty hieroglyphics.

'The office is bogged?' I read out loud.

Again they all leapt about the room, but before I could suggest Alfred Hitchcock's *The Birds*, Raelene snatched the paper back, angrily carved a correction, and then almost winded me with its return.

'Oh, bugged!' I whispered. 'The office is *bugged*.'

After much eye-rolling, face-fanning and collapsing in chairs as my exhausted colleagues congratulated themselves on their extraordinary patience with the staff idiot, Boris took me by the elbow and led me to my desk. Once there, he slowly bent me over it, until my face was pressed hard up against the cold wall. It was not a comfortable position, and I was very glad that others were present. But instead of some hidden microphone behind my desk, all I could see was a mess of phone wires and a few used tissues. I nodded cheerfully anyway, just so Boris would release me.

'Who?' I asked him, as I massaged the blood back into my cheek.

Boris smiled. Gobsmacked, I looked about the room, at my nodding colleagues, and dared not even whisper her name.

'Why?' I asked Boris, who just tapped his temple, gesturing that his wife was very smart.

If Didi smelt a rat, it was not such a surprise. For some weeks now Boris had been demanding an increase in the number of cash bookings we sacrificed from our sheets each night to subsidise his gambling habit. And the thought of Didi's furrowed brow as she perused our sparse booking sheets over her continental breakfast, patting the fluffy shih-tzu in her lap, now made me feel sick to my stomach.

'Does she know about—?'

Boris shook his head with a reassuring smile.

What a relief. After all, we went to such pains to cover our tracks. Every night we diligently rewrote our sheets, minus the several cash bookings Boris had asked for, collected the cash from various girls, and put it in a separate envelope for him. But my relief dissolved when Boris slowly held up his finger like a gun and, with a strange, unsettling glint in his eye, pointed it at Raelene, then at Pip, at Maxine, and finally at me. Had Didi bugged the office because she suspected one of her own receptionists was stealing from her? Boris giggled with infantile malevolence, as if he found it highly amusing that his volcanic wife suspected her employees before her own husband. And so, abandoning three frightened receptionists at the front line, where they would have to mime for their lives, our commander left for the casino. As soon as he'd gone,

I pressed my head against the wall again. Where was this bloody device? And why was it placed behind *my* desk? Why mine? Hadn't Didi heard? I'd been on *Play School*!

For an hour or so we struggled with our loss of freedom, and sat in sombre silence listening to Didi listening to us, knowing that our every sniff was being broadcast. Not since my first day on the job had I felt so selfconscious as I tried to coerce nervous men into booking an escort for an hour. But by nine o'clock guilt had given way to the indignity of it all, and by ten we were defensively justifying our clandestine activities in a mimed but expressive protest. After all, we whispered, what did Didi expect? Paying us twelve dollars fifty an hour and no overtime? By eleven o'clock we had decided that being on Boris's payroll barely compensated for the injustice of it all.

After one week of sign language, we were exhausted. With every new shift I noticed a growing laxness as everyone became more used to the idea of being bugged and less diligent in their efforts to conceal our secret. After two weeks, we had stopped whispering altogether. It must have sounded incredibly suspicious to Didi, propped up by several frilly pillows and a small Tibetan temple dog, as she struggled to decipher the strange halting language coming through the wires, full of half sentences, omitted words and long pauses.

'Has . . . gone to that booking?'

'Yeah, are we giving it to . . .?'

'This is . . . change from . . . Can you put it in the . . .?'

'I've already given . . . three!'

'Would anyone else like another glass of . . .?'

And then there were the inevitable slips when one of us, usually me, put our foot in it.

'Is Pandora's booking on or off?'

For the next minute Didi would have heard nothing but the percussive sounds of fists thumping wood, hands whacking foreheads, strangled hissed reprimands and primal grunts as one distraught receptionist frantically apologised to her furious co-workers. Patrick always found this modern ballet so hilarious he had to run from the room, leaving a trail of hot tea across the carpet like some weak-bladdered marsupial.

So when Leslie brought in her CD player and suggested we play music to drown out any incriminating conversation, we all gave her inspiring idea the thumbs-up. But none of us anticipated what a challenge it would be confirming bookings over Tupac, the Foo Fighters and Regurgitator. Pip's voice audibly cracked as she described girls' attributes to men over the phone with an angry finger stuck in her free ear. I would have asked Leslie to turn it down, but her enthusiastic rap dancing and deep vocal accompaniment had Patrick and I in stitches.

'I'm sorry?' I asked the woman caller over, *I did your mudder too bitch and she moan just like you.*

'I said, is that music in the background, Merediss?' she shouted. 'It sounds like you're having a party in there.'

Holy mother of brothels. It was Didi.

'No, Didi! No!'

As I jumped to attention and Patrick left another trail of tea across the floor, Pip pushed past Leslie and ripped the CD player cord from the wall, as if she had pulled the plug on loud bands all over the world.

'We just . . . had a radio on . . .' I stuttered, 'to hear . . . Apparently there's been—'

'Okay, Merediss,' Didi interrupted me with a laugh. *With a laugh?* 'I just rang to see if it is busy, and obviously it is not. But let us see,' she added in a sweet, mocking voice, 'if we cannot get more cash bookings, okay?'

'Yes, Didi.'

I hung up and looked at my colleagues with horror. Get more cash bookings. She knew. Didi knew! It was like the moment in *The Fiends* when the lovers think they have killed the wife, until she rises up out of the very bath they drowned her in, sending half the audience straight to the drycleaner's. Didi was not only onto us, she was going to terrorise us with her omnipresence, until one of us cracked like an egg under pressure. Possibly me. I was hyperventilating, describing the hideous, syrupy tone Didi had used as if she was effortlessly wringing the neck of a cat, when Leslie grabbed me by the shoulders and told me to 'get a grip!' And I did. I'd never known a girl with such strong thumbs.

Instead of being alarmed by the news that his wife was warm and getting hotter, Boris paused on the stairs below me, looked up and winked.

'My vife is very smart, Meredit,' he mused. 'I like haffing such a smart vife. She keeps me on my toes.'

Yes, well, she'd hang him by his toes if he didn't join a twelve-step program soon.

'Just do what she says,' he smiled teasingly, 'and get more cash bookings.'

As I watched Boris bounce down the remaining stairs and disappear into his office humming, I had a strange revelation. Perhaps it was not his wife's money that Boris gambled with, but the marriage itself. Not getting caught by Didi must have felt as dangerous and thrilling as shaving Hitler's moustache off as he slept. Although Boris would never have done such a thing. Boris had a lot of time for Hitler. I made the mistake, late one night, of greeting my drunken boss on the stairs with a Nazi salute. And for the next ten minutes I was lectured on Hitler's innovative rearmament policy and what it did for the struggling German economy in the thirties. Gripping the banister like it was a lectern, Boris warned me of the selective memory of war historians, who preferred to concentrate on Hitler's lesser achievements. Like the murder of five million Jews, perhaps.

Once again we surrendered to the idea, and soon we were swearing, laughing, drinking and having a good time, as if we had never known life in an unbugged office. And if Didi did not like what she heard, that was her problem. But did we have any right to feel so indignant about being bugged when we were helping our boss steal from his wife, who employed us in the first place? I needed to throw a dinner party and invite lots of lawyers. But I only knew actors, most of whom had dropped out of second-year law when they realised a jury was too small a house, and never clapped at the end of a long speech.

'Oh, she's vermin! Take her for every penny you can,' cried my friend Simon.

'No, I'm sorry. If you're helping her husband to steal from her, it's theft, and you're an accessory!' shouted Anne.

'Access*a*ry, darling,' Basil corrected her. 'Otherwise you're accusing Meredith of being a handbag, or matching shoes.'

'But if it's his business too, isn't he just stealing from himself?' asked Rosie.

'What about her?' interrupted Seamus. 'It can't be legal to record your staff at work without their consent?'

'She underpays them, bugs them and takes money out of their wages when they make mistakes,' Simon shouted. 'Stuff her!'

'I wish you'd get out before you end up in the harbour,' said Anne, not for the first time. 'How's Patrick Whatsisname?'

'No, she must stay forever,' stated Basil, who had talked like this ever since he played Fortinbras in *Hamlet* in the Park, 'and tell us everything.'

In the absence of less pissed and emotional reasoning, whenever my guilty conscience needed some relief, I just reminded myself of Didi's response when Antoinette had been abused by a man in a bungalow. It may not have been a strong ethical or legal defence but for now it worked a treat.

Ménage à Max

As soon as I saw the tabloids, I knew one of our clients was in trouble. Could this be our Max Deverish who also owned an apartment at the Horizon and whose girlfriend Debbie often booked two girls at a time for them?

According to the papers, Debbie had been Max's mistress for some years. Almost two generations her senior, Max had set Debbie up in a beautiful mansion with a pool and a Jaguar in a fashionable beachside suburb, where she was now bringing up their two small children. But Max had still not left his wife, and one could not witness the stoic, silver-haired Betty Deverish in public, graciously smiling and dignified throughout such an ordeal, without wanting to hug her. One newspaper article suggested Betty had always been aware of her husband's other life, to the point where she would sit outside in their waiting Rolls while Max popped in to check on his other family. Another article claimed that Debbie's family often dined with Betty's, enjoying a friendly rapport. I hoped that all this was true. That everyone knew about everyone, and that some were just having more sex than others.

Max and Debbie occupied a very healthy-looking page on our computer. Although Debbie usually booked two girls to arrive at the Horizon apartment, making it a foursome, Max had also flown solo and rung us direct. And like our other regular multi-millionaires, Max always grumbled about paying the extra twenty-five dollars for the girl's taxi. I couldn't help but wonder if Debbie had originally met Max as an escort herself. When I saw her photo in the papers, I thought she looked like all our blondes rolled into one. And it would certainly not be the first time a student had graduated from part-time escort to full-time mistress. I had also developed a ridiculous suspicion of anyone who'd done 'part-time modelling', and who hung around with old money, and by that I mean old men with money. Actually, I had become suspicious of any woman in high heels whatsoever.

Leslie and I ruminated on the possible lucrative consequences if we were to go to the press with this information, and for a moment we lost ourselves in a frenzy of excitement and what ifs. But then we pulled ourselves together, deciding it was too precarious, too tacky. We looked sadly at the computer screen displaying Max Deverish's address, phone number, mobile number, girls seen and preferences, and with noble restraint, we let it go.

'Patrick,' I said in bed a few hours later, taking a drag of his joint, 'what's your surname?'

'Callaghan,' Patrick answered, eyeing me suspiciously. 'Are you sure you should be doing that?'

'What?' I asked, handing the rolled cigarette back with bursting lungs.

'I thought you said it made you paranoid.'

'Not if I'm with someone I feel safe with,' I gasped, trying not to exhale.

And as Patrick embarked on the story of his first joint at a Led Zeppelin concert, I realised I did not feel as safe with Patrick as I thought. While he continued his humorous anecdote, I found myself laughing mindlessly at anything, hoping Patrick wouldn't notice my compulsion to stroke my nose, just to reassure myself it was still on my face.

'And I finally discovered,' Patrick declared with great excitement, 'which girl brought the *Time* in.'

I had not felt such confused terror since I believed my dog was the devil. Patrick was telling me that one of our girls had brought in to work, not her handbag, not her new lingerie, or even a brush, but time itself.

Time.

It was a broad concept to say the least, and Patrick was waiting for my response.

'Time?' I asked timidly, tapping my nose.

Patrick nodded fervently. 'Which girl do you think brought it in?'

As I looked at Patrick's face, I struggled with images of prostitutes coming into the kitchen, staggering under the weight of enormous ticking clocks, and I tried to speak.

Patrick's shoulders started to shake. 'You've lost it,' he whimpered, weakly pointing at my head. 'You should see your face!'

What was wrong with my face? Was it melting? Oh God, I couldn't feel my arms, and my face was melting like a Dali clock. I wanted to be with my school choir, or back at the wedding anniversary in Punchbowl with my Aunty Dot and the Baptists. But first, I wanted to throw up. And after a desperate battle with the doona, which Patrick found endlessly amusing, I made my way to the toilet, where I paused in front of the mirror, comforted by my reflection with a nose, and then purged to kingdom come.

Apparently it was Yoko who brought in *Time* magazine. Yoko, who giggled and struggled with her English, and insisted on driving herself to bookings even though she couldn't read a map.

'Maybe she just picked it up at a doctor's surgery,' I suggested to Patrick.

'No,' Patrick smiled knowingly. 'I asked her. Yoko bought *Time* for the story on the ethics of molecular cloning. She's studying theoretical biology at Sydney Uni.'

Exploiting chefs a recipe for disaster

At two in the morning one Thursday, I was talking to a very pissed and amusing Dale from Darling Point, who had an unusual and most refreshing request.

'Just send me good company, Meredith. Someone with a sense of humour, and if possible, over thirty-five.'

Hear hear!

'How old are you, Dale,' I asked, 'if you don't mind me asking?'

'Thirty-five. Hey!' Dale shouted. 'How old are you?'

'I'm fifty, Dale, married with three kids.'

'Well why don't you come over? Bring the kids.'

I had a much better idea, even though she was only thirty and her name was Bree.

When Dale rang the following week, I was glad he asked to speak to me. Although just as pissed, Dale didn't sound quite as robust and jolly this time, especially when I asked him if he'd like to see Bree again. It was such an evasive response, I wondered what had happened at their booking, or not happened, as the case may be. Although Bree had an excellent track record, there had been the bizarre toast-eating performance for Graham and Jocelyn. But Dale was much more receptive to my second suggestion, and so loved the fact that Antoinette was forty, I was tempted to tell him the truth.

'And she's busty, Dale, thirty-six double D, slim—'

'Don't care, Meredith,' Dale interrupted. 'If you like her, that's good enough for me.'

'And Meredith!' Dale called out, just before I hung up. 'Tell Antoinette to bring a bottle of wine.'

That's funny, I thought. I hadn't met Dale in person, yet I felt sure I'd had several relationships with him.

Later that evening, I saw Bree in the kitchen and remembered my evasive friend on the phone.

'Bree, how did you go with Dale in Darling Point last week?'

For a moment Bree couldn't recollect which Darling Point Dale was, until I mentioned he liked a drink.

'Oh, him.' She smiled sadly. 'He won't remember me. He was so drunk by the time I got there, um …' Bree winced, 'he'd kind of pissed himself.'

Bree always took at least an hour to get to a booking, and it often caused problems, although not usually of the bladder variety.

'But I don't think he realised,' she added consolingly. 'In fact, after he paid me for the hour, he fell asleep.'

I turned to leave. It was a more tragic scenario than I wanted to hear, and Bree could tell.

'Good-looking guy,' she called out after me, on a more optimistic note.

The third week Dale rang, he asked to speak to me again. This time, although drunk again, Dale insisted he was not ringing to book anyone at all.

'That woman you sent me last week, Meredith—'

'Antoinette?' I asked, straining to recall her state of mind that night.

'Yes, Meredith. Antoinette.' Dale sounded very stern. There was a pause. 'Thank you. Thank you. Thank you.'

'I gather the booking went well, Dale?'

The booking had indeed gone so well, Dale demanded to speak to 'the boss'. I looked up at Boris, who happened to be standing right in front of me, but Boris never spoke to clients under any circumstances, and shook his head. So as Dale continued his pissed but passionate affirmation of Antoinette, I repeated it out loud for 'the boss' to hear.

'Antoinette is the most delicious, demonstrative, caring, sensual, brave …'

At 'delicious', Boris left the room, shaking his head in disgust.

'Dale,' I quickly interrupted while Maxine and Pip were still on other calls. 'Dale, tell me, Dale,' I lowered my voice, 'what does Antoinette do? Exactly?'

I had no shame. I badly wanted to know what Antoinette did, and what Kimberley did too. No man could see either of these women for just one hour and we all wanted to know *why*. But all I got was such an outrageous sequence of groans and ululations as Dale relived the whole earth-moving experience, I ended up suggesting I send Antoinette over immediately.

'Whoa, Meredith!' Dale backtracked suddenly. 'Hold your horses.'

And I did. Me and the horses all turned around and lay in the shade. Despite the indelible impression Antoinette had left on him, Dale said he wanted to try someone else. I felt betrayed, but the horses had seen it coming and reminded me this was the sex industry, not a dating service.

It was a pity, because Antoinette was having one of her 'off' nights, and we would have preferred she was having it at someone else's house. At seven o'clock she'd arrived in her black usherette's uniform with wet hair and damp spirits. After blow-drying her hair, she sat slumped at the kitchen table, glowering at anything that moved. And now she was shuffling around the house in her turned-out slippers, blaming everyone for everything, probably because she'd blown all her money on the pokies again. Although Antoinette's bad nights were never very funny, it did amuse me to go from this frightening spectacle, scowling and spitting insults in the kitchen, to our office, where a receptionist was describing 'a very classy lady, beautifully spoken, and provides an excellent service'.

'Send Coral then,' commanded Dale.

Even though Coral claimed she was only twenty-five, Dale liked the sound of 'feisty', and thought he'd give her a go. But before I could ring Coral I had to run to the toilet, where I nearly collided head on with the cantankerous Antoinette, who reeled back like an angry funnel-web.

'Just been talking about you,' I babbled, crossing my legs in the bathroom doorway. 'Dale from Darling Point thinks you're a goddess!'

I was busting, so I shut the door in Antoinette's face before she could say anything ungoddess-like.

When I came out I found Antoinette sitting at the kitchen table looking contrite and playing with the sugar bowl as she struggled to find the goddess within. It was heartbreaking. I wouldn't make her ask. I stood in the doorway and told Antoinette everything Dale had said about her. She smiled demurely, slightly embarrassed, as she bulldozed sugar from one side of the bowl to the other with a spoon. Although reluctant to show it, Antoinette was visibly moved by Dale's praise of her 'talent'. Only Antoinette used words like *talent* and *skill* when describing the brief of a sex worker, and she seemed pleased to hear that someone else appreciated her craft.

'I'm genuinely surprised,' she said somewhat haughtily, examining her spoon poised in mid air, 'because to tell you the truth, he was such hard work.'

A dangerous undertow in Antoinette's quavering voice reminded me of her stormy disposition on arrival, and of the possibility of hail.

'And he's not a "happy chap", as you described him,' she added frostily, catching my furtive attempt to escape. 'He's sad. Desperately sad and unhappy.'

I totally acquiesced to Antoinette's psychological evaluation of Dale from Darling Point. Antoinette had a PhD in unhappiness. But I really had to go. Dale was no doubt getting more and more shickered by the minute, and I still had not rung Coral to give her the booking. With a final reverential nod, I turned to leave.

'Did he want to make another booking with me?' Antoinette asked before she could stop herself.

'Not tonight,' I lied from the doorway. 'Just rang to sing your praises.'

Suddenly someone poked me in the back. And I screamed again when I saw who it was. 'Coral!'

'Hi kid,' Coral said, giving me a quick wink. 'You coming?' she asked Antoinette.

'Yep,' said Antoinette picking up her bag.

I gawked from one volatile blonde to the other, panicking at their imminent departure.

'Coral and I are just going for a drink at the pub next door,' Antoinette said as she passed me.

But they couldn't! Coral had to go and service Dale in Darling Point, who didn't want to see Antoinette, whom I had just lied to.

'Oh, Coral,' I blurted, 'I think . . . someone's got you a booking!'

'Now?' she retorted.

'Yes.'

'Where?'

332 Exploiting chefs a recipe for disaster

'Not sure.'

'Who?'

She was like a machine gun.

'Not sure.'

'Well can you go get me the details, *please*?' she said, rolling her eyes at her friend and throwing her slight body into the nearest chair.

As Antoinette was busy lighting her cigarette I tried to give Coral subtle signals to follow me *upstairs*, where I could give her the booking in *private*.

'Will you fucking hurry up?' she cried.

'Okay,' I said breezily, and left.

I sometimes wondered why we bothered protecting Antoinette. No one could predict, let alone understand, the baffling tides of her choler, but even on her bad nights, when Antoinette despised us all, we did anything possible to spare her one more disappointment. So after a crisis meeting in the office, Maxine and Pip advised me to pretend the booking had fallen through, let the two girls go for a drink next door, and then ring Coral on her mobile.

'Oh, what is it now?' Coral berated me for interrupting her scotch and soda.

'Got you another booking, Coral,' I sang cheerfully, following my colleagues' advice. 'Patrick's got all the details, and he's waiting outside in the Merc, so, soon as you can, finish your drink, pop outside and hop in the car.'

'Well at least tell me where I'm fucking going!' Coral shouted.

Coral didn't use to speak to us like this. It all started when she had sex with a guy who had cerebral palsy. Just before we moved out of the brothel, Nathan brought in his younger brother, Ollie, for a birthday surprise. Unfortunately, none of the girls felt comfortable enough even to shake hands with the twitching, grunting Ollie, except Coral. And after castigating her colleagues for not knowing what *providing a service* meant, Coral strode into the waiting room, threw her arms around the euphoric, fitting Ollie, and almost pushed him upstairs for a birthday treat he'd never forget. It was an inspiring moment, and Nathan and I loved her for it. But ever since, Coral thought she was the Variety Club, and we were all a bit sick of the attitude. And right now, Coral was sitting on a stool in a pub next door, waiting to hear where she was going.

'Eastern suburbs,' I said quickly, and hung up.

Now I just had to deal with Dale. He had been waiting almost an hour for his feisty blonde with a good sense of humour to arrive, and was driving me mad with persistent, pissed phone calls, threatening to cancel.

'Oh, where is she, Merrimoo?'

'She's near, Dale. So near you could almost touch her!'

Apparently there had been an accident in William Street, and while poor Patrick was stuck with Coral in the tunnel at Kings Cross, I talked Dale through another bottle of wine, a peanut butter sandwich, half a Turkish soap opera on SBS, and now we were making a cup of coffee together. I felt like a Lifeline counsellor.

'So, Dale,' I said, 'you're a cook.'

Dale was a freelance chef, and very successful. Just last week he had cooked a birthday dinner for an international model and her boyfriend, whom Dale considered 'a complete tosser'.

'Him or her?' I asked.

'Both of 'em,' Dale growled.

Then Dale boasted that he had once cooked dinner for Geoffrey Rush. I badly wanted to tell him that Geoffrey Rush had cooked dinner for me, but I didn't.

'I run a bar next to one of the theatres.'

I knew the bar well. My friend Rosie worked there between acting jobs. Dale was now listing all the actors that frequented his bar, including my ex-boyfriend.

'He's not gay, Dale.'

'As a row of tents, Meredith.'

'I think you might be wrong there, Dale.'

'He drinks scotch and coke, he's allergic to peanuts, and he recently propositioned one of my waiters. I know all of them in the Bell Shakespeare Company, Meredith.'

I was devastated. Humphrey might have come out since Christmas, but he had no grasp of classical verse whatsoever. This was becoming one of the most bizarre conversations I'd ever had, so I was relieved when Maxine interrupted us.

Maxine had Patrick on the line, who swore he had dropped the petulant Coral in Darling Point ten minutes ago. But then I remembered, Dale's apartment was in the last of three blocks, right at the end of his driveway. Oh dear. Hopefully Dale would be too drunk to notice his blonde had no sense of humour whatsoever by the time she punched a hole through his door.

'Helicopters!' Dale suddenly shouted in my ear.

He must have been standing on his balcony, because I could barely hear him over the roar of choppers.

'Meredith, you didn't have to do this!' Dale yelled. 'What's she wearing? Don't want to catch someone else's!'

But I could also hear what sounded like someone hammering their heel on wood.

'SHE'S KNOCKING ON YOUR FRONT DOOR, DALE!' I bellowed, much to Pip's flinching annoyance.

When Dale finally heard the knocking too, he hung up without saying goodbye, and I got pats on the back all round before I went to the kitchen to make us a cup of tea.

The next day I did something very unprofessional. Pretending a friend of mine was interested in him, I asked my friend Rosie to tell me all about her boss, Dale.

Rosie leant forward on her elbows.

'You sure it's not you, Mer?' she said. 'Because I've got to warn you, I know he's cute but he's a troubled soul.'

I assured Rosie it wasn't me and, after a moment's reflection, Rosie spilled so much we could barely move for beans. Dale's girlfriend had left him five months ago and the antidepressants had hardly begun to work, Rosie said, before he started washing them down with wine. Lots and lots of wine. As a result, Dale's neglected business was suffering, and his friends were abandoning him in droves. A pity, Rosie sighed, as she had a bit of a crush on him herself.

'Would you say he's desperately sad and unhappy, Rosie?' I asked.

Rosie nodded. 'And a stalker,' she added with pathos. 'His ex-girlfriend's just served an AVO on him.'

Rosie and I stirred our coffees thoughtfully. Neither of us had ever been stalked, by any of our exes. Not even slightly. Which reminded me of something.

'Rosie,' I began quietly, 'have you heard about Humphrey?'

Rosie leant forward and grabbed my hand.

'You've heard,' she said softly. 'He got into the Bell Shakespeare Company.'

I nodded, and Rosie gave my hand a compassionate squeeze.

As the weeks went by, we sent Dale more and more girls. And now that he was ringing every few days, I felt slightly jealous to hear him making the other receptionists laugh. Raelene told me he was particularly fond of Sabrina, our new girl, and had seen her more than twice. 'She's sitting downstairs.' Seconds later, I was standing before a petite blonde in the kitchen. Sabrina was in her mid twenties and had a short straight bob, blue eyes, a Bondi tan, and nothing like the 'big arse' Maxine had spoken of so unkindly.

'Look, I'm sorry,' she gabbled before I could say a word, 'but I don't get it. Two days. No bookings. What's going on? I'm not a dog! This is ridiculous!' She held her hand out to me. 'I'm Sabrina, by the way.'

I could see why Dale liked her. I introduced myself and Sabrina smiled as she shook my hand, and then continued her funny, hyped banter. Sabrina worked in finance, she said, and was trying to break into acting, so needed to make a lot of money to pay for lessons. I always felt depressed when I heard this. By the time Sabrina had sold her car to pay for two hundred photos and various courses, including Jacobean Tragedy for Beginners, a Clowning Workshop full of models, and a masterclass held by some lecherous B-grade American actor in a church hall, she might be lucky enough to get three days work a year.

For the next three weeks it was unusually quiet on the Dale front, until I answered a call at midnight from a particularly pissed and pissed-off chef in Darling Point. Dale just wanted us all to know, he began bitterly, about the double-dealing, disloyal and 'treacherous bitch' we had on our books. Sabrina had offered Dale her services privately, he said, and he hoped this information would end any further employment she got through our agency. In a drunken

rave, Dale told me how their 'private' arrangement had suited both
of them for a while, until things got so serious, Dale suggested
Sabrina move in. Sabrina's response to Dale's offer, and I'm so glad
I was not in the room at the time, was to put her price up.

It was difficult to doubt Dale's story when he could quote
Sabrina's home and mobile phone numbers as well as her real name
and address at Bondi. But when confronted by Sofia and Boris the
following night, Sabrina vehemently denied Dale's version with
such conviction that, if it wasn't the truth, she didn't need acting
lessons. According to Sabrina, Dale fell in love with her over three
bookings, and it was when she *refused* to see him privately that
things got ugly. Sabrina accused Dale of getting her personal details
by going through her bag weeks ago, while she was showering after
a booking, and complained that she had been harassed by abusive
phone calls ever since.

'And,' Sabrina cried, 'he's stalking me!'

Spooky. But Sofia was suspicious. Why hadn't Sabrina reported
this before?

I'd never known summer rain like it. While it poured heavily for
the second week in a row, Boris's office downstairs flooded, and
Dale's life went from bad to worse. I arrived on Friday night just as
a red-eyed Sabrina was leaving. According to my colleagues, a lot
had happened in three days. Apparently Sabrina did not have a
fancy job in finance at all. Sabrina was on unemployment benefits,
and Dale had done a spiteful thing. Earlier in the week he had rung
Centrelink to report Sabrina's undeclared income as a prostitute.
Sofia and Boris did not appreciate the inquiry that followed, and
asked Sabrina to leave straightaway. Which she did, But I gathered
from the maudlin late night phone call from a weeping Dale that
Sabrina had not disappeared from his life without one parting shot.
That morning Dale had been served his second, if somewhat soggy,
AVO.

'How do you feel, Dale?' I asked my miserable caller.

'Want Antoinette again, Meredith,' Dale whimpered pathetically.

It had been a slow night for Antoinette. Not one booking could
we get for her. Leslie nodded at me imploringly when she over-

heard me talking to Dale about his request. Leslie had just had her head bitten off for offering Antoinette a booking in Glebe.

'*Glebe?*' Sofia and I had heard the screech from the kitchen. '*And bump into my twenty-one-year-old son? I'm not going to fucking Glebe!*'

This was the first any of us had heard about a son, or that Glebe was a problem. But we would respect Antoinette's wishes, send someone else, and avoid using the toilet downstairs for as long as we possibly could. When Dale's credit card was rejected, I felt relieved not to be sending a sad, desperate prostitute with gambling debts to a sad, desperate alcoholic with no credit.

'Look, Dale,' I said, 'I think we'd better just forget it.'

But Dale had a better idea and hung up on me to stagger off into the rain in search of his nearest ATM. With Sofia railing at me for nearly losing a booking by encouraging drunk, unhappy clients to 'just forget it', I despondently went in search of Antoinette. And sure enough, she was not impressed about being sent to Dale at Darling Point again.

'Why doesn't he just get himself a fucking girlfriend?' she hissed at the kitchen table, aggressively whacking her face with a powder puff.

'Bleeding, Meredith,' Dale cried on the phone while waiting for Antoinette to arrive. 'Fell over.'

He couldn't remember, but Dale thought he might have tripped on his way to the Handybank.

'Lots of blood, Dale?' I asked, especially for Sofia's benefit.

'Lots of blood, Meredith,' he said sadly. 'Big puddle!'

Antoinette's night was just getting better and better.

I found no comfort in Patrick's arms that morning. All I could think about was Dale, and my final exchange with a bedraggled Antoinette an hour earlier in the kitchen, while I waited for her to rummage through her large black bag.

'I won't see him again,' she said curtly, 'not just because I think he could be violent, but because he's vulnerable, and we're exploiting him.'

Barely able to look at me, Antoinette thrust our money into my hand, and walked away.

As I climbed the stairs clutching Dale's wet, crumpled cash, her words rang in my ears, and I felt dreadful. And now Patrick was holding onto me like a needy child. As the sun came up, with Patrick snoring in my ear, I wondered when, exactly, had I become the driver.

Letting go of Patrick

Finally, the rain had stopped.

'Are you going on the Sorry March tomorrow?' I asked Patrick as I threw on my dressing gown.

'What's that?' he asked, sitting up in my bed, reaching for his morning cigarette.

'You know,' I said, 'the march across Sydney Harbour Bridge tomorrow, to say sorry to the Aborigines.'

'Oh God,' Patrick groaned with a weary smile, lighting his Marlboro, 'you're not into all that are you?'

As I looked at the gangly forty-eight-year-old man sitting up in my bed, scattering ash on my sheets, scoffing at my question, I felt as hollow as one of Patrick's happy pipes.

Some people's bodies let them know something's wrong by erupting in hives, shingles or cold sores. Others drown a troubled conscience with alcohol, or hide behind a smoke screen of dope. When I don't want to face something unpleasant or upsetting, I find myself singing about it. Three weeks before I decided to part with my ex, whose quiet indifference was slowly breaking my heart, I was haunted by the same line of a Joni Mitchell song. 'Don't it always seem to go, that you don't know what you've got till it's gone.' It got the point where he was singing along with me, in harmony, until it was the only conversation we ever had before I left him. And now, as I stood in my kitchen waiting for Patrick's tea to brew, I found myself humming another song . . . 'You and I dance to the beat of a different drum.'

It wasn't that Patrick didn't want to say sorry to the Aborigines. Patrick was from Portsmouth, and didn't think he should apologise to anyone. It was more his lazy dismissal of anything so taxing as having a point of view. And I suddenly felt terrified of being sucked into a vortex of procrastination along with Patrick, Den and Limpy as they disappeared down a dark hole with nothing but a television set and a handful of darts. When I handed Patrick his navy, zip-up jacket at the front door, it now felt as light and frail as he did.

'See you tonight,' I said as I kissed him goodbye.

And for the first time, Patrick did not smile or even wave back at me as he opened our front gate and shut it gently behind him. As I watched him bob down our street with his hands thrust deep in his pockets, I knew that daylight had finally caught up with both of us. And that if Patrick and I had only one thing in common, it was that neither of us wanted reconciliation.

As I washed our breakfast plates and opened the windows, I wondered where such cruel and instant clarity came from. I knew I'd been holding the end of the dream at bay, but I never expected the lights to come up so harshly, or so abruptly, on my tenuous relationship with the gentle driver.

Women who wax

As I stood at the Carrington Road bus stop waiting for the 373 to take me to work, I felt the wave growing larger by the minute, until I had to sit down and breath deeply. The thought of doing one more shift was almost more than I could bear. I considered turning back for home rather than facing another of Sofia's cysts, Maxine's heads or Boris's vitriolic tirades. What was the point of going back to that house one more time? I wasn't sure why, but since Patrick had left my place that morning, everything, even the weather, had changed. I could not possibly send Dale another girl, or speak to Thomas Vomeitz with even a hint of politeness. I got on the bus and paid my fare. And if Didi rang, I thought as I sat up the back, I could not sound remotely terrified if I tried. And if Genevieve stood sulking before me, it would cost me less than nothing to tell her to wake up and get another job. Steam rose from the hot wet pavement as

I walked to Mustafa's for a felafel roll. If Leslie mentioned her father one more time, I'd pull the heads off all her stupid Smurfs. And if Bernard QC wanted new toe jewellery, he could buy his own, and call me back. I climbed our steps and rang the door bell.

'Hi, it's me,' I said.

And as the door magically opened before me, I wondered how many more times it would do so.

Girls would die if they knew the appalling conversations going on upstairs, where disgruntled receptionists discussed their every blemish and bulge.

'I thought you said she was beautiful,' Raelene was challenging Leslie when I arrived.

'She's good till she opens her mouth,' Leslie conceded.

'Fat arse,' Maxine grumbled as she packed up from her day shift.

'She's trashy,' Raelene cried.

'Well, I wouldn't send her out for seven hundred!' Leslie protested.

'Fat arse,' Maxine said again.

But it was always good news to hear we'd recruited another blonde, especially if she was young. So on the pretence of making a coffee, I performed my usual routine of feigning surprise at the unexpected sight of a new face in the lounge room, and introduced myself to Giselle.

The first thing I noticed was how young Giselle was, and the second thing was how extraordinarily pale. Her long slim limbs were all collapsed to one side as she sat on the floor watching television with a slip of a black dress falling off her luminous shoulders. She had long blonde hair, fluffy from too many perms, and looked up at me with a sweet and childish smile. I smiled back, already forming my protest to Leslie back in reception. Giselle was too gawky, pale and freckly to be beautiful, and she had an unfortunate predilection for wearing thick black eyeliner, making her look like a gothic fairy.

'Hi, I'm Giselle,' she said coquettishly, 'and this is Celeste.'

I had already noticed the hand caressing Giselle's long neck belonged to Celeste, who lay on the couch above, purring like the cat who ate the new blonde.

'Yes,' I replied slowly, like a kindergarten teacher, 'Celeste and I have met before.'

Another conquest for Celeste. What had happened to Genevieve, I wondered.

'Haven't you heard?' Raelene said, delighted to be the messenger. 'Celeste got the boot when Genevieve caught her stealing from her!'

'And now she's with Giselle?' I asked.

'Pip sent them on a lesbian booking on Tuesday,' Raelene said, 'and they've been together ever since.'

Leslie knew Giselle from their days at Blue Angels.

'Be careful with big cash bookings,' she warned me. 'Giselle's a coke head. She'll take the money and disappear for days.'

'Fat arse,' muttered Maxine again as she walked out the door.

I almost hoped he wouldn't answer.

'Hi, Patrick,' I said, 'would you take Giselle to the Menzies, when you've dropped off Teresa?'

But Patrick sounded perfectly cheerful on his car phone, despite our strange parting that morning.

'Okey dokey!'

And for the next few hours, I tried to detect whether this unexpected joviality was genuine, or a cover, or perhaps something Patrick had smoked. Whatever it was, I dreaded the long drive home, and the inevitable conversation that awaited us both.

Giselle's feet barely touched the ground that night as we sent her to credit card bookings in hotels all over Sydney.

'Hi! It's me!' she'd sing down the phone with yet another one hour extension, and then sound heartbroken when I had to ask who 'me' was.

I found it slightly disturbing that men responded so strongly to the broken, childlike creature I had met on the lounge room floor.

'It's because she's shaved,' Raelene said.

I looked at her. Shaved?

'Yeah, you know,' Leslie said, 'when girls either shave all their pubes off, or else have them waxed.'

Waxed? The whole caboodle?

Leslie and Raelene gaped in horror at my ignorance.

'Yeah. The full wax!' cried Raelene. She started to laugh. 'For a silky smooth finish.'

'Men love it,' grinned Leslie.

I'd heard of heart shapes and thin lines, trims, and even a triangular thing called the Brazilian, but the full Kojak was news to me. Perhaps I was behind the times, as I'd only recently succumbed to the bikini wax myself. Due to a conspiracy between the lingerie industry and beauty parlours, every bikini or pair of knickers now makes any normal woman look like she's carrying a yak in her pants. But to regress to complete hairlessness, what was that, I asked my bewildered colleagues, if not yet another apology for getting old? We'd lost weight, pumped our faces full of botox, shaved our legs, and now we had to be totally pubeless as well? Why not just walk around in a T-shirt that says *Sorry!* and kill two birds with one stone?

'It just feels nicer, smoother,' Leslie said to me, almost tearfully.

'But doesn't it worry you, Leslie, that a smooth, bald vagina also appeals to some men's fantasies of having sex with prepubescent girls?'

'Nah,' said Raelene, looking at me as if I was deranged. 'Just 'cause he prefers a bald noony, doesn't mean he's a paedophile, Meredith.'

Didn't it? I felt close to tears myself now. And who on earth called it a *noony*? When did that happen? Leaving my alarmed colleagues to assess my sanity, I went to the bathroom to splash some cold water on my face.

At three o'clock I received a call from a rather amused Mr Rogers staying at the Intercontinental.

'Yes, Meredith, I think young Giselle here would like to stay for another hour or so.'

I felt like apologising for not having packed her pyjamas.

'Would that be all right with you?' Mr Rogers inquired.

'Oh yes,' I assured him, 'so long as she's no trouble to you, Mr Rogers.'

'No trouble at all,' he said.

'Wheeeeeee!' came the childish cry from the background, 'I'm never coming home! I'm going to stay for ever and ever and ever!', followed by lots of infantile giggling.

And I just knew that Giselle and her bald noony were jumping up and down on Mr Rogers' big bed.

'As you can hear,' Mr Rogers chortled, 'she's quite happy to stay.'

And I just knew that kind Mr Rogers had lots and lots of lovely white cocaine.

Now that Patrick was in our office, waiting for Raelene to count his pay, I realised that the cheerful demeanour had been a cover-up after all. Even when I spoke to him directly, Patrick could only look at me in fleeting glances, with a wobbly, unsteady smile. I felt unbearably responsible, and no amount of empathy could ease my guilt as I watched him hovering over Raelene's shoulder.

'Do you mind?' she cried, looking up at him, and I had to look away.

If Patrick would only stop smiling. If he could just be angry with me, it would be so much easier. He seemed so utterly defenceless. Even Leslie's friendly jibes now seemed to pierce his vulnerable countenance like arrows as he waited, helplessly, for grumpy Raelene to do her sums.

Having dropped Raelene in Bronte, Patrick and I sat in silence at the traffic lights.

'Patrick—' I began.

'I want to tell you something,' Patrick interrupted me, with some urgency.

I felt sick, and wondered what sexually transmittable disease I might have to be tested for in the morning.

'I've got a proposal for you,' he said, with a shaky smile.

I'd rather the disease and a course of strong antibiotics.

'Not a marriage proposal!' He laughed nervously, but then stopped just as abruptly.

Patrick seemed agitated, as if he couldn't begin until the lights had changed. But as the car took off, so did Patrick, who embarked on one of the most bizarre overtures I'd ever heard in my life.

Patrick's pipes were about to take off. The pipes that took sunshine and lit up windowless bunkers? Yes. The very ones. Patrick was going to patent his idea, and an engineer friend in London was terribly excited about the possibility of imminent success. Potentially huge success! We were talking perhaps millions of dollars here. I nodded supportively, but Patrick's wide eyes and erratic hand movements were beginning to frighten me, and I wondered how such madness had gone so long undetected. Very soon, Patrick was going to fly to London, meet up with this chap, and begin hawking their invention around the traps, before selling it to the highest bidder. And we were talking millions here! I nodded again. And possibly America!

'And here's where you come in,' Patrick announced, with great excitement.

I looked at him in horror.

'With your skills as an actress,' he added, checking to see my reaction.

I tried to smile, but dreaded what potential involvement I could possibly have in Patrick's crack-brained, pipe-dream scheme.

'We were talking about you the other day,' Patrick said, now grinning at me. 'And, you know, if we choose to go with your face to launch our sunshine pipes, well, you could end up being the luckiest winner of all!'

The problem of a few darts paled into insignificance as I tried to imagine my future with Patrick. I saw my face painted like the Tinman's, and my arms and feet protruding from a long metal pipe as I performed the Happy Pipe Dance for a bunch of construction engineers in Portsmouth. And I wanted to get out of the car.

Libby buttered her toast thoughtfully while I stared wildly at the fridge. I had waited two hours for her to get up.

'He's panicking,' Libby said when she had finally digested my extraordinary story. 'He can see what's coming, and he's just desperately trying to hold onto you any way he can.'

But if that was all, why did I feel like catching the first plane to Tasmania, and hiding at my parents' house for a year?

'And he smokes a lot of dope,' Libby said, taking a bite of her toast. 'Some people really lose it on that stuff.'

Yes, that felt closer to the truth. Patrick had lost it. Boy, had he lost it. And how could I give our relationship the decent burial it deserved if Patrick was going to go loopy on me?

Ewan MacGregor's nanny

I was shopping in Coles when my mobile rang.

'What are you doing right now?' asked my concerned house-mate.

I told Libby I was in aisle six, trying to decide between tuna and salmon.

'Well, how would you like to be Ewan MacGregor's nanny?' she asked.

'I wouldn't mind,' I said. 'How would you like to be Uma Thurman's gardener?'

And the more Libby laughed, the more I could believe she wasn't serious.

'Seriously, though,' she said, 'I've just been telling Ewan and Eve all about you. They're looking for a nanny for their little girl, Clara.'

'Ewan MacGregor?' I gulped. 'You've been telling Ewan MacGregor all about me?'

'Listen,' said Libby, now sounding very officious, 'they know you're an out of work actress, but they love that you live with me, and that you've nannied before. And they loved that you were on *Play School*, after I explained what *Play School* was. And if you're interested, they'd like to meet you.'

'Did you tell them I work in a brothel, Libby?'

'Well, no, I didn't think that would help, actually.' Libby paused. 'I mean, would you still want to work in a brothel? Rather than in a mansion in Double Bay, looking after Ewan MacGregor's three-year-old daughter?'

I'd only had about four hours sleep and couldn't decide between brine and oil, let alone if I wanted to leave my brothel for Ewan MacGregor.

'Anyway,' Libby said, 'think about it.'

I was in aisle seven, daydreaming in front of the Huggies, something I had been doing a lot lately, when my mobile rang again.

'Have you thought about it?' Libby asked. ''Cause Eve wants to meet you. Now.'

Twenty minutes later, having abandoned a shopping trolley for a taxi, I was dodging Volvos as I crossed Knox Street in Double Bay while applying lipstick and getting rid of my gum, all at the same time. At first, I thought Libby was chatting with a small girl in pigtails at the corner table of the Cosmopolitan. But I could tell by my housemate's body language, this was no ordinary girl. And as I got closer, the petite creature stood to shake my hand, and smiled. No woman had any right to have such delicate bone structure, or look so young with no make-up, or to wear such a tiny but expensive dress. Eve was an exquisite thing. She had flawless olive skin, her large brown eyes were canopied by the longest eyelashes I had ever seen, and I knew ballet dancers who'd spent hours trying to perfect eyebrows that shape. There was something quite dramatic in the upward sweep of her fine features, and when Eve spoke, I was not at all surprised to hear a French accent.

'Thank you so mush for coming,' she said, and smiled charmingly as she shook my hand.

Within seconds of meeting Eve (pronounced Ev), I had completely forgotten who she was married to. Eve had an almost intimidatingly direct manner but an infectious laugh. When I asked Eve if she worked in the film industry too, she nodded, and told me she was an art director.

'Eve has worked on lots of films,' Libby interjected, 'including *Lock, Stock and Two Smoking Barrels*.'

'Wow,' I said, sounding more like a nanny every second.

'And Eve is currently translating a book,' Libby added.

Eve shook her head in a very dismissive French way, as if it was nothing.

'Eve can speak six languages,' Libby cried. 'Six!' And she laughed at Eve's embarrassed shrug.

Eve then turned to me, touched my arm gently, and told me how sorry she was that she had never seen me on *Playtime*. I assured Eve it was nothing, and it certainly felt like bugger-all. I couldn't get over her youthful appearance. Before I'd heard the mature voice of a woman in her thirties, I would not have looked twice at Eve in a school uniform.

Then it was down to business. Clara, Ewan and Eve's little girl, was three years old, and spoke English and French.

'Which is why we would prefer a nanny who can speak French,' Eve said.

I nodded, assuming they'd had no luck finding one.

'Libby tells me you can speak a little French,' Eve said hopefully.

I looked at Libby, who looked at a passing waiter. It was true that I'd stumbled through Paris asking for the odd baguette. I could teach little Clara to say, 'You must be kidding? Five dollars for a cup of coffee?' And, 'Please don't do that. My husband will kill you.' But not much more.

'That's okay,' Eve said, 'it really doesn't matter, so long as you could spare the occasional afternoon to look after her, or pick her up from creche and bring her home.'

I looked at Libby again, who quickly looked for another waiter. I was tempted to tell Eve that I could drive, just not legally, but then I thought the MacGregors could probably do better than that.

'That's okay,' said Eve again, 'the driving is not so important. Are you coming to this dinner on Saturday night?'

I looked at Libby, who nodded enthusiastically. I was now!

'Good,' said Eve. 'Then you can meet Ewan.'

I think we all knew it was a lost cause, but it was so kind of Eve to ask.

On Saturday morning I rang Didi and told her I had diarrhoea. No one argues with diarrhoea. And it doesn't require a silly voice on the phone. But Didi did not sound at all convinced about my loose bowels, until I told her that Trudy was filling in for me. Then Didi told me to eat nothing but dry toast, drink lots of water, and get a good night's sleep.

As Libby and Peter and I perched on stools at the bar of Pascal's Restaurant in Bondi, sipping our mango daiquiris, I assured my helpful housemate that, if by some miracle the MacGregors did ask me to be Clara's nanny, I would leave the brothel immediately. Libby nodded, but she was more concerned at this moment about getting a table. Our intimate booking for five had suddenly grown to seven, as Baz Luhrmann had just rung to say that he and his wife, Catherine Martin, would be joining us as well. But there wasn't a spare seat, let alone a table, at Pascal's. Even the sweating waiters stood marooned between chairs, miles away from shore, balancing five plates full of squid pasta, roasted zucchini flowers and Jerusalem artichokes provençale.

Three mango daiquiris later, there were still no tables, but by now Libby and I had found the funny side. And when Ewan and Eve finally did arrive, with Baz and his wife in tow, we all greeted each other warmly, like long-lost friends. I got a kiss on both cheeks from Baz, who remembered me from NIDA, where we were both acting students before he became an international film director, and I became a receptionist at a brothel. And when Eve had finished with my cheeks, she introduced me to Ewan, who instantly threw his arms open and hugged me like an old nanny.

'She's a strong-willed little thing,' Ewan shouted in my ear above the deafening noise as we sat on stools at the bar.

And as he and Eve told me about my potential new charge, I tried not to be too distracted by the gaze of sixty hungry eyes behind them, and the commotion as the manager practically frogmarched several lingering patrons out the door.

'Do you have a match, Merridy?' Eve asked.

As a matter of fact I did. And as Ewan MacGregor and his beautiful wife leant into my flame, I nearly died when I saw the gold inscription on their new nanny's lighter. *International Escorts*, and the phone number.

When we were finally seated at our table, I found myself happily sandwiched between my housemate Peter and Catherine Martin. CM, as they call her, made me laugh so much, I forgot all about her production design for *Romeo and Juliet*, *Strictly Ballroom* and *Moulin Rouge*, and punched her in the arm, twice. But after dessert, I had to take a moment to look around the table, just to savour the extraordinary dichotomy of my life right now, on my night off from a brothel in Redfern. I was terribly relieved when Baz graciously offered to pay the bill, which saved me a small deposit on a flat, but felt sad that our night was ending. And while they waited for their coats, our visiting dignitaries once again embraced us warmly before bidding us a fond farewell, and left in their shiny cars, driven by shiny drivers.

For some minutes Libby and Peter and I sat in happy, reflective silence, until our waiter inquired if we would like some liqueurs. It was the kindest and most thoughtful suggestion we'd heard all night, and we told him so over the next three rounds as well.

Sending Dave two dogs

When Libby told me a week later that the MacGregors had found a French nanny with a driving licence, I felt more relieved than disappointed. I knew it was time for me to leave my brothel job, but I still did not know how to leave or, more to the point, how to say goodbye to Urszula, Shelby, Maya and, of course, Antoinette. And then there was the driver, as soon as he came back to earth. It wasn't that I was expecting an emotional farewell. This was the least sentimental environment I'd ever worked in, but also the most sensitive, and I suspected a few of the girls would interpret my departure as some kind of cancellation.

Anyway, I couldn't go. Apart from a few screen tests, I had no job to go to. I'd been told I was too old to play the mother in one nappy ad, despite current statistics, and too young, thank God, to have incontinence for another. That just left the sitcom at Fox. I was still waiting to hear if I was just right to play the nervous idiot in a new show called *Flatchat*. For now, I had to be content to play the third receptionist in a tragicomedy set in Redfern, with a cast of sixty gorgeous women, and hundreds of men.

Some phone calls revealed such a disturbing underbelly of contempt and hatred for women, it left me speechless. I'd known it was out there since I was ten years old, when my big sister told a car full of drunken boys leaning out their windows to piss off. I had never witnessed such contradictory behaviour. One minute they were inviting her to sit on their faces, and the next, they were threatening to punch both our heads in. Ten years later, I realised there was not much contradiction in this kind of behaviour at all. And now, twenty-eight years later, I had to deal with the same men on the phone, and indeed send a girl to provide the very service they'd asked for.

'What can I do for you, Dave?' I asked a very pissed Dave, calling from Star City.

'We want two chicks,' Dave said. 'What ya got?'

'And how many of you are there, Dave?' I asked.

'Juz me an' Jimmy.'

'Have you and Jimmy got two rooms, Dave?'

'Hang on.'

I ate the rest of my felafel roll while I waited for Dave to count his rooms.

He was back.

'We gotta bathroom,' Dave suggested hopefully.

I explained to Dave that none of our girls provided a bathroom service, but that I could try to find two girls who did not mind sharing a bedroom. 'And what sort of women were you and Jimmy looking for tonight, Dave?'

'I don't want no Australian rubbish,' Dave told me defiantly. 'I'll throw up if I 'ave to fuck an Australian bitch ... hang on ... *What*?'

Dave had not had much luck, I gathered, with local girls.

'Jimmy does,' he said, returning to me. 'He wants one with big tits ... *I said with big tits!*' Dave yelled in my ear. 'And blonde. But I want Asian, you got that? I want a small Asian, Meredith. And Meredith?'

'Yes, Dave?'

'I don't want nothin' sloppy. I wanna tight little Asian girl, know what I mean?'

'Gotcha, Dave.'

'You got any that don't speak English?'

I should have lied to Eve and told her I spoke fluent French but was a little deaf. And that I had a licence, but liked to drive very, very slowly.

I'd had my fill of callers like Dave by now. To these men, a prostitute provided not just a blow job, she provided living proof that there were still women out there who knew their place. Women whose financial dependence on men, and sexual accessibility, proved beyond a doubt that they were morally, physically and financially inferior.

'So, one petite Asian for you, Dave, and one busty Australian for Jimmy.'

'*Swap?*' Dave suddenly yelled in my ear. '*Fuck off!* ... Hang on, Meredith, Jimmy wants ta swap. *I don't want ta fuck your bitch! If she swaps she's a dog, mate!*'

'Dave, sorry to interrupt you,' I said, 'but if Jimmy wants to swap, that's going to cost extra.'

'Nah, Meredith,' Dave said. 'Just the tight Asian and the girl with big tits, darl.'

'Okay, Dave,' I said, 'leave it with me for a few minutes and I'll call you straight back.'

'Can we have a discount? Seeing there's two of 'em?'

'They're not avocados, Dave.'

Silence. I should have said pineapples.

Some clients resented that they had to pay at all. They'd spent all night being rejected in bars and clubs all over Sydney, and by the time they rang us at four in the morning, they weren't sure if they wanted to have sex with a woman or punch her. If I could hear it in their voices, I wouldn't send anyone. But sometimes I didn't find out until the girl had returned, and I could see in her face that she'd been treated in such a way as to compensate for every disappointing experience her client had had with women since birth. Such can be the glamorous life of an escort.

Poor Dave. The only Asian women I had at four o'clock in the morning were Corky and Lil, both busty, small Thai women, and both single mothers in their forties. Corky had a reputation for putting one hand down her client's pants as soon as she got one foot in the door, before he could cancel, while she called us on her mobile with the other. And the only 'busty' Australian available right now was Antoinette. Antoinette was in a bad way. She'd had no bookings all night, had fought on the street with her Lebanese paramour, and now she was asleep upstairs while Stanley stood brooding yet again in the dim light of the phone box outside.

STELLLLLAAAA!

I rang Dave back with an update.

'Oh, fuck, Meredith,' Dave protested. '*Hey, Jimmy!*' he shouted again in my ear. '*My Thai bitch is forty! What? ...*' Jimmy had a question. 'How big are Jimmy's tits, Meredith?'

352 Sending Dave two dogs

'Antoinette's a thirty-six double D, Dave,' I said. 'Tell Jimmy that's big. She's a beautiful blonde, provides an excellent—'

'Hang on,' he interrupted me. '*Look! I don't wanna fuck some sloppy cunt you've been in, Jim! I'm fuckin' the Asian cunt for an hour, an' you've got the blonde!* Sorry, Meredith.'

'That's all right, Dave,' I said.

'All right,' Dave sighed with resignation. 'But these two girls, Meredith, tell me the truth. Are they dogs, or what?'

'No, Dave,' I said, 'we find our dogs have too much trouble reaching the buttons in the lifts.'

Silence.

'Well look, Meredith,' Dave said, 'just fuckin' send them. Send me the Thai, and Jimmy'll have the blonde with tits.'

'Okay, Dave. They're on their way.'

There was a flurry of movement from a corner of the office.

'Where am I taking Antoinette?' Patrick asked, standing up with his keys.

'Nowhere at all,' I said. 'Sit down and finish your *Cleo*.'

On the way home that night, I broke it gently to Patrick that I would not be helping him out with his pipes, in London, Portsmouth *or* America, as I was already happily established as an actor, here in Sydney. I hoped that it would be an honest way into a more worthy conversation about the sad demise of our almost relationship, but Patrick was too offended already.

'Funny, isn't it?' he said, with one eye on the road ahead as he gripped the wheel tightly. 'I took you for a more adventurous girl than that.'

Patrick was obviously confusing me with someone more adventurous and completely insane. Perhaps some female dart champion he'd met at the RSL, who wanted to tunnel shade into the desert.

'I was going to tell you more, actually,' he said stiffly, 'but I won't now.'

I didn't know what to say.

'Ah well,' Patrick sighed, pulling up at my house, 'your loss.'

If I ever read about Mort the Millionaire who made a fortune by funnelling sunshine into the caves of Afghanistan with his Happy Pipes, I will be genuinely thrilled for Patrick. But I don't think I'll ever regret my decision. I just didn't want to do the happy pipe dance.

A light at the end of the brothel

That night I dreamt that I was flying. I flew over our old brothel, and looked down as Patrick and various girls came in and out of our busy house. They all looked so delicate, in exquisite dresses of soft gauze and coruscating necklaces. Some of them had huge, pregnant bellies, and they smiled as they took Patrick's hand, hopping in and out of his shiny car. Even Boris looked soft and powdery as he searched for his key to the door on the front porch until Sapphire came out, in her dressing gown, and joined him on the step for a cigarette and a laugh. I felt so happy, watching them all, unseen from above, until I heard the sound of a phone ringing. And there, under the harsh fluorescent light of the phone box across the road, I saw Antoinette's pale face, looking up at me. Holding up a fist full of cash, she beckoned for me to come and collect it from her. As my body fell rapidly towards her, the ringing got louder until, just as I was about to be impaled on a phone box, I woke up to the sound of our phone ringing downstairs.

'Good news, girl!' my agent cried in my ear. 'You got the job!'

Fox studios had cast me as the nervous idiot, and rehearsals would begin the following Tuesday.

Didi sounded none too pleased with my one week's notice, and quite rightly suggested that perhaps I should have told her I was a professional actor at my initial interview a year earlier. I apologised for this oversight, rode the strained pause that followed, and squirmed for the very last time.

'But we have had actresses before, Merediss,' Didi sighed wearily, 'and they have always come back to us. It is a most precarious way to earn a living, is it not?'

Precarious, yes, with paid overtime, meal breaks, sick leave, superannuation, loadings, a union, holiday pay and funny cards on opening night.

I hopped onto the bus and sat up the back, grinning from ear to ear. No one knew what amazing women I had worked with every weekend for nearly a year. I skipped across at the lights, and waved to the Lebanese men in their coffee house playing backgammon. Stunned by this gesture, they gawked back at me with cigarettes hanging from their lips as their arms lifted automatically.

'It's me!' I sang into the intercom for the second last time.

And the large wooden door opened, inviting me in.

I leapt up the stairs to the kitchen, where Patrick stood up a ladder, hammering new locks into the windows.

'Hi!' I called up to my eccentric driver.

'Hi!' he sang back, with a slightly surprised smile.

Then I popped my head into the lounge room to see Urszula and Bree sprawled on the couch, watching television.

'Is it true you're leaving?' Bree asked, looking up dolefully.

I stopped smiling. How did they know already?

'Sofia told us last night,' Urszula said flatly, without taking her eyes from the television.

'I've got an acting job,' I said apologetically, 'and it starts on Tuesday.'

I wanted Urszula to look at me, but she was enjoying my punishment too much.

'We'll miss you,' said Bree.

'I won't,' snapped Urszula, aggressively flicking a channel on the remote.

This was just the reaction I had been dreading. But halfway up the stairs, I heard her strong voice yelling after me.

'*I would, but she's so fooking useless!*'

I greeted my colleagues in the office with restrained euphoria, especially as Sofia was already scowling over some tardy girl's non-appearance. Pip and Maxine looked up from their takeaway dinners, and I could tell by the way their eyes darted nervously from Sofia back to me that they, too, had already heard my news.

'You going to be on television, we hear,' Sofia said, with a derisive snort.

'Yes, Sofia,' I answered confidently. 'I've got a job acting in a new sitcom at Fox.'

Sofia just blew out smoke as if she was not surprised by such treachery. Hopefully it wouldn't be a busy night, and she would retire to her office soon.

'I told you this would happen!' Pip cried, suddenly throwing her arms around my neck with ferocious support.

And then Maxine, who never wanted to be left out, followed suit with a sticky, baklava kiss on my cheek. Sickened by such a display of sentiment, Sofia at last left the room. As soon as she'd gone, my tiny colleagues urgently told me of their big plans to escape also. One spoke of 'tarot cards' while the other mentioned a 'fashion line', and I was quite relieved when all babble was extinguished by the sudden return of our Spanish general.

No matter how hard I tried, though, for the rest of the night I could not hide my exuberant mood. Even when the phones were quiet and the only sound was the relentless banging of Patrick's hammer coming from the kitchen below, I found the funny side.

'There you go, Bree,' I said when the hammering paused, 'see if you can walk now.'

Pip and Maxine fell about laughing, but Sofia would not even smile. Bang, bang, bang went Patrick's hammer again.

'Okay, Celeste,' I said, trying not to laugh at my own joke, 'try bending again.'

'I hope you funnier in your sitcom, darling,' Sofia grumbled, looking disapprovingly at her three hysterical receptionists.

But this only made it worse, and when Patrick appeared innocently at our door, hammer in hand, Maxine actually wet herself.

It was a busy night, so I made the most of every opportunity to go downstairs and say goodbye to any girl dropping off money between bookings. But with every goodbye, a strange pattern began to emerge. I'd barely managed to announce my impending departure when I was told by each girl that she was leaving too, any day, any week, any minute, to live in Byron Bay, or start a hairdressing business, a university course, or a family. Kimberley was going to have a baby with Scott, Heather was going to concentrate on her singing, Delilah was returning to Nigeria to be with her little boy, and Marilyn's boyfriend was going to finance her new beauty parlour business in Newcastle. I wondered if it was just that they didn't wish to be remembered in this context. Anyway, it seemed that we were all leaving, except for Maya, who never thought she deserved anything better, and Shelby, who was sticking to her five-year plan and still had six months to go. And these were the only two girls who bothered to ask where I was going.

'It's just a small role in a little telly thing,' I said to Maya, who smiled sadly at the television set.

Shelby seemed only slightly more interested as she gave my new job an almost convincing nod of approval before clicking shut her glasses case, depositing it in her handbag, and striding out the door to her next booking. But I knew exactly what the financial consultant was thinking. Acting was for dreamers who had no respect for the nest egg, and slept around without getting paid for it.

'Aaahh, Meeeeeredit!' Boris sang in our doorway at two in the morning, holding his arms open like an opera singer.

Sofia looked up from her desk with one eyebrow raised, and we all had the same thought. Was Boris pissed again? But my perfumed Bogart walked towards me too steadily, and his eyes were as clear as clean swimming pools.

'I am so sad when Didi gives me this news when I vake up tonight.'

Maxine and Pip burst into hysterics again, but Boris did not mean this to be a joke and, with a sideways glance, snuffed their giggles like candles.

'I vill miss your friendly smile,' Boris continued his speech, 'and your silly, wobbly English face. Here's your pay.'

I had spent a year telling Boris I was not English, but he wasn't having a bar of it. And now he was making me blush with a long and thoughtful, far-off gaze.

'Yes, Meredit,' he said, caressing my desk affectionately, 'I vill miss you.'

I had given up on Urszula, who hours later still sat sulking in the lounge room. But I was happy to find Antoinette sitting at the kitchen table, counting her money, having just returned from her booking at the Radisson.

'Are you leaving?' she asked distractedly, somewhere between eighty and a hundred dollars.

I nodded.

'What a jerk!' she said, slapping the money down in front of her.

Again, not the reaction I was hoping for.

'If there's one thing I cannot stand,' she protested angrily, 'it's the dickheads in therapy who like to practise a little post-coital analysis of their own on the sex worker. Why can't they just accept they've paid for a quick fuck and get over it?'

Oh good. On my second last night, Antoinette was about to unload again. I quickly sat down.

'And why does every amateur shrink assume all prostitutes must have been abused?' she asked me. 'Look around! Are we all so very damaged?'

Antoinette was possibly the most tortured soul I had ever met in my life, but then maybe she would have been the most tortured librarian, podiatrist or Morris dancer.

'He'll find abused women in any profession if he looks hard enough,' Antoinette growled, handing me our ninety dollars.

'I mean,' she railed again, 'why do people ask such offensive questions? How would you like it if I asked you, "Why did you become an actor? Were you abused?" I mean, do people ever ask you that?'

No, I said.

'Well why not?' she asked me. 'There's not much difference between what you do and what I do, is there?'

Wow. This would be good.

'You're good at pretending,' she continued angrily, 'and you like to make people feel good about themselves, so with your particular skills and craft, you help create an illusion which fulfils someone else's fantasy, and they pay you for it. Surely you've made that comparison since you've been here?'

I hadn't, but she had a point.

'You have good nights and bad nights. Sometimes it flows easily, and you can get lost in the act yourself. Other times, it's the last thing you want to be doing, but the show must go on because it pays your bloody rent.'

Antoinette took a cigarette out of her pack and looked at me quizzically.

'Are you on tomorrow night?'

It was a quiet drive home with Patrick but at least there was none of the awkwardness, or insanity, of recent trips. And as he wove through the empty streets of Randwick, I waited for him to mention my news, or congratulate me, or say anything at all. But instead, my driver cheerfully tapped on the steering wheel and sang along to the radio, until I realised that he was waiting for me to ask the questions.

'Any news on the pipe front?' I said at last.

'Yes! As a matter of fact, there is,' he burst. 'It's all falling into place, but there is one small problem.'

For the next five minutes, underscored by Patrick's pipe monologue, I regressed through all my past relationships in search of a boyfriend who had not put his problems before my achievements. One.

'So you see,' Patrick grimaced as he turned off his engine in my driveway, 'that's why I really need a computer.'

There was an uncomfortable pause. Patrick knew that I had a computer, and I wished he hadn't turned off his engine.

'You don't have one?' I asked coldly.

'Of course not,' Patrick exclaimed, appalled at such a preposterous question. 'How could I afford a computer?'

Give up hooch? Give up Marlboros? Work more shifts? Eat in?

'Somehow,' Patrick sighed, 'I've got to find a thousand dollars. Or someone who could lend me a thousand dollars.'

The first pause was more comfortable than this one.

'And I was wondering ...?' Patrick's voice climbed hopefully.

I was not going to even grace this incredible suggestion with a look, but I could hear Patrick's eyebrows calling me. And when I finally did turn to face his expectant, clownish smile, I had to laugh too.

I could forgive Patrick for scoffing at me because I cared about the plight of the Aborigines, as I hoped that he would forgive me for not recognising a good career opportunity when a stoned dart champion tapped me on the shoulder with a happy pipe. But to be asked for a thousand dollars, by a man who still owed me fifty from our first date, was just too sad for words. Patrick helped make saying goodbye as painless as tearing a soggy bandaid from a soapy knee in a Radox bath on a humid night.

'Goodnight, Patrick,' I said, and shut the door behind me.

One last wild ride

I took my card with me to the toilet again. The phones were so busy, it was the only chance I got to read the girls' messages.

Dear Meredith, You were my favourite Play School presenter. Even though you couldn't sing, you always seemed happy. We will miss you. Love, Deb (Marcelle)

I quickly returned to my seat and pressed one of the many flashing red lights.

'Well come on, for fook's sake, where am I taking Lena?' Urszula barked from her car.

For the first time ever, Patrick had rung in sick. But I barely had a spare moment to analyse the possible meaning of this.

'I told you, Urszula,' I cried, rifling through my papers, 'the Furama!'

'Yes, but which fooking Furama, you dopey slag?' she shouted in my ear.

Urszula had obviously recovered from her previous night's petulance and was now in her element, ferrying girls all over Sydney in her white Land Rover, and barking insults down the phone about the incompetence of certain receptionists.

'Central!' I shouted.

'Thank Christ you're going, you useless bint!' she yelled back, and hung up.

But I didn't mind as I sat on the toilet two hours later, laughing at Urszula's childishly drawn stick figure on skates, and once again read her funny, affectionate message, under her mobile phone number, demanding that I keep in touch. The girls had also given me a box of chocolates and a bottle of champagne: the good St James no less, once reserved for one-hour bookings at our brothel. I didn't know if they had bought it as a joke, or if it had been lying around Sofia's office ever since the move. But the card went flying in the air when my sentimental toilet break was interrupted by a violent banging on the door.

'Meredith!' Raelene shouted. 'What are you doing in there? Mr Moroney's on the phone again, and he's really pissed off.'

Mr Moroney, a well-spoken man with an incredibly deep voice, had called at three in the morning from Room 408 at the Hilton with an unusual request. Sounding like he might break into 'Old Man River' at any moment, the baritoned Mr Moroney asked me if he could be frank, before informing me of his somewhat delicate predicament. He would love to see an Asian girl, Mr Moroney said, but only one who could accommodate a particularly large penis. I rang Min straightaway, who assured me that Hoshi was the girl for the job.

'You sure, Min?' I asked her.

I had never seen Hoshi, but she sounded all of five on the phone.

'Hoshi, dali,' Min croaked, reassuringly. And tittering at my predicament, she hung up.

At the time, it felt as if I was sending a small Japanese mouse to a large African elephant. And according to the angry but articulate elephant, now reprimanding me for my lack of honesty, respect and sensitivity, that's exactly what I had done. I felt awful, especially when I spoke to Hoshi on the phone.

'Was man too big, Hoshi?'

'No!' Hoshi giggled, '*Man too big!*' Hoshi's English had never been very good. 'Me only little.'

Yeah, you only little, Min only lie, me only cop it.

'Was he a basketball player?' Raelene asked sympathetically. 'We get a few of those.'

'No,' I said despondently. 'He sounded more like the head of the United Nations than a Chicago Bull.'

At five o'clock in the morning, Sofia announced that, as it was my last night, I could leave on time for once. I looked at my tired colleagues, Raelene and Trudy, who smiled warmly and nodded in agreement. But before I could object, the phones started up again and, obeying a commanding wave from Sofia, I began packing up my things. Five minutes later, the taxi company still had me on hold.

'What you doing, darling?' Sofia asked in the tone she always used when I was doing something wrong.

'You said I could go,' I said, wavering.

'Yes.' But I was still doing it wrong. 'And what you doing?'

'I'm calling a taxi, Sofia.'

'Why you do that? Urszula drive you home, darling. She's the driver tonight.'

I was so used to Patrick driving me home, it felt wrong to ask Urszula for a lift.

'But Urszula's taking Celeste to a booking,' I said, pointing to the board.

'So? You go for the ride, and then she takes you home. That's what she's paid for! Run!'

The thought of going with Urszula and Celeste to the very door of a booking in my final hour was suddenly very thrilling.

'Okay!'

Piled high with my chocolates, champagne and my bag, and promising to keep in touch, I hastily hugged and kissed my colleagues goodbye and ran downstairs in search of Antoinette. I found our petite, mature, classy blonde sitting alone at the kitchen table, and I stood before her in the doorway, panting. I wanted to put my things down, but then Antoinette was not the hugging kind, and Urszula's car horn hooted impatiently from below.

'Well, good luck,' she said, smiling up at me awkwardly.

'I'll never forget you, Antoinette,' I said, finally finding her through two fans of pink cellophane.

We nodded fondly at each other's feet.

'I've been very grateful for your presence in this house,' Antoinette said, smiling with some difficulty, 'at times, very much.'

At that moment, it didn't seem important that I couldn't think of anything to say to Antoinette. My eyes welled up with tears, and she could plainly see how much she had affected me. With one last look at the messy halo of golden hair, and her faltering smile, I turned and ran down the stairs for the very last time.

I ran out the door just in time to stop Urszula from blasting the horn again, and climbed into the back of her compact home. Despite their hurry, Urszula seemed very pleased to have me on board, and so did Celeste, who was looking particularly beautiful tonight. Celeste's hair was up, and she wore a long, black rayon evening dress with red flowers all over it. She looked like a Hemingway. Not Ernest. Or Margot. That just left Mariel. Celeste looked like Mariel Hemingway, I thought as I leant forward between them.

'Where are we going?' I asked, rubbing my thighs with excitement. Before I realised, and stopped.

'Matraville!' they chorused with mock cheer.

Patrick lived in Matraville, wherever that was. I made a little joke about how hilarious it would be if Celeste turned up to find Patrick waiting for her in his boxer shorts. And I laughed so loud I'm sure they both guessed I had been sleeping with him half the year. But Celeste and Urszula were too busy chatting about Rex's latest leg injury, which explained his absence.

'Poor darling,' Celeste pouted in her theatrical way.

I loved the way Celeste called everyone 'darling', despite her young twenty years.

'Is this guy a regular, Celeste?' I interrupted them.

'What, darling? No. Well, I'll know when I get there.'

Back to dogs. Dogs they had loved. Dogs that bit. Dogs that had died.

'Will we wait outside for Celeste to start the booking?' I asked Urszula.

'Yes. Why? You in a hurry?' Urszula asked, glancing at me suspiciously in the mirror.

'No!'

Back to dogs. Dogs that were psychic. Dogs that were phobic. No one wanted to talk about work. Or my last night.

I had no idea where we were. We'd gone through Maroubra, which was the end of the world as I knew it.

'Wow! Look at those enormous fir trees,' I interrupted again.

Inside the grounds of the large factory on our left, enclosed by miles of serious metal fencing and barbed-wire, stood a row of beautiful, enormous fir trees.

'You should see them decked out at Christmas,' said Urszula. 'Not a bad job for a bunch of rapists and embezzlers,' she sneered, lighting her cigarette with one hand.

I didn't understand.

'That's Long Bay, darling.'

I had only ever heard of Long Bay Prison on the news, when murderers escaped. This trip was getting better and better.

'We're not dropping you here, are we, Celeste?' I laughed at my second pathetic joke for the night.

'Well ...' said Urszula, now wrestling with a street directory, the wheel and her cigarette, 'Trudy did say turn left after Matraville High ...'

'Oh, no ...' groaned Celeste. 'I'm not going to a fucking halfway?'

Urszula slowed down to turn left. We didn't talk about dogs now. While Celeste became increasingly tense, Urszula explained to me that a halfway was a block of council flats, just outside the prison, where inmates were allowed to live semi-supervised.

As we turned into a dark narrow street, I felt sick for Celeste, who was now unusually quiet.

'Hang on, hang on,' protested Urszula hopefully, 'it's a street off to the right. Yes, here it is.'

But our hearts sank as we turned into a dark, treeless cul-de-sac housing several foreboding council flat blocks, and not a parked car in sight. Urszula pulled up and the three of us sat in silence, taking in the fluorescent-lit paths that led to several looming, cold brick towers full of criminals. A solitary bed sheet on one balcony flapped in the breeze.

'Oh, baby. I am sorry,' Urszula said at last.

'Thanks,' Celeste said flatly as she got out and slammed her door.

'Bye, Celeste!' I called out after her.

But I don't think Celeste cared, just at that point, that she might never see me again.

364 One last wild ride

It was a perverse sight watching her, dressed so elegantly, walk tall and proud along the narrow footpath towards the central building. From its dark doorway, a man wearing only a short dressing gown appeared, and stood under the porch light to collect his delivery. Urszula and I watched Celeste stride past him, haughtily, salvaging some last moments of dignity before he followed her inside.

'Poor Celeste,' I said.

'Oh, bollocks,' Urszula scoffed. 'Carries on like a fooking princess, that one.'

Although Celeste could be extremely grandiose – 'Fetch me a glass of water, will you, darling?' – I felt sorry for her now.

'He shouldn't have seen us, Urszula. Now he knows she didn't catch the taxi he's paid for.'

'No, it's good he's seen us,' Urszula growled. 'Now he won't try any foony business.'

Just then Urszula's mobile rang, sending my head almost through the ceiling. Urszula had one of those earpieces so that she could talk hands-free.

'Yes ... yes ... she's all right then?' she asked urgently.

It was Sofia, confirming that Celeste had rung from the man's room.

'He give her taxi money?' she asked. 'Good ... Right. I'm driving Meredith home.'

And off we went, leaving Celeste inside a halfway at Long Bay, possibly with a rapist, but I clung on to the hope that he'd just stolen a bicycle. And that he had some cocaine. Celeste liked cocaine.

We were driving back towards Coogee, very leisurely, discussing the possibility of another rollerblading expedition at the park the following weekend, when Urszula's phone rang again.

'Yes?' she shouted. 'Speak slowly!'

Urszula hit the brakes. 'Tell Celeste I'm out the front!'

And we were off. Urszula swung the car to the right, throwing me hard against my door and sending everything on her dashboard into my lap.

'Hold on, Meredith!'

But before I could cry, 'Dear God, I don't want to die outside Long Bay with a prostitute!' Urszula ploughed over the nature strip, turned back down the other side, and put her foot to the floor.

'Celeste's in trouble!'

She'd better be! I had only ever experienced such fear hitting an air pocket flying Air India. Suddenly there were bends in the road that weren't there before. Where did they come from? At every one I thought we'd roll, so I held onto the ceiling. It just felt better. There were those stupid fir trees they decorated at Christmas. What was the point? My whole life flashed before me. A good life! I should have drunk more milk! This was going to kill my parents! I was holding something wet. What was it? Ugh! One of Rex's old tennis balls. The car swerved dangerously out of control. Sofia was going to die of remorse for not letting me call that taxi on my very last night. There was no way we could make that left turn at this speed. I knew it! Urszula hit the brakes, reversed so fast I lost a kilo, swung into the narrow street, skidded, swerved right into the cul-de-sac, and we screeched to a stop.

Now what was going to happen? Urszula looked wild. Was she going to go inside? And if so, should I go with her? Or should I stay here, on my own in criminal cul-de-sac with the doors locked waiting for some psychopath to bounce poor Celeste's head on the roof? Oh, why was I here, for God's sake? I was an actress in a sitcom at Fox! Urszula must have hit her redial button, because for one mad minute I thought she was shouting at me.

'What's happening? Am I going in? … Yes! Ring me back!'

Apparently another man had arrived just as Celeste was about to start her booking. A 'friend', who just wanted to watch. Celeste had grabbed her bag, locked herself in the toilet and rung the office on her mobile. While Raelene calmed Celeste on one line, Sofia was arguing with the obstinate client on the other, and Urszula and I sat outside, waiting.

It was alarming how many men had tried to get away with this sort of thing during my tenure at the brothel.

'Are you the only one there, Larry?'

Larry would promise he was, but then the girl would turn up to find Harry and Garry there as well. I remembered a buck's night call I'd answered, when I had to explain the difference between a stripper and an escort.

'Ow orright, Merra,' Bazza groaned, 'send's one a them, then.'

I had explained to Bazza that we could only send a girl if there was *one* man in the room.

'It's okay, Merry, s'just me! All on me own. S'just me, love.'

I refused, of course, but then we had to go through the tedium of answering Bazza calling on every other line, pretending he was on his own. To get rid of him we just upped the price.

'Eight hundred bucks an hour?' Bazza finally cried, and the unmistakable pissed roar of several incredulous bucks could be heard protesting violently in the background.

Finally, Raelene rang Urszula. Celeste was staying. The second man had gone, and she was going ahead with the booking. Unbelievable. If I had just been through that, I would be fit for nothing stiff but a scotch. Urszula didn't move, though. I assumed she wanted the satisfaction of seeing one man leave the building.

'It's like a stakeout, isn't it, Urszula?' I whispered excitedly.

Silence.

'Urszula? I'm sure he's gone. Maybe he just lived next door.'

'No,' Urszula growled, reluctantly starting the engine again. 'If I know Celeste, he's still in there.'

As we drove away for the second time, Urszula enlightened me with one last trick of the trade.

'Meredith, when a girl rings the agency to say there's two of them, as you know, the agency will tell the client his friend has to go. But if the girl discovers the friend's got cash, she might, if she's a greedy, stupid fook, tell the agency he's gone, pocket the extra dosh, and let both of them have her.'

'Wow!' I gushed. 'Isn't that dangerous?'

'Meredith, have you not learnt one thing since you've been with us?' At high speed, Urszula turned directly to face me. 'It's a fooking dangerous profession!'

I was so relieved when Urszula pulled up outside my house.

'Now just because you're going off to become a famous actress,'

Urszula said as she clasped me to her breast, 'don't you go forgetting a bunch of tarts just down the road in Redfern.'

No, I said.

'*Play School*, for fook's sake,' she said, laughing, when I had one leg out the door. 'How the fook did you journey from singing on *Play School* to working in a brothel?'

'How do any of us end up in a brothel?' I asked, laughing too.

'Oh, one of our brothers takes money off his friends to poke his sister,' she said.

For a split second, Urszula looked almost as surprised as me.

'I'll tell you all about it, Meredith,' she growled affectionately, starting her engine again, 'next time you come to the park.'

Long after the Land Rover had disappeared out of our street, I stood in our driveway, savouring my final arrival home from work at dawn. I did not mind that I had left my chocolates and champagne in the back of Urszula's car, so long as I had my card. My card! I fell to my knees on the concrete and frantically searched in my bag for the card with all the messages from the girls and receptionists I had worked with for the last eleven months. And there it was, just where I had left it, lodged in the middle of my book for protection. As I stood in our driveway with the sky getting lighter and the birds singing around me, I impatiently opened the envelope again, to read Antoinette's crooked hand-written message one more time.

Dear Meredith, Thanks for putting up with me. If ever you see me again, please say hello. My name is Sandra.

Acknowledgements

The best part of my journey as a first time writer was discovering the faith my friends had in me, even when none of us, including me, knew exactly what it was I was writing. I want to thank especially my dear friend Nadine Garner, whose thoughtful and often illuminating insights have helped me out of many a trough, personal and literary. And to Simon, Sioban, Annie, Sara, Susan, Ritchie, Elaine, Jonathan and Perry for their support and for just being there. I could not have written this book at all if it had not been for the extraordinary consideration and restraint shown by my housemates and good friends, Libby Sharpe and Peter O'Brien. I could often hear them begging Daisy the dog to stop barking, so as not to disturb the great artist upstairs working on her first filmscript, sitcom, mini-series, or whatever the hell I kept deciding it was. (Thanks especially to Libby for leading me by the hand under the many petticoats and into the magical, colourful world of *Moulin Rouge*, where I met more of her delightful co-horts.)

Thanks to my agent, Robyn Gardiner (and Margaret too), for overcoming her initial concern about me working in a brothel, and for always being so encouraging, and for making me laugh. And thanks to Garth Nix and Fiona Inglis for all their help and guidance, and to Alex Mohan and Bernadette Foley for their fantastic response.

Thanks to Spocky Wick Knock (John), Virginia, Emma, Mum and Dad, for their love.

I would like to thank the wonderful women at Allen and Unwin in Melbourne for their incredible collective care and creative talent. For the last twelve months I have been tenderly nurtured and watered constantly by Sue Hines, knocked into shape by my scrupulous and brilliant editor Rachel Lawson, and thoroughly polished by Jo Jarrah, whose response to my book was so generous I'm still floating. Thanks to Andrea McNamara for her positive input, and to Jennifer Castles for alerting Sue to my first manuscript, and for bringing us all together in the first place.

Last of all, I would like to thank all the women I met and worked with at the brothel. It was the most interesting and happy year of my life, and that's because I got to know a group of very brave, bright and funny women who work on the front line of the sex industry. I hope this book helps make people aware that, contrary to popular belief, many women freely choose to work as prostitutes, and choose therefore to provide the most confrontingly personal service imaginable, without discrimination. I thank them for an experience I will always cherish, and for inspiring my first attempt at writing a book.

		Nidei's Present	
1	Sandy & Niel	25	cheque
2	Lou & Jo	26	$
3	Rod & LeSlay	26	$
4	Vidu & Bill	25.	$
5	Liz & Craig	25.	$
6	Anne Marie & Andrew Peters	40	$

Petzel. Wellington Suphs